Zune™

FOR

DUMMIES®

by Brian Johnson, Duncan Mackenzie, and Harvey Chute

BICENTENNIAL

1807

WILEY

2007

BICENTENNIAL

Wiley Publishing, Inc.

Zune™ For Dummies®

Published by
Wiley Publishing, Inc.
111 River Street
Hoboken, NJ 07030-5774
www.wiley.com

Copyright © 2007 by Wiley Publishing, Inc., Indianapolis, Indiana

Published by Wiley Publishing, Inc., Indianapolis, Indiana

Published simultaneously in Canada

For general information on our other products and services, please contact our Customer Care Department within the U.S. at 800-762-2974, outside the U.S. at 317-572-3993, or fax 317-572-4002.

For technical support, please visit www.wiley.com/techsupport.

Wiley also publishes its books in a variety of electronic formats. Some content that appears in print may not be available in electronic books.

Library of Congress Control Number: 2007926002

ISBN: 978-0-470-12045-3

Manufactured in the United States of America

10 9 8 7 6 5 4 3 2 1

WILEY

About the Authors

Brian Johnson is a product manager for Microsoft. He's the author of a number of technology books including (with Duncan) *Xbox 360 For Dummies*. You can find out more about Brian by visiting his blog at `http://bufferoverrun.net`.

Duncan Mackenzie is a software developer at Microsoft working on several Web video sites, including `http://on10.net` and `http://channel9.msdn.com`. When he isn't working or writing, he spends most of his time with his wife and two kids, and when they are asleep he fires up the Xbox 360. At any given moment you may find him online playing Viva Piñata, Oblivion or Halo 3. He has a habit of watching TV show episodes on his Zune, including "Star Trek: Enterprise" and "Avatar: The Last Airbender". You can contact Duncan through his Web site, `www.duncanmackenzie.net`.

Harvey Chute is owner and editor of Zunerama.com, an online resource center for Zune owners. He moderates Zunerama's user boards, oversees the site's technical support section, conducts photo reviews of Zune players and accessories, and writes the site's daily Zune blog. A project manager and software developer for a national systems integration and consulting company, Harvey has authored over fifty internal technical documents, white papers, and consulting deliverables. His interests include software development, gadgets, music, photography, woodworking, running, snowboarding, and enjoying life with his wife and three daughters.

Dedication

Brian: To my family.

Duncan: As always, this book is dedicated to my wife. She keeps me going and puts up with all my hobbies, my electronics and my late nights spent working.

Harvey: For my wife, Carrie.

Authors' Acknowledgments

We would like to thank the excellent staff at Wiley who did all the hard work to put this book together. First, we would like to thank Melody Layne, our Acquisitions Editor, who kick started this project and kept it going all the way along. We would also like to extend a big "thank you" to Paul Levesque, the project editor, who took our collective thoughts and turned them into a real book. Thanks also to Andy Hollandbeck and Laura Miller, the copy editors for this project, and the rest of the Wiley staff.

Brian and Duncan would also like to extend a big thanks to our technical reviewer and coauthor Harvey Chute, who checked our facts and then jumped on board to write a few chapters himself.

Harvey would like to acknowledge the members of Zunerama's forums, for their insight, helpfulness, and passion for all things Zune!

Publisher's Acknowledgments

We're proud of this book; please send us your comments through our online registration form located at www.dummies.com/register.

Some of the people who helped bring this book to market include the following:

Acquisitions, Editorial, and Media Development

Project Editor: Paul Levesque

Acquisitions Editor: Melody Layne

Copy Editors: Andy Hollandbeck and Laura Miller

Technical Editor: Harvey Chute

Editorial Manager: Leah Cameron

Media Development Manager: Laura VanWinkle

Editorial Assistant: Amanda Foxworth

Sr. Editorial Assistant: Cherie Case

Cartoons: Rich Tennant (www.the5thwave.com)

Composition Services

Project Coordinator: Jennifer Theriot

Layout and Graphics: Claudia Bell, Shawn Frazier, Brooke Graczyk, Joyce Haughey, Barbara Moore, Heather Ryan

Proofreaders: Aptara, Jessica Kramer

Indexer: Aptara

Anniversary Logo Design: Richard Pacifico

Publishing and Editorial for Technology Dummies

    Richard Swadley, Vice President and Executive Group Publisher

    Andy Cummings, Vice President and Publisher

    Mary Bednarek, Executive Acquisitions Director

    Mary C. Corder, Editorial Director

Publishing for Consumer Dummies

    Diane Graves Steele, Vice President and Publisher

    Joyce Pepple, Acquisitions Director

Composition Services

    Gerry Fahey, Vice President of Production Services

    Debbie Stailey, Director of Composition Services

Contents at a Glance

Table of Contents

Introduction

· ·

*W*elcome to the Zune! Before we get started, we figure we should tell you a little bit about this book and its authors. You could say that Brian and I (Duncan) are big fans of digital media — we've ripped our entire music collections; we live for moving TV and movie digital files around our home networks; and between our two houses, we probably have five different types of digital video recorders (DVRs, such as TiVo). We also love gadgets. Cell phones, music players, video cameras . . . if it's small, cool, and electronic, we've tried it. Given our interests, we both knew we'd be snapping up a Zune the moment they came out, even though we already have some Portable Media Centers (early Zune-like devices from Microsoft), iPods, and MP3 players between us. As we heard more about the specs for the unit, we decided that to get the most out of the Zune, people are going to need a guide — and a *Zune For Dummies* book seemed like the best way to meet that need. After we plunged into the project in earnest, we decided to invite Harvey Chute, the Zune master of Zunerama (www.zunerama.com), along for the ride to offer his perspective on the community side of the Zune.

So, the three of us have collectively come up with a book we hope can help just about anyone get up and running quickly with the Zune. We also wrote this book to help parents understand the device and what they need to know about its features before giving or lending it to their children. Whoever you are, though, the goal of this book is to help you get the most from your Zune!

About This Book

This book is designed to get new users up and running quickly with the Zune, as well as help any user master the more advanced features of both the device and the accompanying Zune software. The person who just brought home the Zune box and needs to get some of his or her music onto the device should find this book helpful, as can a parent who wants an overview of the Zune so he or she can make good, informed decisions about how to monitor and control his or her children's Zune usage. Finally, gamers — folks near and dear to our hearts — can find info in these pages on how to use their Zunes and Zune Marketplace music right from their Xbox 360s.

We've worked to make this book a really good guide for Zune owners, with step-by-step instructions where appropriate. We've collected the most interesting and useful tips, and give advice on all the different topics that matter to a Zune owner.

Because the Zune experience focuses on the social element, this book helps new Zune owners discover the possibilities for a community built around the device and around their music.

How to Use This Book

You can read this book from cover to cover, or you can pick and choose the pieces of information you're looking for by skipping through the book as needed.

If you get this book before you get your Zune, you can go ahead and start preparing for the arrival of your new device. You can review Chapter 1 to find out what to expect when you bring the box home and open it up. You can also go ahead and download the Zune software and get yourself set up with an account with Zune Marketplace (covered in Chapters 2 and 7). Check out Chapter 19, as well, to see what add-ons you can get for your Zune, ranging from cool cases to fancy docking units.

If you're a parent who's getting a Zune for the family or for an individual child, be sure to check out Chapter 18 first and then Chapter 7. Chapter 18 gives specific information for parents about controlling the use of the Zune, deciding how to deal with online music purchasing, and other issues unique to a family situation. Chapter 7 introduces the online side of the Zune experience, including the Zune Pass subscription service, Microsoft Points, and more.

Interested in recording your own digital video? Then flip to Chapter 9. Heard about podcasts and want to get them on your Zune? Chapter 10 should have everything you need.

How This Book Is Organized

Zune For Dummies is divided into four parts. Each of these parts is designed to help you understand a different aspect of the Zune experience.

Part I: Getting Started

The first chapter in this part of the book, Chapter 1, explains a little bit about what you can do with the Zune before you even hook it up to your computer. After you do have your Zune unpacked and charged up, we cover hooking it up to your computer, getting you all set up with the Zune software, and helping you get logged in to Zune Marketplace, the Zune's online music store, in Chapter 2. Finally, in Chapter 3, we run through the various settings and options on the Zune device itself.

Part II: Managing Your Zune Content

The Zune device can hold a lot of content, including music, video, and photos. This part focuses on getting all that content organized on your PC, imported into the Zune software, and synchronized over to the Zune. In Chapters 4, 7, and 8, we take you through the process of getting all your favorite music onto your Zune, including music that's already on your machine, music you need to rip off of CDs, and music you want to download from Zune Marketplace. We cover tracking down videos on your machine and on the Web in Chapter 5, and if making your own videos is more your style, we cover that in Chapter 9! Chapter 6 takes care of photos and Chapter 10 talks about podcasts, complete with an intro to the podcasting world, details on how to find and subscribe to the feed(s) you're interested in, and some suggestions on the best way to get podcasts onto the Zune whenever those podcasts are updated.

Part III: Enjoying Your Content

This part covers using your music, videos, and photos — on your Zune, on your PC, and through external systems such as an Xbox 360 (Chapter 13). Chapter 12 talks about navigating through all your videos on the Zune, along with the full set of controls for watching videos on the device. We show you the best way to get your Zune going while you're in the car (Chapter 14), while travelling (Chapter 15), or using your home stereo system (Chapter 11). Chapter 16 does its part by introducing you to the Zune community — they're just waiting to welcome you aboard!

Part IV: The Part of Tens

This part contains lists we thought Zune owners might find useful. Dive into the Zune's coolest accessories in Chapter 17. Every parent should check out Chapter 18 to find out what you need to know about your child and the Zune. And everyone who cares about keeping their Zune safe needs to read Chapter 19.

Icons Used in This Book

If you're a *For Dummies* fan, you'll quickly recognize the icons in the margins of this book. If you're new to *For Dummies* books, then welcome! Here's a list of the icons scattered throughout this book, along with a little explanation of what each icon means.

This icon indicates you can find a little piece of knowledge here that's going to make your life easier, so be sure to take a look. Using the info these icons point out can make you seem oh so smart.

When you see this icon, try to remember the information it shows you. That way, you can save time (and headaches) later. (Sort of like that 30 days hath . . . whatever.)

The Warning icon tells you to be very careful or something bad might happen. You don't want to lose all the data on your device, do you? You can probably find a warning about that somewhere in this book.

This icon indicates you're looking at a piece of geek data that you can either read or choose to ignore.

Where to Go from Here

Hook up your Zune. Rip some CDs and DVDs. Visit the Web sites mentioned in this book. You can use the Zune as just another music player, or you can make it a gateway to a cool new world of digital content online. Hopefully, this book can make getting your Zune up and running, putting all your favorite content on board, and finding great new media to watch or listen to a breeze.

Part I

Getting Started

The 5th Wave
By Rich Tennant

"I hope you're doing something online. An indie band like yours shouldn't just be playing street corners."

In this part . . .

This part is all about getting you up and running with your Zune. After you go out and buy a Zune, then bring it home, you need to open up the packaging and start playing with your new toy.

Chapter 1 is all about the out-of-box experience. Here, you can find out what comes with your Zune and how to power up your Zune for the first time. Chapter 1 also covers basic device usage, including a walkthrough of all the preloaded content on your device and details on hooking up your Zune for charging.

Chapter 2 dives into the Zune software; first, getting it installed and updated, then hooking up your device to your PC. You can find out how to update the firmware on your Zune, how to name your Zune, and how to create your very own account with Zune Marketplace.

Chapter 3 finishes this part off with coverage of all the settings on the Zune device itself. From turning on shuffle to configuring your wireless privacy, we take you through all the settings.

Chapter 1

First Steps with Your Zune

*I*f you're reading this book, then you either recently purchased a Zune or are seriously considering getting one. Either way, it's time to find out what a Zune can do! In this chapter, you can take a look at what you gain when you get your hands on a Zune — or figure out how to get ahold of one if you haven't picked one up yet.

Entertainment on the Go

So, the big question you're asking yourself is this: What is this Zune thing and what can it do for me? The first thing to realize is that a Zune is so much more than just a music player; it's a full-blown entertainment unit that has 30GB of memory and just happens to fit in your pocket. Any one of the Zune devices — they come in three different colors but are otherwise the same — is capable of doing a ton of great things right out of the box. What kinds of great things? Well, check out this list:

✔ Take all your music, photos, and videos with you everywhere you go, which means you can

  • Store 500 hours (at standard settings) of music so that you can listen on the go.

  • Tune into FM radio stations, set your station presets, and even receive station information (station call letters or music format, for example) on the fly.

- Store thousands of photos in full color so you can browse through them any time you want. (You can even start up your slideshow and flip through your photos automatically.)

- Store anywhere from 30 to 100 hours (depending on your settings) worth of movies, TV shows, and other video content . . . and watch it all on a bright display.

✔ Hook up to Marketplace and never buy another CD again . . . or buy CDs and rip them to your Zune. It's up to you! You can use any or all of these options:

- Getting bored with your own music but don't want to buy more CDs? You can subscribe to Zune Marketplace and listen to new music whenever you want for a set monthly price.

- Buy songs and albums from Zune Marketplace one at a time, often for less than you'd pay for the CD in the store.

- Copy your existing music, or music from new CDs you buy, right onto your Zune, and add new music whenever you get it.

✔ Share your Zune experience with your friends and family:

- Use the built-in wireless features to find and connect to other nearby Zunes and share music and photos.

- Fire up your Web browser and go online to check out the ever-expanding roster of Zune chat forums out there.

- Hook your Zune up to a stereo system (with a mini-plug-to-RCA cable or something similar) or a set of speakers to listen to your music with your friends, or hook it up to your TV (which requires an audio/video cable) to share photos and videos.

Getting Your Hands on a Zune

If you haven't already purchased your Zune, you need to make only a couple of decisions: What color should I get, and where should I buy it?

The big decision: Black, white, or brown?

There is currently only one Zune model, but it *does* come in three different colors: black, white, and brown. When you see a Zune up close and personal, though, you'll realize that the colors are more complex than just a single tone. The outside of each Zune is actually made up of multiple layers of material. The outer layer is semitranslucent and has a slightly different color than the rest of the unit. This interesting design produces a color that changes slightly depending on the light and the angle at which you hold your Zune, an effect that many people are calling *doubleshot*.

So, technically, each and every Zune has more than one color, but you still have to decide if you're (overall) a white, black, or brown type. Other than the color, there's no difference in the three styles of device, so pick whichever color suits you best. Brown is a relatively unusual color for an electronic device, but perhaps that will make your Zune stand out a bit more from the other music players out there. A lot of rumors are flying around about new colors, especially pink. At the time we wrote this book, nothing had been confirmed, but check out www.zune.net (click on Meet Zune) to see if any new colors are available.

Where to buy your Zune?

Just like with color, where to buy your Zune isn't a technical decision. There's no difference between the Zunes being sold by different stores, so your decision should depend on the price and the level of after-sale support that you can expect to receive. Many people avoid buying larger ticket items online, but for something in the range of a Zune, there are few worries.

Personally, though, we prefer using a local chain store, such as Best Buy or Circuit City, for two main reasons:

- ✔ First, if something is wrong with the unit right when you open the box, you can be confident that they'll take care of the problem without any need to call Microsoft support (and possibly having to mail the unit in to be replaced or fixed).

- ✔ Second, we just really like to get our purchases right into our hands when we're buying something that we're this excited about. (Okay, so we're into instant gratification!)

Regardless of your personal preferences about online shopping, we suggest you check out www.pricegrabber.com before you buy. On this site, you can compare the prices (including shipping and taxes) across hundreds of different online retailers. Find the best price (from a store with a high star rating and a large number of positive reviews, to be sure), and the savings might be enough to get you over any fear of online purchasing.

Opening the box

So you've bought yourself a Zune (or better yet, you've been given one as a gift), and you've ripped the shrink wrap off the funky brown box with the distinctive orange bottom. Now what? Well, first, go ahead and open this thing up and take a look at what you get!

After you have that outer layer of plastic off, you can slide the brown case up to reveal yet another funky piece of packaging, this one with the slightly hard-to-understand (but easy-to-remember) tag line, "Welcome to the Social." Ignoring the writing for a moment, lift that front flap to expose your Zune. The device sits in a recessed pocket in the front of the package (see Figure 1-1), and you should see a small ribbon sticking out from the bottom of it. Pull carefully on that ribbon (not too hard or it will rip, and you'll feel all sad for damaging an otherwise perfect Zune storage box), and the Zune should lift right up and out of the packaging.

Now, if you check out the area to either side of where the Zune was sitting, you'll find that two flaps open to reveal little secret compartments. On one side, you'll find a pair of headphones, and on the other side, you'll find a special USB cable that you'll need to hook your Zune up to a PC.

You (smart person that you are) may have spotted those pockets immediately, but we know a large number of people who didn't notice them until they were already totally frustrated from searching the package for a pair of headphones.

Figure 1-1:
Liberate
your Zune
from its
cardboard
confinement.

Now, if you look on the very top of the inner box, you'll find an opening behind where the Zune sits, and inside that area, you'll find

- ✔ A Product Guide and a Start Guide (very basic usage information)
- ✔ The software CD

    You find out all about installing and getting started with the software in Chapter 2.

- ✔ A sleek little bag for your Zune
- ✔ A Zune sticker (or not — the stickers were a limited-time item)

    Run outside right now and stick it on your car, or your parents' car, or a friend's car, or on your bike . . . just stick it somewhere!

You can ignore almost all these goodies for now; just take out your Zune (it should be wrapped in its own plastic, so unwrap it now and peel the plastic sticker off the screen) and the headphones. It's time to try out your new toy and see what it can do.

Checking the battery

Turn your Zune on by pressing the Play/Pause button (see Figure 1-2) to make the display light up.

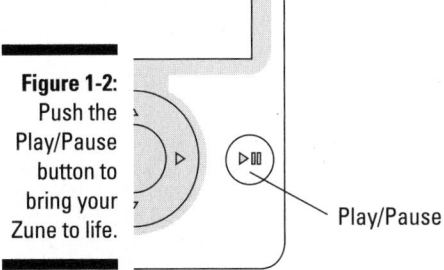

Figure 1-2: Push the Play/Pause button to bring your Zune to life.

Play/Pause

If the display doesn't light up at this point, your battery might be completely drained (more on that in a moment), or your Zune could be locked.

TIP

If the Hold switch at the top of your Zune is in the Locked position, as shown in Figure 1-3, slide it gently to the left to unlock it and then try the Play/Pause button again.

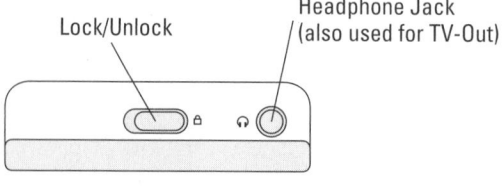

Headphone Jack
(also used for TV-Out)

Lock/Unlock

Figure 1-3:
Unlock your
Zune before
taking it for
a drive.

If your Zune display does light up, check out the lower-right corner to see the current battery status. (See Figure 1-4.)

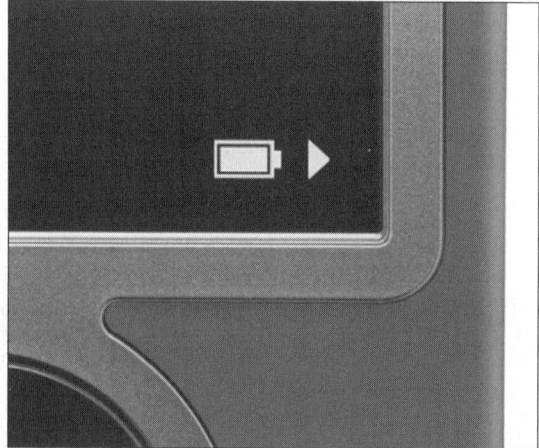

Figure 1-4:
Checking
out the
Zune juice.

If half or less of this bar is filled in, your battery is low. If you have more than half, you can go ahead and start using your Zune now; otherwise, it's probably a good idea to charge it for a couple of hours before going any further. To find out how to take care of this (very basic) chore, check out the following section.

Charging your Zune

When you were unpacking the Zune, you probably were amazed to discover that there wasn't any sort of power cord anywhere. There's a simple reason for that — there *is* no Zune power cord. You charge a Zune by using the same USB cable (called the sync cable) you use to hook it up to your PC.

To charge your Zune, plug the wide connector on the sync cable, shown in Figure 1-5, into the bottom of your device. Make sure that the Zune logo is facing up and that your Zune itself is lying face-up, with the screen visible. (The connectors fit right only if everything's facing in the right direction.)

Don't force the connector in; just push gently until you hear a click. Then go ahead and plug the other end (the standard USB connector) into an available USB port on your PC.

Figure 1-5:
The sync cable plugs into the bottom of the Zune.

You may want to use a USB port on the back of your PC because the front ports may be underpowered and could cause you problems in charging and syncing your Zune.

If your PC is running and you're logged in at this point, you'll likely receive a prompt like the one in Figure 1-6, asking if you want to try to find a driver for your Zune device. Just click the Cancel button at the bottom; we show you how to set up your Zune drivers and software in Chapter 2.

What if my Zune won't charge?

If you're unlucky enough that the battery doesn't appear to be charging, the USB port you're using may not have enough power. If your Zune battery won't charge, try these fixes to figure out how to get your Zune to charge properly:

✔ If you're plugged into a USB hub, try plugging directly into a port on your PC.

✔ If you're already plugged into a front panel port on your PC, try switching to a rear-panel port.

✔ If you have a powered USB hub available (one that uses an AC adapter in addition to a connection to your PC), try hooking up to a port on that hub.

✔ Try unplugging any other USB devices from your PC or hub. One of those other devices might be interfering with your Zune's ability to charge.

✔ Try a port on another system . . . such as your Xbox 360. (A running Xbox 360 provides enough power on its USB ports to charge the Zune; we cover other ways your Zune and your Xbox 360 can work together in Chapter 13.)

If none of the preceding fix attempts work, and you can't get your Zune to charge via any USB port you have, then you have two options:

✔ If the Zune never started up at all, you should take it back to the store where you purchased it. Why take chances? Even if some voodoo charm gets it charged up in some way, you shouldn't have to wander around trying to figure out how to get it working.

✔ If the Zune did start up and was working for a while, but is now low on battery and you can't find a USB port that will charge it, you could get a docking station, such as the Microsoft dock or one of several others that are available (see Chapter 17 for more information on accessories for the Zune), or you could get a USB charger, such as Zip LinQ's model (shown in the following figure), which is currently available for less than ten dollars.

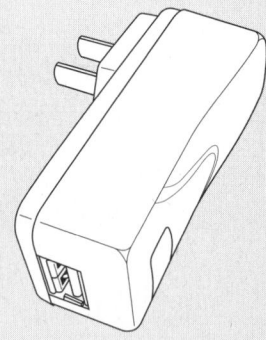

Figure 1-6:
Don't try
to install
drivers
until you set
up the
software.

After you connect the sync cable, check to see if your Zune is charging. If it is, the little battery icon does a shape shift, as shown in Figure 1-7.

Figure 1-7:
The dots
show you
that your
Zune is
charging.

Putting Your Zune through Its Paces

Okay, we're going to assume you have your Zune up and running. Time to fill you in on the basic navigation and usage instructions for the Zune — while taking you on a tour of the preloaded music, photos, and videos.

Starting your Zune is as easy as pressing any button (unless it's locked, of course), but what about turning it off? Turns out you don't ever have to shut it completely off. If you just leave it inactive (not playing music, video, or a photo slideshow) for more than 30 seconds, it goes into a low-power state, and shortly after that, it goes into a suspended sleep state. From either of these states, pressing any key brings it back to full power instantly. After approximately a day in the sleep mode, the device goes into a deep sleep to conserve battery life even more. There's little difference between the sleep and deep sleep modes, except that the device starts up a bit more slowly from a deep sleep and has forgotten what you were doing when you last used it. (When your Zune's in either the low-power state or sleep mode, it starts up right at the song, video, or picture you were on when it powered down.)

When it's turned on after being in deep sleep mode, it goes to the startup screen with the Zune logo.

If you want, you can put your Zune to sleep immediately by pressing and holding the Play/Pause button for about three seconds. Here are some other handy tips about stopping and starting your Zune:

- ✔ In normal usage, tap any key on the Zune to wake it up and light up the display. If it's been left idle for a long time, tap the Play/Pause key to wake it up.

- ✔ Leave the Zune alone for more than a few seconds, and the screen dims down to save battery power. (You can tweak how long it'll take before this dimming down takes place — we show you how in Chapter 3.)

- ✔ The Zune won't dim if it's playing video, which is nice because that would be really annoying.

- ✔ Keep in mind that, after being inactive and paused for more than a minute, the Zune *will* go to sleep (which is still not powered down completely, but it's very close), and that after about a day, the Zune goes into a deep sleep (or sooner if it's very low on battery power).

- ✔ Left asleep, a fully charged Zune should retain battery power for a week (possibly two).

The key to making your way through the Zune's menus and through your content is the control pad below the screen on your Zune. This control pad (see Figure 1-8) is a circle, but you can press it only on the four distinct sides (or on the center OK button). It doesn't turn, and sliding your finger around it won't do anything; it's not a wheel.

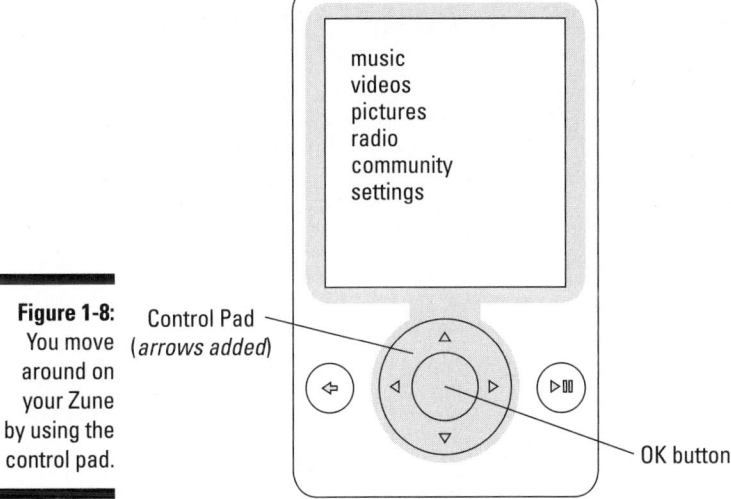

Figure 1-8: You move around on your Zune by using the control pad.

Control Pad (*arrows added*)

OK button

When you're viewing menus, you press up and down on the control pad to move up and down on the list of options. Press left or right on the control pad to move between types of lists, such as between viewing your music by Album, Genre, or Song. After you find a menu item that you want to select, just press the OK button to select it.

When you're listening to music or watching a video, press up and down on the control pad to adjust the volume. As you can see in the "Checking out the videos" section later in this chapter, you need to rotate the Zune 90 degrees to the left when you watch video or view photos; the control pad adjusts its behavior depending on what you're doing. Volume control is always up and down relative to how the screen is supposed to be rotated (see Figure 1-9).

Figure 1-9: Left/right and up/down functionality depends on the mode you're in.

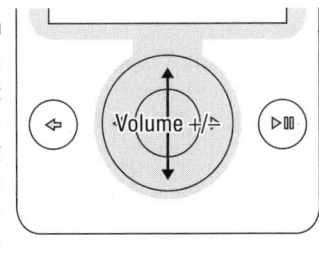

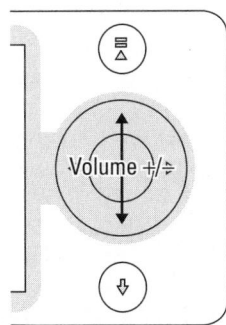

Although we definitely spend more time talking about rebooting later, we do want you to know that if you ever need to completely reboot your Zune, you can do so by holding down the Back button and Down on the control pad, as shown in Figure 1-10.

Figure 1-10:
The super-
secret
button
combo to
reboot a
Zune.

Back and Down together will reboot your Zune

Get out those headphones

It's time to dig out the funky headphones, plug them in, and check out some content. While you have them out, did you notice that the headphones were magnetic? Yep, that's right . . . those pesky ear buds will be staying nice and close due to magnetic backs. Whenever you aren't using them, let their backs click together, making them easier to wrap up and keep untangled. The headphones also act as the antenna when you're listening to FM radio stations, and the Zune doesn't get very good reception without them.

If you're at all like us and aren't really into the kinds of prepackaged headphones you get right out of any box, you'll be happy to know that any headphones should work fine as antennas.

Exploring the preloaded music

For many people, the Zune is all about music. When you add in the wireless sharing features along with the Zune Marketplace, you'll see that it's also very much about discovering new music. In that spirit, the folks at Microsoft preloaded your Zune with quite a few off-the-beaten-track tunes for your listening pleasure. Here's the full list of preloaded songs:

- Band of Horses, "Wicked Gil" (Sub Pop Records)
- Bitter:Sweet, "The Mating Game" (Quango Music Group)
- CSS, "Alala (Microsoft edit)" (Sub Pop Records)

- Darkel, "At The End of The Sky (edit)" (Astralwerks)
- Every Move a Picture, "Signs of Life" (V2)
- Small Sins, "Stay" (Astralwerks)
- The Adored, "Tell Me Tell Me" (V2)
- The Rakes, "Open Book" (V2)
- The Thermals, "A Pillar of Salt" (Sub Pop Records)

Those in the know will immediately recognize most of these bands as indie faves — that is, bands that generally record for independent record labels. This is a great selection of music for anyone who's tired of what he or she hears on the radio and is on the lookout for some new favorite bands. Each track has a different vibe, but the set works well, as a whole, as a great mix of pop and rock songs from a variety of new artists.

To dig into these tracks yourself, use the control pad below the screen. Just follow these steps:

1. **Start out on the home page, the first screen of the Zune.**

   If you aren't on the home page, you can press Back again and again until you make it all the way back home, or you can press and hold the Back button for a few seconds, which will take you right there. This is a great way to get back to the home page, no matter how deep you are in the Zune menu hierarchy.

2. **Use down or up on the control pad to select Music from the home page menu. Press the center button of the control pad (the OK button) to confirm your choice.**

   What you see — a list of albums, artists, playlists, genres, or songs — depends on what you viewed the last time you were in this section. (If you've never clicked the Music item before, you most likely see a list of albums.)

   Whatever list you're viewing, you can now navigate the menu choices in two different directions. Moving up and down (pressing the top and bottom areas on the control pad) moves you through the current list of items (albums, for example); moving left and right switches what list you're viewing (from albums to artists, genres to songs, and so on). Figure 1-11 shows how this works in the music section.

3. **To get to your preloaded content, click the right side of the navigation area until you have the Songs list selected.**

   Because there's only one song by each band and from each album on the Zune, viewing by album or artist just makes you go through an extra step to get to your music.

Figure 1-11:
Switching
views by
pressing left
or right lets
you move
from albums
to artists
without
having to
go back a
step first.

4. **Select the song you're interested in from the Song list and then press the Play/Pause button to play that song, or press the OK button in the center of the control pad for more information about the song.**

Rock on!

If you want to play all of your preloaded content without having to select each one individually, select the Shuffle All option at the top of the Song list. Doing so plays the tracks in random order. (You can find out more about the music features of your Zune in Chapter 4.)

Checking out the videos

Your Zune comes preloaded with quite a few different videos, most of which are music videos in the same style as the preloaded music. (In fact, one of the videos is by CSS, a band that's also highlighted in the Music section.) Check out the music videos first:

- 30 Seconds to Mars, "The Kill" (Virgin Records)
- BT, "1.618" (DTS Entertainment)
- Chad VanGaalen, "Red Hot Drops" (Sub Pop Records)

✔ Coldcut featuring Roots Manuva, "True Skool" (Ninja Tune)

✔ CSS, "Let's Make Love and Listen to Death From Above" (Sub Pop Records)

✔ Fruit Bats, "Live: The Wind That Blew My Heart Away" (Sub Pop Records)

✔ Grandaddy, "Elevate Myself" (V2)

✔ Hot Chip, "Over and Over" (Astralwerks Records)

✔ Kraak & Smaak featuring Dez, "Keep Me Home" (Quango Music Group)

✔ Kinski, "Live: The Snowy Parts of Scandinavia" (Sub Pop Records)

✔ Paul Oakenfold, "Faster Kill Pussycat (Featuring Brittany Murphy)" (Maverick Records)

✔ Serena-Maneesh, "Drain Cosmetics" (Playlouderecordings)

Microsoft has also preloaded onto your Zune three cool action videos that feature some extreme skateboarding, mountain biking, and snowboarding/skiing. Here are the details:

✔ 5 Boro: "A New York Skateboarding Minute" (Skateboarding)

✔ Radical Films: "Kranked — Progression" (Mountain Biking)

✔ TGRTV: "The North Face" (Skiing/Snowboarding)

These videos may not be your cup of tea, but they're great for showing off the Zune's big and bright display until you've had a chance to load some of your own videos onto it!

To play a video, follow these steps:

1. **Start out on the home page, the first screen of the Zune.**

   If you aren't on the home page, you can press Back again and again until you make it all the way back to home, or you can press and hold the Back button for a few seconds, which will take you right there. This is a great way to get back to the home page, no matter how deep you are in the Zune menu hierarchy.

2. **Use down or up on the control pad to select Video from the home page menu. Press the center (OK) button on the control pad to confirm your choice.**

   When you first open the Videos section, a list of All Videos appears, but you can navigate the menu choices in two different directions. Moving up and down (pressing the top and bottom areas on the control pad) moves you through the current list of items (the All Videos list, for example); moving left and right switches which list you're viewing (from All Videos to subcategories such as Music Videos and Movies, each of which shows a filtered view of the video content).

3. **To get to your preloaded content, make sure you have the All Videos list selected.**

   Browse through this list to find all the videos on your device.

4. **Select the video you're interested in from the All Video list and then press the OK button in the center of the control pad to see the details about that video.**

   The Detail view appears, which you can see in Figure 1-12, showing a description of the video.

5. **Select Play to start the video.**

   If you aren't interested in the details of the video, you can press the Play/Pause button right on the All Videos list, and the video starts playing without showing the detailed information.

Browsing through and watching videos is covered in more detail in Chapter 12.

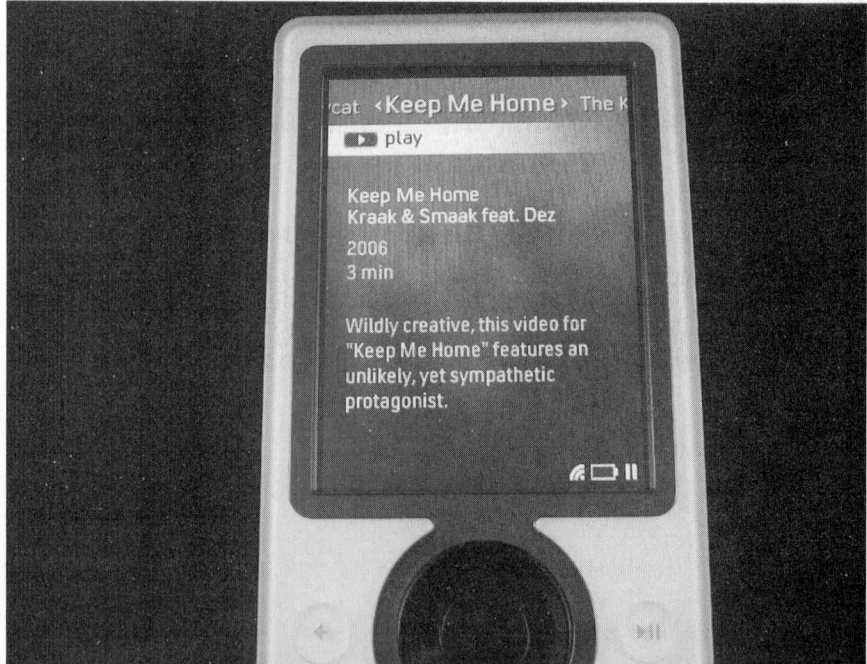

Figure 1-12:
A video's Detail page shows you the length, date, and description of the video.

Flipping through the photos

The last bit of preloaded content covers the photo angle actually, three different photo angles. You get a set of DJ photos (pictures of DJ equipment, such as record players and stacks of vinyl records), a set of graffiti photos (colorful wall art), and a collection of poster art highlighting various rock bands. Follow these steps to check out the cool eye candy:

1. **Start out on the home page, the first screen of the Zune.**

   If you aren't on the home page, press and hold the Back button for a few seconds, which will take you right there.

2. **Use down or up on the control pad to select Pictures from the home page menu. Press the center (OK) button on the control pad to confirm your choice.**

   The View by Folder list appears. This view shows you all the preloaded photos in their three groups (DJ photos, graffiti photos, and poster art). If you press left or right on the control pad, the View by Date list appears. This list is handy when you're looking at your own personal photos, but it isn't very useful for the preloaded ones.

3. **Pick Play Slideshow from the top of the screen to start up a slideshow of all the photos across all the folders, or use the control pad to select one of the three folders and press the OK button to view the contents of that folder.**

   If you view a single folder, you get a thumbnail view (see Figure 1-13) showing up to 30 pictures at once. (In the case of the preloaded photos, you get to see them all.) You can use the control pad to select an individual picture to view or select Play Slideshow at the top of the screen to start a slideshow of the current folder.

No matter how you view a photo or a slideshow of photos, the images are displayed in widescreen (or *landscape*) view, so you need to turn the Zune 90 degrees to the left to view them (or turn your head 90 degrees to the right — whatever's easier for you). Chapter 6 digs into the photo features of your Zune in much more detail.

Figure 1-13:
The photo folder view shows you up to 30 pictures at a time.

Tuning in the radio

It isn't really *preloaded* content, but the other way you can use your Zune right out of the box is to tune into some local radio stations. Pick the Radio option from the home page to switch to a cool Tuner view (see Figure 1-14).

Remember that the headphones of the Zune are also its antenna, so if you're going to use the radio feature, make sure they're hooked up.

Press left or right on the control pad to seek between stations. When your Zune finds a station, you may get some extra info above and below the tuning band. Not every station transmits this extra data, which usually includes the station's call letters and sometimes the currently playing song, but many do! We chat more about that info, and the rest of the radio features, in Chapter 4.

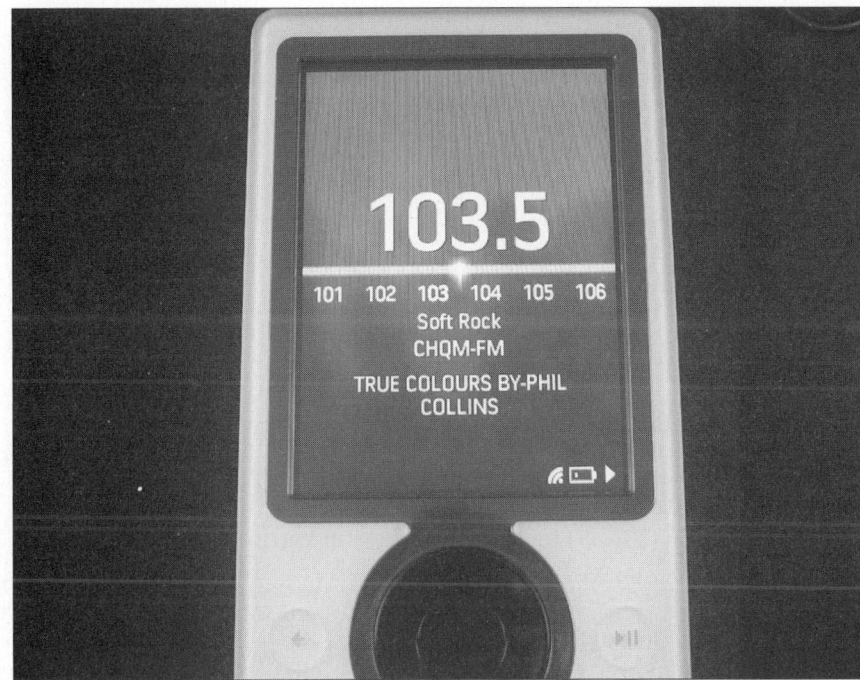

Figure 1-14:
The hottest-
looking
tuning dial
I've ever
seen.

What's Next?

You can rely on your Zune's preloaded content for only so long — did you really plan on getting by with just nine pieces of preloaded music, for example? — so Chapter 2 shows you how to install the Zune software and hook your device up to your PC so you can load some content of your own. If we were you, we'd go to Chapter 2 right now.

Chapter 2

Installing the Zune Software

● ●

In This Chapter

▶ Installing the Zune software

▶ Getting familiar with the Zune software

▶ Browsing the Zune Marketplace

▶ Discovering Zune features

▶ Getting a Zune account

● ●

*A*fter you do the unboxing-your-Zune thing (see Chapter 1), you probably want to add your own music, videos, and pictures. We do all that and more in this chapter — right after we show you what's what on the Zune CD and walk you through getting all the Zune software transferred to your PC.

A Zune CD Overview

First things first. If you plugged in your Zune when you first got it, as described in Chapter 1, it's charged and ready to go. To add content to your Zune, you need to install the software that comes on the Zune's companion CD-ROM. This is important because the drivers that allow the PC to talk to the Zune need to be installed before the Zune can be used with the software.

So, if your Zune is currently plugged into your PC, go ahead and unplug it now so you can install the Zune software.

The Zune CD contains the Zune player software that's used to add music to your Zune. The Zune is a little different than many other Windows-based MP3 players in that its software has to be installed before you can add your own music to the device. This software allows you to set up and manage playlists, purchase new content from Marketplace, and manage music and other content on your PC.

The CD provides the Zune software installer and some other goodies that can enhance your Zune experience.

Walking through the Installation Process

If you've ever installed anything from a CD onto your PC, most of what follows in this section won't come as much of a surprise. Still, the devil is in the details, so we decided to document the major steps along the way.

Speaking of details, be sure to get your PC up to date by going to `http://windowsupdate.microsoft.com` and getting the latest patches for Windows *before* you install the Zune software. Having an updated PC will give you a warm and fuzzy feeling.

When you insert the Zune CD into your PC, the computer normally prompts you to run the Zune installer automatically. Go ahead and let that run to get things started. Eventually, the Welcome screen of the Zune Setup Wizard should appear, as shown in Figure 2-1.

If you have Autorun disabled on your PC, you'll first have to use Windows Explorer to navigate to the Zune CD-ROM on your PC and then double-click the Zune installer file — named, appropriately enough, `ZuneSetup.exe`. Doing so gets you to the wizard's Welcome screen, as well.

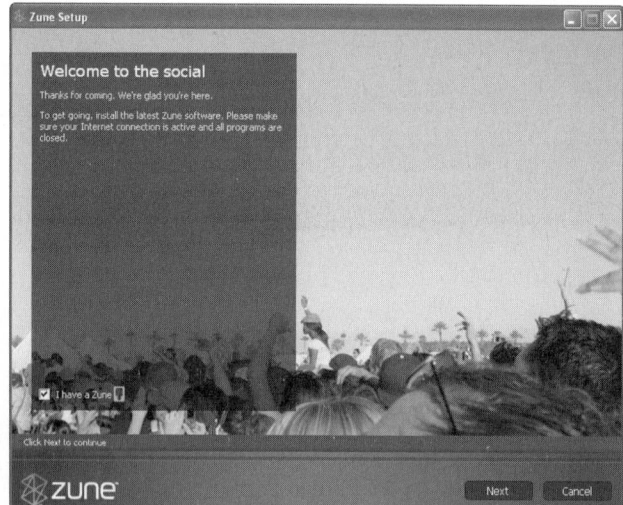

Figure 2-1:
The first step in a little Zune magic.

Time to move beyond all the warm welcomes and actually get some work done. Follow these steps:

1. **With the Welcome display on-screen, click the Next button to get the installation process started.**

   A progress bar appears at the bottom of the setup program while files are copied from the CD to your hard drive. Sit back and relax as the progress bar fills up to 100 percent, which is when you'll be prompted to plug your Zune into your PC, as shown in Figure 2-2.

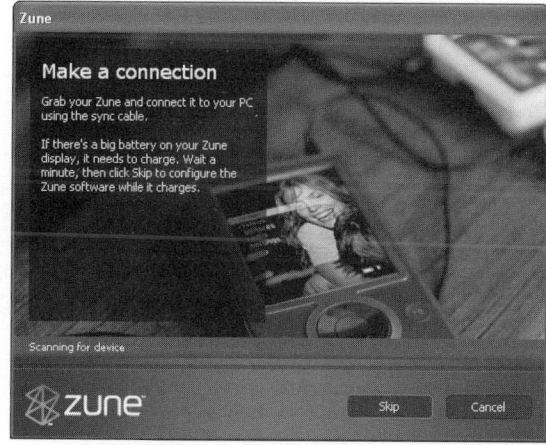

Figure 2-2:
The Zune Setup screen prompts you to plug in your Zune.

2. **Follow the prompt by first plugging the adapter end of your Zune sync cable — the wider, flatter part — into the bottom of your Zune (see Figure 2-3) and then plugging the standard USB end — the rectangular end — into the USB port on your PC, as shown in Figure 2-4.**

   Sometimes, the USB ports in the back of the PC perform a little better than those in the front. If you're experiencing performance issues, try changing the USB port to which you're connecting your Zune.

   With the Zune plugged into your PC, the Zune starts charging, and Windows automatically installs the appropriate Zune drivers on the PC. The installation program has also been scanning for your Zune, and when it finds it, one of the first things the installation program does is prompt you to update the Zune's firmware, if necessary, as shown in Figure 2-5. (*Firmware* is the software that runs on the Zune device itself.)

Figure 2-3:
The Zune
end of the
sync cable.

If your Zune doesn't have enough charge in it to update itself in the next few steps, you can still navigate the steps. After the battery is at an acceptable level, you can update its internal software.

Figure 2-4:
The rectan-
gular USB
port on
a PC.

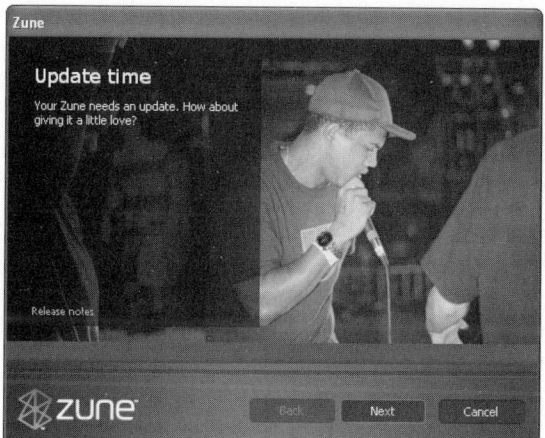

Figure 2-5:
Updating
the Zune's
firmware.

3. **Click the Next button in the Update Time screen to update your firmware.**

As the firmware is being updated, you see the screen shown in Figure 2-6.

Updating your Zune's firmware is a very important part of the setup process. Be sure to take your time and do this very carefully. If you don't follow the instructions, you could damage your player, so be sure to do just what the screens tell you to do at this point. Don't move or disconnect the Zune during the update.

Figure 2-6:
The setup
screen
warns you
not to move
your Zune,
so hands off!

Did we mention that you shouldn't move or unplug the Zune while it's updating? We know you might be tempted, and we also know that it might seem like a very long wait; that's okay, just keep waiting. If you're not sure what to do while you wait, here are some suggestions:

- Get a snack.

- Go to the bathroom.

- Page through this book and get familiar with all of the cool stuff you're going to be doing with your Zune after you get through this boring part!

After your Zune is updated, the installer screen changes to the Name that Zune screen, shown in Figure 2-7. You can rest easy now. You did it!

Figure 2-7:
Pin a moniker on your Zune.

You're occasionally prompted to update your Zune firmware during the life of the product. Keep in mind that you shouldn't move or unplug the Zune when you update the firmware then, either.

4. Enter a name for your Zune in the Name field and then click Next.

This is the name that others will see when you make wireless connections with them for music and picture sharing.

You might already see your first name listed as the Zune's default name. That'll work, but if your friends know you better by a nickname, or if you have a lot of friends with the same name as you, it might be better to give your Zune a name that's unique. Why? Well, as you can see in Chapter 16, that name shows up on other people's Zunes when you start socializing. Having a unique name makes it much easier to let people know exactly who you are. (You're free to name your Zune anything you want, but keep in mind that a Zune name is a relatively public thing, so maybe you don't want to choose "Chronic Bed Wetter" if you want to avoid snide remarks. "Zune Cleaver" or "Zune Carter Cash" would, of course, be entirely appropriate.)

5. **On the screen that appears, choose your synchronization options (as shown in Figure 2-8) and then click Next.**

   Synchronizing here means getting your existing music, pictures, and video — stuff already on your hard drive — copied to your Zune.

   Your music files are synchronized by default. If you want to synchronize your video and your pictures to your Zune, as well, check the boxes associated with those items. If not, you can add them later after you've discovered a little bit more about what it means to add a lot of video and pictures to your Zune.

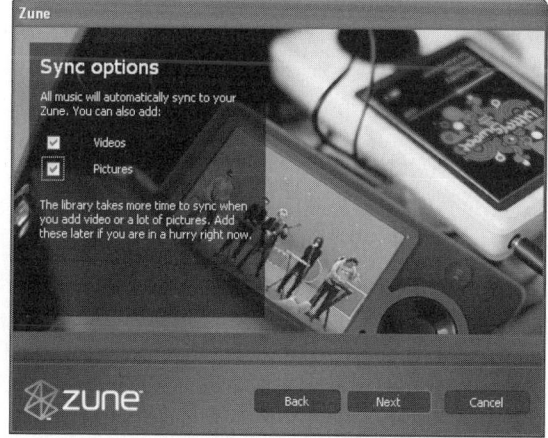

Figure 2-8: Adding your media to your Zune.

If you have a lot of pictures (say, over 1,000), or if you have a lot of video files, hold off on synchronizing them for now; we show you how to optimize your pictures and video for your Zune in Chapter 3.

6. **In the screen that appears, choose how you want the sync process to build your Zune library.**

   Your choices are shown in Figure 2-9. You can accept the defaults — the Express library settings — and just continue with the sync, or you can do a custom synchronization, which lets you choose certain options to set when you build your library.

The following options are set if you choose the Express option:

- Make Zune the default player on your PC for a number of media data types.

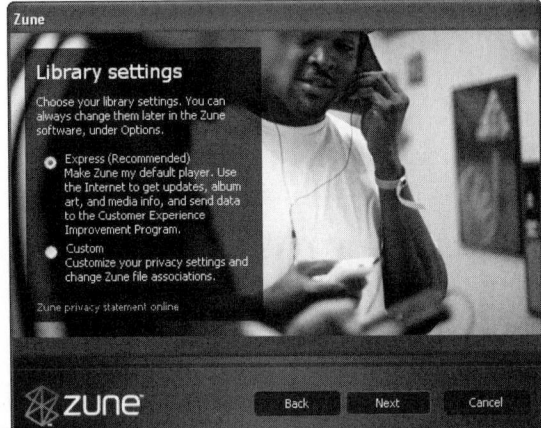

- Get Zune updates from the Internet automatically.

- Get album art and media information from the Internet automatically.

- Send data back to the Microsoft Customer Experience Improvement Program.

7. **(Optional) If you choose Custom in Step 6, customize your installation by clicking the links on the screen shown in Figure 2-10. Then click Next.**

The following list clues you in on your options:

- **Privacy:** Following this link gets you to the Privacy tab of the Options window, shown in Figure 2-11. Actually, there's not much to this tab. You can opt out of the Zune Customer Experience Improvement Plan — a setup that sends anonymous usage data back to Microsoft so they can improve the product by knowing how customers are using it — by deselecting the check box. And you can clear caches for your CDs and other media-related stuff by clicking the Clear Caches button. (A *cache* is local storage that holds a copy of the media files you've played on the machine. If you're especially concerned about keeping the content you view and listen to private, then you may want to clear the cache.) Other than that, there's not much to Privacy settings. Make your choices and then click OK.

- **File Types:** Following this link gets you to the File Types tab of the Options window, as shown in Figure 2-12. It turns out that the Zune software on your PC, in addition to being the host application for your Zune device, can also act as a stand-alone media player, comparable to Windows Media Player. The File Types tab lets you choose which types of files are opened by the Zune player by default.

You can choose to associate any, all, or none of the file types listed in the box. You might have another favorite player that you want to use for a particular file type. Unchecking that type here doesn't change whether the file is played on the Zune, only whether the Zune player is invoked when the file is double-clicked on the PC.

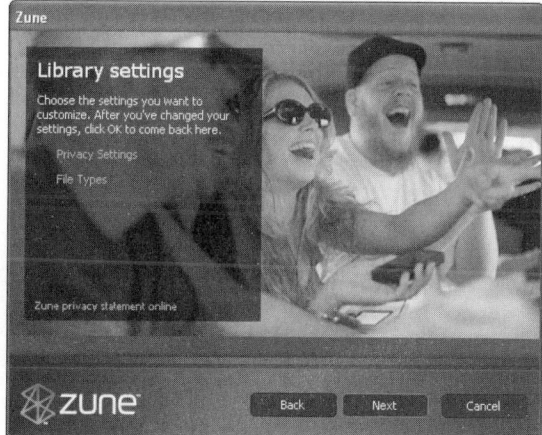

Figure 2-10:
Accessing
the custom
options.

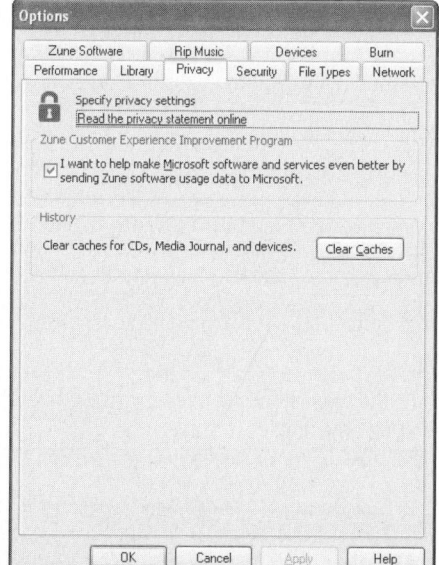

Figure 2-11:
The Zune
privacy
settings.

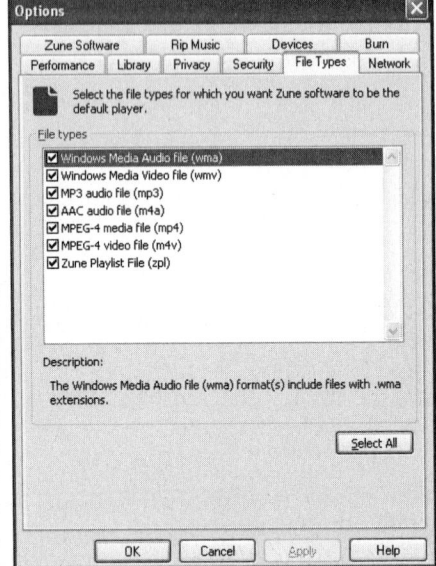

Figure 2-12:
Choosing
the default
file types
played by
the Zune
software on
your PC.

Table 2-1 shows the file types that are associated with the Zune software on the PC by default if you leave all of the options checked or if you use the Express option in the installer.

Table 2-1   File Types Associated with the Zune Player on the PC

Extension	Description
WMA	Windows Media Audio file format
WMV	Windows Media Video file format
MP3	Common audio file format used on the Internet
AAC	Audio file format commonly used by Apple iPod/iTunes
MP4	Video file format commonly used on the Internet
M4V	Video file format commonly used in mobile devices, such as mobile phones
ZPL	Zune playlist file, the playlist format used by the Zune player on the PC and on the Zune device itself

TIP

On this screen, you should check all of these items unless there's a specific player that you know you want to keep using for a particular file format. The Zune player makes a great player for all of these file types, and it should have no problem with any of them. After you make your selections, click OK.

After completing the Library Settings screen, the Zune Setup Wizard advances to the Stream to Xbox 360 screen, as shown n Figure 2-13.

8. **In the Stream to Xbox 360 screen, use the check boxes to set whether you want to *stream* (or broadcast) music, video, or pictures over your home network using your Xbox 360; then click Next.**

We have a lot more information about streaming to your Xbox 360 in Chapter 13, but for now, we recommend, if you do have an Xbox 360, that you go ahead and check all three boxes. Doing so puts a tiny program on your computer that allows the Xbox 360 to find and communicate with the Zune software on your PC.

Clicking Next brings up a version of the screen shown in Figure 2-14. This screen lets you know that the content on your computer is being indexed and converted as necessary for play on your Zune device.

Figure 2-13:
Set these
options to
stream
content
to your
Xbox 360.

9. **After the Build Your Library screen tells you that your library is complete, click Next.**

REMEMBER

You're set. Your media has now been added to your Zune device.

The library build takes longer to index if you have a lot of content.

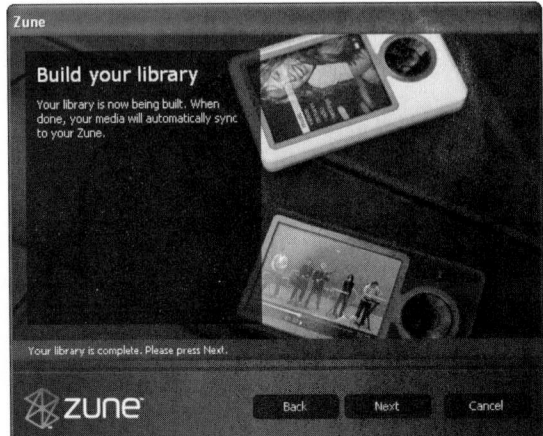

Figure 2-14:
The installer
builds the
Zune library.

When the installer builds the Zune library, it does so by searching for content in the My Music, My Videos, and My Pictures folders. Don't worry if you have your content stored outside of your PC's standard music and media folders. We show you how to add those files to your Zune library in Chapter 3.

So, you have your media files transferred to your Zune. Good work! We'd love to tell you that you're done, but we're not really through with the whole installation thing yet. You still need to create a Zune account — you know, that little item that gives you access to thousands of songs from the Zune Marketplace? Nevertheless, this is as good a time as any to insert a logical break in the installation process and start over with a new numbered list. (Otherwise, we'd have a list with 47 numbered steps in it, and who'd want to do that?)

What is streaming?

Streaming is a technology that lets you play music, video, or picture files over your home network and through a device such as your Xbox 360. This technology doesn't copy your content to the Xbox 360 in a way you can access from the console later. Rather, it plays the content by sending bits of it over the network to play out a little bit at a time, sort of like a broadcast. When the 360 gets the content from the PC, it starts to cache it locally (in a temporary file) until it has enough stored up that it can play the content continuously without pausing. This way, you get to enjoy the content stored on your PC, and you don't have to worry about clogging up your Xbox 360 with a lot of extra files.

Setting Up Your Zune Account

We assume here that you've been dutifully making your way through the Zune Setup Wizard (as spelled out in the preceding section) and have now gotten to the really exciting part where you create your own Zune account. If that's true, and you've been good and clicked the Next button on the Build Your Library screen of the wizard, the next screen you see is your first look at the Zune software actually running on the PC, as shown in Figure 2-15. Just so you know what to expect, here's a brief rundown of what's involved in creating a new account:

✔ You need to create a Zune Tag.

✔ You need to either register your current Windows Live ID with Zune.net or create a new one from scratch.

  Not sure what a Windows Live ID is? Don't worry; we tell you all about it later in this section.

✔ You need to create a new Zune account.

✔ You have the chance to purchase Microsoft Points or choose a Zune Pass subscription, if you so desire.

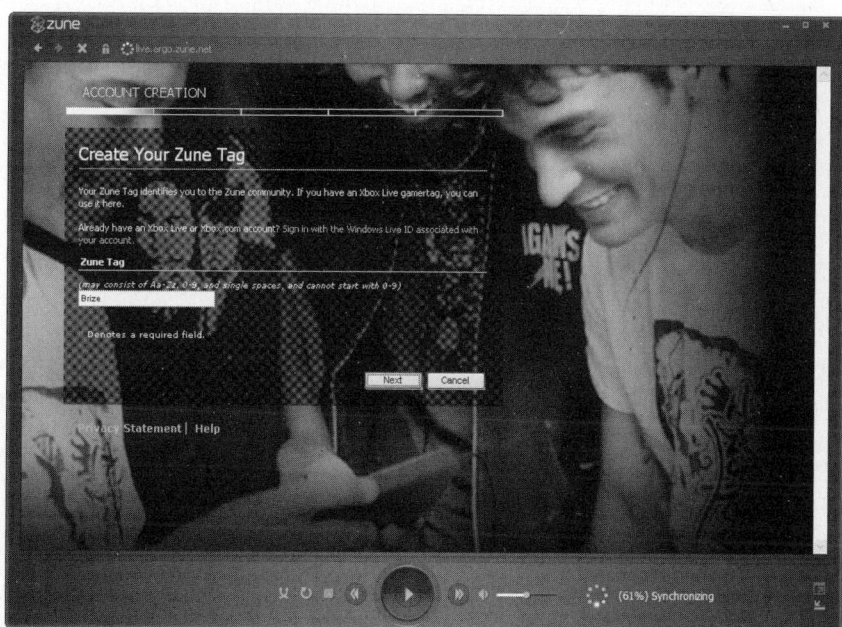

Figure 2-15: Creating a new Zune Tag.

Keeping up with the captia

A *captia* is a security device designed to prevent computer programs from being able to create dummy accounts on a system. Spammers — people who send all of that lovely, unsolicited e-mail to everyone — love to create fake e-mail accounts because they can use them to send their spam. The captia — with its strange, floating numbers and letters — prevents these programs from automatically creating a new account because computer programs have difficulty seeing the letters and numbers in the captia.

Unfortunately, many people have trouble reading the captia, also. To help with this, you have two options:

✔ If you have trouble reading the characters in the captia picture, you can get a new set of characters by clicking the button with the two arrows on it. (See the following figure.)

✔ If you have a lot of difficulty reading the captia, you can click the speaker button, which turns your picture captia into an audio captia, as shown in the following figure. When you click the Play button, a set of numbers is played through your PC's speakers, and you can type them into the Numbers text box.

To get this party started, just follow these steps:

1. **Enter your Zune Tag in the appropriate field (refer to Figure 2-15) and then click Next.**

   Your Zune Tag is the handle by which you'll be known in the Zune community as more community-based features are added to the Zune experience.

   You can come up with a completely new Zune Tag, or you can use your Xbox 360 Gamer Tag if you register using the same Windows Live ID account (an Xbox Live or Xbox.com account, for example) associated with your Gamer Tag.

2. **In the screen of the wizard that appears, indicate whether you have a current Windows Live ID and then click Next.**

   If you read the fine print in Figure 2-16, you see that if you have a Hotmail or MSN e-mail address, you already have a Windows Live ID. (This ID used to be called a Microsoft Passport.) If such is the case, then choose the first option on the screen here and click Next. You can then skip the Purchasing and Subscriptions section if your billing information is up to date and go straight to Step 5.

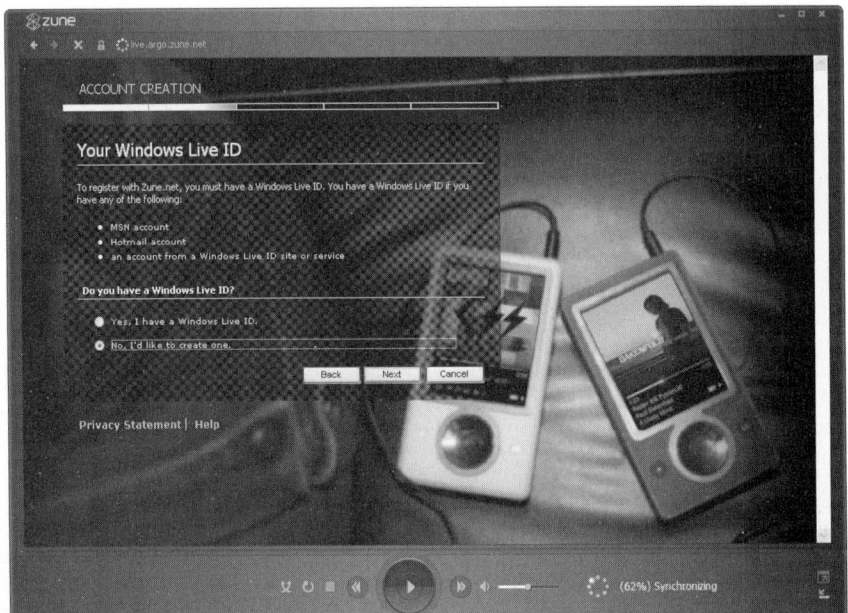

Figure 2-16:
Creating a
new Zune
account.

If you don't already have a Windows Live ID, choose the second option
and click Next. You see the screen in Figure 2-17.

3. **If you check the second option in Step 2, enter the information to
   create a new Windows Live ID in the appropriate fields of the Create
   Your Windows Live ID screen and then click I Accept.**

The Create Your Windows Live ID screen is pretty straightforward. It
really just wants the tried-and-true stuff: e-mail address, password
(twice), the ubiquitous password reset question (and answer), the weird
Type the Characters That You See in This Picture part — also known as
the *captia* (see the sidebar "Keeping up with the captia," in this chapter,
for its interesting tale) — and of course, the I Accept button. (That last
one is to keep the lawyers happy.)

You may need to scroll to see all of the items on the screen in
Figure 2-17.

As you complete these steps, here are a few suggestions that are guaranteed to make your life easier later on down the line:

- **Write down your account information and store it in a safe
  place.** This is important because it's really hard to figure this stuff
  out later, and I promise that if you need to use the information you
  write down later, you'll send us an e-mail thanking us for telling
  you to write this down.

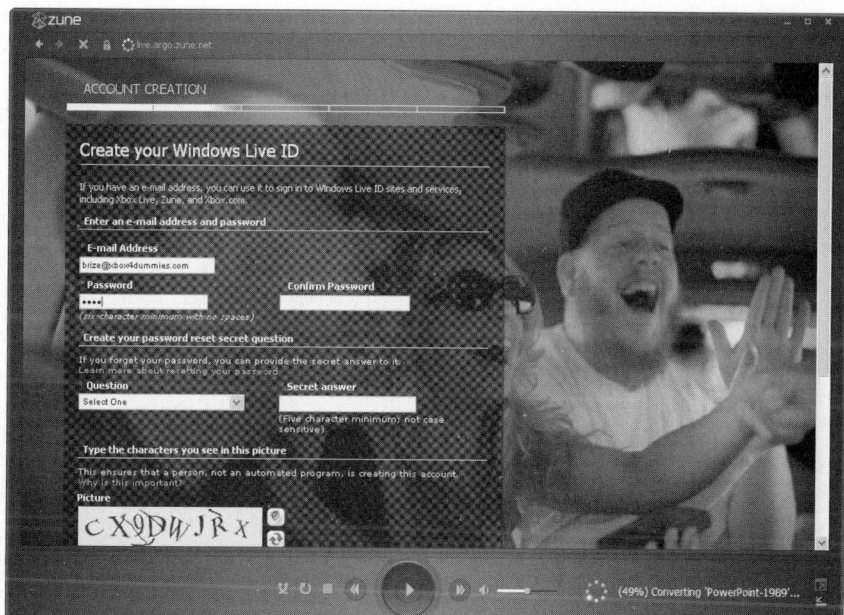

- **Use a strong password.** Words that are found in the dictionary (*any* dictionary) are usually not that great as passwords. They're easy to remember, but hackers can figure them out more easily than you might think. Try coming up with a password that uses numbers, letters, capital letters, and other characters on your keyboard. This account will be associated with your money, so keep it as safe as you can.

- **Use a secret question and answer that nobody else can figure out.** It's actually okay to lie on this one if it keeps your answer safe and you can remember the answer. (See our first tip about writing stuff down.)

Making a point

What are Microsoft Points? They've actually been around since the launch of the Xbox 360, and the Xbox Live Marketplace has used them as currency to buy content for the console. Points have now spread to the Zune, and you can use them to purchase music and other content through Zune Marketplace.

How much is a Microsoft Point worth? Well, that depends on what country you live in. In general, 100 Microsoft Points costs more than 100 pennies, but after you buy them, they seem easier to spend than dollars!

After you add all the data to the screen in Figure 2-17 and click I Accept, you're shown the Create Your Account screen, shown in Figure 2-18.

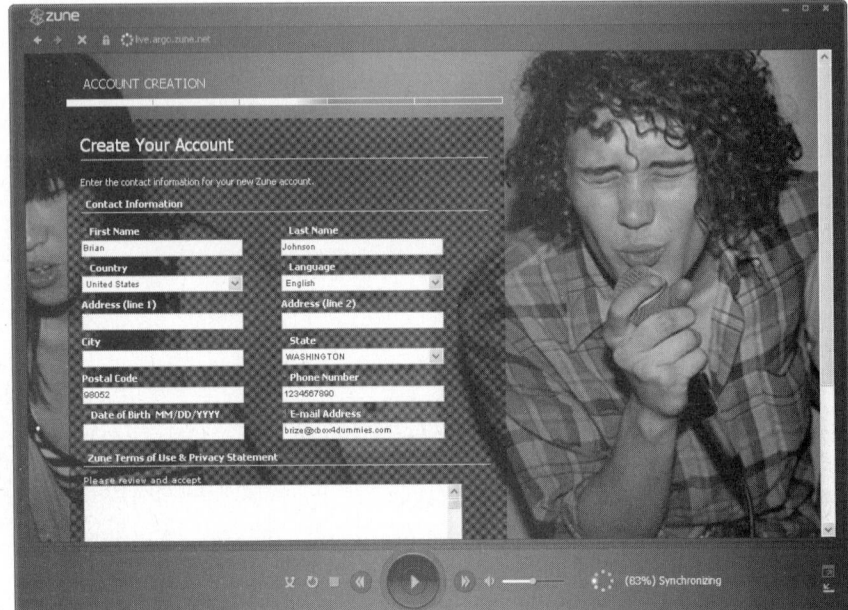

Figure 2-18: Adding your personal data to your Windows Live ID account.

4. **Enter the personal data you want to associate with your Windows Live ID into the appropriate fields and then click the I Accept button.**

Again, nothing too out-of-the-ordinary here. Name, address, e-mail, terms of use — the usual stuff.

This is another screen that you might need to scroll to read.

5. **With your account now created, use the screen that appears (see Figure 2-19) to choose how you want to purchase new music.**

Your choices are as follows:

- **The Pay as You Go option:** To purchase Microsoft Points during this installation process, click the Purchase Points button at the bottom-left of the screen and follow the instructions for purchasing Points for Zune Marketplace. You can purchase Points with a credit card in various increments, depending on your location.

- **The Get a Zune Pass option:** A Zune Pass subscription is a good way to get all the music you could possibly listen to at one fixed price. To purchase a Zune Pass subscription, click the Subscribe to Zune button at the bottom-center of the screen. The Subscribe to Zune screen, shown in Figure 2-20, appears. This screen lists the Zune Pass subscription prices and offers.

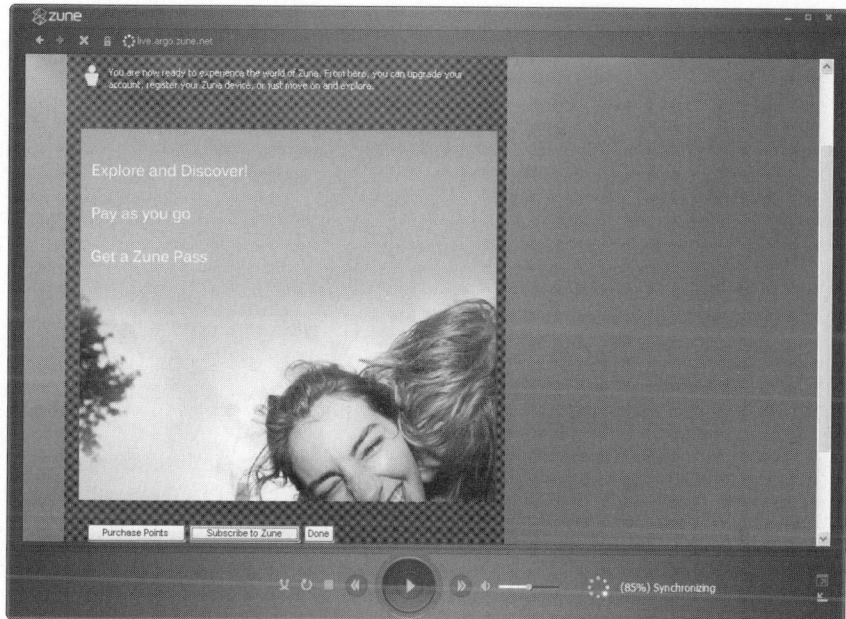

Figure 2-19:
Purchase
points or a
subscription
during the
setup
process.

Check your package for a special coupon that allows you to experience a Zune Pass subscription for 14 days for free.

Figure 2-20:
Choosing a
Zune Pass
subscription.

- **The Explore and Discover option:** This option is perfect for those who don't want to commit to anything just yet. Just click the Done button in the lower-right corner, and you're free to Zune with what you've got.

For the sake of argument — or at least for the sake of our example — we assume you want to go the subscription route.

6. **Choose the subscription level you want in the Subscribe to Zune screen and then click Next.**

Zune Pass subscriptions come in two flavors. A monthly pass and a three-month pass. In general, you can save some money if you go with the three-month pass.

Things change fast in the Zune world, so be sure to look for other Zune Pass options in the future!

You can also purchase subscriptions at many different music, electronics, and game stores, and you get a redemption code that you can enter at this point, if you have it.

The prices shown here can change at any time. Check the Zune store for current pricing information.

7. **In the screen that appears (see Figure 2-21), add your credit card information to complete your purchase.**

Purchasing versus subscription

You should be aware of some differences between music purchasing and a music subscription before you make your decision about how you want to spend your money. Table 2-2 lists the differences between content purchased with points and music that you can listen to via your subscription.

Differences between Purchasing and Subscriptions

Feature	Purchased	Subscription
All the content you can hear at one low price		X
Play music on your Zune	X	X
Play music on your PC	X	X
Copy music to a CD-ROM		X
Music expires when subscription expires		X
Music protected by DRM	X	X

8. **In the confirmation screen that appears (see Figure 2-22), click the Finish button to complete the setup of your Zune.**

Whew!

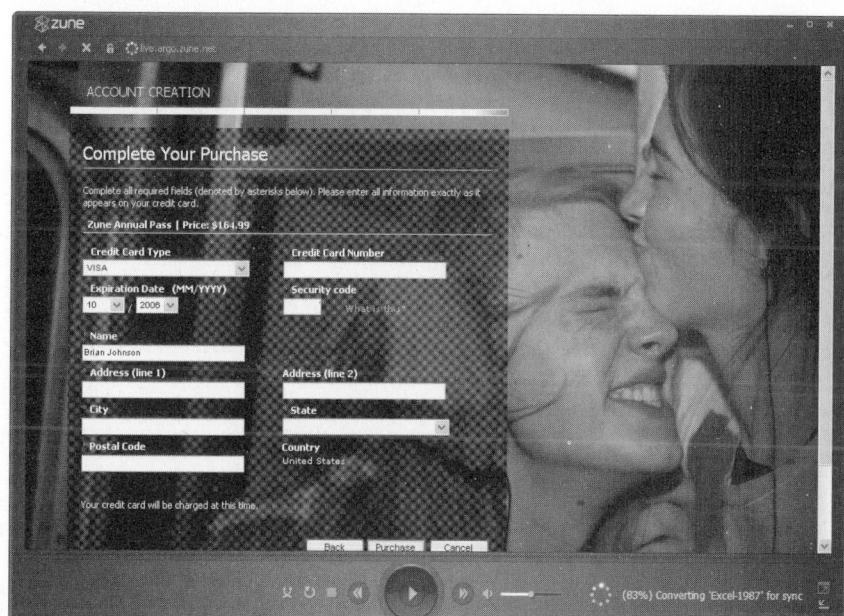

Figure 2-21: Show them the money!

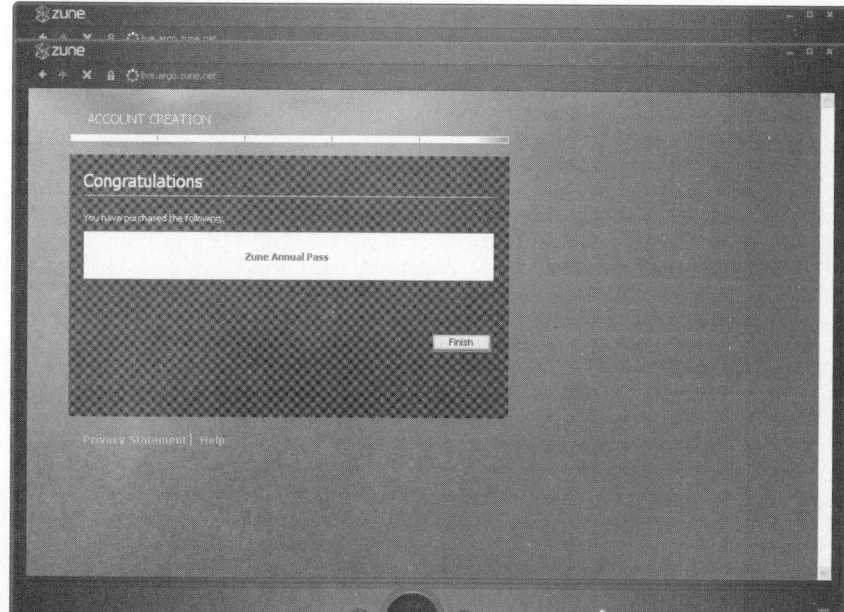

Figure 2-22: It's confirmed: You're now part of the Zune community.

During the synchronization process, some of your content needs to be transcoded into a format that the Zune can understand. Depending on how much content was in your media folders when you started this process, your Zune may take a while to get that content. While you're waiting, why not view the Zune Marketplace and see what's there?

Browse the Zune Marketplace

Okay, the moment you've been waiting for: Click the Marketplace item in the Zune software's Navigation pane (on the left) to check out the Zune Marketplace. You can see Zune Marketplace in all its glory in Figure 2-23. This is where you can purchase and download new music for your Zune, and boy does it have a ton of features. (Too many features to cover right now, but we get to every minor detail in Chapter 7.) For now, we just want to show you how things are laid out and fill you in on how you can navigate and find the content that you're looking for.

While you look at the Zune Marketplace, notice that the home page is broken down into specific areas:

- **Main:** In this section, you see the currently highlighted artists and links to featured content on Zune Marketplace.

- **New Releases:** This section is for new content on Zune Marketplace. Check it often for updated content.

- **Playlists:** Here, you can find groups of related songs that somebody in their infinite wisdom put together for you. (Sometimes these "somebodies" are your favorite artists moonlighting as your personal DJ.) You can purchase the songs on these playlists, or you can download them via your Zune Pass subscription.

- **Featured Artists:** These are the hottest artists featured on Zune Marketplace.

- **Top Songs, Top Albums, Top Artists:** What's everyone listening to? Check out the rightmost side of the Zune Marketplace screen, where the most requested songs, albums, and artists have found a home. This section gives you a great way to see what you might be missing.

There's definitely a lot to the Zune Marketplace, so don't think that the preceding list is in any way a definitive list of its many treasures. That comes with Chapter 7.

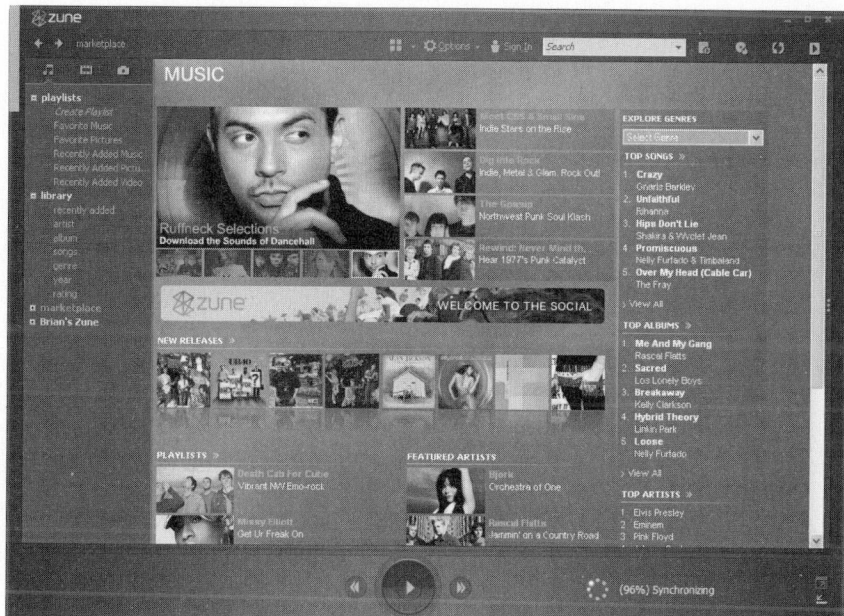

Figure 2-23:
The Zune
Marketplace
on your PC.

Take Off and Go

After your Zune has completed the synchronization process, you can unplug it and hit the road. If you ever run low on battery power or want to transfer new content from your PC to your Zune, just use the Zune USB cable to plug your Zune back into your PC; synchronization and charging take place automatically.

It's a good idea to get into the habit of charging your Zune before you go running off to places unknown.

Now that you've installed the Zune software on your PC, you can purchase new music anytime via the Zune Marketplace. Of course, you can get music and content onto Zune in other ways, and we talk about those ways over the course of the next few chapters.

Chapter 3

Handling the Zune Interface

*I*n this chapter, we tell you all about the various buttons and other gizmos on your Zune device →ll the stuff that's collectively known as the *user interface*. When it comes to user interfaces, the one on the Zune is pretty straightforward, but it might be a little confusing if you're used to the Apple iPod or another medium or MP3 player.

Surely a Zune Has More than One Button!

The first thing you may notice about the Zune is the big round button in the lower quarter of the device. This button, along with the smaller buttons nestled to the left and right of it, are your controls for the Zune.

The buttons are laid out in such a way that you shouldn't need to switch gears based on the mode your Zune is in. For example, it doesn't matter whether you're navigating through your music choices, video choices, or picture choices — the *process* (which button you push when) is essentially the same. After you get the hang of it, making your way around a Zune's features effectively is no problem.

Figure 3-1 shows the Zune with its various controls nicely labeled. The following list takes a breezy look at what each of these controls does — generally speaking.

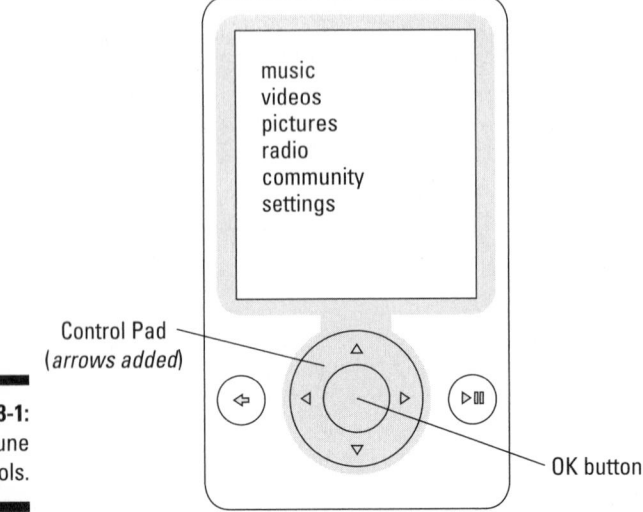

Control Pad
(*arrows added*)

OK button

Figure 3-1:
The Zune
controls.

✔ **Back:** This button's purpose is to move you back through the menu system. If you're looking at a screen showing the specific song you're listening to, pressing the Back button backs you up through the menu to the general list of songs, and pressing it again takes you all the way back to the main menu.

The Back button takes you back to the preceding menu. If you want to move to the preceding item at the same level — sideways, as it were — press Left on the control pad.

Holding the Back button down for a couple seconds takes you directly to the main menu of the Zune. With this quick menu access, you can switch from one feature to another on the device in no time.

✔ **Up, Left, Right, and Down:** You can move around by using the control pad that surrounds the OK button on the screen. (Think of it as a high tech version of the cinder track around the football field at your old high school.) This track is actually a rocker button, meaning that pressing the top, left, right, and bottom parts of the button translates into quite distinct actions — namely, moving the selection on the screen up, left, right, and down.

If you've used an iPod, you might think you can spin your thumb around the Zune's track button to make something happen. It doesn't work. This control is click-only.

✔ **OK:** The button in the center of the big circle is the OK button. This button works like a computer button that you click. If an item is selected and you press the OK button, the next screen or action associated with the labeled selection appears.

✔ **Play/Pause:** This Play button does what you'd expect — click it, and your Zune immediately plays the currently selected song or video. You can also use this button to pause the currently playing song. Just press the button while a song is playing, and the song pauses. Press it again, and the song plays again. Kind of like that game Red Light/Green Light you used to play at camp.

The Play button does one more thing — it actually puts your Zune to sleep if you hold it down for five seconds. This ability helps save the battery when you're not listening to music, watching video, or looking at pictures.

✔ **Lock:** At the top of the Zune, you can see the Hold switch. Engaging this switch disables the rest of the buttons on the Zune. Why would you want to do that? Here are two big reasons to lock your Zune:

- **Preventing accidents:** You probably want to avoid buttons being pressed accidentally, which can put a speed bump in your Zune-content enjoyment. You can accidentally press a button when you stick your Zune in a coat pocket while you're out for a walk or doing some physical activity, such as skiing, for example.

- **Storage:** You definitely want to lock the Zune before throwing it in your backpack, shoulder bag, briefcase, fanny pack, or whatever for transport. You don't want your Zune waking up when you're not using it and draining the battery. So lock your Zune before you put it away.

Taking Care of Your Basic Settings

Everything is adjustable in our technology-driven world, and the Zune is no exception. Sure, you can do tons of stuff with your Zune by using all the default settings from the factory, but what's the fun of that? The real Zune experience comes with customizing your feature settings just the way you want them.

So, where does all this customizing take place? At the Settings screen, as shown in Figure 3-2. To get to the Settings screen, follow these steps:

1. **Hold down the Back button to pull up the main menu (if you're not at the main menu already, of course!).**

2. **Press the Down button until the Settings item is selected in the main menu and then press the OK button.**

   The Settings menu appears.

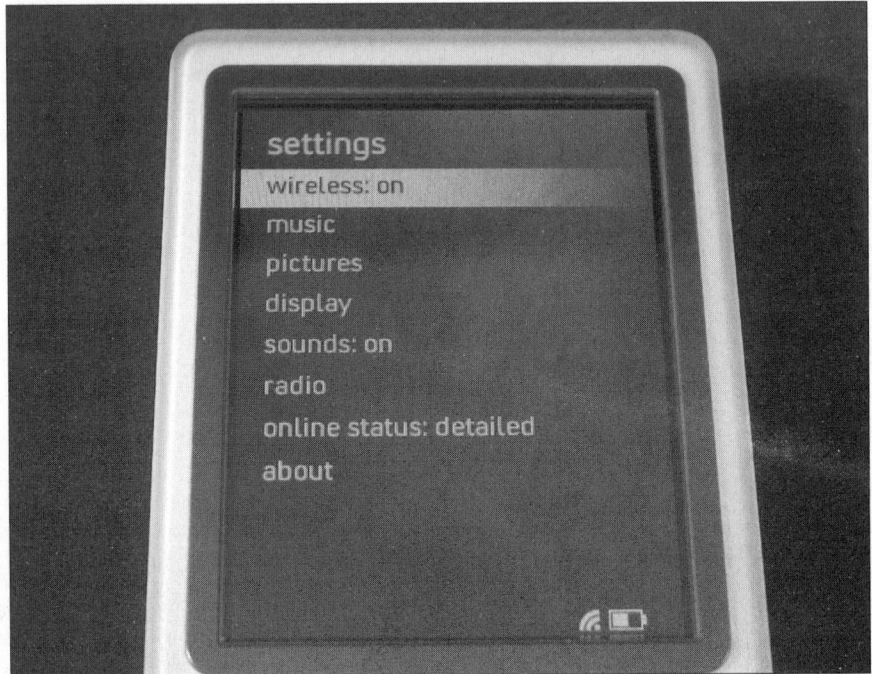

Figure 3-2:
The Settings
screen is
where you
set your
Zune.

The Settings menu features this list of items:

- ✔ Wireless
- ✔ Music
- ✔ Pictures
- ✔ Display
- ✔ Sounds
- ✔ Radio
- ✔ Online Status
- ✔ About

One of the great things about the Zune is that it's fully updatable, so you can expect this list to change in the future as new features are added to the devices through firmware updates.

The following sections walk you through these items, so you can find out the kind of stuff you can customize and how to do it.

The Wireless setting

The Wireless option is a toggle that turns your Zune's WiFi feature on and off. Turning this setting to Off conserves your battery power, but it also disables the social aspect of the Zune, which is all about sharing music and pictures with others. (Okay, if you're out in the woods all by yourself, it probably makes sense to toggle the Wireless option to Off.)

When the Zune Wireless is enabled, you see Wireless: On in the Settings menu. When Wireless is disabled, you see Wireless: Off.

Toggling this setting on and off is pretty simple. If you see Wireless: On in the Settings menu, press OK to toggle this setting to Wireless: Off. And, if you see Wireless: Off, you press (you guessed it!) the OK button to toggle this setting to Wireless: On.

You may run into two big reasons to turn Wireless off on your Zune:

- **Air Travel:** On most flights, you're required to turn off the wireless features of your personal electronics during air travel, including WiFi and Bluetooth on your phones, laptops, and PDAs. Now, you can add the WiFi on your Zune music player to that list. This policy may be different in different countries and on different flights, so be sure you understand what the rules are before you get on your plane. If the policy isn't clear, go ahead and shut off Wireless, just to be on the safe side.

- **Personal Security:** Okay, this may sound a bit cloak-and-dagger, but if you're out in public and your Zune Wireless is enabled, there's a slight chance that evildoers looking for something to steal might use a Zune to try to find other Zunes nearby. It's highly unlikely, but still possible, that a less-than-reputable individual could use your Zune to discover the name of the person who owns another Zune in the area. Armed with such information, that less-than-reputable individual could approach a Zune owner and pretend to know that person by his or her first name, thus gaining his or her confidence.

Turn off your Wireless when you don't want to socialize with others, such as during your commute to work. Doing so saves your battery and keeps others from finding out details about you that you might not want to share. (Such as the fact that you have a Zune in your pocket!)

The Music setting

The Music setting is actually your doorway to another menu sporting the Shuffle, Repeat, and Equalizer settings. You toggle these settings the same way you toggle the Wireless setting; just select the item and keep pressing the OK button to switch from on to off to on again. The following sections tell you what each of these settings does.

Shuffle

The Shuffle item determines whether playback on your Zune is randomized or whether the music is played back in the order that's shown when you begin to play the content. For example, if Shuffle is turned on when you select a particular artist and you choose Play All, your Zune plays back that artist's music in random order.

When you browse music by Artists, Playlists, Songs, Genres, or Albums, the first item under each of these headings is Shuffle All. You can shuffle music in any of the categories, or you can turn on Shuffle from the Music settings.

To toggle the Shuffle option on your Zune, follow these steps:

1. **In the Settings menu, choose Music and press OK.**

2. **Select the Shuffle item and then press OK.**

   If the Shuffle setting is on, the Shuffle item changes from Shuffle: On to Shuffle: Off. If the Shuffle setting is off, the item changes from Shuffle: Off to Shuffle: On.

Repeat

The Repeat setting determines whether a particular selection of music plays over again after it's finished. For example, if Repeat is on, an album or a selection starts over automatically after it's played through the first time.

To toggle the Repeat setting on your Zune, follow these steps:

1. **In the Settings menu, choose Music and press OK.**

2. **Select the Repeat item and then press Enter.**

   The Repeat setting toggles between Repeat: On and Repeat: Off.

Be careful when you use this setting. If you leave an album playing on your Zune with Repeat on, the Zune never goes to sleep on its own. It just keeps playing the content until your batteries finally run out of juice!

Equalizer

The Equalizer setting changes the sound of the music played on your Zune — bumping up the bass, for example, or goosing the treble range. Eight equalizer settings ship by default with the original Zune:

✔ Acoustic

✔ Classical

✔ Electronic

✔ Hip Hop

✔ Jazz

✔ Pop

✔ Rock

✔ None

Equalizer settings are like seasoning for your food. Think of it this way: For good old American steak-and-potatoes food, you may want to use a bit of salt and pepper; for Chinese food, you may want to rely on soy sauce; and Mexican food cries out for jalapenos. Just as you want the right seasoning for your food, you want the right Equalizer settings for your music. The Jazz setting brings out the trumpets and the sax, the Rock setting pushes the guitars forward, and the Hip Hop setting brings out the bass.

Keep in mind that seasonings, as well as equalizer settings, are often matters of personal preference. If you like soy sauce on your enchiladas or ketchup on your scrambled eggs, more power to you. And if you think your Rock setting works great for John Coltrane, go for it. Feel free to experiment, mixing and matching your Equalizer settings as you see fit.

To toggle between Equalizer settings, follow these steps:

1. **Start playing a song of the type you listen to most often.**

2. **Press the Back button to get back to the main menu.**

3. **Select Settings and then press the OK button.**

4. **In the Settings menu, choose Music and press the OK button.**

5. **Select the Equalizer item and then press OK.**

   The Equalizer toggles through the various setting options when you press the OK button. Listen carefully to each option for a few seconds to determine which sound you want from your Zune.

6. **Select the setting you want to keep and then press the Back button to return to the main menu.**

We all hear things differently, and the Equalizer setting that you choose can probably make all the music you listen to more enjoyable, regardless of whether the setting's genre and the music's genre match up. But keep in mind that you can switch Equalizer settings almost as easily as switching from one tune to another. That way, you can match your settings to whatever you're playing at the moment — say, the Troggs "Wild Thing" or Evgeny Kissin's performance of Beethoven's "Moonlight Sonata."

The Pictures setting

The Pictures setting has two options you can set. You can change the amount of time (the *transition* period) that a picture is displayed by default in a slideshow, and you can set whether your pictures are shown in random order *(shuffled)* during a slideshow. Here are the Pictures setting's options:

✔ **Transitions:** You can set your transitions to occur every 3, 5, 7, 10, 15, or 30 seconds.

To change the default transition time on your slideshows:

1. **Choose Pictures in the Settings menu.**

2. **With the Transitions item selected, continue to press OK until you reach the time value you want.**

3. **Press the Back button to return to the main menu.**

✔ **Shuffle:** As with the Shuffle setting in Music, the Shuffle setting here randomizes the picture playback during a slideshow on your Zune.

To toggle the Shuffle setting on or off for slideshows on your Zune:

1. **Choose Pictures in the Settings menu.**

2. **With the Shuffle item selected, press OK.**

The Display setting

The Display setting has a number of important options associated with it. Here, you can change the current Zune theme, set the backlight and brightness, and set whether the TV Out option is enabled — for playback on the big screen — as well as what type of television you're using.

Themes

The Zune ships with three default *themes* — little decorating schemes for the look and feel of your new favorite media player. Admittedly, all three themes are pretty non-descript because they were designed mostly to make the menus easy to read rather than as a major fashion statement, but feel free to try them out.

To change the theme on your Zune, follow these steps:

1. **In the Settings menu, choose Display and press OK.**
2. **Select the Themes item and then press Enter.**
3. **Choose the theme you want and then press OK.**

   Your choices here are Haze, Night, and Amber.

   To change the theme again, press OK to get back to the Themes menu and choose a new theme.

If you've chosen a picture to use as a background, as we describe in Chapter 6, you lose that background when you change the theme on the device. To get the picture back, you need to browse to the picture and set it as the background image again.

Backlight

The backlight on your Zune provides the illumination necessary for you to see what's on the screen. It takes power, so you can make it shut off automatically while you're playing music to save the battery. The Backlight setting determines how long you want to leave the backlight on when you browse through music or pictures. (The backlight stays on continuously when you're playing video.)

You can toggle the Backlight setting to 1, 5, 15, or 30 seconds, 1 minute, or Always On.

To change the amount of time the Backlight stays on, follow these steps:

1. **In the Settings menu, choose Display and press OK.**
2. **Select Backlight.**
3. **Press Enter to change the Backlight value.**

   The value of the Backlight setting changes each time you press the OK button.

4. **Set the value to an amount of time you're comfortable with and then press the Back button to return to the main menu.**

The timer for the backlight resets when you use the Up, Down, Left, and Right buttons to navigate the menus. If the backlight shuts off before you finish reading through the items you're looking at, change the Backlight value to something higher so you're not interrupted.

Brightness

In the Zune world, *brightness* refers to the brightness of your actual Zune display. The Brightness option lets you toggle between Low, Medium, and High.

To change the brightness of your Zune display, follow these steps:

1. **In the Settings menu, choose Display and press OK.**

2. **In the Display menu, choose Brightness.**

3. **Press OK to toggle through the various Brightness values.**

   The screen brightness changes immediately to reflect your selection.

4. **After finding a selection you like, press the Back button to return to the main menu.**

The higher the brightness of the display, the faster your battery runs down.

If you use your Zune outdoors a lot, a higher brightness can make your Zune easier to read in bright sunlight.

TV Out

If you use the TV Output adapter we describe in Chapter 11, you need to set the TV Out setting to On to get the video signal to go through to the TV.

This setting sends the video to the television only — nothing gets sent to the display on your Zune. When you change this setting to On, you get the following warning:

> *To return display to Zune, hold Play/Pause to turn it off and then press any button to turn it back on.*

If you change the TV Out setting and you're not connected to a TV, you can possibly turn your Zune display off and then have no idea that the device is running. If you change this setting and can't get the screen to react, hold down the Play/Pause button for a few seconds to turn the device off completely — which automatically resets the TV Out to Off. Then press any other button to fire up your Zune.

Because the TV Out setting can be potentially confusing if not set correctly, visit Chapter 11 for a complete description of how to use it.

TV System

The TV System setting lets you toggle the TV Out signal between *PAL* and *NTSC,* two distinct (and mutually exclusive) broadcast television standards. In general, TV systems in North America use NTSC as the signal standard, and PAL is used in most other countries throughout the world.

To change the TV System setting on your Zune, follow these steps:

1. **In the Settings menu, choose Display and press OK.**

2. **Select the TV System item.**

3. **Press OK to toggle between TV System: NTSC and TV System: PAL.**

4. **After selecting the correct system for your television, press the Back button to return to the main menu.**

Go to Chapter 11 for more information about the TV System and the settings associated with this feature.

The Sounds setting

No, this setting doesn't have anything to do with your music's volume. By default, you hear little clicks when you press buttons and otherwise navigate through the Zune user interface. If these clicks start getting on you nerves, you can toggle them off.

To change the Sounds setting, follow these steps:

1. **In the Settings menu, choose Sounds.**

2. **Press OK to toggle the Sounds setting between Sounds: On and Sounds: Off.**

3. **After making your selection, press the Back button to return to the main menu.**

Unless you have superhuman hearing, you can hear Zune sounds only through the headset, so you probably don't hear a difference after you change the Sounds setting until you put your earphones in.

The Radio setting

The Radio setting lets you choose the radio band that you want to listen to with your Zune. This setting lets you choose between North America, Europe, and Japan.

To change the Radio setting on the Zune, follow these steps:

1. **In the Settings menu, choose Radio and press OK**

2. **In the Radio menu, choose the setting that matches your current location and then press OK.**

3. **After making your selection, press the Back button to return to the main menu.**

If you travel a lot, your stations are saved on a per-location basis. You can have a set of European favorites, as well as a set of North American favorites.

The Online Status setting

The Online Status option lets you set how much information you want to share when taking advantage of the community feature. You might be perfectly willing to let your friends find your Zune, but you don't want them to know what you're listening to. In that case, Basic status is perfect for you. But if you want the Zune world to know you're rocking to '70s disco classics all day and all night, set your Online Status to Detailed.

Figure 3-3 shows you the difference between having your Online Status set to Detailed versus having it set to Basic.

To toggle between Detailed and Basic status on your Zune, follow these steps:

1. **In the Settings menu, choose Online Status.**

2. **Press OK to toggle between Online Status: Basic and Online Status: Detailed.**

3. **After making your selection, press the Back button to return to the main menu.**

Remember, having people know what you're listening to is what Zuning is all about. If some friendly Zune users know you're listening to something they like, they might approach you and ask you to share!

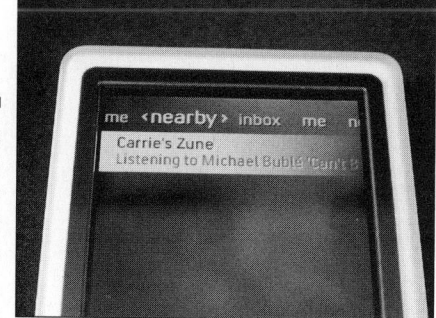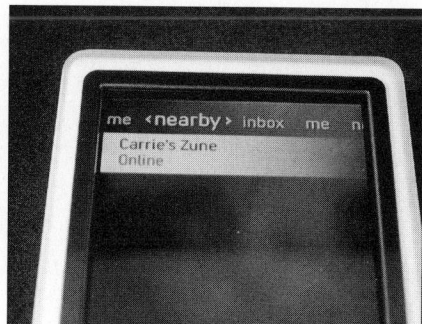

Figure 3-3:
Detailed
and Basic
community
status on
the Zune.

The About setting

The About setting might seem like the most boring option on the whole device. It's not really an option, anyway. It's more like information. Although we have to admit it's not the most exciting section, it is one of the most useful.

The About option provides information about the Zune, its storage capacity, and some legal stuff you may want to look at. The following sections cover each of these features in detail.

Zune

The Zune screen shows the product version numbers, your Zune serial number, and other information about the device. You need this information if you ever have to talk to Technical Support about your Zune device.

To get to the Zune screen, follow these steps:

1. **In the Settings menu, choose About and press OK.**

2. **From the About menu, choose Zune and press OK.**

3. **After getting the info you need, press the Back button to return to the main menu.**

Storage

The Storage screen, as shown in Figure 3-4, tells you how many songs, pictures, and videos you have on your Zune. It also tells you how much space you've used on the device and how much is still available. If you ever catch yourself wondering how many tunes you actually have, use the Storage screen to find out.

storage
2176 songs
5043 pictures
32 videos

14.22 GB used
13.54 GB free

Figure 3-4:
The Storage
screen tells
you how
much of
what is on
your Zune.

To get to the Storage screen, follow these steps:

1. **In the Settings menu, choose About and press OK.**

2. **From the About menu, choose Storage and then press OK.**

3. **After you find the info you're looking for, press the Back button to return to the main menu.**

Legal

If you're interested in finding out about the fascinating legal aspects of your Zune, be sure to visit your Zune's Legal screen.

To get to the Legal screen, follow these steps:

1. **In the Settings menu, choose About and press OK.**

2. **From the About menu, choose Legal and then press OK.**

3. **After reading all the legal verbiage, press the Back button to return to the main menu.**

Part II
Managing Your Zune Content

The 5th Wave   By Rich Tennant

"I could tell you more about myself, but I think the playlist on my Zune says more about me than mere words can."

In this part . . .

The Zune device can hold a lot of content, including music, video, and photos. This part focuses on finding your way through all that content — on your PC as well as on your Zune.

Chapters 4, 5, and 6 cover finding all the content (music, videos, and pictures) on your PC and making sure it all gets into the Zune software's library. These chapters also talk about synchronizing that information onto your Zune, including how to use the basic manual and automatic synchronization settings.

In Chapter 7, we dig deep into the Zune Marketplace, including details about the subscription-based option for purchasing content. Then, Chapter 8 gets you looking for music for your library; this time, though, you're not just finding it, you're ripping it off your own CDs.

Chapter 9 takes you a fair ways outside the normal Zune experience. It covers how to get yourself into the world of digital video. Check it out if you want to know about your options when it comes to getting a digital video camera or video editing software. We even give some tips about how (and where) to publish your videos online.

Podcast support is a very popular device feature that didn't quite make into this first version of the Zune, but you can still download both video and audio podcasts onto your Zune. Chapter 10 covers the steps for finding, downloading, and syncing podcasts, and it includes some podcast recommendations of our very own.

Chapter 4

Importing the Music You Love

• •

In This Chapter

▶ Understanding how digital music files work

▶ Introducing the Zune library — and synchronization

▶ Making sure you find all the music on your computer

▶ Keeping your Zune in sync with your computer

▶ Listening to the FM radio on your Zune

• •

With wireless sharing and a rich online marketplace, your Zune can help you discover new music, but the core of your experience is surely going to be tied up with all that great music you already have and love. In this chapter, we take a look at all the music file formats that you can put onto your Zune. We cover how to set up your Zune software to find all your music, and we go over the basics of getting your content synchronized (synced) to your device. Because one or two of your local radio stations are likely a great source of the music you love, we cover the full usage of the radio feature, as well.

Getting a Handle on Digital Music Files

When looking at any digital music player (or any Web site that provides music for download, for that matter), you're going to come up against a variety of different music formats (encodings) and quality levels (often simplified to bit rate). Formats and quality levels are, in fact, two different but related topics. *Format* describes how the audio has been converted (and usually compressed) into digital bits, and *quality* indicates how close the digital bits are to the original source. In addition to format and quality, you'll also run into a few other (quite mysterious-looking) terms, such as DRM and VBR. We explain DRM in the section "Digital Rights Management (DRM)," later in this chapter. And we tackle VBR in the sidebar "Variable Bit Rate (VBR) and lossless encodings," later in this chapter.

Music formats

Although you've probably encountered several different formats and a wide range of quality settings during your ramblings on the World Wide Web, the one format we're pretty sure everyone's already heard about is the MP3 format. In fact, it's so popular that it's often used to describe digital music in general, and people often refer to their digital music player as an MP3 player, regardless of what format(s) it's capable of playing. In fact, MP3 is just one of many possible audio formats. MP3 is short for MPEG-1 Audio Layer 3, and MPEG stands for the Moving Picture Experts Group (an organization primarily known for their video compression formats such as MPEG-2, which is the format used on DVDs).

Another popular format is WMA (Windows Media Audio), which is owned by Microsoft and is also widely used on the Web. You often run into Windows Media Audio (and Windows Media Video, which we cover in Chapter 5) when you get media through online stores (for reasons that we explain in the section "Digital Rights Management (DRM)," later in this chapter). Other popular audio formats include

- **AAC:** AAC is short for Advanced Audio Coding and is the native format used for audio that you download through iTunes.

- **WAV:** WAV is short for waveform and is the basic audio format used by Windows. This format is often used for storing recorded voice files and small sound files for computer programs, but it's not commonly used for music.

- **(Ogg) Vorbis:** Vorbis is the name of a relatively new audio encoding format that doesn't cost the music creator anything to use, unlike MP3, which requires a licensing fee. Vorbis promises better audio quality at lower bit rates than some of the other formats.

  Okay, we know that the common name for this format is actually Ogg Vorbis — which explains the Ogg-in-parentheses bit in the preceding bullet — but, technically, the audio encoding technology itself is known as just Vorbis and the format of the actual files used to store Vorbis audio is known as Ogg. And don't ask us who came up with such bizarre terms as Ogg and Vorbis, or why. Nobody really knows for sure, but we're guessing Ogg was some kind of inside joke.

Your Zune can play video only in the WMV format, but it can play music in WMA, MP3, and AAC formats. This built-in feature means that your existing MP3 or AAC files won't need to be converted when you sync them from your PC to your Zune.

Music quality

When talking about digital music, quality doesn't really depend on the kind of format used. (Okay, some geeks will argue back and forth about the virtues and vices of file formats, but trust us, they're just nitpicking.) Sound quality really depends on the amount of data per second (or *bit rate,* measured in Kbps — kilobits per second) being used to digitally store the music; the more data used, the closer the music gets to the original source. Because quality is based on the amount of data used per second of music, you have to make a trade-off between quality and file size. The higher the quality, the larger the file.

Although you can encode music at almost any bit rate, most music is encoded at one of the rates shown in Table 4-1.

Table 4-1	Bit Rates and File Sizes
Bit Rate	*File Size for an Average CD*
64 Kbps (kilobits per second)	28MB (megabytes)
96 Kbps	42MB
128 Kbps	56MB
160 Kbps	69MB
192 Kbps	86MB
256 Kbps	115MB
320 Kbps	144MB

Most music you find in the digital world is encoded at lower than 192 Kbps, with many people choosing 96 or 128 Kbps as their encoding settings. Consider using 192 Kbps as the minimum encoding setting for converting any of your own music into digital files. (See Chapter 8 for more info on ripping music from your own CDs.) We can't tell the difference between an encoded music file and the original CD at 192 Kbps; it might be a higher or lower point for you, but if you aren't sure, 192 Kbps is a good place to start. Whatever bit rate you choose, you have to make a trade-off between audio quality and storage space on your computer. You can rip your music and store it on your PC at a higher bit rate than the rate you use for your Zune, but then you have to convert your music before you can synchronize it.

Encoding a song into two different formats at the same bit rate produces two files of similar size with a similar level of quality. You'll hear some difference in the sound of the two files (the high notes in one file might sound more tinny than the high notes in another file, for example), though, because each format converts the music in different ways. In our opinion, it really boils down to personal preference as to which format produces the best sound; some people say that WMA files sound better than MP3, some say the opposite, and others can't hear any difference at all.

We personally prefer the sound of WMA files, so if you don't already have a preference, you may want to pick that option when ripping CDs (which we talk about in Chapter 8) or downloading audio files (such as podcasts) from other Web sites.

Digital Rights Management (DRM)

When the whole digital music technology caught on, a huge amount of music was (and still is) shared between users all over the Internet. This no-rules period of digital music downloading (during which the original Napster file-sharing service became extremely popular) was a real concern for many record labels and artists. Their product was being distributed without any money going back into their pockets, so you can imagine that they don't want the same thing to happen with music you download for use on your Zune.

The Zune, Windows Media Player, and other applications (such as iTunes) use the technology called Digital Rights Management (DRM) to control how a certain media file is used. DRM allows albums to be sold online and the Zune to offer a subscription service because only the original purchaser can use music files protected by DRM. If you send a DRM file to your friend, he or she can't play that file. In fact, you're restricted in how you use the file, as well; you can play it on only a certain number of PCs, for example. There's more than one type of DRM, and support for each variety of rights management is different for each media format. Windows Media files, such as WMA (audio) and WMV (video), support Microsoft's implementation of DRM — the technology that the Zune uses. The other major style of DRM in use today, Fair Play, protects music and video purchased from Apple's iTunes store.

The different types of rights management systems on the Web can make buying music online confusing, so keep the following in mind:

- ✔ The Zune device and the Zune software are DRM-specific and thus can't access Fair Play–protected files (files purchased through iTunes).

- ✔ If you purchase your Windows Media–protected files directly from the Zune Marketplace, your Zune will play those files smashingly (duh!).

- ✔ Your Zune (and Zune software) has no trouble accessing any non-DRMed content (such as WMA files that you've ripped from your own CDs or MP3 files that you have on your machine) that you may want to add to your Zune.

Why won't my PlaysForSure WMA files play on my Zune?

One of the most discussed facts about the Zune has been its inability to play music purchased from PlaysForSure-compatible online stores. Loyal customers who previously used (or are still using) players from iRiver, Creative, Samsung, and many others may have a large investment in music purchased from the Urge, Napster, MSN, or Wal-Mart online stores. All this music will still work for them on their PC and on their existing music player(s), but it doesn't work on the Zune.

Why is this? With the Zune, Microsoft was going for an all-in-one experience in which you get the player, the software, and the content

(the music and videos) from a single source. This approach is supposedly designed to make things better for you, the Zune owner; if you have a problem with any part of this integrated system, you can turn to the same place — Zune Support. In our personal opinion, this benefit seems questionable. We would understand if Microsoft strongly encouraged the use of Zune Marketplace and the Zune software (even setting them up as the default when people buy the device), but making all our existing purchased digital media unusable on our hot new Zune is a bad deal.

✔ Saving the worst (or at least the most controversial) for last, any other DRMed Windows Media content you may have on your machine — including music from Napster and Urge, two online stores that have provided content to Microsoft's Windows Media Player — don't work with the Zune. (Ouch!)

Using the library feature of your Zune software, you can quickly find out what protection is on a particular file that you've added to your collection by looking at its Media Usage Rights information. To access this information, follow these steps:

1. **Launch your Zune software on your PC.**

   To launch this software, open the All Programs menu, select the Zune folder, and then click Zune; or click the Zune icon on your Quick Launch toolbar.

2. **Select the media type you want to view (Music, Photos, or Videos) from above the navigation pane, then click Library from the list of items in the navigation pane.**

3. **Right-click the file in the library (see Figure 4-1) and select Properties from the menu that appears.**

   The Properties dialog box appears.

Figure 4-1:
Select the
Properties
menu item
to get
detailed
information
about a
music file.

4. **In the Properties dialog box, click the Media Usage Rights tab to see the current status of your song or video.**

Depending on the file's protection status, a message in the dialog box either tells you that the file isn't protected (see Figure 4-2) or gives you a description of how you can use the protected file (see Figure 4-3).

Figure 4-2: A
non-DRMed
file has no
restrictions
on its use.

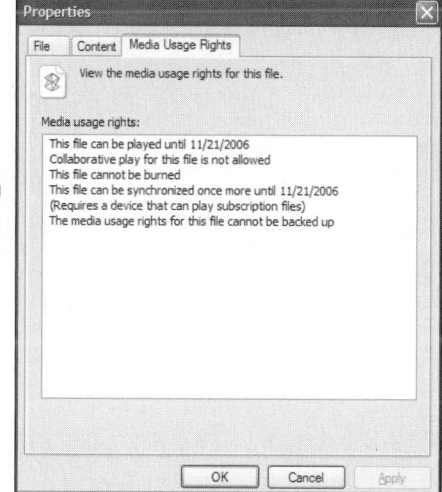

Figure 4-3:
The Media
Usage
Rights tab
shows what
you can and
can't do
with a
media file.

Variable Bit Rate (VBR) and lossless encodings

For years, bit-rate technology was based on the standard method of encoding known as Constant Bit Rate (CBR). CBR indicates that an entire music file is encoded at the same bit rate. Another method of encoding has recently come down the pike, and it's known as Variable Bit Rate encoding (VBR). This method uses different bit rates, depending on the complexity of different parts of a single music file. Silent or simple passages might be encoded at a much lower rate than other parts of the same music file. VBR encoding isn't very common right now, but it's capable of producing higher-quality sound with less data, so you may start seeing it more and more.

You may run into another type of encoding known as lossless encoding. Normally, the act of encoding music into a digital file reduces the music's quality to some degree, saving space by producing a close, but not exact, copy of the music. A lossless encoding format, on the other hand, converts all of the audio information into the new file. Lossless encoding may save you some space by creating a digital file at least a bit smaller than the original file, but lossless encoding can't save anywhere near the amount of space that MP3 or WMA encoding can. In practice, the human ear can't distinguish between lossless encoding and normal encoding with a high-enough bit rate. Exactly how high a bit rate you need depends on the encoding. You can find detailed information on the quality of different codecs at different bit rates at www.soundexpert.info, but 192 Kbps should produce suitable results. The large file size and relatively small difference in perceived audio quality means you rarely find music encoded using the lossless method.

Music files (MP3, WMA, or AAC) that have been encoded by using either VBR or lossless methods should play fine in the Zune software and will be converted when they're synchronized with your Zune device.

The Library and Synchronization

Storing all your music files in an appropriate file format on your computer is all fine and dandy, but the real fun starts when you get your music files onto your Zune. The process itself is pretty simple, as long as you remember the two major parts of the transfer process: the library and synchronization (often called syncing).

As you make your way through the following sections, keep these points in mind:

✔ The library is a crucial — perhaps *the* crucial — part of your Zune software; it's the catalog of all of your music, photos, and video content.

✔ Be careful with terminology. The library is a great catalog of your stuff, but it doesn't actually store your stuff. Your computer's hard drive, or possibly somewhere else on your home network, takes care of the actual file storage. The library is, technically speaking, a directory that knows where to find everything that's listed in it, rather than a repository for all your great content.

✔ The first step in getting content onto your Zune is getting it catalogued in your computer's library.

✔ To get content from your computer onto your Zune, you don't just copy it (by using the drag-and-drop method, for example); you need to *synchronize* the library with your device so that both have the same content.

The following sections discuss some of the ways your music gets added (and catalogued) in your Zune library.

Scouring the universe (or at least your hard drive) for music

Getting your first batch of music into your Zune is pretty much a no-brainer. As part of the initial Zune software installation (which you can read about in Chapter 2), you're prompted to let the software search for any content (music files, image files, video files, whatever) that might conceivably make a nice addition to your Zune library. The neat part about your Zune software, though, is that it stays on the lookout for potential new additions to your library, adding any additions that it sees (or you see) fit. It does this by taking advantage of its Monitored Folders feature.

Using monitored folders

The Zune software's monitored folders do exactly what their name implies. They act as your personal spy service, on the lookout for new music, video, or photo files. To view the current list of folders, follow these steps:

1. **Choose Options➪Library➪More Options from the Zune software's main menu, as shown in Figure 4-4.**

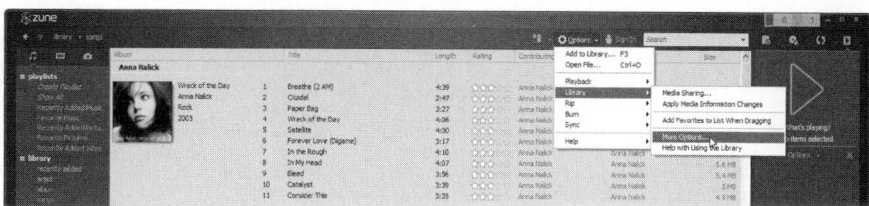

Figure 4-4:
The Options menu gives you access to detailed settings for the library.

The General Options dialog box appears.

2. **In the Library tab of the General Options dialog box, click the Monitor Folders button.**

The Add to Library dialog box appears, displaying the current folder list, as shown in Figure 4-5.

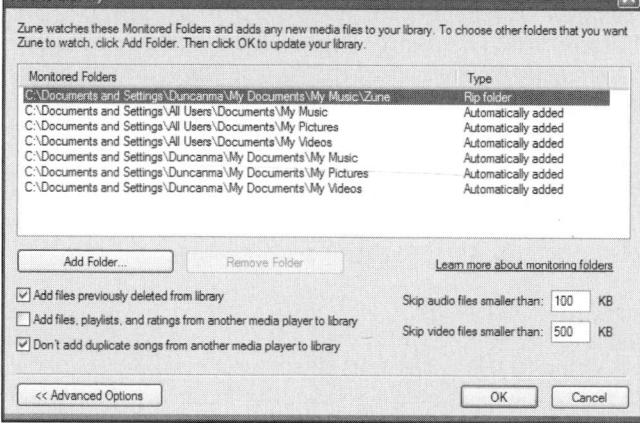

Figure 4-5:
The Add to Library dialog box allows you to view, add, and remove monitored folders.

You can actually get to the Add to Library dialog box in several other ways — pressing the F3 key on your keyboard, choosing Options➪Add to Library from the main menu, or right-clicking the Library heading from the Navigation pane (along the left-hand side of the software) and picking Add to Library from the menu that appears.

When you first install the Zune software — which we talk about in Chapter 2 — it adds some common locations for music, videos, and photos into your Monitored Folders list and then scans those locations to populate the library with anything it can find. Some of the locations added include

- The My Music, My Videos, and My Pictures folders

- The Shared Music, Shared Videos, and Shared Pictures folders

These locations are the defaults used by a variety of other applications, so you probably have at least some content in one of these folders already. If you store your content in a folder other than one of these default locations, then add that folder to your Monitored Folders list.

3. To add a new folder to your list, click the Add Folder button.

The Locate dialog box appears.

Monitored folders aren't divided based on media type, so if you add a new folder to the list of folders to watch, Zune will find any music, photo, and video files added to that location.

4. In the Locate dialog box, browse to the folder you want to add and then click OK.

Your new folder is added to the Monitored Folders list.

Whether you add a folder, remove a folder, or do nothing to the list, closing the Add to Library dialog box causes the Zune software to begin a scan of all monitored folders (see Figure 4-6). This scan can take a long time, but if you click Close to close the dialog box, the scan continues in the background while you go back to using the Zune software.

Closing the dialog box slows down the scan a bit, so if you're eager to get all of your music into the Zune library, you may want to just let the scan run its course.

Figure 4-6:
Closing the
Add to
Library
dialog box
starts a full
scan of all
monitored
folders.

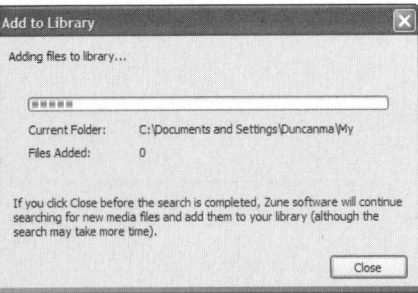

After the initial addition of a folder, updates become automatic. When a file is added or modified within any one of the folders on your list, it's added or updated in the library. These updates may not happen immediately, but they should occur within a short period of time — we've generally seen updates

occurring within 10 to 15 minutes, assuming the Zune software is running —
without you needing to do anything.

Importing your iTunes library

If you have iTunes, you may already have a lot of music that you've ripped
from CDs, audio/video files from podcasts, and other content already stored
in your iTunes library. Some of that content may be DRMed, such as music
that you purchased through the iTunes store, which means the Zune software
can't play it back and you can't synchronize it onto your Zune device. (Check
out our DRM discussion in the section "Digital Rights Management (DRM),"
earlier in this chapter, for more info.) Not all of your content is likely to be
DRMed, though; if you've ripped your own CDs or downloaded podcasts, that
content should work fine. To make sure this content gets into your Zune
library, you need to ensure that it's being scanned/monitored so that all its
content can get catalogued.

By default, your My Music folder is automatically included and scanned by
the Zune software. Because the My Music folder is where the iTunes software
stores all downloaded and ripped content by default (in a subdirectory called
iTunes, of all things, as shown in Figure 4-7), all non-DRMed iTunes content —
even podcasts and video files — gets added automatically to your Zune
library.

Zune software doesn't import your content from iTunes itself, Zune just happens to scan the iTunes content because it's located in the My Music folder.

 If you change your default iTunes Music folder (see Figure 4-7), then add that
location to your Monitored Folders list to ensure all of your iTunes content is
included in your Zune library. (Check out the preceding section for more on
adding folders to your Monitored Folders list.)

Importing from Windows Media Player

If you use Windows Media Player (WMP) to listen to music, rip CDs, or do
anything else, then you can use the Zune software to automatically import
settings, Monitored Folder lists, and all of your existing library information
(including all the media in your library, your ratings, and your playlists)
directly from WMP. Just follow these steps:

1. **In the Add to Library dialog box (refer to Figure 4-5), select the check
   box to the left of the Add Files, Playlists, and Ratings from Another
   Media Player to Library option.**

2. **Click OK to close the dialog box.**

   The Zune software imports your current library of information
   from WMP.

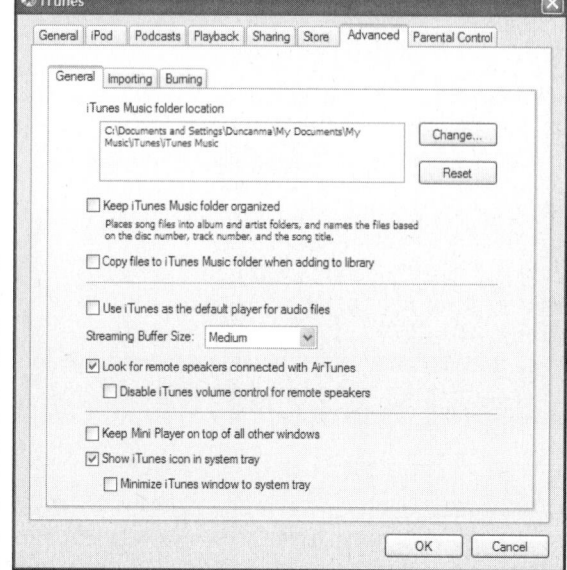

Figure 4-7:
iTunes
stores
music,
podcasts,
and video
files in the
My Music
folder.

Setting Up to Sync

The way things work with a Zune — as with most portable media players — is that you first get your content nicely organized in the Zune library (stored safely on your PC's hard drive), and then you sync the content onto your Zune.

The good, the bad, and the ugly of automatic synchronization

By default, your Zune software is set up to automatically synchronize all your music right onto your Zune. You just have to connect your Zune to your PC — by using the handy sync cable — and then Zune software takes over. All your music content — and maybe your photos and videos, depending on what options you chose when setting up your Zune for the first time (see Figure 4-8) — makes the trip from your hard drive to your Zune.

Automatic synchronization may be a perfect solution for you, but it has some drawbacks and can be a bit tricky to use. Here's a breakdown of the positives and negatives. On the positive side

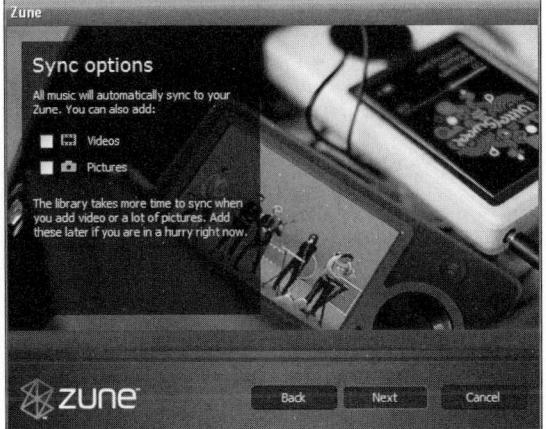

✔ If you set up your Zune with an automatic synchronization for all music, new content — content that you download or rip from a CD — will just automatically appear on your Zune whenever you hook it up to your PC. You don't have to remember to copy that new CD you just bought and ripped; it just happens. The same goes for videos and photos — everything new that ends up in your Zune library will be compressed and copied to the Zune.

✔ Because you're going to sync all of your content, the Zune can be smart and start converting your media ahead of time, even when it isn't connected to your PC.

On the negative side, automatic syncing does exactly what it promises to do — it keeps your Zune in sync with your library, even if that means deleting content from your Zune. We're not fans of any feature that might possibly delete something we want to keep, and with no undo feature, we think it's just too risky. Here are some specific issues we have with auto-sync:

✔ **Losing content:** If any of your content is removed from the Zune library stored on your PC — perhaps the content is on a USB-attached hard drive that you forgot to hook up today — then the automatic sync will remove it from your Zune, as well. You really notice this change if you set up your Zune software on a new PC — one that doesn't have all the same music available — and then decide to hook your Zune up to that PC.

✔ **Unwanted content:** Perhaps "all your music" includes the past year's worth of voicemails, a gazillion system alert files (all 1.5 seconds long), or 15 albums of children's music that you never play anymore. You may not want to remove these files from your PC, but you sure as heck don't want them on your Zune.

> ✓ **The space issue:** Maybe you have so many digital music files that sync-
> ing them all onto your Zune would completely fill the Zune — leaving no
> space for any of your video or photo content.

If you connect your Zune to a new computer as a guest, you don't have to
worry about automatic synchronization — it's not enabled for a guest connection. And as a guest, you can still edit the Zune's content, copy new content onto it, and charge it to boot, so a guest connection should work in most
cases. But if you choose the Sync with Your Library on This PC option (see
Figure 4-9), automatic sync is the default and every song that's on your Zune,
but not on that new PC, will be removed from the Zune.

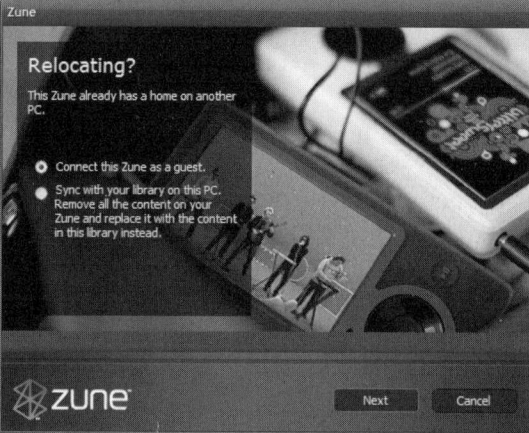

Figure 4-9:
If you
connect
your Zune to
another PC
running
the Zune
software,
you get this
prompt.

"Automatic" doesn't have to mean all your content, though; you can actually
customize your synchronization. You can tweak your syncing experience by
making it fully manual or by customizing the automatic sync so that you have
a bit more control over the process. The following sections show you how.

Manual synchronization

If "manual" makes you think of "manual labor," think again. It sounds like a lot
more work than it is because manual synchronization means only that you
pick out which albums, artists, or songs (or which videos and photos) to
copy onto your device. Nothing is copied over unless you specifically request
that content be copied.

In order to get from automatic to manual, you have to change your Zune's default synchronization settings. (The default is all automatic, all the time.) Follow these steps to undo the auto-synchronization settings that Zune has created for you:

1. **Launch the Zune software (if it isn't already running).**

2. **Connect your Zune to your PC.**

   If you're connecting your Zune for the first time, head to Chapter 2. Make sure you don't select either the Pictures or Videos option (refer to Figure 4-8).

   After your Zune is connected, it may start to auto-sync. If it does, cancel the sync operation by following these steps:

   1. **Close any open dialog box (such as the Zune Setup dialog box that checks for updates).**

   2. **Click the Stop Sync button at the bottom of the List pane (along the right side of the Zune software window).**

   If you turned off the automatic sync at an earlier time, you don't need to cancel anything.

3. **Right-click the name of your Zune device in the Navigation pane (along the left side of the Zune software window) and choose Set Up Sync from the menu that appears.**

   The Device Setup dialog box appears, as shown in Figure 4-10.

4. **Uncheck the Sync This Device Automatically option, then click Finish to exit the Device Setup dialog box.**

After turning off automatic synchronization, go ahead and try out the manual process. With your Zune still connected, select the Sync button (the button with a picture of two arrows, one going up and one heading down) at the top of the List pane of the Zune software window, as shown in Figure 4-11. Doing so opens a Sync List pane in this right-hand section, which essentially acts as a holding area for the content you decide you want synced.

With the Sync List pane visible, you can access your library by using the expanding links in the Navigation pane (on the left side of the Zune software window). You can view your music (song, playlist, album, whatever), your photos, or your videos in the center area of the Zune software window by selecting these links. After you select a link, you only need to drag a song, a playlist, an album, or an entire artist from the Music section onto the sync list. (Of course, you can do the same thing with a photo or folder from the

Pictures section, or some video files from the Videos section.) After you have the list filled up with your choice of content, click the Start Sync button, as shown in Figure 4-12, and all that content starts copying to the Zune.

Uncheck this option.

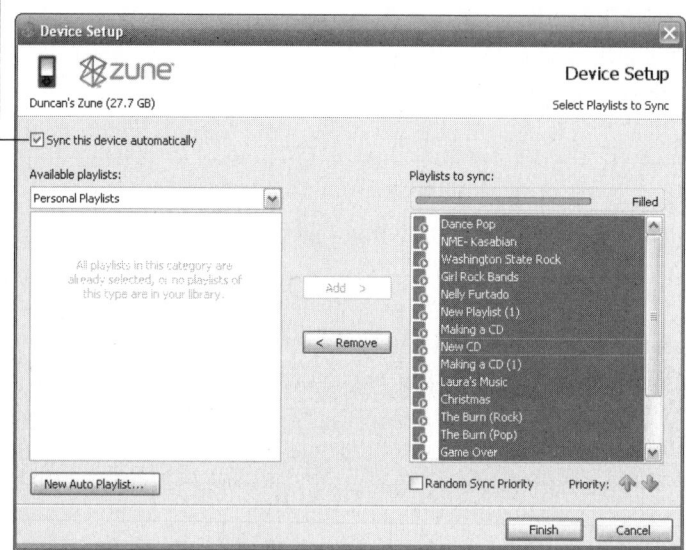

Figure 4-10:
The Device
Setup dialog
box lets
you choose
which
(if any)
playlists
should be
automati-
cally
synchro-
nized.

The Zune software is usually smart enough to automatically convert your music and video files to the correct format, if necessary

While your content is being copied, you can view the current progress by selecting the Sync Results option from under your Zune's name in the Navigation pane, as shown in Figure 4-13.

The Sync Results screen shows you all of the content being synced to your Zune, complete with the progress of each file, from conversion to copying (see Figure 4-14).

You can't add an item to or remove an item from the sync list after synchro-nization has started. To change the sync list, click the Stop Sync button, adjust your sync list as desired, and then click the Start Sync button.

Sync button

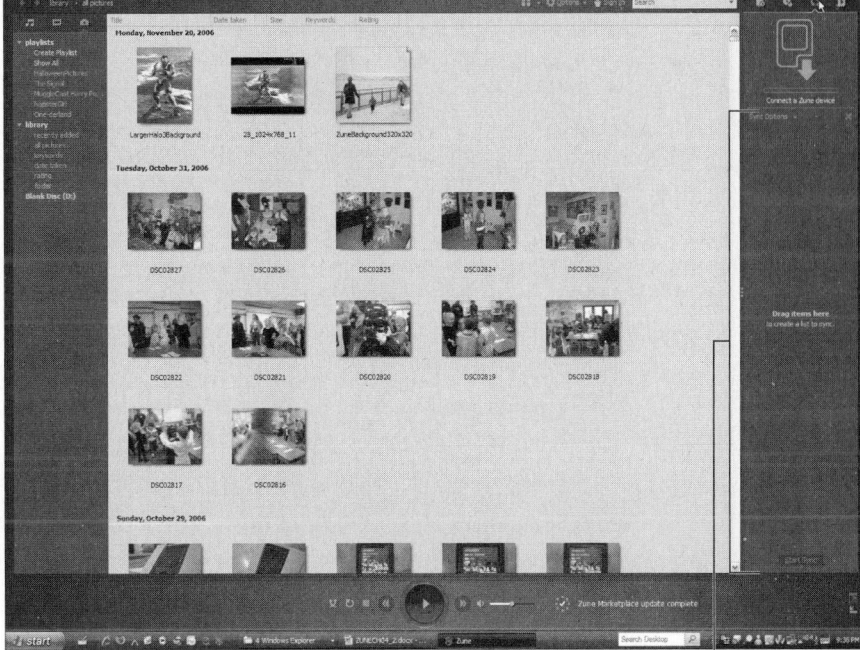

Figure 4-11:
Selecting
the Sync
button
makes a
sync list
displaying
all the
content
queued up
to copy to
your device
appear.

Sync List pane

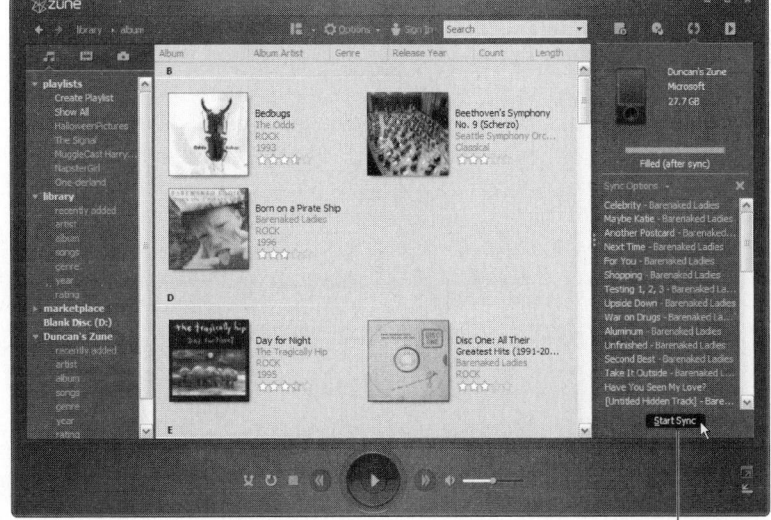

Figure 4-12:
After you
add your
selected
content to
your sync
list, click
Start Sync.

Start Sync button

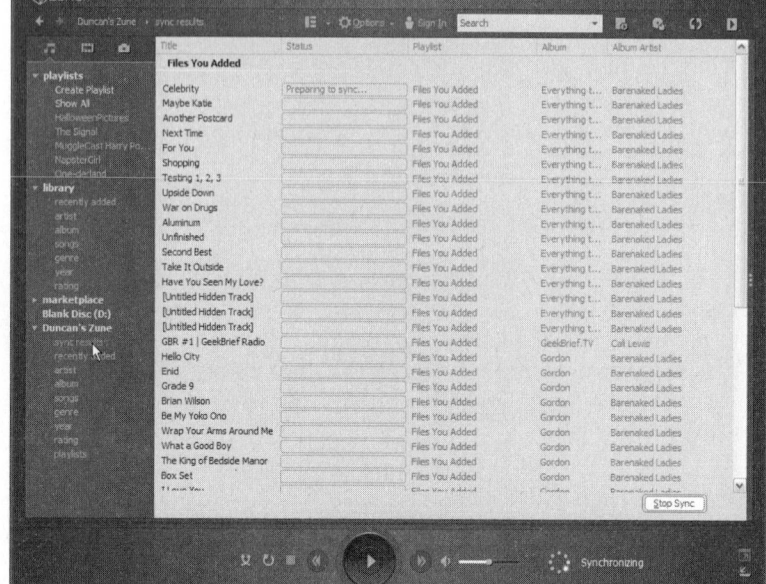

Figure 4-13:
The Sync
Results
option
appears
during or
after a
synchro-
nization.

Figure 4-14:
The Sync
Results
screen
shows you
the status of
files being
copied to
the Zune.

Automatic synchronization

Keeping in mind the negative side of automatic synchronization — check out the section "The good, the bad, and the ugly of automatic synchronization," earlier in this chapter, for more on the negatives — auto-syncing is still a good method of keeping your Zune up to date with the content on your PC. Instead of synchronizing all your music, all your videos, and all your photos, you can set up automatic synchronization to sync only selected playlists of content. You end up with more control than you have with the default behavior of syncing everything. If you want to set your machine up to automatically synchronize whenever you connect, you can choose from a variety of methods. You might want to create and sync a normal playlist, or you might like the idea of a dynamic playlist that you can use in different ways to sync exactly the right content onto your Zune. The following sections explain how you can play with your playlists.

Using normal playlists

To illustrate syncing by playlist(s), you need to have at least one playlist created. Follow these steps to create a playlist:

1. **Click the Now Playing button (a picture of a right-pointing triangle within a square) above the List pane on the right side of the Zune software screen.**

   The Device Setup dialog box appears. (Refer to Figure 4-10.)

2. **Drag a song, album, photo, or video into the List pane — anything will work!**

3. **After you have at least one item listed in the What's Playing? area, choose Save Playlist As from the Playback Options menu displayed in the List pane, as shown in Figure 4-15.**

   A Save As dialog box appears.

4. **In the Save As dialog box, specify a name for your new playlist, leave the location as-is, and then click Save.**

   We recommend leaving the Save location alone because the Zune should default to the standard location in which all of your playlists are stored. In our case, we set the filename to New, which then appears under the Playlists option in the Navigation pane.

Now that you have a playlist, you can set up your Zune to always keep itself current with the contents of just that specific playlist — if you add content, it gets synced to the device; if you remove content from the list, it gets removed from the device. To set up this arrangement, just follow these steps:

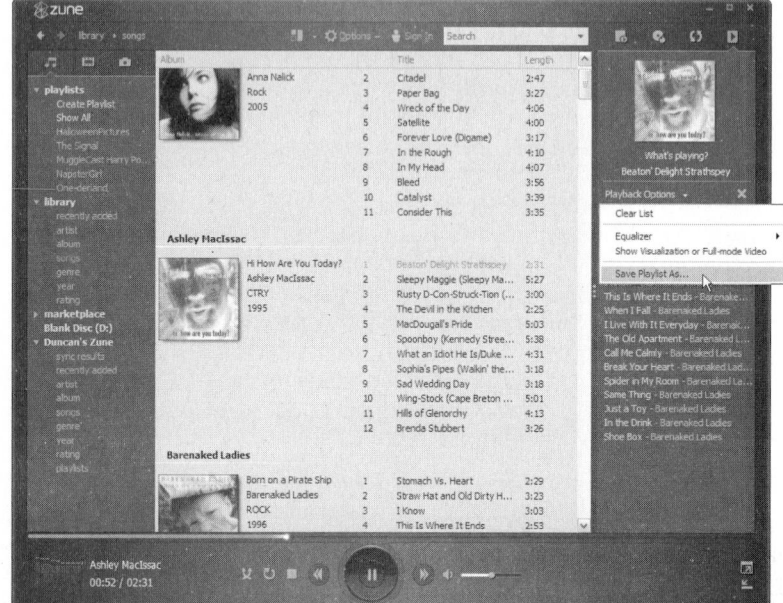

1. **Right-click the name of your Zune in the Navigation pane and choose Set Up Sync from the menu that appears.**

   The Device Setup dialog box makes an appearance (see Figure 4-16).

2. **In the Device Setup dialog box, select the new playlist and then click the Add button to move the new playlist to the Playlists to Sync field.**

   Playlists added to this field are automatically synced.

If you have more than one playlist set up to automatically sync, you can set their order of priority by moving them up and down in the Playlists to Sync list. Higher priority lists sync first, so if you run out of space on your Zune, they're more likely to make it onto the device.

Creating auto playlists

Normal playlists are manually created, so if you've set up Zune to auto-sync using normal playlists, you still need to manually add content to the appropriate playlist in order to get that content onto your Zune. This approach gives you a great deal of control, but it doesn't really give you any of the benefits of automatic content synchronization; you're probably better off with manual synchronization.

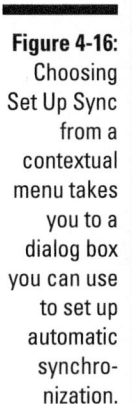 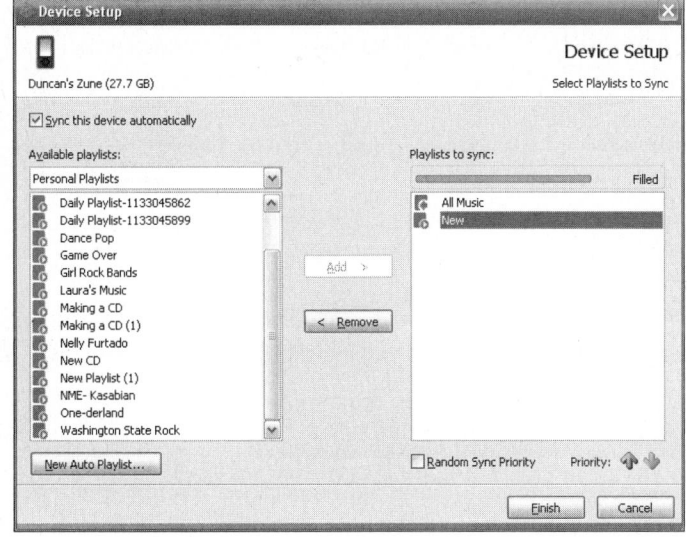

You can save yourself the work of manually updating the playlists by creating one or more *auto playlists* — playlists that don't contain any specific content, but instead contain only a definition of criteria that content has to meet to be included. Some examples of auto playlists include "all content rated 4 or 5 stars in my library" or "all music in the genres Rock or Pop." Regardless of the criteria, the actual list of content is the result of a query against your library, so any new content that meets that criteria will automatically appear in that playlist.

To create a new auto playlist, follow these steps:

1. **Right-click the Playlists item in the Navigation pane of the Zune soft-ware (see Figure 4-17) and choose Create Auto Playlist from the menu that appears.**

Figure 4-17:
Creating a
new auto
playlist.

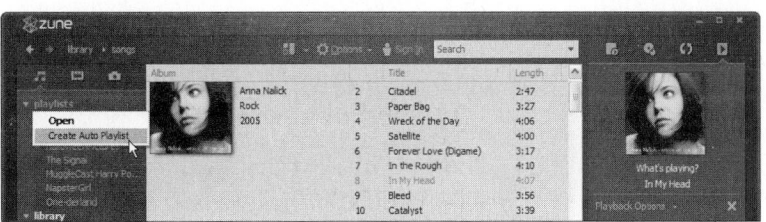

The New Auto Playlist dialog box appears.

2. **Enter a name for your new playlist in the Name field and specify a series of filters that determine what your new playlist will contain.**

   You can change these filters by clicking the plus (+) symbol to add new filters and by clicking existing filters and then removing or editing them (see Figure 4-18).

   Some of the possible criteria include the bit rate of the content, the rating (number of stars), the date on which it was last modified, and the genre of music.

3. **After making your selections, click OK to save your selections and close the New Auto Playlist dialog box.**

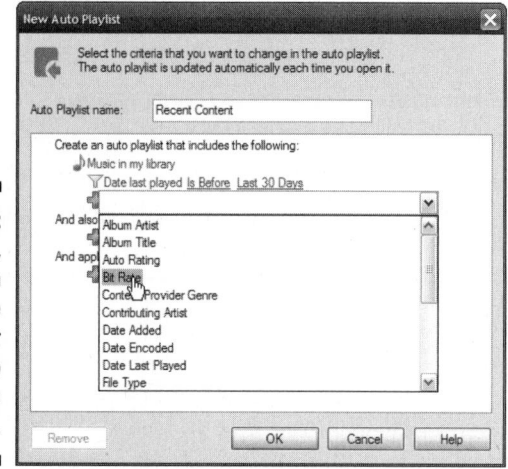

Figure 4-18: Using filters, you can create whatever type of auto playlist you need.

Whatever auto playlists you create, you can add them to the Playlists to Sync area in the Device Setup dialog box (shown in Figure 4-16), enabling a dynamic flow of content onto your device. Even if you aren't using automatic synchronization, auto playlists can still be manually synchronized onto your Zune just by dragging the playlist into the sync list and then clicking Start Sync.

Using FM Radio

When you need to listen to the news, or when you just need to break out of your own music from time to time, you'll be happy to find that your Zune includes the ability to tune into FM radio frequencies. In fact, it can tune into the specific frequency ranges used in Europe, Japan, and North America, which is a plus for travelers. (Check out Chapter 3 for details on how to switch between the three regions' FM radio settings.)

Tuning into your favorite stations

With the FM feature, you probably first want to find a station to listen to — an easy task that uses the Zune's tuning options. Follow these simple steps to find a radio station with your Zune:

1. **Select Radio from the main menu of your Zune device and then press the OK button.**

   Make sure you have a pair of headphones plugged in because the Zune uses the headphone cable as its FM antenna, and you may not be able to tune in a station without them.

2. **Press left or right on the control pad to seek out the next available radio station up or down the FM band.**

After you tune into a radio station, you probably see a bit of additional information on the screen, such as the station's call letters (KEXP, for example) or maybe some information about the current show or song. Figure 4-19 shows an example.

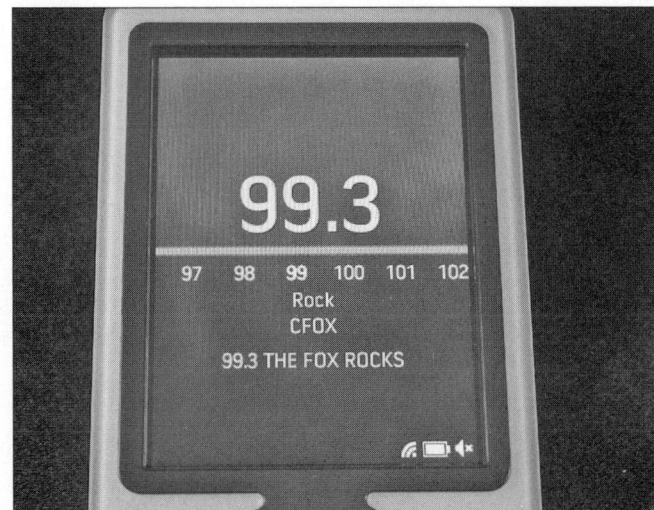

Figure 4-19: Your Zune receives extra info, in addition to the normal FM audio.

This information is provided by a service known as RDS or RBDS (Radio Data Service or Radio Broadcast Data System, respectively), where additional information from a radio station is encoded into the FM signal. RDS originated in Europe and wasn't widely supported in North America for quite a few years. Because of its origins, you'd previously find this feature only on stereo brands that were popular in the European market (such as Blaupunkt), but it's now becoming common across many different brands.

To seek or not to seek

When you press left or right on the control pad to move between radio stations, you may find that you're moving up or down by more than just one position on the FM band. Pressing left or right on the control pad seeks to the next frequency on which the Zune can pick up a signal. (Remember that without your headphones, reception can be very poor.) This functionality, which you commonly find on car stereos and other digital FM tuners, saves you time by taking you through only those frequencies with a strong enough signal to listen to. Holding down left or right on the control pad for a second or more takes you between presets (saved radio stations) that you've set up on your Zune, which is a really quick way to flip between your favorite stations.

If you're trying to tune into a specific frequency, though, this Seek feature can get in the way because it can just skip over the frequency you want if the signal isn't strong enough. If you can't get to the frequency you want, don't worry — you can turn the Seek feature off. Just follow these steps:

1. **While in the Radio mode on your Zune, press the OK button.**

   A small Settings screen appears, as shown in Figure 4-20.

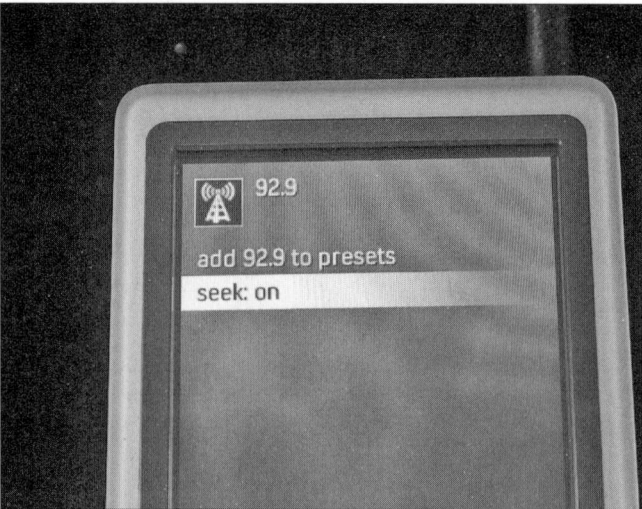

Figure 4-20: When you're in Radio mode, press the OK button to display the Settings menu.

2. **Navigate down to the Seek: On line and press the OK button to turn the feature's setting to Off.**

3. **Press the Back button on your Zune to return to the Radio screen.**

With the Seek feature off, pressing the left or right button moves you through the FM frequency one step at a time (moving up or down by 0.2 on the dial), and holding either direction down just makes you move faster through the frequencies.

Setting presets

With the Seek feature turned on or off, after you find a station that you want to save for future use, you can create a preset for that station. Follow these steps to create a preset:

1. **Tune in to the station you want to save.**

2. **Press the OK button to bring up the small Settings screen.**

   Be sure to just press the button; don't hold it down — holding it down doesn't do anything at all.

   At the top of this screen, you see an Add <frequency> to Presets option.

3. **Select that option to create a new preset for the current frequency.**

4. **Press the Back button to get back to the tuning interface.**

5. **Repeat Steps 1 through 4 as needed until you set up all the radio presets you want.**

You can tune or seek to the left or right with the Settings screen still open, making for a great way to quickly add a bunch of presets. With the Add <frequency> to Preset option selected in the Settings screen, press left or right on the control pad to tune up or down, and then just press the OK button at each of the desired frequencies to add them to your list of presets.

After you create one or more presets, you can jump between them by holding down left or right on the control pad for a second or more. Jumping between presets in this way works only if Seek is off, though; presets don't work if it's on. You can also reach a specific preset by pressing the OK button and then selecting the desired station from the list that appears (see Figure 4-21). You don't have a limit on the number of presets you can create, only on the number of addressable frequencies in the FM band.

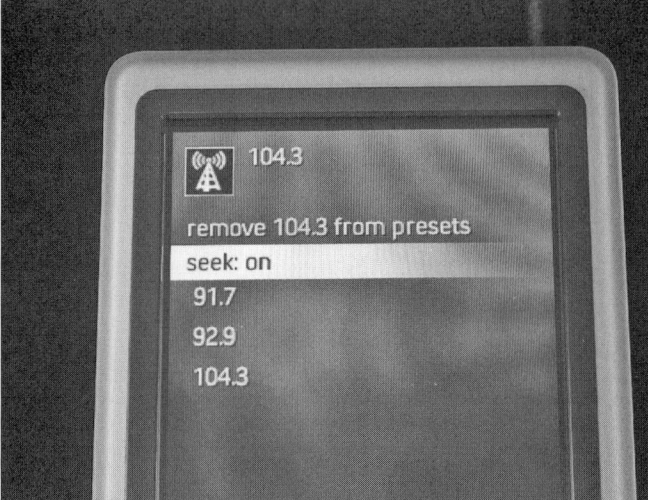

Figure 4-21:
The Settings
menu
displays
all your
available
presets.

Chapter 5

Getting Video onto Your Zune

. . . .

In This Chapter

▶ Finding the videos on your machine

▶ Figuring out video formats

▶ Converting videos for use on the Zune

▶ Understanding copyright

▶ Getting DVDs onto your Zune

▶ Getting TV onto your Zune (from TiVo or Media Center)

. . . .

*W*ithout video, your Zune is a fancy music player with one of the biggest and brightest screens available; you just aren't taking advantage of everything it can do if you're not adding video to the mix. TV shows, movies, Web videos, and more are all great content to store on your Zune.

Finding Videos Already on Your Machine

In Chapter 4, we show you how to add folders to your library's Monitored Folders list, and we also point out the many folders that get added by default as part of your Zune software installation. In terms of your Zune software hunting down stuff to add to your Zune device, the software doesn't treat video files any differently than music files or picture files; it adds any file it finds in a format that the Zune can understand to the library and then syncs that file to your Zune.

When video is turned into a digital file, it gets saved as a specific file format, normally one that involves compression so that a large amount of video data can be saved into a smaller amount of space. We discuss the full list of video file types that the Zune software can understand in the section "What file extensions can and can't tell you," later in this chapter, but the supported formats include QuickTime movie files (.mov), MPEG 4 video files (.mp4), and, of course, Windows Media files (.wmv).

If you have any content on your machine in any of those formats in any of your monitored folders (see Chapter 4), that content should already be in your library. Check out the full list of what the Zune software has found by clicking the View Video icon along the top of the Navigation pane, as shown in Figure 5-1.

Just like with music and photos, the Zune software adds your My Videos folder to the Monitored Folders list automatically, along with your iTunes folder (if you use iTunes), which is located in your My Music folder. If you have videos in either of these places (if you subscribe to one or more video podcasts through iTunes, for example), the Zune software should find them and add them to the library.

If you have additional folders that contain video (for example, I put video files for my Media Center PC in `C:\videos_mce`), make sure to add them to your Monitored Folders list. (For more on how to do that, see Chapter 4.) Just editing the Monitored Folders list and closing the dialog box starts a full PC scan, which may pick up a few additional files (check out the "Library limitations" sidebar in this chapter for more information).

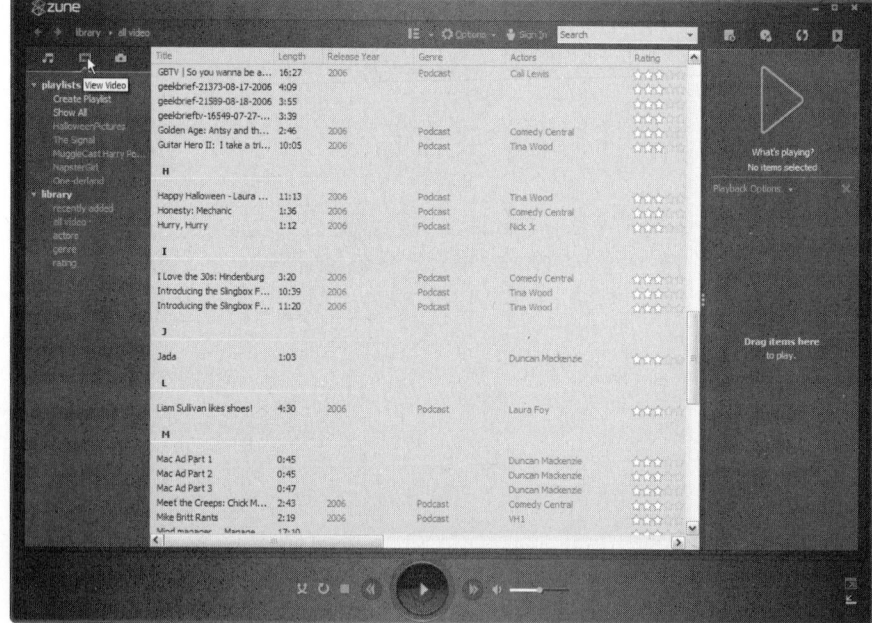

Figure 5-1:
In Video mode, you can browse the videos on your Zune or in your library.

Library limitations

Sometimes media on your hard drive (videos, music, photos) doesn't show up in your library even though it's in one of your monitored folders. This doesn't happen very often, but it happens to enough people enough of the time that you'll probably experience it at some point. Movie files get excluded from the library for a couple reasons:

✔ **The files in question aren't compatible with the Zune software, even though they look like they should be.** MPEG 4 files (`.mp4`) can sometimes be encoded differently than your run-of-the-mill MPEG 4s and thus fail to work with your Zune.

✔ **The files could be copy-protected by Digital Rights Management (DRM).** Movies downloaded from iTunes or Vongo.com are often copy-protected. (For more on Digital Rights Management, see Chapter 4.)

If either compatibility or DRM is the issue, the file won't appear in your Zune library, no matter what you do. If the file isn't protected, plays fine, but still doesn't appear in the library, maybe the folder-monitoring system simply hasn't added it yet or has missed it somehow. If you suspect that the file(s) are valid but just have been missed, you can start a folder scan of all your monitored folders by opening the Add to Library dialog box (right-click the Library item in the Navigation pane and select Add Folder to Library from the menu that appears) and then clicking OK without changing anything. This starts a full scan of all your monitored folders and should pick up any valid files along the way.

After you have video in your library, you can connect your Zune to your PC, drag video files onto the sync list (on the right side of the Zune software window), and then punch the Start Sync button to have the video content synchronized onto your device. Synchronization usually consists of three steps:

1. The software checks to see whether a copy of the file already lives on your Zune.

   If your Zune already has the file, the software doesn't do anything else with it.

2. If your Zune doesn't already hold a copy of the file, and if the file isn't already in the correct format, it's converted into the right format for the Zune.

   In the following section, we discuss what we mean by the right format and what happens when a file is or isn't in that format.

3. The file is copied to the device.

Finding the Right Kinds of Files

Before we jump into a discussion about video formats, you need to recognize the difference between formats that the Zune software (on your PC) *supports* versus formats that the actual Zune device can *understand.* The Zune software supports a much wider range of formats than the device itself does and can usually convert these files into the right format or quality level for your Zune device when you ask it to synchronize.

Although conversion happens automatically, you still need to understand a bit about the process — mostly so that you can avoid it. Converting from one video format to another takes a very long time, so your goal should always be to do one of the following:

- ✔ Grab your video in a format that will work on your Zune as-is.
- ✔ Grab your video in a format that will play in the Zune software.
- ✔ As the least desirable option, grab it in a format that you can convert to a Zune-compatible format by using some other piece of software.

When you look at videos on the Web, the video format is usually described by using one or more of the following criteria:

- ✔ File extension
- ✔ Codec
- ✔ Other various encoding parameters, such as bit rate and resolution

File extensions, codecs, bit rate, and resolution all come into play both when you're looking for video content for your Zune and when you're creating your own movies, so remember the terms that we discuss in the following sections.

What file extensions can and can't tell you

Many people use only the file extension to determine what format a particular video or music file is stored in, and although that method works pretty well, in general, it doesn't really tell the whole story. Table 5-1 shows some common movie file extensions and what they tell you about a file.

Table 5-1	Some Common Movie File Extensions
Extension	*Type of File*
.mov	QuickTime movie file
.wmv	Windows Media Video file
.mpg	MPEG video file; could be MPEG 1, MPEG 2, or MPEG 4
.mp4	MPEG 4 movie file
.avi	Standard video file format on Windows, usually described only as AVI (which stands for Audio Video Interleave)

In reality, you discover very little about your video simply from the file extension because all the formats in Table 5-1 are just containers for other video formats. The video content inside two AVI files could have been compressed using two totally different codecs (more on that term in the following section) or totally different settings (or both). File extensions can give you an idea of how a video has been encoded, but only by looking at the codec and settings can you really know what you're dealing with.

Codecs

The process of converting video into a digital file format is called *encoding;* turning it back into the original format is called *decoding.* The code that handles both of these processes is known as a *codec.* When you watch a DVD, you're seeing the MPEG 2 codec at work because DVD movies are stored on the disc in the MPEG 2 format. If you watch a Web video, it could be using any of hundreds of different codecs that are available on the Internet. Different codecs produce very different files that can be decoded only by using that same codec, and they often have different characteristics. One codec may use more space than another codec to produce the same quality of video; one codec may work better for fast-moving video, such as a sporting event, than another codec.

Just because a file has a familiar extension doesn't mean that it'll work with the Zune software. But in our experience, the Zune software supports the widest range of codecs we've ever seen, so you should try any video you have in that software first, regardless of the codec used.

Need to figure out the codec for a particular file? Right-click it in Windows Explorer and choose Properties from the menu that appears. The Properties dialog box might tell you which codec was used. If that doesn't work, you can also run a free program such as VideoInspector (from www.kcsoftwares.com) that looks at a video file and then tells you exactly what codec it uses.

This kind of program can be really helpful when you're trying to understand why a particular video isn't playing on your machine.

Working with encoding options, parameters, or settings

When a video file is compressed/encoded with a specific codec (such as Windows Media Video 9), a set of options is used to determine the quality and dimensions of the video file. The two terms that you see associated with these options most often are bit rate and resolution:

✓ **Bit rate:** A description of how much data is required for each second of the video; the higher the bit rate, the closer to the original the video quality will be. Some examples of common bit rate values are 512 Kbps (kilobits per second), 1200 Kbps, and 2.5 Mbps (megabits per second; 1 Mbps is equal to 1000 Kbps).

In general, higher is better, up until you hit the bit rate of the original file. You can't increase the quality of a video file, though; after a video file has been encoded to a specific bit rate, such as 512 Kbps, you won't see any improvement in quality by converting that file to a higher bit rate. To produce a higher bit rate version that's truly of higher quality, you need to start with the original source file again. Bit rate is a trade-off between video quality and file size; the higher the bit rate, the more space on disk is required for each second of video. Bit rate determines only how much data is used to store the video; another important factor is the resolution (width and height) of the video file.

✓ **Resolution:** Determines the size of the video on your screen. The two dimensions, height and width, are usually in a ratio of either 4:3 (the standard ratio for television) or 16:9 (the standard ratio for movies, also known as *widescreen*). Videos encoded specifically for use on the Zune will usually be in 4:3 mode with a resolution of 320 pixels (across) by 240 pixels (down), but you might also see 640 x 480 or 1280 x 720, all depending on the source of the content and the purpose for which it was encoded. More pixels is usually better, but if your target is the Zune, it doesn't really matter because it'll be converted down to 320 x 240 on its way to the device, anyway.

The higher the resolution, the higher the bit rate you need to produce good-quality video. If the Zune is your final target, then anything equal to or above a 320 x 240 resolution should work well.

Supported Video Formats

When you're downloading videos off the Web or creating your own videos, you need to understand what can play in the software, what can play on the device, and what can be converted between the two. The following sections dig into the supported content in each location and explain how the conversion process works.

What does the Zune software support?

The Zune software supports a wide range of codecs, bit rates, and resolutions, including MP4 files, QuickTime movies (.mov files), and WMV, as well as MP3, AAC, and WMA for audio files. However, the software doesn't support certain variations within these formats; an MP4 file, for example, can use one of many different available codecs, and not all codecs work with the Zune software. If a video file doesn't appear to be supported by the Zune software, you need to convert it first by using Windows Media Encoder or other third-party software, which we discuss in the section "Converting videos outside the Zune software," later in this chapter. If the video file came from a site that produces a lot of video, though, you may also want to check back on the original site for any other versions of the file available for download. For example, a download intended for the iPod most likely works well in the Zune software and can be successfully converted for your Zune device.

As far as bit rate and resolution go, the Zune software on either of these settings doesn't appear to have any real limit, though very high bit-rate files can sometimes have trouble playing on any machine. (They tend to be huge, so you need a lot of memory to play them.)

What does the Zune device support?

The good thing about your Zune software is that if a video is supported by the software but not by your Zune device, the software tries to convert the video into the right format. This happens a lot because the software understands a much wider range of codecs, bit rates, and resolutions than the Zune device. To be honest, the Zune device itself supports only the Windows Media Video (WMV) codec with a resolution of 320 x 240 (or 320 x 180 for 16:9 widescreen content) and a maximum bit rate of 1500 Kbps.

Although the Zune supports bit rates up to 1500 Kbps, you may not want to always convert videos at that rate. Many people find that videos encoded at a bit rate as low as 800 Kbps still look great on the Zune. Because these videos are half the size of ones encoded at 1500 Kbps, you save on space. Another bonus of the lower bit rate is that you also get better battery life while watching your videos. A lower bit rate takes less power to read from the Zune's internal hard drive, as well as less processing power to decode and play it back. You may have to experiment to find the bit rate that works for you, but we suggest 512 Kbps as a lower limit, 800 Kbps as a nice compromise between quality and file size, and bit rates as high as 1500 Kbps for when you need the absolute highest quality on your Zune.

When video is copied to your Zune, the bit rate used is determined by the video quality setting you've chosen. Checking out and/or changing this setting is easy. Just follow these steps:

1. **Connect your Zune to your PC and launch the Zune software.**

2. **Right-click your Zune's name in the Navigation pane of the interface and choose Advanced Options from the menu that appears.**

   Your Zune's Properties dialog box appears.

3. **Click to the Quality tab and either choose to let the software determine the maximum quality automatically or use the slider to pick your own (see Figure 5-2).**

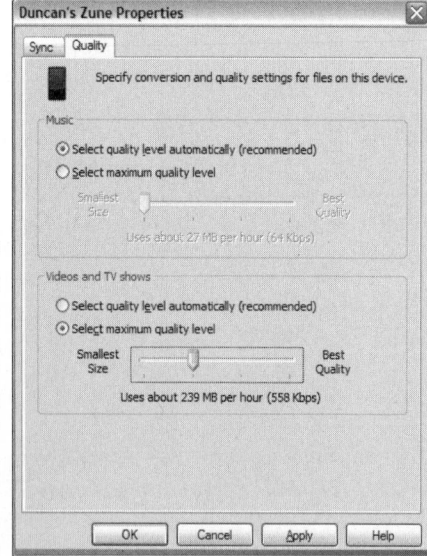

Figure 5-2:
You can adjust the video quality settings while your Zune is connected to your PC.

We normally pull this slider all the way to the right for both music and video, but we've been experimenting with lower settings for video quality and find that you can go down to the 1.11 Mbps setting (one down from the highest quality) without any real noticeable change in quality. You may have more

discerning eyesight than we, though, so try out the lower settings and be pre-
pared to move this slider higher if you find the quality unacceptable.

 The highest bit-rate setting in the video quality slider is 1.69 Mbps, but as we
mention earlier in this section, 1500 Kbps is the maximum bit rate for video.
Is the software wrong, or are we? Neither: The rates corresponding to locations on the slider are for the combination of video and audio, so a 1500 Kbps
video format is combined with a 192 Kbps audio format, making the total bit
rate approximately 1.69 Mbps.

Of course, you're only setting the maximum quality in this dialog box. If your
source video (such as a video podcast from the Web) is already at a lower bit
rate, you're stuck with that bit rate when the file gets converted. (You can't
wave a magic wand and convert the file at your maximum quality setting, in
other words.) If your source videos are WMV and are equal to or under the
maximum quality setting, you don't need to do any conversion at all. If they
aren't already in the right format, you can either let the Zune software convert them or use other software to do the conversion yourself in advance. The
following section covers the process of converting video so that the Zune software doesn't need to convert it again before copying it over to your device.

Converting Videos for Use on the Zune

One of life's harsh realities is that your Zune device supports only one video
format — WMV — and only within a certain range of bit rates (up to 1500
Kbps). If you have video in any other format, such as an MP4 file designed to
work on an iPod or even WMV files in a higher bit rate than the Zune supports, those files need to be converted before they can be copied onto your
Zune. To do the conversion, you have a couple of choices: you can either use
some additional pieces of software to convert the video, or you can just let
the Zune software do the conversion for you. In the following sections, we go
through both types of conversion and then discuss why you might want to
pick one over the other.

Letting the Zune software do it

Having the Zune software convert your files for you is the simplest conversion solution, with no extra software required. Just follow these steps:

1. **Add the video files you want on your Zune to your library in one of
   two ways:**

- Save the files to one of your monitored folders (your My Videos folder is a great spot).

- If the files are already in a folder on your machine somewhere, you can add that folder to your Monitored Folders list (see Chapter 4); then the Zune software can find those files and add them to your library.

2. **Hook your Zune up to the computer and fire up the software.**

3. **Drag the groovy movie files onto the sync list (located on the right side of the Zune software window) and then click Start Sync.**

4. **Click the Sync Results link (under the name of your Zune in the Navigation pane) to see the sync's progress.**

   The Sync Results page (see Figure 5-3), shows you the progress of each video file being converted (if necessary) and then copied over to the Zune.

The great thing about following these steps is that you don't have to really know anything about how the Zune handles video or what format your videos are in. If they need conversion, they're converted; otherwise, they just copy right over. The Zune software can handle most of the common video formats on the Web, although there are so many different variations that odds are it will eventually come up with a file that proves to be too tough a nut to crack.

Figure 5-3: The Sync Results page shows the progress of converting and copying files to your Zune.

Converting videos outside the Zune software

There may come a time when you'll want to convert your video files to the Zune format *before* adding them to the Zune library. You still need to sync them to the Zune in the Zune software, but the conversion step won't be required.

If you're trying to convert TV shows from a Media Center PC (`.drv-ms` files) or movies from DVDs, you can find more specific information in the "Ripping a DVD onto your Zune" and "Zuning into TV" sections, later in this chapter.

If you decide to do video conversion on your own, you can find quite a few software tools to help you handle all sorts of video files. Most of the easy-to-use tools cost money, but Microsoft offers a free professional tool called Windows Media Encoder, which you can use to convert between many popular formats and Windows Media Video. Windows Media Encoder isn't the simplest program to use, but it's definitely the fullest featured and most well-documented free tool you can find. You can download this application from `www.microsoft.com/windows/windowsmedia/forpros/encoder/default.mspx`, and after it's installed, you can find a link to it under Windows Media on your All Programs menu.

To convert a video by using Windows Media Encoder, follow these steps:

1. **Start your favorite Web browser, navigate to `www.crazyaboutzune.com`, and download the file `zune.prx`.**

   This file contains a hardware profile that lets you quickly and automatically adjust a file's video settings to specifically match your Zune hardware. (You don't use this file until Step 12, but the process goes more smoothly and more quickly if you have the file downloaded and ready to go.)

2. **Fire up Windows Media Encoder and double-click Convert a File from the startup screen (see Figure 5-4).**

   The New Session Wizard opens. This wizard lets you pick a file to convert (see Figure 5-5), pick some formatting options, and set the metadata for your file.

3. **Click the Browse button next to the Source File text box.**

   A run-of-the-mill Windows Open dialog box appears.

4. **Navigate to the file you want to convert, select it, and click OK.**

   The Output File text box automatically updates to show where the converted file will be and what it will be called. This output file must bear a

.wmv file extension, but you can specify whatever filename you want for the final file.

5. **Click Next.**

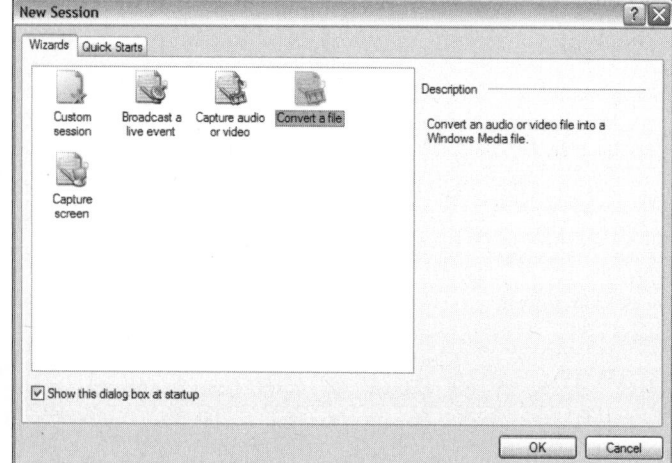

Figure 5-4:
The New Session Wizard gets everything set up for a straight-forward conversion.

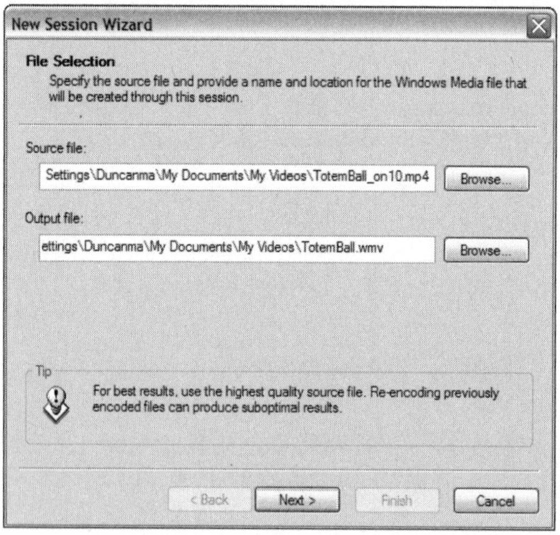

Figure 5-5:
Select your source and destination files for the conversion wizard.

The Content Distribution screen of the wizard appears, listing the various distribution methods available. The file's *distribution method* is how you intend to use it, whether on a portable device, on your PC, or in some other scenario. Each distribution method on this list (see Figure 5-6) represents a group of settings for resolution, bit rate, and other encoding parameters.

6. **Select Windows Media Hardware Profiles from the text box and click Next.**

   In some ways, it doesn't matter what you select here because you can (and will) edit the settings before you actually do your encoding. But selecting Windows Media Hardware Profile gets you pretty close to your goal.

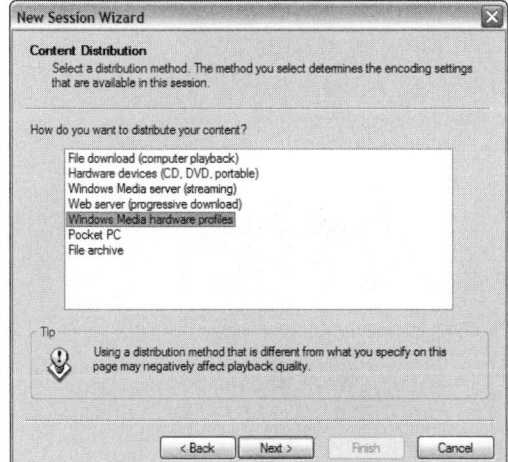

Figure 5-6:
Picking
the right
distribution
method.

The Encoding Options screen appears (see Figure 5-7).

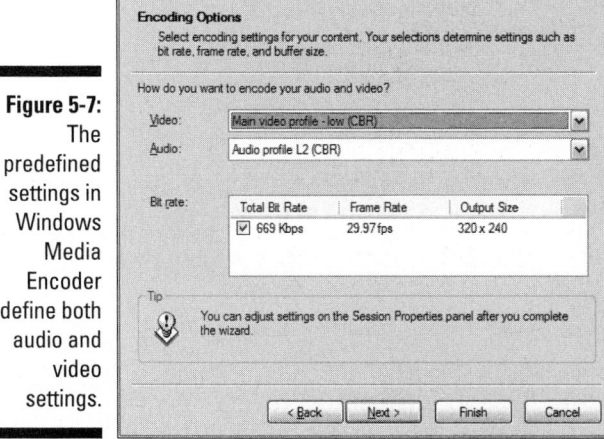

Figure 5-7:
The
predefined
settings in
Windows
Media
Encoder
define both
audio and
video
settings.

7. **In the Encoding Options screen, leave the defaults as they are and click Next.**

   Although you can edit the values at this point, we're going to ask you to just hang tight; you edit them all at once in Step 12, using the `zune.prx` file you download in Step 1.

   The Display Information page makes an appearance (see Figure 5-8).

8. **Enter a title, author, copyright information, and, if you want, a rating and description of the content for your video. Click Next.**

   The information you enter here becomes the metadata that's saved with the final, converted file. The information in these metadata fields will show up on the Zune, in the Zune library, and in the Windows Explorer, so it's important to enter useful and accurate values.

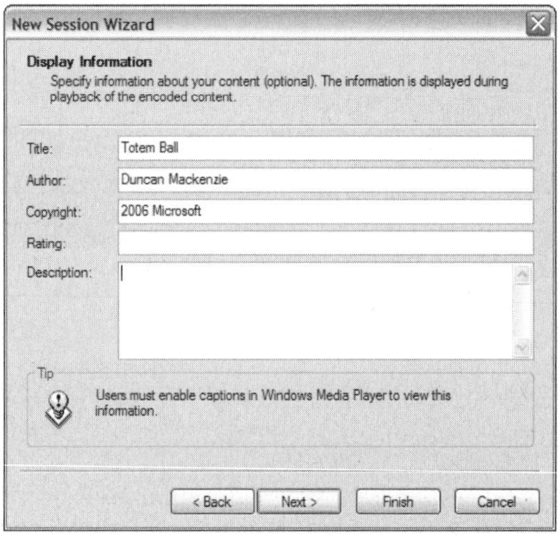

Figure 5-8:
To ensure that your finished file displays as much useful information as possible, fill in the metadata fields before completing the wizard.

> **New Session Wizard**
>
> **Display Information**
> Specify information about your content (optional). The information is displayed during playback of the encoded content.
>
> Title: Totem Ball
> Author: Duncan Mackenzie
> Copyright: 2006 Microsoft
> Rating:
> Description:
>
> Tip
> Users must enable captions in Windows Media Player to view this information.
>
> < Back   Next >   Finish   Cancel

The Settings Review window appears, summarizing all of your choices, as shown in Figure 5-9.

9. **In the Settings Review window, make sure the Begin Converting When I Click Finish check box is *not* selected. Then click Finish.**

   By deselecting that check box, you give yourself the opportunity to edit the conversion settings before starting the process.

   Clicking Finish in the New Session Wizard switches you to the Project view's Session Properties dialog box in Windows Media Encoder. From this window, you can edit any of the project settings that you set during the wizard, including the compression settings.

10. **In the Session Properties dialog box, switch to the Compression tab and click the Edit button.**

   The Custom Encoding Settings dialog box, shown in Figure 5-10, appears.

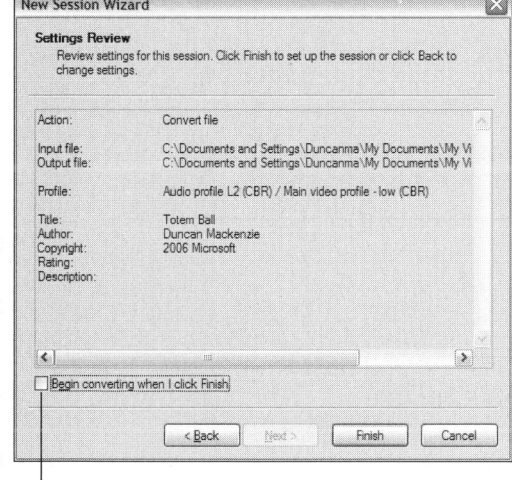

Figure 5-9:
You don't
want to
start the
conversion
just yet!

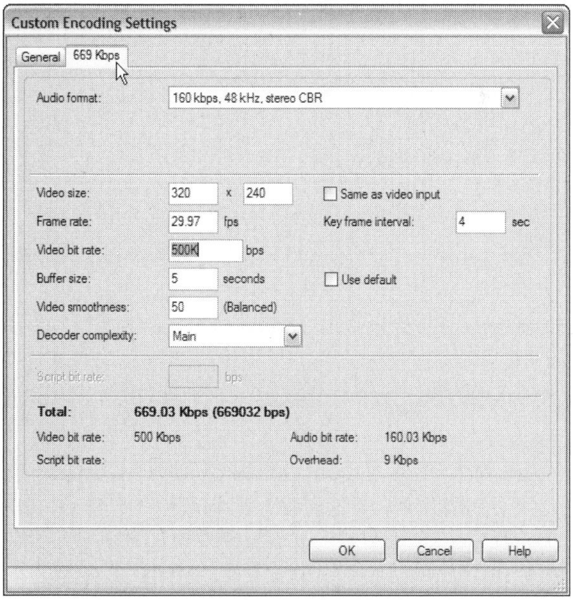

Begin Converting When I Click Finish check box

Figure 5-10:
Set up the
file's bit
rate and
resolution
settings to
get it just
right.

From here, you can manually edit each setting to produce the best file for your Zune (or whatever other device you have), but a quicker way is to just import a profile containing all the encoding settings you need — a profile suspiciously like the profile you download in Step 1!

11. **In the Custom Encoding Settings window, switch to the General tab and then click Import Profile.**

12. **Browse to the `zune.prx` file, select it, and then click Open (see Figure 5-11).**

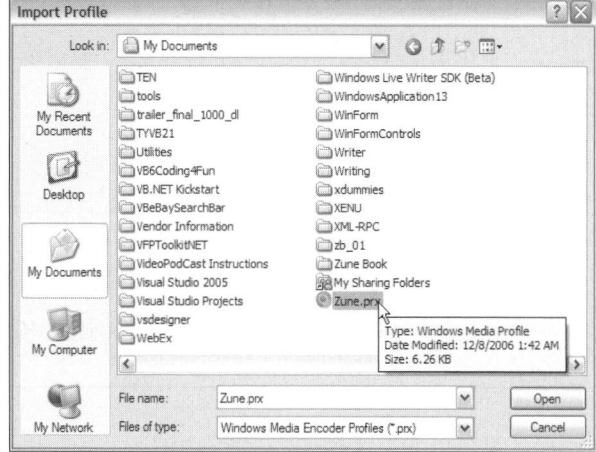

Figure 5-11:
The Zune profile (`zune.prx`) is your ticket to good conversions.

After you import the profile settings, all of the encoding options change to a perfect profile for the Zune. From this point, you can still edit the settings as you want, especially if you save this project to use as the starting point for any future conversions. But, generally, you shouldn't need to do any more fiddling with these settings; they'll work as they are.

13. **Click OK to save your settings and close the Custom Encoding Settings dialog box.**

The Session Properties dialog box comes to the fore.

14. **In the Session Properties dialog box, click Apply and then click Start Encoding on the application's toolbar to start the actual conversion process.**

Depending on the file you choose to convert, this process can take quite some time, but when the conversion is done, you should be able to add the completed file to your Zune library and sync it to your device without forcing the Zune software to perform any conversions.

Getting Movies and TV onto Your Zune

The two main types of video that people load onto their Zunes are movies and TV. Both of these types of content have different issues and require different techniques, although they certainly share the common video concepts and converting issues discussed in the preceding sections of this chapter. In the following sections, we go through these two common types of content and detail processes for getting them onto your Zune.

Another great source of video content is the Internet. We cover a particular form of Web video known as the podcast in Chapter 10.

Ripping a DVD onto your Zune

There's nothing quite like having your own movies along with you on a plane, on the bus, or even just sitting at home away from the TV. The Zune software won't do anything with a movie on DVD: It won't pull it onto your computer, and it definitely won't sync it over to your Zune. It's up to you to *rip* (copy from the disc onto a hard drive) the movie off the DVD yourself, which presents both some technical and some legal questions. The legal question is worth dealing with first, so you can decide if you're even interested in heading down the DVD-ripping path.

Copyright issues

If you're going to rip video from homemade DVD movies, you don't have to worry about any legal issues; you can do whatever you want with your own videos. Ripping the latest new release off DVD isn't quite so clearly legitimate.

Many people consider ripping a movie from a DVD onto your computer similar to ripping music off a CD — completely within your fair-use rights for a product that you own. It's a little trickier with DVDs, though, because DVDs use encryption technologies to make copying their content a tad more difficult; most commercial CDs don't even bother with such technology. This slight difference may not seem like much, but it's led to a lot of debate and back and forth among lawyers — that's what you get when the law is complicated and you're right in the middle of a legal gray area. When all's said and done, though, you're not likely to have any issues if you

✔ Stick to ripping only DVDs that you own.

✔ Rip a copy only for yourself.

✔ Don't distribute that copy in any way.

Ripping rental DVDs isn't okay, and neither is ripping your own DVDs to your computer and then selling the original DVDs. In both of these cases, you end up with a digital copy of a DVD that you don't own, which means that you don't have any fair-use argument. If you get caught, prepare for fines, court battles, and possible jail time.

Our three little rules outlined in the preceding list apply to ripping music, as well: Rip music off of CDs that you own, and don't sell the CD (or the music files) afterward unless you also remove the digital files from your PCs and portable devices. The only real difference is that Microsoft software *will* rip music from your CD collection for you.

Even though it's a common activity and many people agree that it constitutes fair use, we're not lawyers and can't offer you any real advice — advice that's really worth anything, at least — about the legality of ripping DVDs. Use your own best judgment, and if you decide to rip DVDs, keep to the guidelines described in the preceding list to keep the process as legitimate as possible. If you're interested in learning more about this issue, a Web search on "fair use DeCSS" will return more information.

Ripping a movie from a DVD onto your machine

Movies are stored on a DVD as MPEG 2 files, compressed at varying bit rates depending on the type and length of the movie. The individual video files on the DVD are stored in a folder called Video_TS and named with a .vob extension. On a nonprotected DVD (such as one that you make with your own home videos), you can just copy one or more of these VOB files from the DVD onto your PC, rename them with an .mpg extension, and probably play them in Windows Media Player or in another video player, such as Nero Showtime.

Most consumer DVDs are protected, though, which means that you can't just copy the files from them. The encryption system that DVDs started out using (and many still do) is known as CSS (Content Scrambling System), but newer DVDs may use a different encryption system. To copy the VOB file off of a protected/encrypted DVD, you can use one of several free software programs, such as DVD43 or DVD Encrypter, but these programs are hard to find and relatively hard to use. Instead of that process, we recommend using a commercial application such as Xilisoft's (www.xilisoft.com) DVD to Zune Converter or DVD Ripper application, or Cucusoft Technologies' (www.cucusoft.com) DVD to Zune Converter. All these applications, as their names imply, copy a DVD movie from the disc and turn it into a file that can play on your Zune. All these products cost around $30 each, but although you can use other methods to accomplish the same result without any cost at all, we think the simplicity of using a single program is well worth a few Hamiltons.

Although I (Duncan Mackenzie speaking here) have heard good reports about all these programs, I personally use the Xilisoft application and have found it to work well on a large number of my DVDs so far. Using this application, I walk you through the steps to turn a DVD movie into a file that can be synced right to your Zune without any conversion required:

1. **Go to `www.xilisoft.com/downloads.html` to see a list of available products with free trials available for download.**

2. **Find the DVD to Zune Converter entry and click Free Trial to download the converter program.**

3. **After the file has been downloaded, double-click its icon and follow the on-screen instructions to install the application onto your computer.**

4. **Put the DVD you want to rip into your DVD drive.**

   If the DVD tries to launch any interfaces, start playing, or install anything, quit or cancel those applications.

5. **Launch the DVD to Zune Converter by choosing Start➪All Programs➪ Xilisoft➪DVD to Zune Converter 4➪Xilisoft DVD to Zune Converter 4.**

   The DVD to Zune Converter's window opens.

6. **Click the DVD button near the bottom of the program's window (see Figure 5-12).**

Figure 5-12:
Open your DVD by clicking the DVD button in the DVD to Zune Converter.

DVD button

A standard file-browsing dialog box appears.

7. **Navigate to your DVD drive and then click OK.**

If you aren't sure which drive your DVD is in, look for one that has a `VIDEO_TS` folder, as shown in Figure 5-13.

Figure 5-13: DVDs have a `VIDEO_TS` and some-times an `AUDIO_TS` folder at the top (or first) level of the disc.

After you select your DVD drive, the converter loads up all the titles on the disc and lists all the file information. (Each main feature and extra on the DVD shows up as an individual title.) You can select each title and click the preview buttons in the lower-right corner of the application to see what that title is. Normally, the main movie is the longest item in the list, such as the nearly two-hour-long entry shown in Figure 5-14.

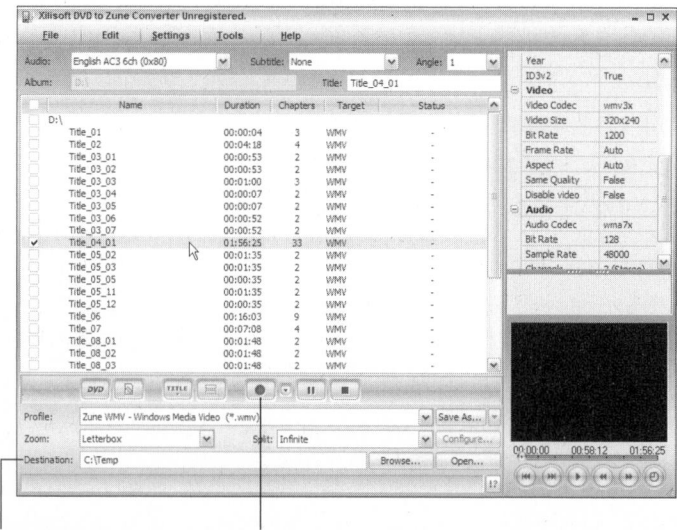

Figure 5-14: Most DVDs contain a number of titles; generally, you want to rip the longest one.

Destination field   Record button

The software uses a set of default values for its settings, including bit rate (1200 Kbps) and resolution (320 x 240), that you can change if you'd rather rip to a higher-quality file (for example, set the bit rate to 1500 Kbps) or a lower-quality file (800 Kbps produces good-quality video while saving you some space). To change these settings, follow these steps:

1. **Select one or more titles in the list shown in Figure 5-14.**

   Under the Video section of the two-column grid on the far right of the window, you find the bit-rate and resolution settings. You can also see many other settings, all of which you should leave alone unless you know what you're doing; changing any one of the shown settings could possibly make the video output unusable on your Zune.

2. **Adjust the bit rate and resolution to the settings you want.**

   You can raise the bit rate all the way up to 2000 Kbps and the resolution up to 640 x 480 if you want, but with those settings, the video will need to be converted before it can be synchronized to your device.

8. **Click the check box to the left of a title to indicate that you want to rip that particular item.**

   By default, the software rips the movie into the C:\Temp folder, but you can enter in any path you want. At this point, this is just a trial version, but if you buy the software, you'll want to change the Destination either to a monitored folder (such as your My Videos folder) or to a folder that you then add to your Zune's list of monitored folders. To enter in a different path, either type the path you want into the Destination field or click the Browse button (to the right of the Destination field) to pick a folder.

9. **Click the red Record button to start the ripping process.**

   You see a Registration dialog box (see Figure 5-15).

10. **Click Later to skip the registration for now.**

    At this point, the software isn't registered, so it rips only the first five minutes of any title you pick. But if you do decide to pay for the software, you can register it when you rip your first DVD.

    The DVD to Zune Converter does its thing and leaves you with a WMV file that you can add to your Zune library and synchronize to your Zune.

If you decide that you like the results of this test rip, and if you think that you'll need to rip DVDs on an ongoing basis, select the Buy Registration Code command from the application's Help menu.

Registration

Registration Info

Name:

License Code:

Buy Xilisoft DVD to Zune Converter

Tech Support

Anytime, even you are in trail, you have hard question,
you can contact our support team at

support@xilisoft.com

We provide free technical assistance.

OK   Later

Figure 5-15:
Until you
register,
you're
limited to
only five
minutes
of video
encoding.

Zuning into TV

Aside from movies, the other major source of video content for your Zune is
probably television. Getting your favorite TV shows onto the Zune can be
tricky, though, depending on your current setup for watching and recording
television.

If you use a TiVo (Series2), a computer that runs Windows XP Media Center
Edition, or a Windows Vista computer running the Ultimate or Home Premium
edition, you're really close to a solution. Both systems do a great job of digi-
tizing TV content, but you need to take one more step before you can get a
show onto your Zune. The following sections tell you how to take that step
for each setup.

TiVo to Go

If you have a TiVo DVR, you can get an additional feature called TiVo to Go
(www.tivo.com/4.9.4.1.asp) and a program called TiVo Desktop that
together allow you to pull files from your TiVo over to a Windows XP desktop.
The shows you pull over end up in a folder on your PC, and from there, you
can add them to the library in your Zune software. Unfortunately, the files
produced by this process aren't immediately compatible with the Zune, but
the Zune software or a third-party conversion utility can convert them before
synchronization (check out the section "Converting Videos for Use on the
Zune," earlier in this chapter, for the lowdown on how to make this conversion).

You don't have to pay anything for any of this software, but you do need a
Series2 (or later) TiVo — and you need it on your home network to transfer
TV shows to your PC.

Media Center PC and DVR 2 WMV

If you have a Media Center PC, your shows are already sitting right there in your PC, but if you try to add them into your Zune library, the library won't accept them. At the time this book was written, the Zune software couldn't understand or convert .dvr-ms files, the format that Media Center records television into. Luckily, a few applications out there can convert these files into the more usable WMV format. The most popular of these programs is DVR 2 WMV, which you can find at http://thegreenbutton.com/files. This application (and many others) is based on a Windows Media Encoder profile, which describes the destination format in the form of a .prx file. In DVR 2 WMV, you can pick from one of several choices or select a .prx file, as shown in Figure 5-16.

Figure 5-16:
DVR 2 WMV
lets you pick
a custom
.prx file,
and it uses
those
settings to
do its
conversion.

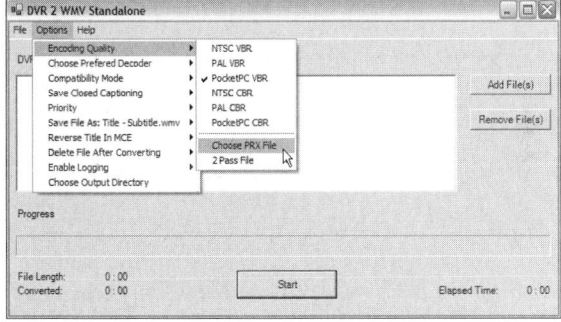

If you don't have a .prx file that you want to use, you can either select a profile that should work well, such as Pocket PC VBR/CBR, or grab a Zune .prx file from www.crazyaboutzune.com. (If you performed the steps in the "Converting videos outside the Zune software" section, earlier in this chapter, you already have one!) Regardless of which encoding settings you use, the DVR 2 WMV application uses those settings when accessed as a normal Windows application, as a command-line (DOS style) utility, or as a plug-in to Windows Media Center Edition.

Finding Out More

This chapter gives you a good start into getting videos onto your Zune, but there's always more you can do. Check out Chapter 10 for information on downloading video podcasts and Web videos, and getting them synchronized onto your device. If you make your own home movies, you can use Movie Maker, the video editing software that's included free with Windows, to convert your videos into the right format for the Zune. (For more on creating your own videos, check out Chapter 9.)

Chapter 6

Adding Pictures to Your Zune

. . . .

In This Chapter

▶ Using your Zune software to view pictures on your PC

▶ Viewing pictures on your Zune

▶ Making cool custom Zune backgrounds

▶ Making a special folder for Zune pictures

▶ Organizing your Zune photos with auto playlists

▶ Creating custom photo playlists

▶ Sharing your pictures with other Zuners

. . . .

*O*ne of the great features of the Zune is its ability to view and share your favorite photos. In this chapter, we take a look at what you can do with photos on your Zune. We show you how to get photos onto your Zune and how to share the photos with other Zuners, and we share some tips for how you can use the photo feature in new and unique ways.

In the first part of this chapter, we assume that you synchronize pictures with your Zune by default; if you don't, skip to the "About Syncing Pictures" section and add some pictures to your Zune.

Pictures in Zune

There are two ways you can view pictures with Zune. First, you can look at pictures in your library by using the Zune desktop application. Of course, the second way to look at pictures is to use the Zune player itself.

Pictures in the Zune desktop

The Zune desktop application has a great photo-viewing application built right in. This photo-viewing app lets you view pictures, create playlists, and play slideshows from right within the Zune software itself. Of course, this functionality complements the picture-viewing features of your Zune player. You can see photos in the Zune desktop application in Figure 6-1.

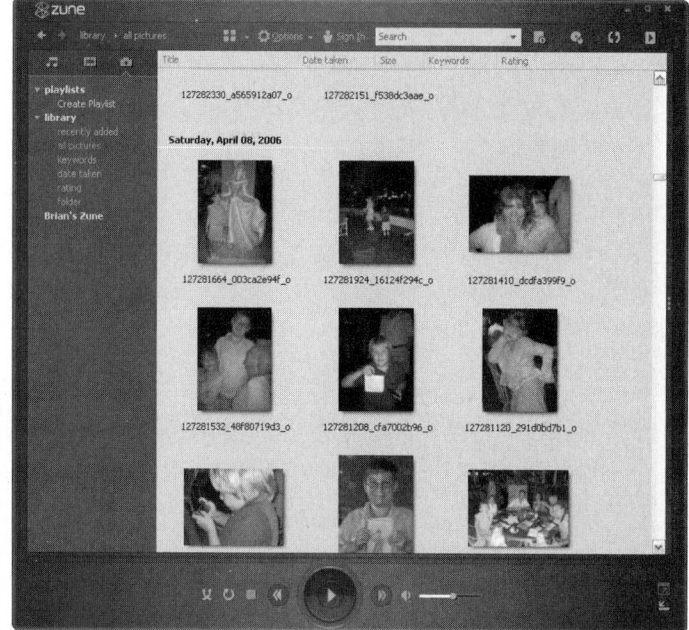

Figure 6-1:
You can view photos in the Zune desktop application.

To view photos in the Zune desktop application, follow these steps:

1. **Fire up the Zune software and click the View Pictures icon (the cute little camera) in the Media selector bar in the upper-left part of the screen.**

   Now, under the Library heading in the Zune software's Navigation pane, you'll see different ways to view your pictures (All, Keywords, Date Taken, and so on).

2. **Click the option under the Library heading you want to use to view your pictures.**

   Note the different column headings (Title, Date Taken, Size, Keywords, Rating) at the top of the View window. You can use these column headings to sort the photos according to different criteria. Say you want to see the latest pictures first, all you have to do is click on the Date Taken column heading until the triangle in that heading points down. These quick sorts can make it much easier to find the pictures you're looking for.

3. To view the pictures as a slideshow, press the Play button at the base of the screen.

Figure 6-2 shows the Zune desktop application with the photo viewer open.

Figure 6-2:
Photos in
the Zune
desktop
application.

The Zune desktop application lets you look at photos in three different ways, as shown in Figure 6-3:

- ✔ **Icon view** shows a thumbnail of the photo with the name of the photo beneath.

- ✔ **Tile view** shows the photo thumbnail with the name to the right of the photo. This view also shows the date and the rating that have been added to the photo.

- ✔ **Details view** adds more information to the list, but doesn't show a thumbnail of the photos in the list; so you get more information, but you don't get to see the images while you work with them.

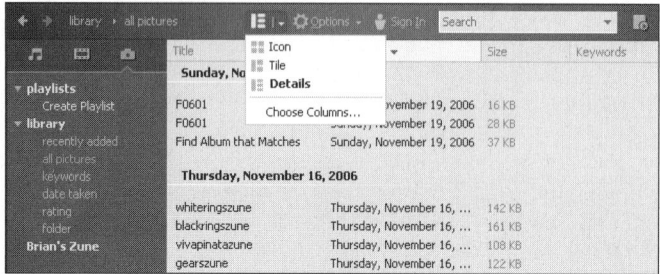

Figure 6-3:
Choose the
view for
photos in
the toolbar
above the
photo list.

You can see a thumbnail of the currently selected picture in the Now Playing list in the bottom left of the Zune window.

What's Playing Now

The items shown in a desktop slideshow are the items in the What's Playing Now list in the Zune desktop application. You can see this list in Figure 6-4. The Watch What's Playing Now button above this window is a rectangle with a small triangle in it. Click this button to toggle between hiding and showing the What's Playing Now list.

Watch What's Playing Now button

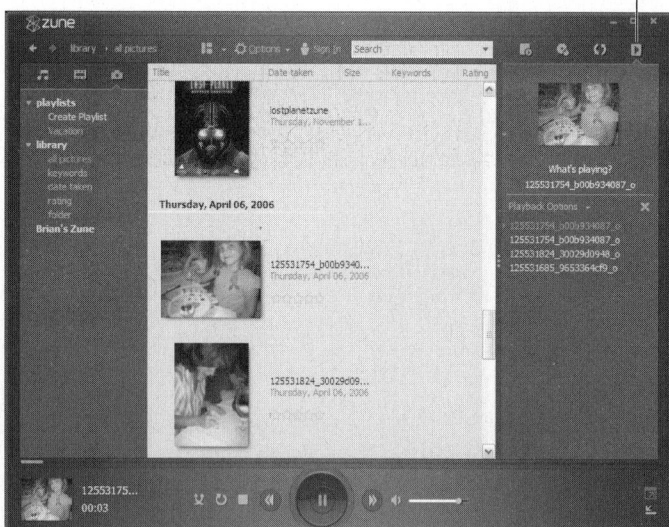

Figure 6-4:
The What's
Playing
Now list in
the Zune
photo view.

In the What's Playing Now panel, clicking the big X at the top clears the list so that you can add just the photos you want to see. You can add photos by dragging selected pictures from the main panel or by dragging a whole collection from the library list to the left.

After you have the pictures you want in the What's Playing Now list, you view them as a slideshow by pressing the Play button at the bottom of the screen. (Refer to Figure 6-2.) If you'd like to view your images in full-screen mode, click the View Full Screen button in the lower right of the player window.

You can see what the full-screen mode for the Zune desktop player looks like in Figure 6-5.

To exit full-screen mode, click the View Full Screen button again or press the Esc key on your keyboard.

When you're viewing a picture and you're not in full-screen mode, you can get back to the photo list in the Zune desktop by clicking the Back button in the upper left of the Zune window.

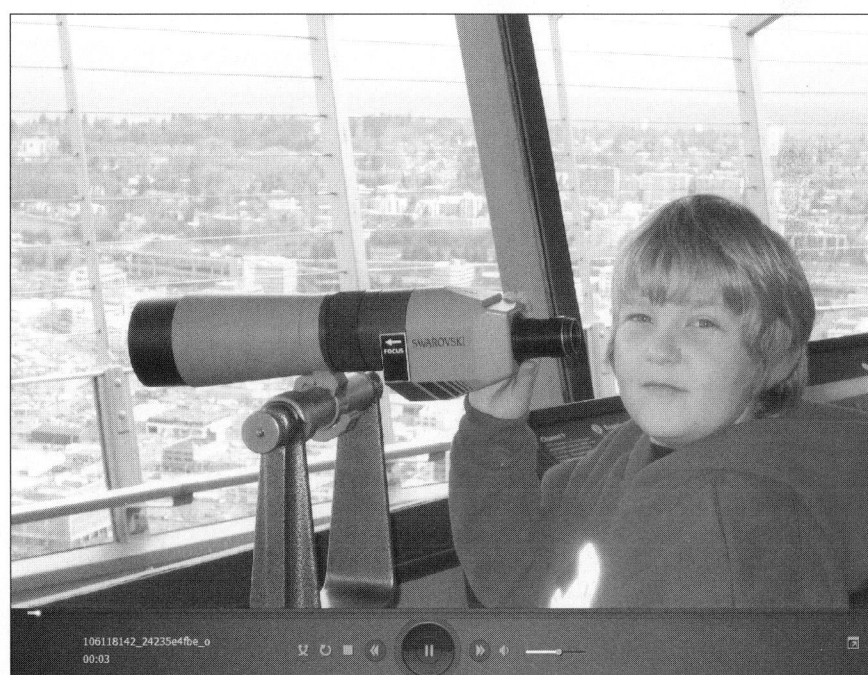

Figure 6-5: Viewing pictures full screen with the Zune desktop player.

Making Zune backgrounds

On the Zune, any picture on the device can be set as the background for all the menus, providing a great way to customize the look of your Zune. The screen on your Zune is 240 pixels wide and 320 pixels high (holding it in "portrait mode," with the navigation pad at the bottom), so those are the proportions you want to shoot for as a background. But if you're making your own background images, there are a couple of things you should be aware of:

- If the image isn't 320 x 240 to begin with, it will be cropped to portrait mode.

- Whenever you leave the main page, the image is zoomed in a bit on all four sides.

Given a 320 x 320 square photo, the accompanying figure shows what happens when it is displayed as a background.

The outermost rectangle is what you end up seeing on the Zune's screen when you are on the home page. This is the standard 240 x 320 image

you'd expect, taken from the middle of the picture. The next smaller rectangle is the slightly zoomed-in image you see when you navigate to any page other than the home page. What this means is that the image might be slightly distorted on any page but the home page. View your custom backgrounds on your Zune to see whether the effect is noticeable with the pictures that you create for backgrounds.

Zune viewer controls

The controls at the bottom of the screen are pretty straightforward. You can see them labeled in Figure 6-6 and described in the following list:

- **Preview:** Shows a thumbnail of the current photo. This disappears in full-screen mode.

- **Turn Shuffle On:** When toggled to On, shows pictures in random order.

- **Turn Repeat On:** When toggled on, repeats the slideshow from the beginning after the last slide in the list.

- **Stop:** Stops the show at the current slide.

- **Back:** Goes back one slide in the list.

- **Play:** Plays the slideshow. When the slideshow is playing, clicking this button causes the show to pause. Click it again to continue.

✔ **Forward:** Move forward one slide in the list.

✔ **Volume:** Controls the volume when you're playing music while viewing photos. (The speaker button next to the volume control is a mute button.)

✔ **View Full Screen:** Switches Zune to full-screen mode.

✔ **Switch to Compact Mode:** Switches Zune to compact mode. (This shows the controls only, so it isn't very useful when viewing photos!)

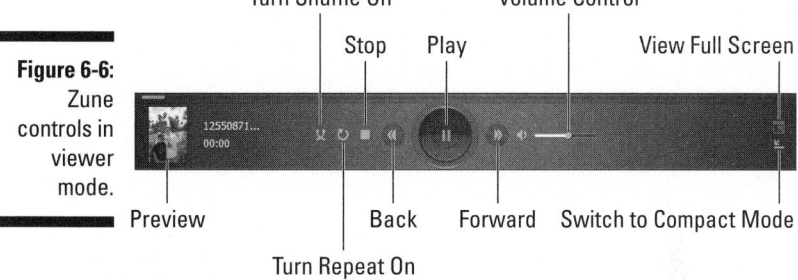

Turn Shuffle On Volume Control

Stop Play View Full Screen

Figure 6-6:
Zune
controls in
viewer
mode.

Preview Back Forward Switch to Compact Mode

Turn Repeat On

Pictures on your Zune device

The pictures that are added to your Zune desktop are copied to your Zune when you sync with your PC. These pictures are optimized by default, meaning that the pictures are compressed and resized to make them take up less space yet still look great on your Zune.

After you sync your Zune to your PC, you can find your photos in the Pictures section of your Zune. To get to this section, click Pictures from the Zune main menu.

Working with folders

By default, you see a list of folders in the Picture section of your Zune. If all of your pictures are in a single folder, that folder will be the one that you see in this section. Selecting a folder and pressing the OK button on the Zune opens the folder and shows you a list of pictures in the folder. Picture folders can also include subfolders (folders within other folders), so you can drill into those in the same way.

You can also view your pictures by date. This option lets you see the pictures on your Zune sorted by month.

To view a single picture on the Zune, select the picture from the list and click it.

To view all of the pictures in a folder or view as a slideshow, click the Play Slideshow selection at the top of the screen, as show in Figure 6-7. This starts a slideshow of pictures in the currently open folder.

Your Zune device view options

When you view a picture on the Zune, the view is in landscape orientation, meaning that you need to turn your Zune sideways to view the photos normally.

Clicking OK while you're viewing a picture brings up the menu shown in Figure 6-8.

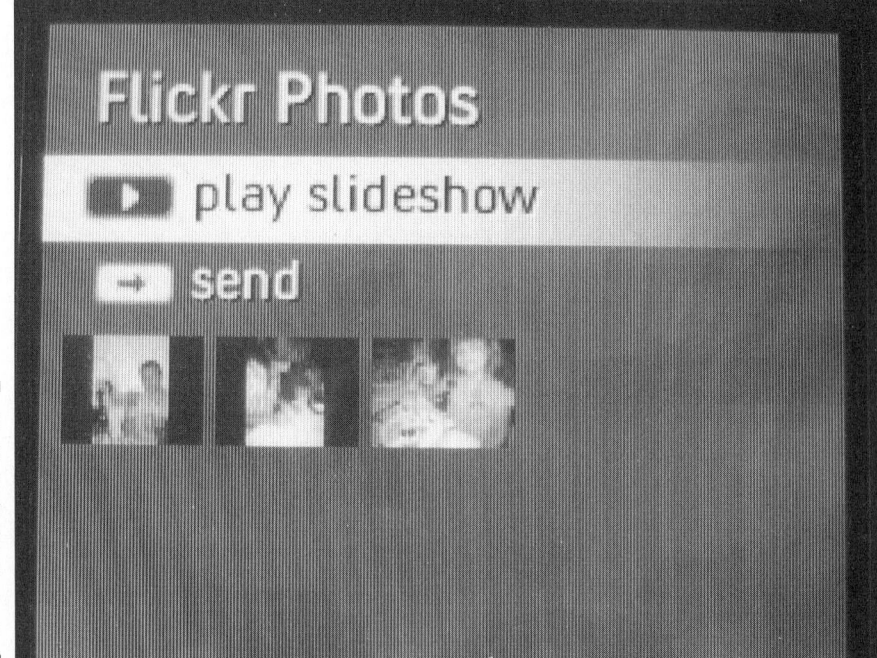

Figure 6-7:
Click the Play Slideshow item to view the pictures in the current view.

Figure 6-8:
Options for
an individual
picture.

The Picture menu gives you a number of options:

- **Zoom In:** Lets you zoom in on a specific area in a picture to get a closer look. To use this feature, click the Zoom In item and then move around the picture by using the circle on the Zune.

- **Shuffle:** By default, this is set to Off for photos, but selecting this item and clicking lets you toggle this between Off and On. When this option is On, photos in the slideshow appear in a random order.

- **Apply as Background:** This item lets you turn any picture that you're viewing into the background for your Zune device. Just click this item, and the picture gets set as your background. See the sidebar, "Making Zune backgrounds," for more information.

- **End Slideshow:** Ends the currently running slideshow and takes you back to the main menu.

- **Send:** Sends the current photo to a nearby Zune device via wireless sharing.

- **Flag:** Flags the current photo. This causes the photo to be marked for your Zune inbox. (The inbox is your own special place for storing an item like a picture or a song so you can quickly access it later — to send to a friend, for example.

TIP

You can get back to the Zune main menu at any time by holding down the Back button.

About Syncing Pictures

The following sections cover picture organization in a slightly more advanced way. Read through them to figure out how to add just the items you want to your Zune.

Pictures from your PC are synchronized to your Zune based on a couple of different factors. These factors include the location of your picture files and the playlists associated with pictures in the Zune desktop application. What this means is that you need to tweak these two settings to control the pictures added to your Zune device.

Auto playlists

Auto playlists are content collections based on criteria that you set. The one (default) playlist associated with pictures that you'll find in the Zune desktop application is the All Pictures playlist. This playlist adds all of the pictures in any of the picture folders recognized by the Zune desktop application to your Zune device. Later in the chapter, we show you how to create your own custom auto playlist.

Picture folders

Picture folders are folders on your PC that contain pictures that you want to synchronize to your Zune device. By default, the Zune desktop software looks for your pictures in your My Pictures folder — but don't assume you have to stick with the default. You can store pictures in folders anywhere on your hard drive and then have the Zune software track down the images. The next section shows you how.

Adding a picture folder

The Zune desktop application copies files to the device based on the folders that you've chosen for synchronization. You can find these settings in the Add to Library dialog box. To add picture folders to your Zune through the Zune desktop software, follow these steps:

1. **In the Zune desktop application, click the Options button in the main menu.**

2. **In the drop-down menu that appears, click Add to Library.**

   You see the Add to Library dialog box.

3. **In the Add to Library dialog box, click the Add Folder button.**

   Doing so opens the Add Folder dialog box.

4. **Navigate to (and select) the folder containing the pictures that you want to add to your Zune.**

   For example, if you have a picture folder named Vacation on your C: drive, you would click My Computer, then click Local Disk (C:), and then scroll down to the folder named Vacation and click that.

5. **Click OK and the folder you selected (`C:\Vacation` in this example) is added to the Add to Library dialog box.**

The pictures that get added to the Vacation folder will now automatically be synchronized to your Zune — if you have picture synchronization enabled. (For more on synchronization options, see Chapters 2 and 4.)

 You might not want to sync all of your pictures to your Zune. Create a folder for Zune pictures and sync just that folder. This will make it much easier to show off and share your favorites with others.

Controlling the photos added to Zune

Digital cameras have really changed the way we all do photography. We can now take thousands of photos easily, store them digitally on our PCs, and display them publicly on our Web sites. Of course, we can also put those photos on our Zunes and enjoy them when we're on the road.

When you first set up the Zune, as described in Chapter 2, you're given the option of synchronizing your pictures, along with other content on your PC. If you choose to synchronize your pictures at that time, the Zune software searches your machine for picture files and adds them to an auto playlist called All Pictures.

The default location for pictures on a user's PC is the My Pictures folder, located in the My Documents folder on your PC. If that's where your pictures are stored, and you have the All Pictures playlist set to sync, then all of your pictures will be added to your Zune — if there's enough space. We don't know about you, but we really have a lot more pictures on our computers than we want to add to our Zunes. You can reduce the number of pictures synced to your Zune by creating a custom auto playlist for all your syncing purposes. In order to do that, however, you first have to tell your Zune that it should no longer use the default All Pictures playlist as the basis for syncing. Here's how that's done:

1. **In the Navigation pane on the left side of the Zune softwarewindow, right-click your Zune's name — for example, Brian's Zune — and choose Set Up Sync from the contextual menu that appears.**

   This brings up the Device Setup dialog box. You see the playlists that you've already set up to sync in the Playlists to Sync section.

2. **If the All Pictures playlist is listed in the Playlists to Sync area, click on it to select it.**

   The Remove button becomes active when you do this.

3. **Click the Remove button to remove this list from your synchronized playlists.**

Now if you sync, you won't have any pictures on your Zune at all! Fix that by making a custom auto playlist that syncs only the pictures you've taken in the last couple months:

1. **Again, in the Navigation pane on the left side of the Zune software window, right-click your Zune's name and choose Set Up Sync from the contextual menu that appears.**

   The Device Setup dialog box makes another appearance.

2. **Click the New Auto Playlist button to bring up the New Auto Playlist dialog box.**

   In the New Auto Playlist dialog box, Music in My Library is there by default.

3. **Remove the Music in My Library entry by selecting it and clicking Remove.**

   You are setting up this auto playlist to just sync photos, so you don't need to include any music content from your library. You'll rely on other playlists — either default or customized — to sync your music.

4. **Click the green plus sign and choose Pictures in My Library from the contextual menu that appears.**

   A Pictures in My Library entry is added to the list.

5. **Click the plus sign next to the Click Here to Add Criteria link and choose Date Added to My Library from the contextual menu that appears.**

6. **Click the Last 30 Days criterion and change that to 6 months by choosing that option from the drop-down menu that appears.**

7. **Type a name for your playlist in the Auto Playlist Name box.**

   The New Auto Playlist dialog box should look like the one in Figure 6-9.

8. **Click OK to add this to the Device Setup dialog box. Then click Finish.**

Now when you synchronize your Zune device, only those photos taken in the last six months will be added to your device. Of course, you can set up an auto playlist based on many other criteria, including Keywords, Month Taken and Year Taken, but it will work in much the same way as this.

The whole idea of syncing is that your PC and Zune device talk to each other and figure out what may already have been transferred over during a previous sync session. So if you're worried about lots of duplicate images showing up on your Zune after syncing, don't — worry, that is.

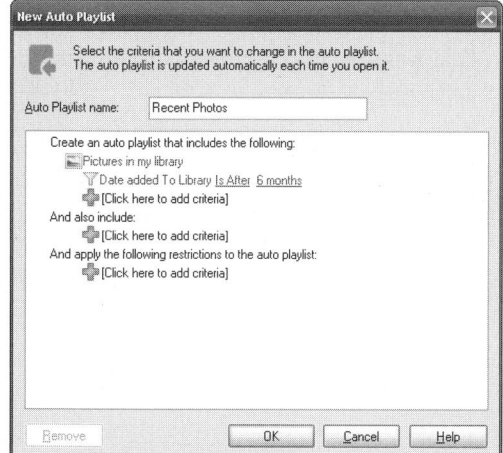

Figure 6-9:
Creating an
auto playlist
for pictures.

Making playlists

One final way to organize your photos in Zune is to create a custom playlist. Just keep in mind that this doesn't have anything to do with the sync playlists covered in the previous section. Rather than using a playlist to organize the way files get moved around, we're going to use a playlist to create logical groupings so that it's easier to organize and view just the pictures that you want.

To create a new playlist, follow these steps:

1. **In the Zune desktop application, click the Camera icon to switch to View Pictures mode.**

2. **Click Create Playlist in the Navigation pane on the left side of the Zune software window.**

   This makes the title editable, and you can type a title — Vacation, for example.

3. **Name your playlist and press Enter to set the title.**

4. **Find and select the photos that you want to add to the playlist.**

   You can select photos one at a time or as a group by holding down the Ctrl key as you select pictures.

5. **Right-click the selected picture(s) and choose Add To⇨*Your Playlist* from the contextual menu, as shown in Figure 6-10.**

   Of course, the menu doesn't actually say *Your Playlist;* it shows the name you assigned to the new playlist back in Step 3.

   The pictures you chose will now be available from the playlist you created. The pictures aren't moved to new folders, they're just grouped together.

Figure 6-10:
Adding
selected
pictures to a
custom
playlist.

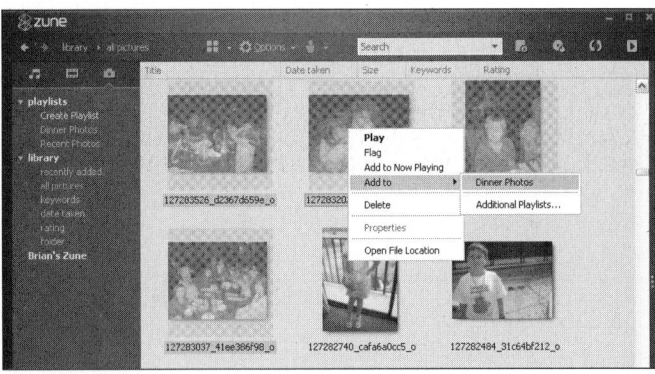

You can have multiple playlists, and synchronize them all to your Zune. For example, you could have an auto playlist for recent pictures, a separate playlist of family photos, another playlist of scenic pictures, and perhaps another playlist for Zune background images. Just follow the above procedure to set up the playlists, and add them to your Playlist list.

Transferring Photos between Zunes

One of the best features of the Zune is the ability to share the stuff you have with others via the WiFi built right into the devices. Sharing pictures between Zunes is easy, be it a single picture or a whole folder. Just follow these steps:

1. **On your Zune device, click the picture that you want to share.**

2. **With the picture in full-screen view, click OK to bring up the picture menu.**

   If you're not already in full-screen view, select an image and click the OK button to get there.

3. **From the menu, choose Send and then click.**

   Your Zune searches for nearby Zune devices.

4. **Choose the device you want to send the picture to and click Send.**

   Your picture is sent wirelessly to your friend's Zune device. Your friend can now view that picture, delete it, or even make it the background for her Zune device.

Unfortunately, your friend can enjoy the picture you send only on the Zune device itself. She can't transfer the picture to her own desktop.

Chapter 7

Buying Music in Zune Marketplace

*W*hat's Zune Marketplace? Here's the short answer to that question: Zune Marketplace is your one-stop shop for music that you can purchase and play on your Zune player. In Marketplace, you can purchase music by the song or by the album. You can do your purchasing on a pay-as-you-go basis, or you can *subscribe* to music through Zune Marketplace, meaning that, after you pay a single monthly fee, you're free to download all the music you want from Marketplace's millions of tunes.

That's the short answer. The longer answer takes up the rest of this chapter. The following list gives you some pointers to keep in mind when you're exploring the Zune Marketplace possibilities:

✔ Zune Marketplace takes care of tracking what you've purchased and what you've downloaded, all associated with your Zune account.

✔ Any music you purchase from Zune Marketplace works only on the Zune player and the PCs you've activated. (We talk about how to activate PCs in the section, "Adding and removing subscribed machines," later in this chapter.)

✔ You can access Zune Marketplace only through the Zune desktop software.

✔ Zune Marketplace looks pretty cool, as you can see for yourself in Figure 7-1. Just click the Marketplace link in the Navigation area of your Zune desktop application to get there.

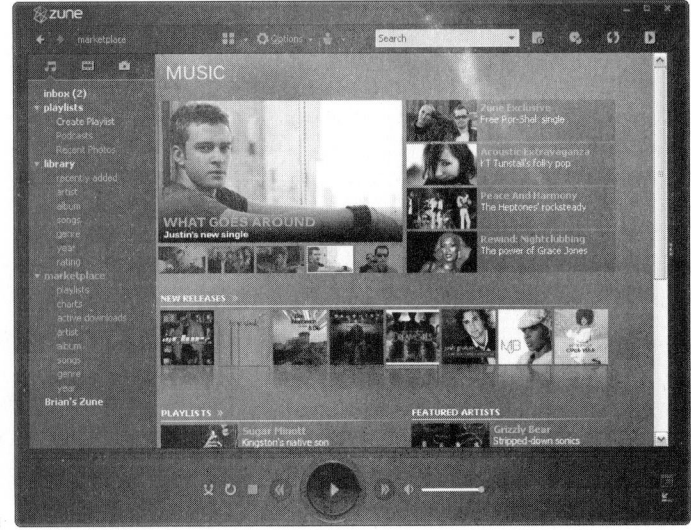

Figure 7-1:
You can find
all sorts
of music
in Zune
Market-
place.

Exploring Music in Zune Marketplace

Before you start buying music, you need to find the music that you want to buy. In the following sections, we look at some of the different ways you can go about finding the music that you want to preview, purchase, and download from Zune Marketplace.

When you dive into the music in Zune Marketplace, you can find music that you haven't heard in years, explore new music and genres, and browse playlists compiled by music experts that can give you all kinds of new ideas and insights into music.

You can find music in Zune Marketplace in a number of ways:

✔ Search by song title, album title, or artist.

✔ View the music charts to find the most popular music.

✔ Browse by artist, genre, or release year.

Choose the search method that works best for how you want to find your music. You can browse if you feel like exploring, but you can also search and sort if you know exactly what you're looking for.

Searching for music

If you already know the title of the song, album, or artist you're interested in, you can most easily track said song, album, or artist by using the Zune search box in the top-right of your Zune desktop software. If you want to find out whether the Zune service has a particular song, album, or artist available, follow these steps:

1. **Click inside the search box at the top-right of the Zune desktop application.**

2. **Type the name of the song, album, or artist that you're looking for.**

   For example, we typed **U2**.

3. **Choose what you want to view from the results listed in the main panel of the desktop application.**

   You can see the results of our U2 search in Figure 7-2.

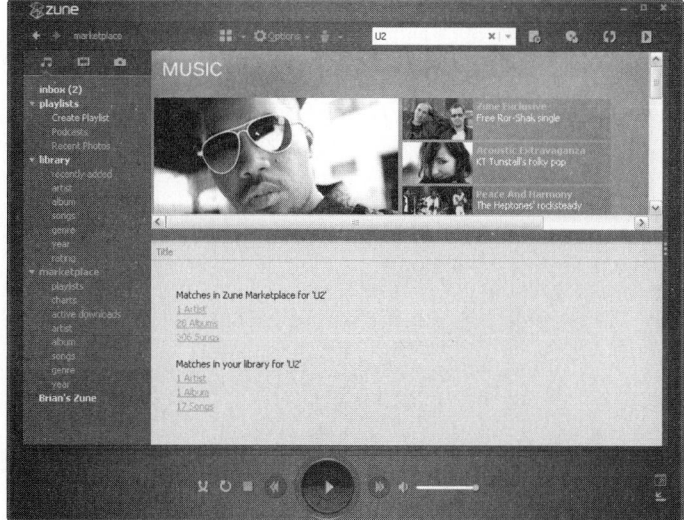

Figure 7-2:
Use the search box at the top of the Zune software to search for artists and songs.

The search box in the Zune software is dynamic, so as you type in your search, you see the results update dynamically in the main panel.

The search box has a feature that lets you narrow down the results of your search. By clicking the down arrow to the right of the search box, a drop-down menu appears, displaying the number of items in the categories of Artists, Albums, and Songs. In addition, if you hover over the Library item, as shown in Figure 7-3, you can see the number of items containing the search word currently in your library.

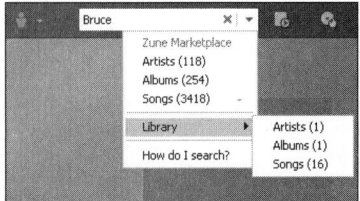

Figure 7-3: Narrow your results in the search box's drop-down menu.

Checking out Marketplace playlists

Marketplace playlists are music selections grouped together by any number of criteria. The Zune team creates some of these playlists, and guest artists and celebrities who want to share their musical ideas with others also create their own playlists. You can see the Marketplace Zune playlist section in Figure 7-4.

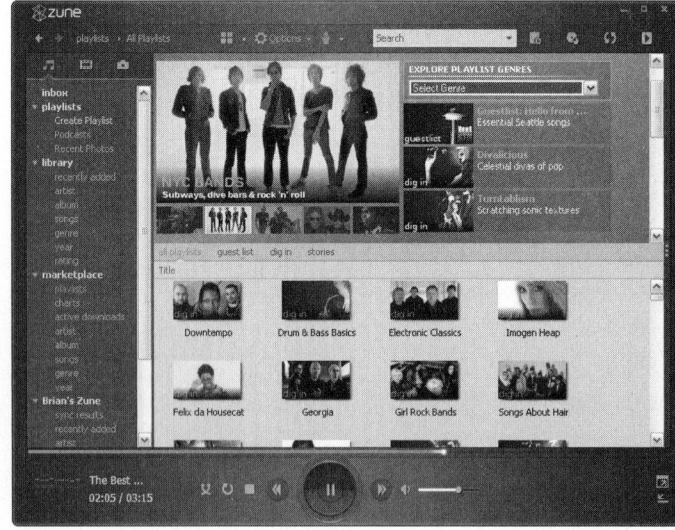

Figure 7-4: Playlists can be based on almost any common musical trait.

Playlists change regularly on Zune Marketplace. They can be based on common musical traits ranging from style ('60s garage bands, for example), to nationalities (French pop), to a common theme (pirate music), to whatever some famous person might have on high Zune rotation that day.

To check out a playlist, follow these steps:

1. **Click the Playlists link in the Marketplace section of your Zune software's left navigation bar.**

   A selection of playlists appears in the details pane.

2. **Browse the list of playlists and double-click one that seems interesting to you.**

   The playlist duly appears onscreen.

   You can review the tunes in the playlist and decide whether you want to purchase some tracks or, if you're a Zune Pass subscriber, just download or play the music in the playlist right then and there. (You can read more about actually purchasing music, as well as getting a Zune Pass, in the section, "Making Music Purchases," later in this chapter.)

   Figure 7-5 shows a typical playlist.

Figure 7-5:
A playlist in Zune Marketplace is a collection of songs related by a particular theme — in this case, drum & bass style music.

Clicking the Guest List option from the main Playlists page shows you the current celebrity and guest playlists in Zune Marketplace.

You can dig deeper into Playlists from the main Playlists page. Choose a genre from the Explore Playlist Genres drop-down menu, and you get to see playlists of that specific music type. For example, Figure 7-6 shows the current playlists from the Country genre in Zune Marketplace.

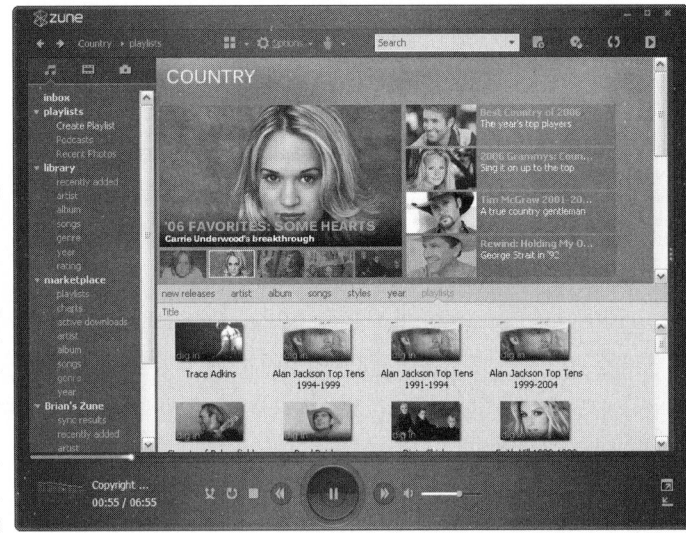

Figure 7-6:
You can browse the Country playlists (or any other genre) in Zune Marketplace.

Going to the charts

For music fans, there's really nothing like digging into the charts to find fun and popular music. Zune Marketplace has a great Charts page that not only lets you see the music that's currently the most popular on the Billboard charts, but also the music that's the most popular in Zune Marketplace.

You can see a shot of Zune Marketplace Charts page in Figure 7-7.

To check out a Billboard chart from the past, you just need to specify the year you want to view and the specific chart you want to see. To see a Billboard chart of days gone by, follow these steps:

1. **In the Billboard Explore Charts section of the main Charts page, choose the year you want to explore from the drop-down menu.**

2. **From the Select a Billboard Chart drop-down menu, choose the chart you want to see.**

   A variety of charts are available, including

   • All Billboard Charts

- R&B/Hip-Hop Album Titles
- The Billboard 200 Titles
- Top Christian Titles
- Top Classical Titles
- Top Country Album Titles
- Top Gospel Album Titles
- Top Latin Pop Album Titles
- Adult Contemporary Titles
- Hot 100 Songs
- Hot Country Audience Titles
- Hot Dance Club Play Titles
- Hot Latin Song Titles
- Hot R&B/Hip-Hop Song Titles
- Hot Rap Track Titles
- Modern Rock Track Titles

Different years have different charts. So, for example, you won't find any rap charts in 1950!

3. Click the Get Chart button.

The requested chart appears.

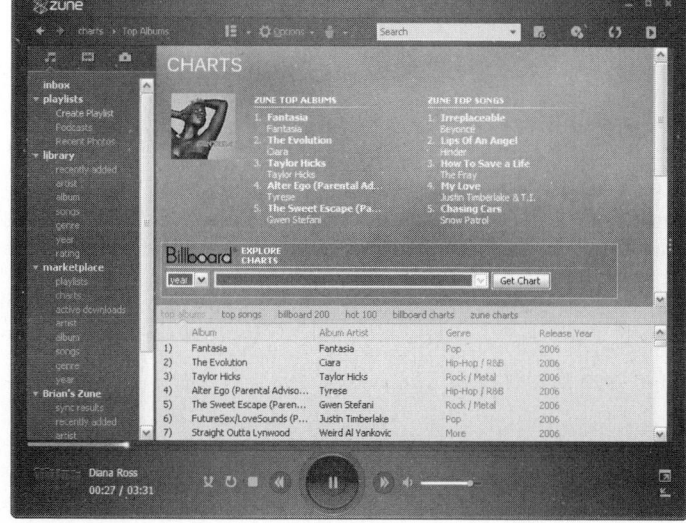

Figure 7-7:
The main Zune Marketplace Charts page shows the top Zune and Billboard songs.

Visiting the artists

A lot of times, you want to find music from a favorite artist — and it wouldn't hurt if you could maybe find out a little bit more about an artist you caught wind of and the music that he or she creates. Marketplace makes browsing for artists easy; just follow these steps:

1. **Click the Artist link in Zune Marketplace navigation pane on the left side of the Zune software.**

   A list of artists appears in the Details pane, sorted by popularity. Beside each artist is a "stack" of his or her albums.

2. **Scroll down to browse the most popular artists available from Zune Marketplace, as shown in Figure 7-8.**

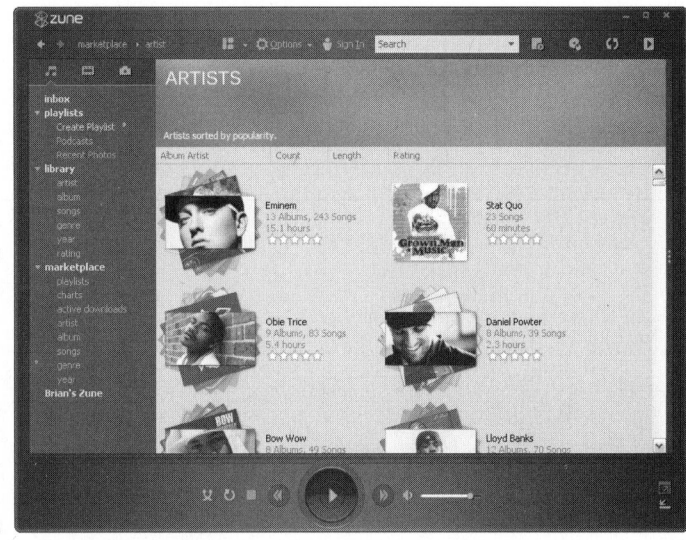

Figure 7-8:
You can browse the most popular artists on Zune Marketplace.

3. **Double-click an artist's name (or the image of his or her stack of albums) to open that artist's page.**

   You can see Jay-Z's page in Figure 7-9.

If you can't find the artist you want by browsing, use the search box at the top of the Zune software window.

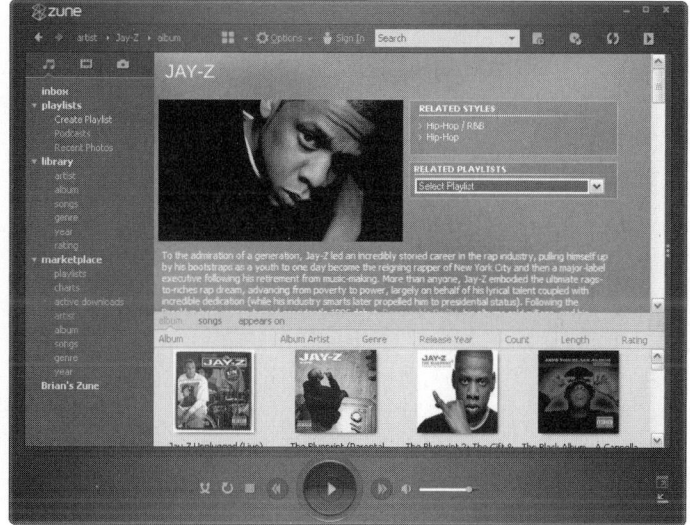

Figure 7-9:
The artist
page for
Jay-Z lists
his albums
and includes
a personal
biography.

Don't forget to check out the Related Playlists drop-down menu associated
with the artists you check out. These playlists are collections of songs from
your selected artist as well as other artists representing a similar music style,
genre, or period. The related playlists can help you discover additional music
similar to the artist you're looking at.

Browsing by album

Browsing by album lets you view a list of the most popular albums on Zune
Marketplace. When you double-click an album, you see information about the
album, along with a list of album tracks. From this page, you can preview
the tracks on the album, purchase the album in its entirety, or pick up just
one track (or a few selected tracks). If you're a Zune Pass subscriber
(which we talk about in the section, "Subscribing to the Zune service with
Zune Pass," later in this chapter), you can listen to entire album tracks
(no preview snippets here) or download the album to your PC for syncing
to your Zune.

Figure 7-10 shows the Marketplace Album view in the Zune desktop
application.

Figure 7-10:
Check out an
interesting
album page
in Zune
Market-
place.

Searching songs

Clicking the Songs link under Marketplace in the Navigation pane gives you a
list of the top songs available in Zune Marketplace. For each top song, the
complete album track list is provided, as shown in Figure 7-11.

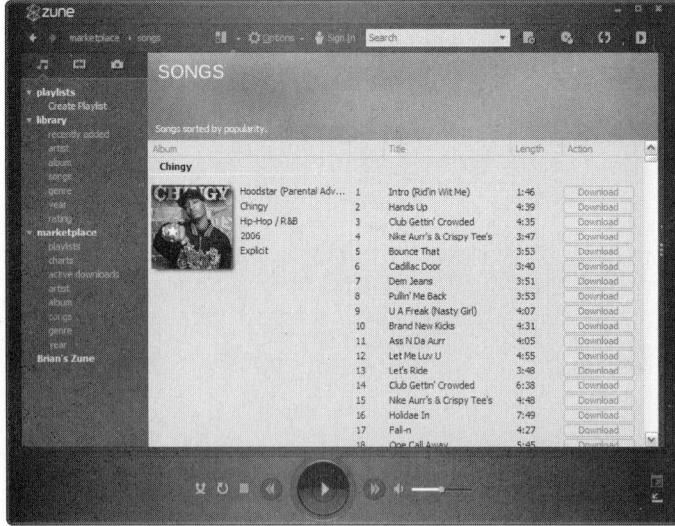

Figure 7-11:
The Songs
list in
Marketplace
displays
tunes in
open
albums.

For a better look at the most popular songs available from Zune Marketplace, view the songs by Chart (which you can figure out how to do in the section, "Going to the charts," earlier in this chapter). These charts give you a much clearer list.

Browsing by genre

Marketplace's Genre category lets you look at music grouped by type. Double-clicking a type opens a genre page that includes music of that particular genre, along with suggestions and playlists you can listen to. You can choose from the following genres:

- ✔ Country
- ✔ Electronic/Dance
- ✔ Hip-Hop/R&B
- ✔ Latin
- ✔ More
- ✔ Pop
- ✔ Reggae/Dancehall
- ✔ Rock/Metal
- ✔ World

Be sure to check out the rather cryptically named More option. With this option, you can find music that doesn't necessarily fit into the other genres, such as comedy albums, movie soundtracks, classical music, and even game soundtracks. This list includes a lot of weird and wonderful stuff. Don't miss it!

Browsing by year

You can browse Zune Marketplace music by sorting everything by release year, as shown in Figure 7-12. If you know which years you want to look through, this sorting option can make finding music from that time period a snap.

After you double-click a year, the music for that year appears, sorted by the most popular albums.

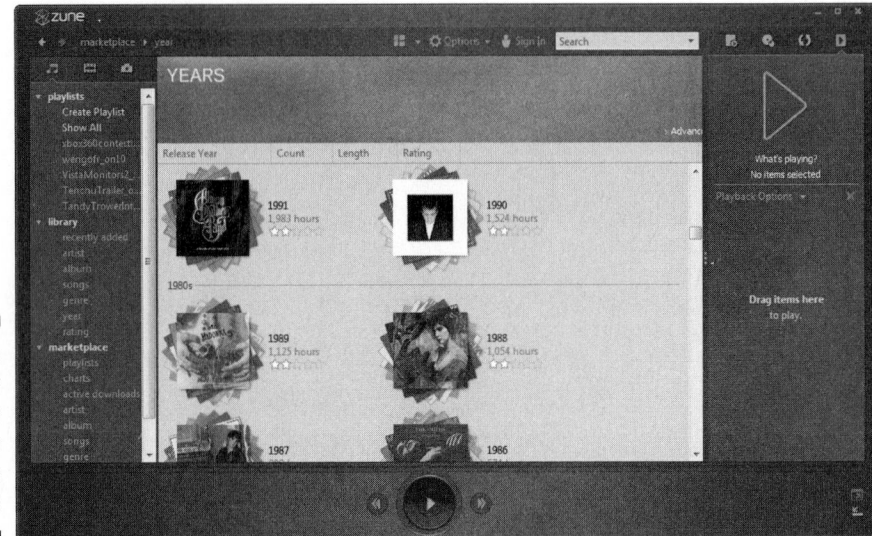

Figure 7-12:
Sort music
in Zune
marketplace
by release
year.

Making Music Purchases

Time to get to the whole filthy lucre part of Zune Marketplace. At some point, you'll have to hand over some of your hard-earned cash if you want to get some tunes into your Zune. To purchase music or to subscribe to *Zune Pass* — Zune Marketplace's subscription service — you need to create a Zune Tag and associate it with a Windows Live ID account. (Check out Chapter 2 for more on Zune Tags and IDs.) Your Windows Live ID account holds your *Microsoft Points* — the currency Microsoft uses for Zune Marketplace transactions — and the credit card associated with your Live ID account gets the Zune Pass bill.

You only need to set up your Zune Tag, and Windows Live ID account, once. You had an opportunity to do so when you installed the Zune software, so you may already be set. If not, you can create your Zune Tag and Windows Live ID account by following these steps:

1. **Fire up your Zune desktop application and then click the Sign In button in the main menu.**

   The Signing In to Zune dialog box appears.

2. **In the Signing In to Zune dialog box, click the Create New Account link.**

   The Zune Account Creation Wizard makes an appearance.

3. **Let the Zune Account Creation Wizard walk you through the creation of a new account.**

Part of the Windows Live ID account creation process involves providing Microsoft with an e-mail address and password. A word to the wise: Be sure to write down the e-mail address and password you give and store it somewhere safe, just in case your memory cells fail and you end up forgetting your password. (If you forget where you stored the password, though, you're up the proverbial creek without a paddle.)

Subscribing to the Zune service with Zune Pass

One of the more enticing features of Zune Marketplace is *Zune Pass,* the Zune subscription service. Zune Pass lets you download unlimited music from Zune Marketplace to your Zune or your PC (where you can listen to that music through the Zune player software). It's an all-you-can-eat service that can be a simple, powerful way to get your hands on a lot of music without having to pay for individual tracks.

How does Zune Pass work? Simple. Pay a monthly subscription fee, and you can download all the music you want from Zune Marketplace. There's no limit to the number of songs or albums you can download from Zune Marketplace with your Zune Pass. (***Note:*** Some songs and albums are not eligible for downloading with Zune Pass — evidently because of music label restrictions — but the vast majority of music on the service is available.) When you're a Zune Pass subscriber, the Zune desktop software checks to see if you're paid up for the month and then it allows you to download and play music from Marketplace. If your subscription expires, you can't play the music you've downloaded anymore.

You can listen to music you've downloaded as part of your Zune Pass service only for as long as you stay subscribed to the service. Let your subscription lapse, and those downloaded music files shut down as tight as clams. And, you can't burn any of the subscription tunes to a CD.

Is a Zune Pass subscription right for you?

Whether you want to spend money on a Zune Pass subscription is a matter of personal preference, but it's also a matter of convenience. Consider the following features when you're thinking about a Zune Pass subscription:

✔ If you accidentally delete all the music on your PC, you can re-download your favorite songs.

✔ You can explore music in ways you may have only dreamed about. With a Zune Pass, you can listen to a lot of music that you might never lay the cash down for. If you don't like a song you decided to try out, just delete it.

So, what are the negatives of a Zune Pass subscription? Here they are, all in one place:

✔ You rent the music you download, instead of purchasing it. You can't keep the music after you stop paying for the subscription.

✔ You can't burn CDs of the music you download.

✔ The monthly fee can seem expensive, especially if you don't listen to any new music for a month or two.

So what do we recommend? The cost of a subscription is roughly equivalent to the cost of two albums. If you don't check out new music on a regular basis, just buy the albums you're listening to and forget about a subscription. If you're constantly updating your music collection, you might find getting your music through a subscription more convenient (and cheaper).

Choosing a Zune Pass subscription

You can subscribe to Zune Pass easily — just follow these steps:

1. **In the Zune desktop software, click the Sign In icon in the main menu.**

   The Sign In screen appears.

2. **In the Sign In screen, enter both your Windows Live ID username and password and then click OK.**

   You're returned to the Zune software window, and the Sign-In icon is now colored orange — indicating that you're now signed in to Marketplace.

3. **Click the small pull-down arrow beside the orange Sign-In icon, and select Account Management from the menu that appears.**

   The Account Summary page appears.

   4. **On the Account Summary page, click the Zune Pass button.**

   The Get a Zune Pass Subscription page makes an appearance.

   5. **On the Get a Zune Pass Subscription page (see Figure 7-13), choose the subscription type that you want and click the Next button.**

   You may need to scroll to the bottom of the page to see the button.

   You have the following three choices for a Zune Pass subscription:

   > **Pay a monthly fee.** With this option, you're authorizing the folks at Zune to charge your credit card each month for said monthly fee until you tell them otherwise.

   > **Pay for three months at a time.** Just like the one month option, this signs you up for an automatically renewing charge every three months.

   > **Use a prepaid subscription card.** If you have a prepaid Microsoft Points card or a promotional code for a prepaid Zune subscription, you can enter the 25-digit code from that card. Microsoft Points cards are available at consumer electronics retailers, and can be used for Xbox Live purchases or for Zune Marketplace.

   After you've purchased or extended your Zune Pass subscription, you'll see a confirmation page confirming your changes. Congratulations — you're now a Zune Pass user and can go to town downloading music that strikes your fancy in Zune Marketplace!

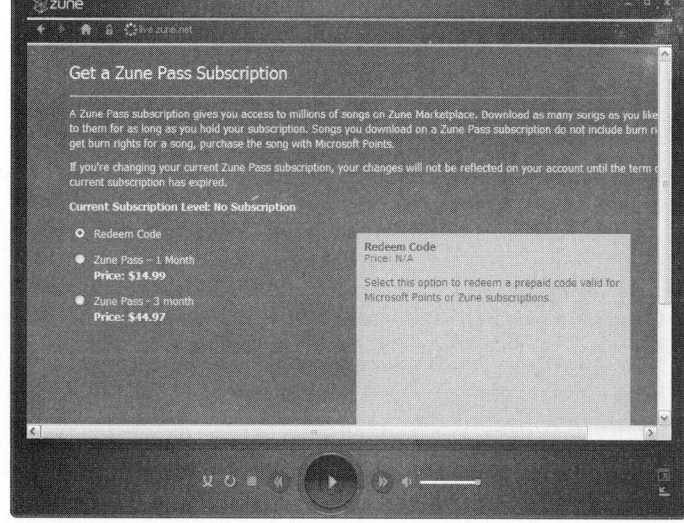

Figure 7-13: Choose the Zune Pass subscription that you want in the Zune Pass Subscription page.

Using the Zune Pass service

After you subscribe to Zune Pass, new options become available in the Zune desktop application. You can stream and download a wide range of Zune content, so you can explore all sorts of new music. With Zune Pass, you can listen to full tracks, streamed to your PC from Zune Marketplace — as opposed to the 30-second samples that you can hear if you don't have a Zune Pass subscription.

Streaming Zune content lets you listen to music from Zune Marketplace without actually downloading that music to your machine. Streaming lets you listen to an entire song or even an album, before you decide whether you want to add it to your library and then sync it to your Zune.

To stream an album, follow these steps:

1. **From within Marketplace, find an album or track that you want to listen to.**

   You can do this by searching for an artist or album, or by browsing the Marketplace playlists and charts. (Click Playlists or Charts under Marketplace in the Navigation pane.)

2. **Double-click the album or artist to see the list of tracks for that album.**

3a. **To listen to a single song, right-click the song title and then choose Play from the menu that appears.**

3b. **To listen to the entire album, just click the Play Album button in the album's header information at the top of the screen or right-click any track and choose Play All from the menu that appears.**

You can see these streaming options displayed in Figure 7-14.

If you've already reviewed the music you want to download or if you're not afraid to jump right in without a preview, you can start downloading music from your Zune Pass subscription right away.

To download music by using your Zune Pass subscription, follow these steps:

1. **From within Marketplace, find the song or album you want to download.**

2a. **To download a single song, click the Download button next to the song title.**

2b. **To download an entire album, click the Download Album button next to the album art.**

After you download music on your Zune Pass, that music is added to your Zune the next time you synchronize your device.

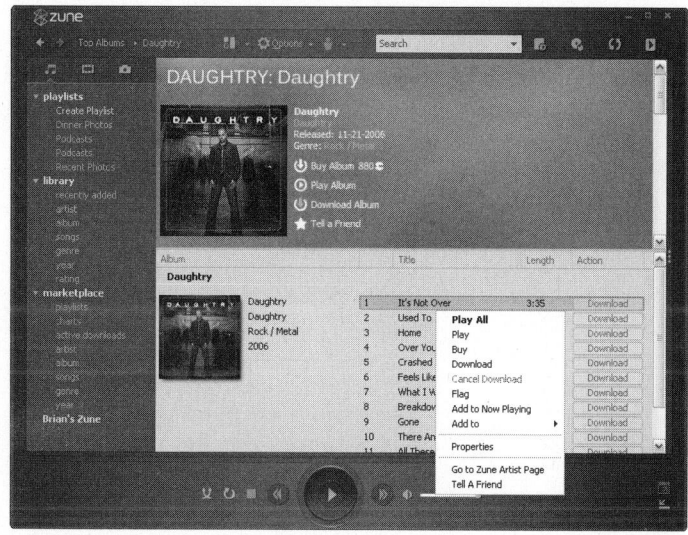

Figure 7-14:
Stream a
song or an
entire album
by using
Zune Pass.

Canceling your Zune Pass service

If you're paying for your Zune Pass by the month, you may want to cancel the service someday — or at least put it on hold for a while. To cancel your Zune Pass service, follow these steps:

1. **If you're already signed in, you can jump to Step 3; otherwise, click the Sign In button in the Zune desktop application.**

   The Sign In screen appears.

2. **In the Sign In screen, enter both your Windows Live ID username and password and then click OK.**

   The home page of Zune Marketplace appears.

3. **Click the Account Options button and choose Account Management from the menu that appears.**

   The Account Summary page appears, with a listing of options and buttons to take you into different areas of managing your account.

   Note: If you're already signed in, you can select Account Management right from the Sign In menu.

4. **On the Account Summary page, click the Zune Pass button.**

   The Update Your Zune Subscription page appears.

5. **On the Update Your Zune Subscription page, click Cancel Subscription and then click Next.**

   Your subscription is canceled.

Be careful! When you click Next, your subscription is cancelled immediately. If you change your mind, though, you can easily restart your subscription by going through the setup steps (which we outline in the section, "Choosing a Zune Pass subscription," earlier in this chapter) again.

Microsoft Points

Subscriptions aren't the only way to go in Marketplace. You can also use cold hard cash — or, at least, Microsoft's equivalent of cash. Songs and albums that you purchase through Zune Marketplace are priced using Microsoft Points. You use Microsoft Points to purchase content in both Zune Marketplace and on Xbox Live Marketplace.

Zune Pass subscriptions don't use Microsoft Points; for a Zune Pass subscription, you use your local currency.

Microsoft Points work on a varying exchange rate, depending on what country you're purchasing them from. In some countries, you pay taxes on Microsoft Points; in others, you don't. But the price per song in Microsoft Points stays constant, no matter what country you're in.

Most of the individual songs in Zune Marketplace are currently priced at 79 points. Some newer and premium content costs more.

Albums are generally priced at 880 points, but double albums and special editions cost extra. If you want to see the price of an album in Microsoft Points, check out the details for the album in Zune Marketplace, as shown in Figure 7-15.

Okay, we understand that a huge global conglomerate (such as Microsoft) can probably run an online store more easily by using a global currency (such as Points), but you may find calculating that conversion for your own budgeting purposes a little challenging. To help you make relatively pain-free conversions, use the online converter for Microsoft Points at www.mspconverter.com (as shown in Figure 7-16).

Album price   Song price

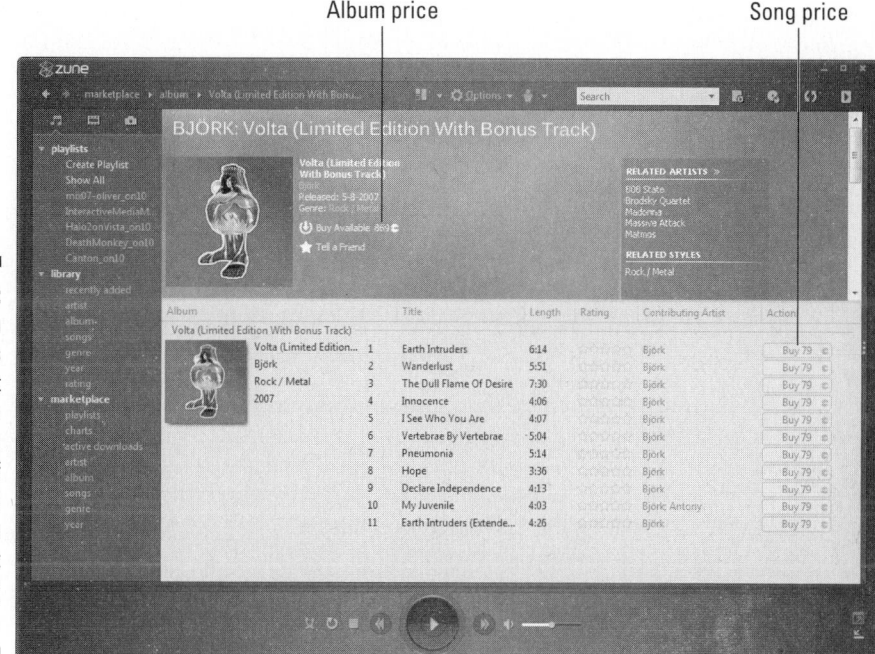

Figure 7-15:
The album
price is
listed next
to the album
cover and
the price of
individual
songs is
shown next
to the song
listing.

Figure 7-16:
Figure out
what your
Points
translate
to in real
money at the
Microsoft
Points
Converter.

The www.mspconverter.com site is privately run — Microsoft doesn't control it. The price shown in the official Zune Add Microsoft Points window (as shown later in Figure 7-17) is the definitive source for the price of your Microsoft points.

To purchase Microsoft Points for your account, follow these steps:

1. **If you haven't already done so, sign in to Zune Marketplace by clicking the Sign In button, entering your user ID and password, and clicking OK.**

2. **After signing in, click the Sign In button again and then choose Account Management from the menu that appears.**

   The Account Summary window opens.

3. **In the Account Summary window, click the Purchase Points button.**

   You're prompted for your Windows Live ID and password.

4. **Enter your ID and password and click Sign In.**

   The Add Microsoft Points window appears onscreen, as shown in Figure 7-17.

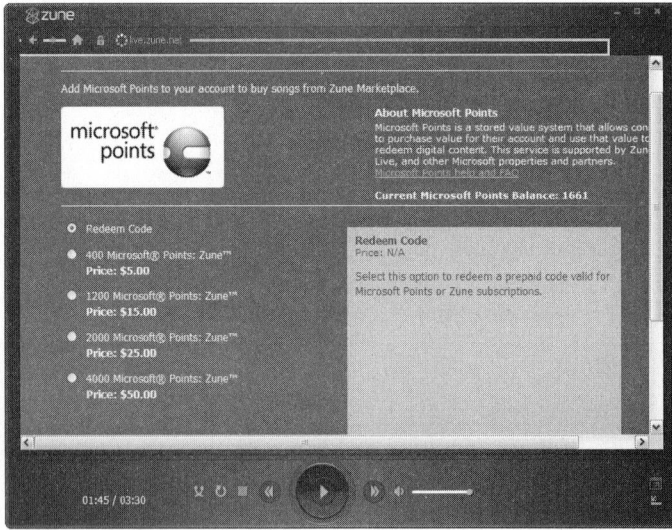

Figure 7-17: Choose how many Points you want to add to your account in the Add Microsoft Points window.

5. **Choose the number of points that you want to purchase and then click Next.**

   The Complete Your Purchase window appears.

6. **Choose a credit card associated with your Windows Live ID account in the Complete Your Purchase window.**

   If you want to add a new credit card, click Add New Credit Card. If you want to update the billing information for one of your existing cards, select that card and click Edit Payment Options.

7. **Click Purchase to pay for your points.**

   Your Microsoft Points are added to your account, and you can use them to make music purchases in Zune Marketplace. You can also use these same points with an Xbox 360 to purchase videos and other types of downloadable content.

Previewing music

One of the coolest things about checking out music on Zune Marketplace is that you can preview that music before you buy it. And, if you have a Zune Pass subscription, you can listen to a whole song or album before you decide to download it.

You can preview music easily in Zune Marketplace. To preview a song, just follow these steps:

1. **Find the song you want to preview.**

2. **Double-click the song to play a 30-second preview.**

   You can now decide whether you want to buy the song based on the snippet you just heard.

A Zune Pass gives you much more that just a 30-second preview. If you have a Zune Pass and double-click a song, you get to hear the whole thing!

After you preview a song, you can purchase that song very quickly and easily in Zune Marketplace. We discuss that process in the following section.

Buying a song

Okay, it's time to commit and actually buy something. You can make a Zune Marketplace purchase (dangerously) easily. To purchase a song from Zune Marketplace, just follow these steps:

1. **Find the song you want to buy.**

2. **Click the Buy button located to the right of the song title.**

   Note that this button normally says Download if you are a Zune Pass subscriber because you do not have to pay to download an individual song.

   The label on the Buy button changes from Buy to Confirm, as shown in Figure 7-18. If you're a Zune Pass subscriber, there is no confirmation step, the button changes directly to Downloading.

   The Buy button conveniently lists the price of the song in Microsoft Points, so you know what you're getting into.

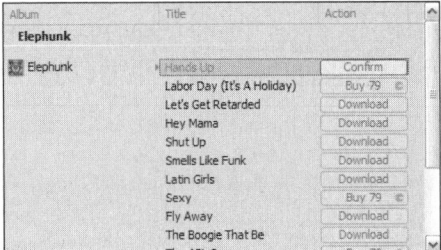

Figure 7-18: Confirm your purchase by clicking the Confirm button.

3. **Click the Confirm button to complete the purchase.**

   Your song does what you've told it to and downloads. You can monitor the download process with the help of a progress bar that appears in the Action column to the right of the song title, like the one shown in Figure 7-19. After the song finishes downloading, play and enjoy.

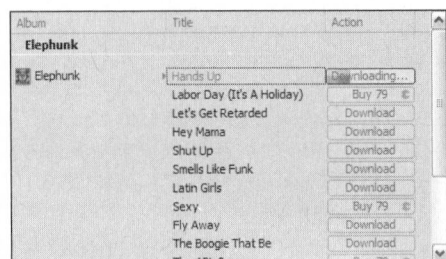

Figure 7-19: The progress bar lets you know how your download is going.

If you're a Zune Pass subscriber, you can just download the song directly — no need to purchase it. But if you do want to buy it — for example, because you want to burn it to a CD — you can right-click a song that you want to purchase and then choose Buy from the pop-up menu that appears.

Buying an album

You can buy a whole album very much like you purchase a song, which we discuss in the preceding section. To buy an album, follow these steps:

1. **After searching for an album, double-click the album's icon in the Search Results pane.**

   A Details window for the album appears, as shown in Figure 7-20.

Figure 7-20:
Click Buy
Album to
purchase
an album
in Zune
Market-
place.

2. **Click the Buy Album button to make your purchase.**

   A pop-up window prompts you to confirm your purchase. When you click Confirm, the points are deducted from your account, and the album is downloaded automatically to your PC.

Caring for Your Music Collection

Digital music collections take a lot of time to build, and they also tend to take up a lot of space. Unless you have a backup option, like an external hard drive or something similar, they're generally hard to back up after they get past a certain size. If you rip your own music (as we describe in Chapter 8), you really have no choices here. Either you back up the music you've ripped or risk having to put a lot of time into re-ripping that music if the unthinkable happens and your hard drive does nasty things to you (like failing and losing all your files).

If you purchase your music through Zune Marketplace, you have another way to recover files if you've somehow lost them on your PC. You can restore the music that you've purchased, and if you're a Zune Pass subscriber, you can restore the music that you've downloaded as part of your Zune Pass subscription.

Restoring your music

You may need to restore music if you buy a new PC and want to transfer your music to that PC for listening and syncing to your Zune device. In this situation, purchasing your music through Zune Marketplace really pays off. You can easily restore your music (downloading it all to the new machine) in just a few clicks.

To restore your purchased Zune tracks, follow these steps:

1. **If you haven't already done so, sign in to Zune Marketplace by clicking the Sign In button, entering your user ID and password, and clicking OK.**

2. **After signing in, click the Sign In button again and then choose Account Management from the shortcut menu that appears.**

   The Account Summary window appears.

3. **In the Music and Purchases section of the Account Management window, click Restore Library.**

   You'll see the Restore Library — Step 1 page.

4. **In the Restore Library screen, click Begin Scan.**

   The software scans your music directory, comparing the contents of your music directory with the purchases and downloads that you've made from Zune Marketplace.

   On the next page that appears, you see a list of music you've purchased that isn't presently on your PC.

5. **In the new page that appears, choose the music you want to re-sync with your PC (by checking the boxes next to the desired songs) and press the Sync button.**

   The music you selected is restored to your PC.

If you've purchased or downloaded a lot of music from Zune Marketplace, give the Zune desktop software ample time to download your music. The download can take a while, depending on your connection speed.

Adding and removing subscribed machines

If you're a Zune Pass subscriber, you can access your content from up to three PCs. For music you've purchased by using Microsoft Points, you can have up to five PCs active at any given time.

You can add a PC to your Zune Marketplace account easily. Just install the Zune software on the PC that you want to add and sign in with your Windows Live ID. If you hit your limit of subscribed PCs and want to switch one out, you first need to remove a PC from your list of authorized computers by using your Account Management options.

To remove a PC from your list of active machines, follow these steps:

1. **If you haven't already done so, sign in to Zune Marketplace by clicking the Sign In button, entering your user ID and password, and clicking OK.**

2. **After signing in, click the Sign In button again and then choose Account Management from the menu that appears.**

   The Account Summary window appears.

3. **On the Account Summary page, click Rights Management.**

   The PC Management window appears, with an explanation of the authorized computer model and a list of your currently authorized computers.

4. **In the PC Management window, click the Remove button to the right of the name of the PC you want to remove from the list.**

   You can now add a new machine to your list of PC Names (by signing in and attempting to play your Zune Pass material on it).

You can remove a PC from this list only once every 30 days, so be sure you know which machine you want to deactivate. If you deactivate the wrong PC, you can add it back immediately (by signing in and playing protected music on it), but if you have added a machine by accident then you may have to wait 30 days to remove it. You can call Zune support if you need to get around the 30 day limitation, just go to `www.zune.net/support/contactsupport` to find a contact number.

Chapter 8

Ripping CDs with Zune

. . . .

. . . .

Compact discs have been around for a long time, and most people have built up pretty good CD collections over the years. Although it's becoming more and more common to just purchase music online, CDs have an advantage when it comes to quality — but, boy, can they take up space.

Thanks to modern technology, however, you can now get your CDs out of the way pretty easily — and keep them in nearly pristine condition — by ripping your music to your computer and then putting your CDs in storage.

In this chapter, we show you how to rip music to your computer by using the Zune desktop software and we talk about getting your current music into your Zune.

Ripping CDs

To create digital music files from your CD collection, you need to copy the music from the CD. (Okay, okay, the hip term for copying music files is *ripping* music files.) During the ripping process, the full fidelity music files are copied from the disc and saved in one of the standard compressed media formats — MP3, WMA, AAC, or Ogg. (For more on digital file formats, see Chapter 4.)

Ripping a CD with the default settings

The Zune desktop player wouldn't be a true, top-flight player if it couldn't rip CDs — it kind of goes with the territory. The Zune software — which, by the way, uses the WMA file compression format to store your music — makes ripping pretty easy. Just follow these steps:

1. **Connect your computer to the Internet — if it's not already connected.**

   If you have an Internet connection, the Zune software can then download useful details, such as track names and album art, for the CD that you're ripping.

2. **Insert the CD into the CD tray of your PC.**

   Your Zune auto-detects the CD, and a screen that looks like Figure 8-1 appears.

Figure 8-1:
The Zune desktop software is ready to rip this CD.

3. **To begin ripping the CD, click the Start Rip button in the lower-right of the window.**

   Zune begins to rip the CD, as shown in Figure 8-2.

   In a few minutes, your music is copied to your library, and you can remove the CD from your PC. The next time you sync, the newly ripped songs get copied onto your Zune. Now you can enjoy your music anytime, whether it's on your Zune or your PC.

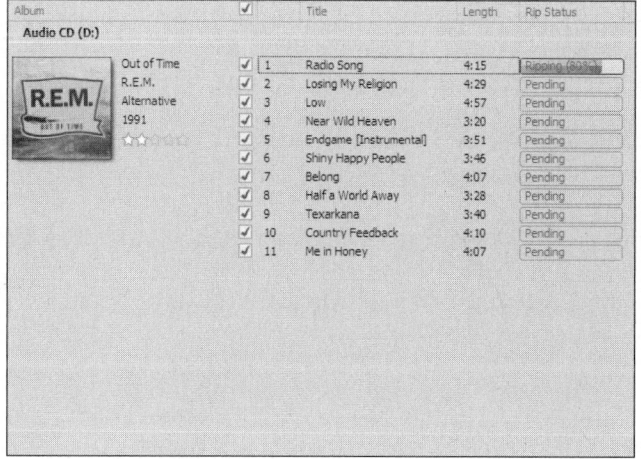

Album	✓		Title	Length	Rip Status
Audio CD (D:)					
Out of Time	✓	1	Radio Song	4:15	Ripping (80%)
R.E.M.	✓	2	Losing My Religion	4:29	Pending
Alternative	✓	3	Low	4:57	Pending
1991	✓	4	Near Wild Heaven	3:20	Pending
	✓	5	Endgame [Instrumental]	3:51	Pending
	✓	6	Shiny Happy People	3:46	Pending
	✓	7	Belong	4:07	Pending
	✓	8	Half a World Away	3:28	Pending
	✓	9	Texarkana	3:40	Pending
	✓	10	Country Feedback	4:10	Pending
	✓	11	Me in Honey	4:07	Pending

Figure 8-2:
You can see the progress of the rip as each song is copied by the Zune software.

Ripping options

If you can rip a CD using default settings, it stands to reason that you can use some customized settings, as well. Foremost among all things tweakable is your choice of digital file formats. (We cover file formats in some detail in Chapter 4, so you may want to flip back to that chapter and bone up a bit on formats before continuing.) You probably should get your rip settings how you like them right from the start. If you don't, think of the hassle if you rip hundreds of files to a certain level of compression — or file format — that you later want to change for some reason; it could take forever to copy that music back to your PC.

Again, the default file format for music ripped by the Zune desktop software is Windows Media Audio (WMA), but you can make other choices and set those choices in a couple of ways, as the following list makes clear:

✓ **Windows Media Audio (WMA):** Okay, we might as well start with the old standby. WMA is the Zune default for a reason — it's actually quite good if you're looking for a good clear music format with decent compression. So, no complaints about the format, as such, but it's not quite as generic and therefore not as universally accepted — as the MP3 format.

The default compression for WMA in Zune is 128 bit compression, which is a trade off between space concerns and the quality of the playback. Some people are very sensitive to audio quality and insist on 192 bit compression, but others frankly can't tell the difference between compression rates and appreciate the lower file sizes. At 128 bits per second, an average CD ripped by the Zune software to WMA comes in at about 56 megabytes, whereas it would be around 84 megabytes at 192 bits per second.

Because the quality at 192 is so much better, it's usually best to use the highest bit rate possible, depending on how much space is on your PC.

✔ **Windows Media Audio Lossless:** The Windows Media Audio Lossless format copies the music from your CD at full fidelity. This might make a good format if you're an audiophile and have a lot of extra disc space, but be aware that a CD ripped to WMA Lossless needs anywhere from 206 to 411 megabytes of storage space.

✔ **MP3:** In the Zune software, the MP3 format is your final option for ripping your CDs. Default compression for the MP3 format is the same as for Windows Media Audio. The bit rate is 128 by default, and the total space that a CD takes up at this bit rate is around 57 megabytes.

Changing rip settings

You use the Rip Music tab in the Zune Options dialog box to change the settings for ripping your music. The following options are tweakable:

✔ The location for storing your ripped music files

✔ How you want to name the ripped files

✔ The default file format used

✔ Whether to rip the CD as soon as it's inserted

✔ Whether to eject the CD after it's been ripped

✔ The compression rate for the ripped music

You can get to the Rip Music tab in the Options dialog box by clicking the Options button and then clicking Rip and More Options from the submenus. The Rip Music tab is shown in Figure 8-3.

The following sections describe how to change the Rip Music tab's options.

Setting a ripped music file location

By default, the Zune desktop player copies your ripped music to your My Music/Zune folder on your PC. To change the location to something different, follow these steps:

1. **Click the Change button on the Rip Music tab.**

   The Browse for Folder dialog box appears, as shown in Figure 8-4.

2. **Using the Browse for Folder dialog box, navigate to the folder you want to use for storing your music.**

If you want to create a new folder, navigate to the folder in which you want to create the new folder and click the Make New Folder button. Type in a name for the new folder.

3. Press OK to save the change.

Your new location is saved, and you're brought back to the Rip Music tab of the Options dialog box.

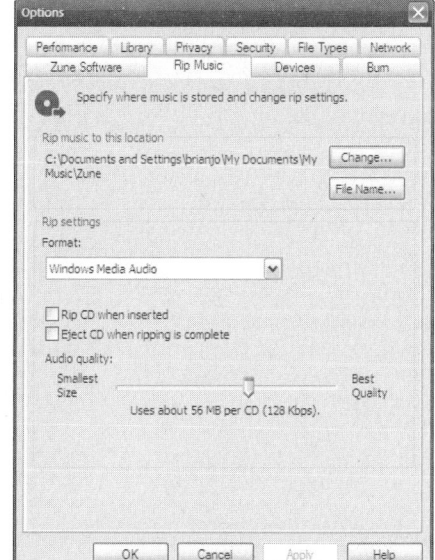

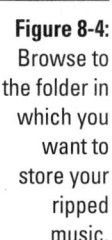

Figure 8-3:
Use the Rip Music tab in the Options dialog box to change your rip settings.

Figure 8-4:
Browse to the folder in which you want to store your ripped music.

Changing the default filenames for ripped music

The default name for any music file in Zune is the track number of the song on the CD followed by the name of the song. You may think that info is enough to name your music files, but you can add a lot more to the filename if you want. To change the default filename used for ripped music, follow these steps:

1. **In the Options dialog box, click the File Name button on the Rip Music tab.**

   The File Name Options dialog box, as shown in Figure 8-5, appears.

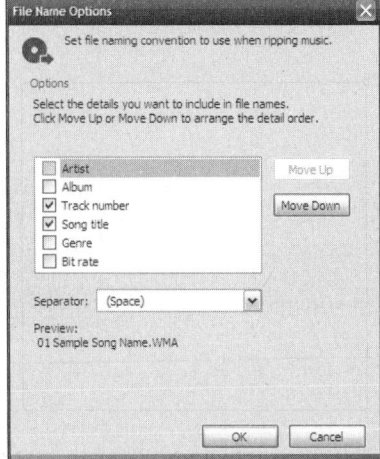

Figure 8-5: You can change how your files are named by using the File Name Options dialog box.

2. **Choose the details that you want to add to the song title.**

   You can add the following details:

   - Artist
   - Album
   - Track number (default)
   - Song title (default)
   - Genre
   - Bit rate

Filename changes affect just the actual filename. These changes don't affect how the song looks in your library. Even if you stick with a simple filename, you can view all this added info in the Zune desktop player.

3. **Choose the separator you want to use between the details in the filenames.**

   You can choose from:

   - (Space)
   - - (Dash)
   - * (Dot)
   - _ (Underscore)

We recommend keeping the track numbers in the titles. If you do, you can much more easily figure out the original order of track listings on a CD when you're working with the files outside your Zune software.

4. **Press OK to save the changes.**

   Your new file naming convention is saved, and you're brought back to the Rip Music tab of the Options dialog box.

Choosing your music format

Use the Format drop-down menu in the Rip Music tab to choose the file format you want to use when ripping music. You can choose from Windows Media Audio (WMA), Windows Media Audio Lossless, and MP3.

We talk about the virtues of each of these formats throughout the chapter — as well as back in Chapter 4.

Setting the audio quality

Each of the Zune file formats we describe in this chapter have varying degrees of compression that you can set by using a slider on the Rip Music tab of the Options dialog box. You can check out Table 8-1 for bit rates (and associated file sizes) for each of Zune's supported ripping formats.

Table 8-1	Music Ripping Compression Options in Zune	
Format	**Bit Rate (in Kbps)**	**CD Size (in MB)**
Windows Media Audio	48–192	22–86
Windows Media Audio Lossless	470–940	206–411
MP3	128–320	57–144

Deciding whether to use the Rip CD When Inserted and Eject CD When Ripping Is Complete options

The final two ripping options in the Rip Music tab we want to mention are the Rip CD When Inserted and Eject CD When Ripping Is Complete check boxes. By setting these options, you can just keep inserting new CDs over and over to rip all the music in your collection. To start your CD-burning marathon, follow these steps:

1. **Set your ripping options, as we describe in the preceding sections.**

2. **Check the Rip CD When Inserted and Eject CD When Ripping Is Complete check boxes to make them active.**

3. **Click OK to save your settings and close the Options dialog box.**

4. **With the Zune desktop software running, insert a music CD.**

   The Zune desktop application rips the music to the specifications you set and saves it in the location you specified.

5. **When the CD is ejected, just insert another music CD to continue the process.**

As you can imagine, you can get through a large music collection relatively quickly by copying the CDs in this way.

You probably don't want to leave the Rip CD When Inserted and Eject CD When Ripping Is Complete options checked all the time. Save the automation for when you have a big stack of CDs in front of you. If you don't, every CD you insert starts ripping whether you want it to or not.

Obtaining CD and song information

When you rip a popular CD to your PC by using the Zune software, the software looks up the CD in an online database and downloads the CD's title and track information, which is then saved with the song information. Most of the time, this process works very well, and your Zune gets all the info you need about the music you're trying to rip.

Sometimes, though, the info about the music that you're ripping hasn't been added to the database (maybe it's from an independent artist) or some ambiguity leads to incorrect information for an album. When your Zune software can't find the correct particulars for your CD, you need to add or change the information yourself. Use the Find Album Information dialog box in Zune to adjust a CD's information by following these steps:

1. **In the Details pane of the Zune desktop application, right-click the icon for the album whose information you want to change and then choose Change Album from the menu that appears.**

   The Find Album Information dialog box appears, as shown in Figure 8-6.

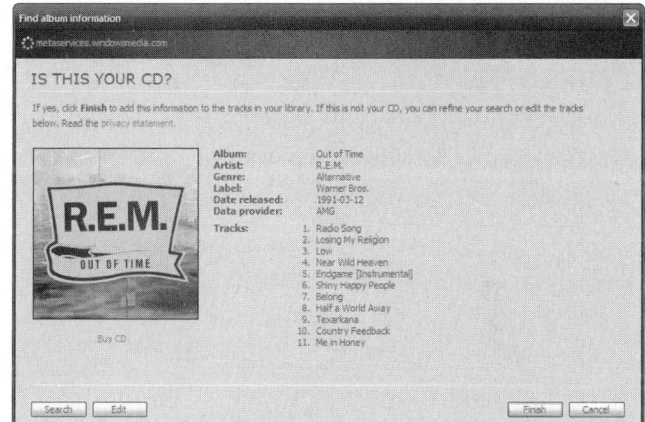

Figure 8-6: The Find Album Information dialog box first verifies the CD you want to edit.

2. **Click the Edit button.**

   The Edit CD Information dialog box appears, as shown in Figure 8-7.

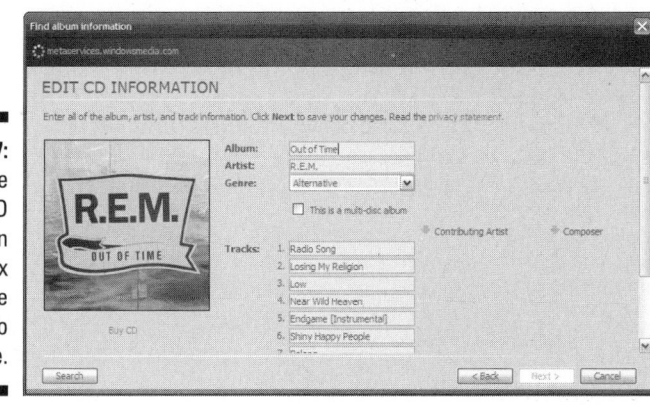

Figure 8-7: Use the Edit CD Information dialog box to change album info in Zune.

3. **Edit the CD information fields as appropriate.**

   You can actually change a lot of information by using the Find Album Information dialog box. The following items are editable:

   - Album
   - Artist
   - Genre
   - Tracks

   By clicking the arrows to the left of the Contributing Artist and Composer items, you can open more fields for those options.

 If your Genre playlists don't show the music that you expect, check to see whether your music has the assigned Genres that you want. If your tunes aren't in the Genre in which you want them, change the Genre assignments as appropriate.

   The Zune software's database is actually quite extensive. We tried to outsmart the software by using some of the most obscure music we had in our collections, but the database (correctly) tracked down the info every time.

Getting Your Current Music into a Zune Format

If you have an existing music collection in a format not supported by Zune, you have a couple options for getting that music into your Zune:

- **Starting from scratch:** You can re-rip the CDs, using the Zune software this time. Re-ripping can give you a chance to clean up your collection a bit — making your ripped files uniform by using a single product to perform the rip is a good start.

- **Transcoding:** You can obtain software that can transcode your music files from one format to another in order to make the music playable on your Zune. For example, you might want to use this kind of software if you've ripped some of your music in Ogg format and stored the original CDs in some inconvenient place, making re-ripping not an option.

If you're interested in transcoding a library of music, one solution for this is the Xilisoft Audio Converter, as shown in Figure 8-8. This utility lets you select a file of one type, say OGG, and convert that file to one that can be played on your Zune.

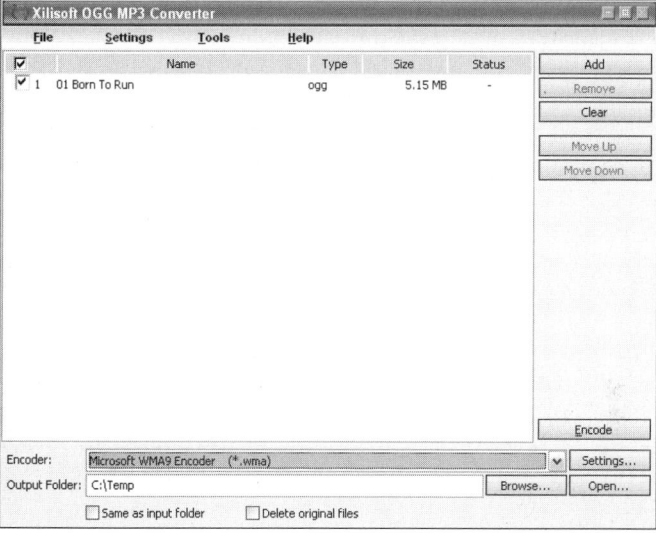

Figure 8-8:
The Xilisoft
Audio
Converter
can trans-
code files
between
WM3, MP3,
OGG, and
other
formats.

To use the Xilisoft converter to change a file from OGG to MP3, follow these steps:

1. **In the Xilisoft OGG MP3 application, click the Add button in the top right of the screen.**

2. **In the Browse dialog box that appears, navigate to the folder containing the music that you want to convert.**

3. **Select the files you want to convert and click Open to add them to the converter.**

4. **Choose the encoder you want to use to transcode the added files from the Encoder drop-down list box.**

5. **To change the default quality settings for the encoder, click the Settings button and make your changes in the Properties dialog box.**

6. **Choose the output folder for your transcoded files in the Output Folder text box.**

7. **Click Encode to transcode your files.**

The Xilisoft converters are quite good and come highly recommended.

Changing your files from one compressed format to another isn't usually the best way to re-encode your data. The best way to do this would be to use the original CDs and just re-rip your music. That said, sometimes you don't have easy access to your CDs and so converters are a good alternative.

You can download a trial copy of the Xilisoft Audio Converter from the Xilisoft Web site at `www.xilisoft.com/audio-converter.html`.

Chapter 9

Making Your Own Videos

*I*f you've spent any time at all on the Web, you've surely come across tons of videos in digital form, including a large amount of user-generated content, such as the videos on YouTube and elsewhere. How can so many people, amateurs in the video business, produce so much content? Why is it such a growing trend right now?

The world of digital video (or DV, for short) has matured to the point where anyone who's comfortable using a camera and a computer can be his or her own digital Martin Scorsese. Consumer-level video cameras (another way of saying "entry level" or "not for professionals") have gotten steadily cheaper, and the quality of these lower-end cameras has continued to increase. The end result is that most people who want to make a movie can go ahead and make it.

Of course, we're over-generalizing a bit here. The price of computers and cameras (along with the technical knowledge required) still makes video production out of the reach of most of the world's population. In the first-world countries, though — countries such as the United States and much of Europe and Asia — amateur video production is at an all-time high.

As a Zune owner, you're in a great position to get into the world of digital video. You can start out as a viewer, checking out the video available online from a variety of sources (see Chapter 10 for more on finding some great video podcasts online). Perhaps you'll be motivated to create your own videos. The following section takes you through the first step in your video-making adventures — deciding what type of content you want to create.

What Do You Want to Make?

The different videos on the Internet generally fall into one of a few major categories. The following sections cover each of these categories, along with some real-life examples.

Home movies

Home movies include your standard film of the kids having their birthday party, you and your friends out at the lake enjoying yourselves, or even the footage of someone's wedding. Until recently, these sorts of home movies were nearly the only type of video that regular people made, and they still represent the bulk of video footage being shot by nonprofessionals. Although a majority of amateur movies fall into this category, you can describe only a relatively small number of the online video content (especially the popular content) as a home movie. Home movies aren't really intended for publishing out onto the Internet, visible to the world. Although you may decide to publish a few of your home movies on the Web, you probably intend for just a few friends and family to see them.

Monologues/rants

Upset about something? Have an opinion, but no one's listening? Grab a camera, point it at yourself, and then let fly with your thoughts and opinions on whatever topic you want. This type of content is basically the standard style of a blog, recorded onto video. For a really good example of this type of video, check out `www.youtube.com/profile?user=lonelygirl15` (see Figure 9-1).

If you have something to say, and you want absolutely everyone to be able to see it, then posting a video of your thoughts on the Web is definitely the way to go.

News updates

Traditional journalism still exists on the Web, with NBC, ABC, and others putting their daily news shows online for you to view. But many other people have decided to start providing news updates for you online — and if they can do it, so can you. In general, these videos are less polished and more casual than traditional news, but that's a big part of their appeal to most of their viewers. Some of the best examples of this type of content include GeekBrief TV (`http://geekbrief.tv`, shown in Figure 9-2) and Rocketboom (www.rocketboom.com, shown in Figure 9-3). You can find many other informal online news reports, of course, many of which also cross into the category discussed in the following section, "Interviews and discussions."

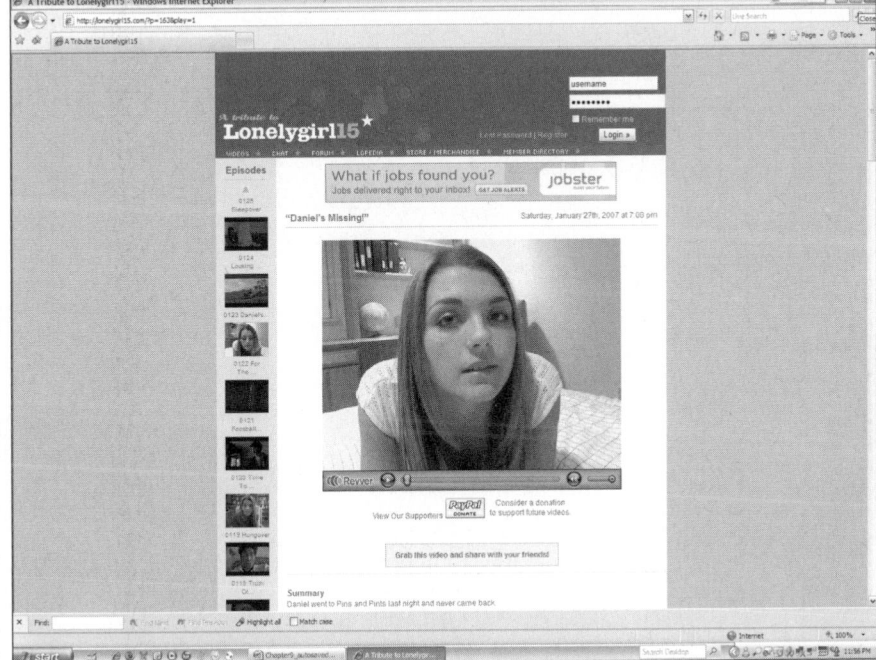

Figure 9-1: Although LonelyGirl15 turned out to be fake, it's still a classic example of the online monologue.

Figure 9-2: Cali Lewis from GeekBrief TV delivers your daily tech news in a light-hearted style.

Figure 9-3:
Rocketboom
delivers
news in a
traditional
TV format
but at a
much
quicker
pace.

Interviews and discussions

The sites `http://Channel9.msdn.com` and `www.on10.net` both provide some videos that match up with your standard talk show style interview (such as you see on Larry King or Oprah, for example). Similar to the news updates category, most of these videos are done by citizen journalists, folks who have arranged interviews with interesting people and then published those interviews, essentially sneaking into a world of content that was previously reserved for TV networks and newspaper writers. Check out `www.scobleshow.com` for some sample interviews. (Okay, many of the interviews center around a particular product or technology and therefore could find a home in the demonstrations and how-to category, as well. The following section covers that category.) If you're interested in doing this type of video, you need to find someone worth interviewing and then convince him or her that an interview with you would be worth his or her time.

Demonstrations and how-to videos

Demonstrations and how-to videos can focus on comedy (showing what happens when breath mints are added to diet cola); demonstrate how to use a new product; or give you detailed instructions about cooking, fitness, electronics, or just about anything else. In this style of video, the content really fits the medium; no one wants to read about how to do a perfect push-up, but a two-minute video can illustrate the move from several angles. You can find so many different videos online that illustrate this point, but check out `www.youtube.com/profile?user=zedomax` if you want to see some really good DIY content.

Performances

Today's digital video revolution has ushered in one truly seismic change in the entertainment industry — it's given both amateurs and professionals alike a platform they can use to get their performances on the Web. A garage band can record their own music video and put it up for everyone to see. Or a fan can record a show at a local club (something that more and more performers are allowing), then go home and upload it for people on the other side of the country to check out. Of course, official music, comedy, and sporting videos are being done and released online all the time, as well, by all sorts of companies, but the bulk of online content comes from the amateur recordings. Enter the keyword "standup" on YouTube for a huge number of videos, most of which are stand-up routines from both unknown and well-known comics (`www.youtube.com/results?search_query=Standup`).

Traditional movie and TV content

Although a lot of commercial TV shows and movies end up online, a lot of regular Joes and Jodis are using consumer-level cameras and technology to create an increasingly larger number of new shows and movies for the Web. Homemade Hollywood isn't unique to the world of digital filmmaking; enterprising would-be filmmakers have used VHS cameras to make full-length films in the past, but digital video makes the process that much easier. The high video quality and professional editing features now available have opened up the floodgates for original content that compares favorably with what you can find on commercial networks. If the idea of shows and movies produced with a minimal budget and equipment from Best Buy interests you, then check out some of the shows on `www.podshow.com`, such as *Port City P.D.* (`www.podshow.com/shows/?show_id=3114`).

You might also want to check out Robert Rodriguez's book *Rebel Without a Crew* (Dutton). Rodriguez, the director of many popular films (including *Desperado* and *Spy Kids*), tells how he made his first big movie without a crew and with a budget of only $7,000.

Picking a Video Camera

The first thing you need to get in order to make a video is some form of camera — unless, of course, you already have one lying around. If you're planning a trip to your local electronics stores in search of a new camera, keep in mind that consumer-level cameras are available in three main categories:

- MiniDV cameras
- Hard-drive or Flash-based cameras
- Webcams, camera phones, and still cameras that can do movies

The following sections give you the facts on each type of camera.

MiniDV cameras

MiniDV refers to handheld cameras that use the MiniDV format of digital video tape. MiniDV is the standard for consumer cameras today, utilizing small tapes capable of recording 60 to 90 minutes of high-quality video and audio. Most MiniDV cameras record in standard definition (normal television quality, 640 x 480 pixels), but some support high-definition recording onto the same type of tape (most MiniDVs that support high definition record in the 720p format of high definition, which is 1280 x 720 pixels).

As you step up into higher-level cameras, such as the kind used by on-site reporters and even some filmmakers, MiniDV is still a very popular format. Because of its wide popularity, you may want to make MiniDV the only tape format that you use. MiniDV tapes, and services that can accept these tapes, are widely available in most places in the world. You may see cameras that use older tape formats, such as 8mm or Hi-8, but you should stick with MiniDV.

You can find MiniDV cameras available in a wide range of prices, but here is a selection of camera models at a few select price points:

- **Panasonic PV-GS29 (around $200):** A pretty standard entry-level MiniDV camcorder with high optical zoom and standard definition.
- **Panasonic PV-GS300 (around $500):** Essentially the same as the GS29, but it also includes a 3CCD sensor. 3CCD indicates that the camera uses three sensors to pick up the incoming image instead of just one, which results in much better image quality.
- **Panasonic Pro AG-DVC7 (around $1,000):** Edges into the lower end of professional camcorders. The Panasonic Pro drops the handheld

thing and goes for more of a shoulder style of camera. Generally, it has more features that appeal to professionals, including more options for controlling focus, white balance, and audio settings yourself (as compared to cheaper cameras that are nearly completely automatic). This class of camera usually produces better quality video because it uses better components, such as higher-end lenses, in the camera's construction.

✔ **JVC GY-HD110U High Definition Camera (over $5,000):** If digital video isn't just a hobby for you, then you probably want to save your pennies and step up into a camera such as this one. This type of camera can produce high-definition video (usually 1280 x 720 pixels, normally referred to as 720p), but keep in mind that recording in HD means that you also need to capture to your computer and edit the video in HD, as well, which can add even more cost to the process.

Hard-drive and Flash-based cameras

This category of camera records directly to digital storage, without the use of tape. Such cameras record either to a hard drive or to some form of Flash memory card, such as Compact Flash (CF) or Secure Digital (SD). These cameras have features similar to MiniDV cameras, but they do have a couple of important differences:

✔ **Recording:** Recording isn't done on tapes (as it is with MiniDV cameras), but on the camera's own storage space. Hard-drive-based cameras often let you record six or more hours of high-quality video (and much more at a lower quality level), and Flash-based cameras may be capable of a half hour of video per gigabyte of memory (these cameras usually use 1GB–4GB cards).

✔ **Ease of use:** Given the technology underlying hard-drive and Flash-based cameras, you're generally able to record longer than you can with MiniDV cameras — no need to switch tapes — and it's generally easier to transfer the video files to your computer.

Hard-drive and Flash-based cameras sound great, right? Well, you should know about a few issues:

✔ **Cost:** Such added convenience doesn't come cheap. A good hard-drive-based camera costs you more than a similar model that uses MiniDV tapes.

✔ **Quality:** The video quality could potentially be lower because the video is being recorded in a compressed format. And, depending on the camera and the settings you use, your video may be compressed to a higher degree than you want.

To avoid low-quality video footage when you use a hard-drive or Flash-based camera, make sure you record at the highest possible quality setting. Don't let the temptation of doubling the number of hours of video you can record lead you astray.

✓ **Equipment needs:** When you use a tape-based camera, you can carry as many tapes with you as you need. Sure, you have to swap them out, but you can record for however long you need without having to transfer any of that content onto a computer.

With a hard-drive-based camera, you need a PC onto which you can transfer content every time you fill up the camera. For Flash-based cameras, you could certainly carry multiple Flash memory cards around, but a MiniDV tape can cost up to 50 times less than a memory card of similar size. If you plan to record an hour or less of video and have a computer available at all times, a hard-drive-based camera can work wonders. But for a traveling documentary filmmaker, filling up 20 MiniDV tapes might be a lot easier.

In this category, we can recommend only the two camera models that we use, but you can find many other models available — and more are coming every day. Both of these recommendations are for hard-drive-based cameras because the only Flash-based cameras we've used produced poor quality video that was extremely difficult to work with on a PC. Here are the hard-drive cameras that get our recommendation:

✓ **JVC Everio GZ-MG30 (around $400):** This camera has worked quite well for us, but the picture quality is definitely not as high as any of the Panasonic MiniDV cameras listed in the preceding section. Battery life is around an hour with the standard battery, so you definitely need to upgrade to an extended battery.

✓ **JVC Everio GZ-MG505 (around $1,100):** The main difference between this camera and the GZ-MG30 is this camera's use of 3CCD image sensors, making the video quality on this camera much better, rivaling the MiniDV cameras that we've used. Battery life is a big issue, though, so plan to spend an extra $50 or so to pick up an extended-life battery.

Webcams, camera phones, and other options

These days, you no longer need to have a video camcorder around if you want to record video. You can turn to your trusty digital camera, a computer Web camera, or even your cell phone. Admittedly, the final result may be of fairly low quality and resolution, but if you simply want to get some video content online quickly and easily, the low-quality approach may be just perfect for you. (Low quality usually means a small file size and therefore quick playback online.)

Despite the lack of quality, this type of video may still serve your purpose. In fact, at least one person has even used a cell-phone camera to create a full music video. But his phone, the Nokia N93 shoots full VGA-size (640 x 480) video at 30 frames per second, far beyond your average cell-phone-shot video. Check out his story at `http://on10.net/tags/Mike+Hodgkinson`.

Getting Video from Your Camera to Your PC

The exact steps for copying video depend on your camera, but the following sections give you the basic procedure for each type of camera.

From a tape-based camera

For MiniDV (tape-based) cameras, the camera has either a FireWire or USB (or both) port available so that you can connect it to your PC. If you connect via FireWire, you shouldn't need any drivers. But if you're using a USB port, you may need to install something before your camera will show up as a camera on your computer. After you install the correct drivers (if you need to), your camera should appear in your My Computer folder, as shown in Figure 9-4.

After you connect your camera to your computer, you need to capture the content from the tape into digital form on your computer. You can make this conversion by using a wide variety of software, including whatever software came with your camera. Windows Movie Maker, available on Windows XP and Vista, is one such capture software. Because, if you have Windows, you get Movie Maker for free, we show you how to capture video using this program. Just follow these steps:

1. **First disconnect your camera (unplug the cable that's connected to the computer) and then reconnect it.**

   A dialog box appears asking what you want to do with this device.

2. One of the choices listed in the AutoPlay dialog box is to capture video using Windows Movie Maker. Choose that option and click OK to continue.

If the Video Capture Wizard dialog box doesn't appear but the camera shows up in your My Computer folder, run Windows Movie Maker manually by choosing Start⇨All Programs⇨Windows Movie Maker. After Movie Maker is loaded, you can start capturing video by choosing File⇨Capture Video from Movie Maker's main menu.

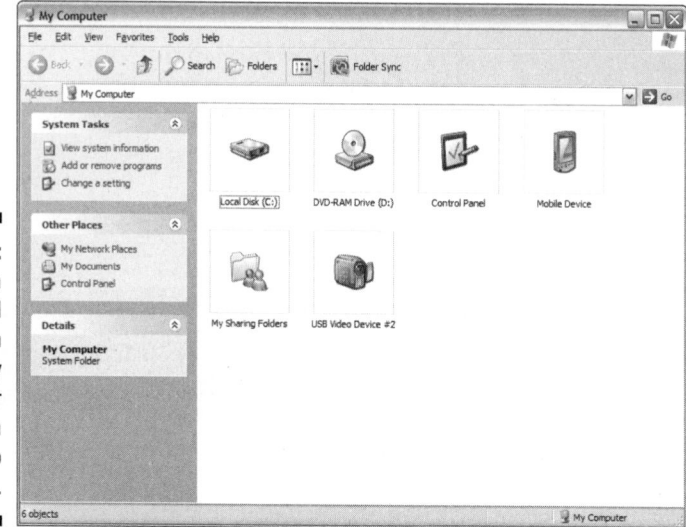

Figure 9-4:
Your camera should appear in your My Computer folder as a video device.

Regardless of how you get into Movie Maker, you end up working your way through the Video Capture Wizard.

3. In the Video Capture Wizard, pick a name for your video and choose how you want to import that video.

You can choose between two options:

- **The whole tape:** Automatically import the entire tape. If you choose this option, Movie Maker rewinds the tape to the start and captures everything on that tape.

- **Pick and choose:** Import only specific sections that you manually fast-forward and rewind to set up.

If you're using Windows Vista, you get an additional choice — whether to save the imported video as a single file or create a file for every scene that the software detects during import. A new scene starts with a change in location, lighting, or other elements significant enough to suggest that you'd probably treat it as disconnected from the footage immediately before and after it. We don't really see the benefits of creating many small files because you can split up a large video as needed easily enough while you're editing. For that reason, and to be consistent with the behavior in the XP version of Movie Maker, we suggest you stick with the single-file option.

The Vista version of Windows Movie Maker adds several new features, but it removes your ability to choose at what bit rate you want to capture the video. In XP, you get to choose from one of several possible bit rates (with description names such as High Quality Video and Video For Local Playback, as shown in Figure 9-5), depending on your final destination.

Under Vista, all video is captured at around 4 Mbps, which should be high enough for nearly any purpose. Choosing a bit rate may seem confusing, but it can save space on your computer; if you're making a video for the Web, you don't really need to capture the video at HD or DVD quality.

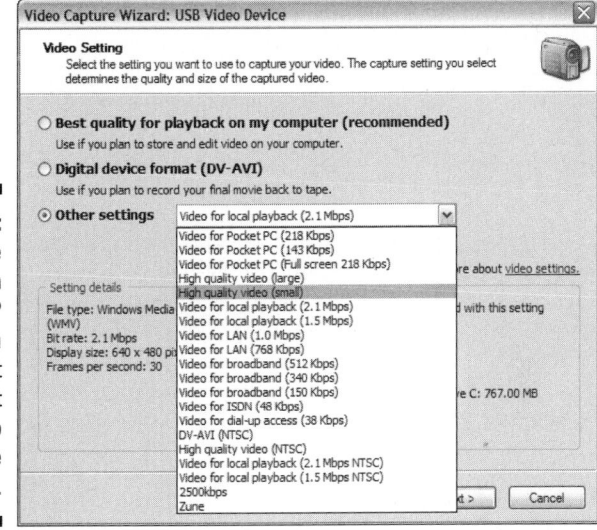

Figure 9-5: Movie Maker on Windows XP gives you a choice of bit rates at which to capture your video.

From a camera that uses digital video files

For hard-drive or Flash-based cameras, or camera phones, you don't need to capture the video to get it onto your computer — that video is already a digital video file. You just need to get that file from the device — or from the device's memory card — onto your PC. Normally, you make this transfer through a

USB connection (Figure 9-6 shows how a video file from one type of camera phone appears on a computer), although you may also have to remove a memory card and place it into some form of memory-card reader. Check the documentation for your specific camera (or phone) to find out what you need to do to transfer photos and videos from your device to your computer.

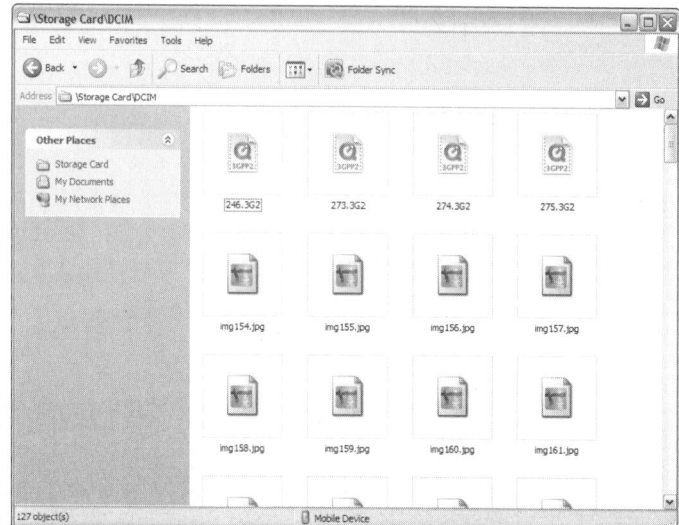

Figure 9-6: Video and image files on a camera phone don't need to be captured, just copied.

Web cameras usually have some software included with them to handle the capture of video, but Windows Movie Maker may recognize a Web camera as just another video camera. Check to see if Movie Maker recognizes the camera first (if it doesn't, you get an error message after choosing Import from Digital Camera from the File menu) and follow the instructions in the preceding section to capture video. If that doesn't work, install and use whatever software came with the Web camera.

Editing Your Video

However you get the video onto your machine, the next step is to edit it, assuming you don't want to just put it up online or onto your Zune exactly as you filmed it. You can find a lot of video editing software out there — some of it inexpensive, some quite pricey — so we really can't cover all the options. We do want to show you at least one way to edit video, so we talk about Windows Movie Maker.

If you use Windows Movie Maker to capture your video (from MiniDV, for example), that video is already in a *collection* (a grouping of video files) inside Movie Maker.

If you're using a file-based (hard-drive or Flash) camera, just copy the videos from the camera onto your local machine and then drag the videos into the Movie Maker Imported Video area (or, in Movie Maker, choose File⇨Import into Collections). You can do a lot with Movie Maker. In fact, you can find entire books written about using it, and it's covered in general video-editing books, such as Keith Underdahl's *Digital Video For Dummies,* 4th Edition (Wiley Publishing, Inc.). But this book sticks to the essentials. To edit your video by using Movie Maker, follow these steps:

1. **Start playing a clip by double-clicking its thumbnail in the Imported Media area.**

2. **When the clip reaches a spot at which you want to slice the video into two pieces (one that contains all the content up to the current time and one that contains the remainder), click the Split button under the video preview, as shown in Figure 9-7.**

Figure 9-7:
The most basic action in Windows Movie Maker is the split.

Two thumbnails appear in the Imported Media area, but the file itself hasn't actually changed.

The name of the first half of the split is the same as the name of the original clip, and the name of the second half is the name of the first half with a number stuck at the end. So you probably want to rename each side of your split operation with some descriptive text (for example, "Introduction to the Zune" and "Zune Demo"). Continue splitting as necessary until you create all the clips that you need.

3. **Drag the clips into the Timeline view at the bottom of the Movie Maker window in the order that you want for your final output, as shown in Figure 9-8. After you have the timeline populated, you can view it by clicking in the Timeline area and then clicking Play on the preview window.**

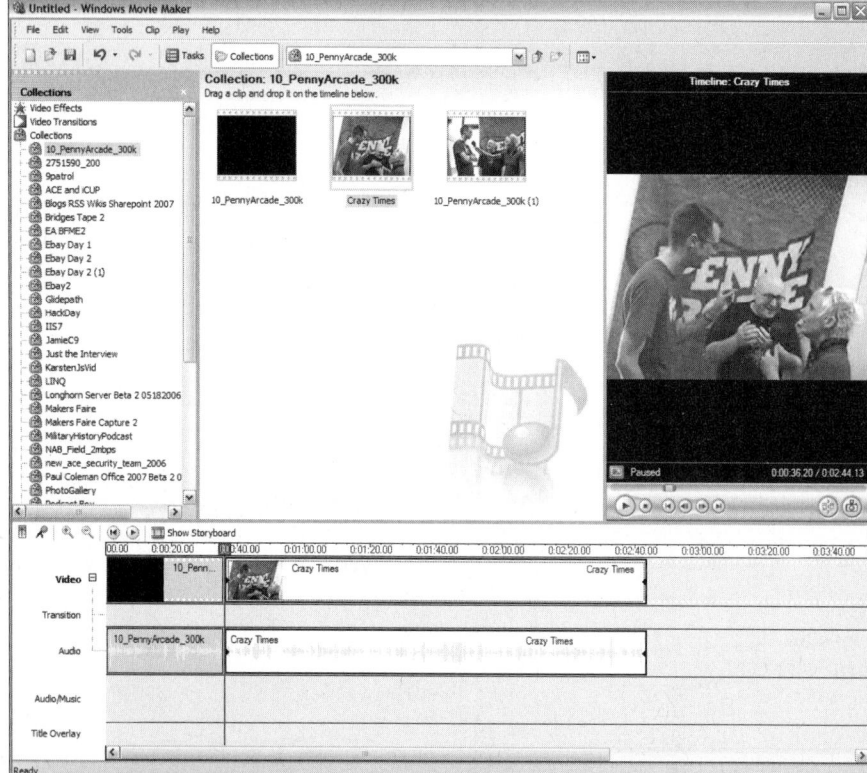

Figure 9-8:
You can view your Movie Maker project as a timeline or storyboard.

4. **If desired, insert an effect (such as a fade) between individual clips.**

To insert an effect, follow these steps:

1. **Pick Video Transitions from the list on the left-hand side of the window.**

2. **Drag the desired effect from the center area of the window where all the transition icons are displayed (see Figure 9-9) into the area between clips on the Storyboard view of the movie at the bottom of the window.**

You can choose from a lot of neat transitions, including page turning and dissolves. Don't use any of them. In general, you should leave fancy transitions to people who have already mastered the art of editing their videos and know how to use them without making their work look amateurish or like an '80s music video. Using the Spin transition is tempting, but please resist the urge.

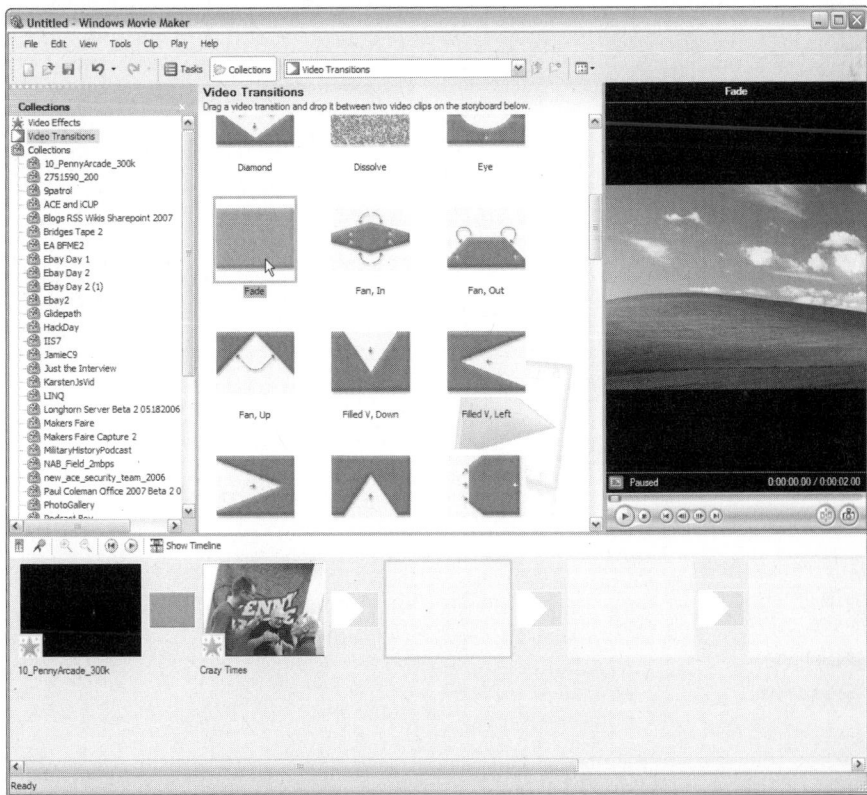

Figure 9-9:
You have many options for transitions between your clips.

If you want to add a Fade In from Black or Fade Out transition to the beginning or end of your video, right-click a particular item on the storyboard and pick Fade In or Fade Out from the menu that appears (see Figure 9-10).

5. **To add audio, import an audio file (`.wma`, `.mp3`, or `.wav`) into Movie Maker by following these steps:**

   1. **Drag the file into the Imported Media area.**

   2. **Drag the file from its new position in the Imported Media area onto the Audio/Music area in Timeline view.**

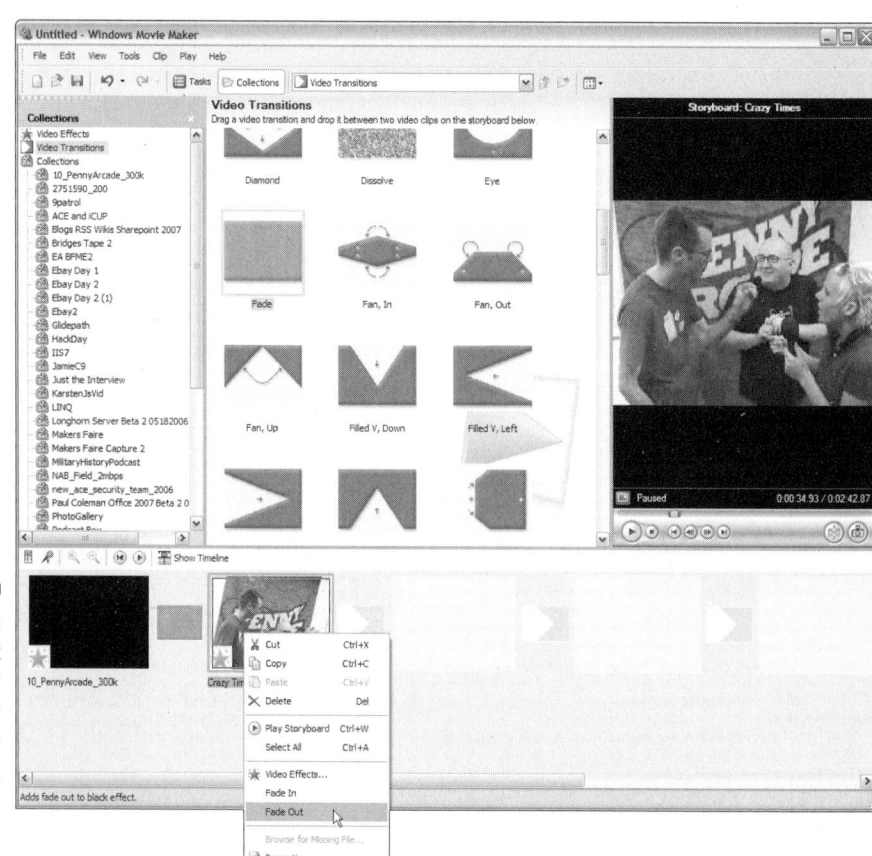

Figure 9-10: You can set a Fade In or Fade Out for a particular clip by using the right-click menu.

You can't use protected music, such as the tunes you buy from the Zune Marketplace; you can use only music that you rip from your own CDs or download from a source that doesn't place any DRM protection on the files.

6. **After you finish editing your video, choose File➪Publish Movie from the main menu to save the finished product as a .wmv file.**

Exactly what settings you use when saving your file depends on what you want to do with your new masterpiece. In the following section, we cover the best settings for burning your work to a DVD, uploading it to Soapbox, or putting it onto your Zune.

Sharing Your Video

After you create the next great video, you probably want to show your work to someone. . . . The only question is, how? Well, if your target audience is somewhere far away (or if you're hoping to show your brilliance to everyone in the world), you probably need to upload your video to the Internet. If your intended audience is close by, perhaps a DVD would be in order. And if you see your audience every day, you may just want to put the video onto your Zune.

Posting your video online

You can post video on a lot of different sites, but not that many of those sites can accept the WMV output that Movie Maker produces. If you want to find a converter and produce an MPEG4 version of your video, YouTube is one possible option. Otherwise, we suggest you check out MSN Soapbox (http://soapbox.msn.com).

Soapbox lets you upload any WMV that's less than 100MB in size. When publishing your movie out of Movie Maker, make sure to pick a profile or custom setting that produces a video under that limit. Alternatively, if you don't want to compress the video past a certain point, you can split up your creation into chunks small enough that each one can be made into an individual post on Soapbox.

Follow these steps to post your video on Soapbox:

1. **At http://soapbox.msn.com, sign up for an account by using your Windows Live ID.**

   If you don't have a Windows Live ID (the evolution of the Microsoft Passport brand), you can register for one by clicking on the link next to Don't Have a Windows Live ID?

2. **Click Upload Video.**

   The Upload Video screen appears.

3. **Fill out the Upload Video form (see Figure 9-11) and click Browse to find your local copy of the video.**

   The form asks for a name, description, and tags (categories) for your video.

   Changing the Soapbox Permission option to Private (it's set to Public by default) means that your video won't show up in a Search or Browse. People can still get to it via a link, so you can post or send your link around. But the Private setting makes your video less likely to be seen by a few thousand random people.

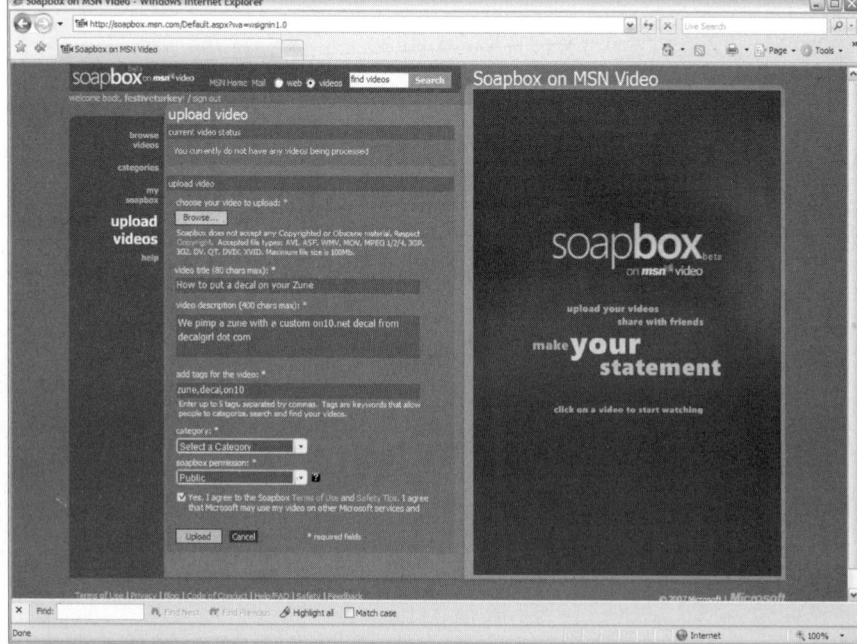

Figure 9-11:
You have to provide some details about your video before Soapbox lets you upload it.

4. **After you fill out the form, click Upload to start sending the video to the Soapbox server.**

   This process can take some time, but you can continue to browse around in the Soapbox site while your video transfers.

   After your video uploads to Soapbox, the Soapbox service *processes* the video (converts your uploaded video into the formats that Soapbox uses). You can leave the site while your video is processed, if you want.

In the end, you have a video entry of your very own on Soapbox. From that entry (see Figure 9-12), you can grab a couple of very useful bits of text:

✔ **A link to the video:** You can e-mail this link to someone so he or she can check out your work.

✔ **The HTML code to embed your video on a Web page:** Use this html code if you run your own site, blog, or MySpace page. You can use that html to put your Soapbox video right on your own page, where people can play it without ever going to Soapbox themselves (as shown in Figure 9-13).

Figure 9-12:
The Soapbox Share tab gives you a variety of ways to provide links to your video.

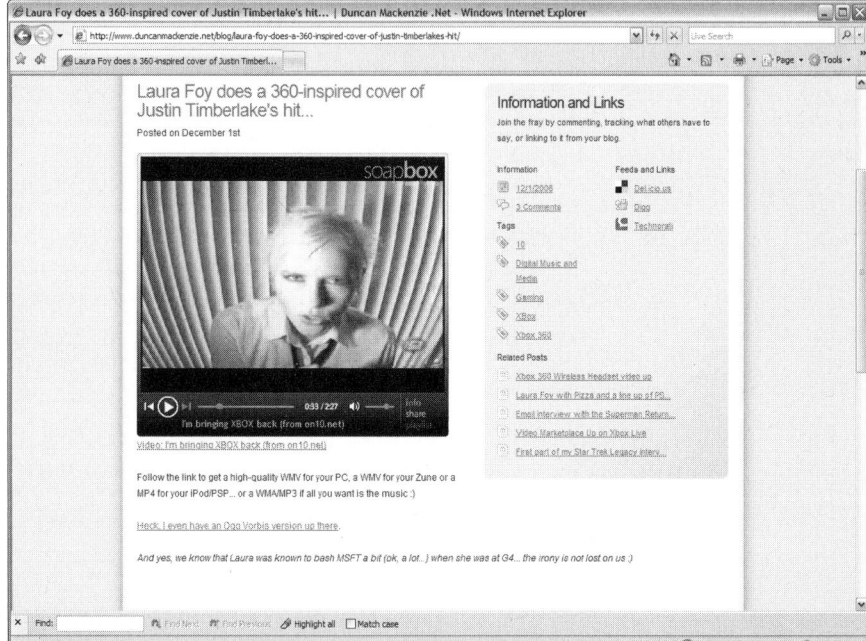

Figure 9-13:
Embedding the player in your own Web page or blog lets people watch without having to leave your site.

Burning a DVD of your video

Getting your finished video onto a DVD is very simple, if you have the right hardware and software. In Vista, the ability to create a video DVD is built right into the operating system, so as long as you have a DVD burner installed, you can just fire up the Windows DVD Maker program, add one or more WMV files to a displayed list (in which you can move videos up and down to control their position on the disc), and then walk through a short wizard to burn the actual DVD. The end result is a real DVD, complete with menu, without any hassle at all.

In fact, you can go right from your Windows Movie Maker project to the DVD Maker without even having to create a WMV file. Just choose File⇨Publish Movie to bring up the Publish Movie Wizard and then select DVD under Where Do You Want to Publish Your Movie? Movie Maker saves your project, then closes itself and opens Windows DVD Maker with the output of your project already added as the content of a new DVD.

Under XP, the DVD-making process isn't quite so easy because XP doesn't ship with any software to burn video onto a DVD. Movie Maker can still output a high-quality WMV file, using a 2 Mbps or higher output setting, that you can then take and use in another program such as Nero Ultra Edition (www.nero.com) or whatever software came with your DVD burner (if any).

Getting your video onto your Zune

Under both XP and Vista, you can add a custom PRX to the list of possible output formats in Windows Movie Maker. If you download the zune.prx file from www.crazyaboutzune.com and copy it to the Shared Profiles folder for Movie Maker, it shows up as a new item in the list of possible output formats when you publish your Movie Maker project out to a file. The Shared Profiles directory is usually located at C:\Program Files\Movie Maker\ Shared\Profiles. Under Vista, this folder probably doesn't exist, but you can just go ahead and create a Profiles folder yourself. Copy zune.prx into that folder, restart Windows Movie Maker, and when you go to publish a video, select the Zune item from the list.

After you get your video into the proper format, just save it in a folder that the Zune software watches, such as your My Videos directory, and it's added to your library automatically. Drag your video into the Sync list the next time you have your Zune hooked up to your PC, click Start Sync, and it should transfer over without even having to be converted on the way.

Finding More Information

Making videos is a complicated process. Even after you master all of the technical issues, you're still just getting started. How to shoot an event, what type of lighting is best, and even how to tell a story are all part of producing a great video. Check out these books for more information:

- ✔ *Digital Video For Dummies,* 4th Edition, by Keith Underdahl (Wiley)
- ✔ *Digital Video Handbook,* by Tom Ang (Dorling Kindersley Publishers Ltd.)

For some quick tips, Tina Wood (one of the hosts from Microsoft's http:// on10.net video site) produced a cute video describing how to shoot video. Check it out online or download it to your Zune at http://on10.net/ blogs/tina/how-to-shoot-video.

Chapter 10

Podcasts

*P*odcasts are a relatively new technology, but the concept is certainly nothing revolutionary. The name itself is a combination of iPod (because that's the device many people use to listen to or watch podcasts) and broadcast (recognizing that it's a publishing mechanism similar to radio or TV), but you can listen to or view podcasts on a wide variety of devices, including the Zune. A podcast is essentially a radio show that gets published on the Internet as a series of episodes. (More and more podcasts use video now, but it was originally an audio-only technology.) The exact content of a podcast isn't really defined, but most podcasts resemble talk radio in many respects; someone spends anywhere from five minutes to over an hour discussing a topic that he or she is interested in. (Podcasts have no length restrictions, but you don't often see an episode that goes over 30 minutes, much less an hour.)

The format of a podcast is often as varied as its content. Sometimes a podcast features multiple people or an expert in the field, but sometimes a regular person who has opinions (just like all of us do) uses a podcast as a way to get his or her thoughts out to the world. Podcasts offer a truly no-rules kind of format.

If you're familiar with blogs, think of podcasts as an audio (or video) blog, with each post available as a media file rather than just text. Despite their similarities (an individual's personal thoughts published in ongoing episodes on the Internet), the nature of audio or video makes podcasts quite different than text blogs, in most cases. For example, you can very easily and naturally include multiple people in a podcast, but if you had the same people having the same discussion in a text blog entry, it would just seem odd and be hard to follow to boot. Over time, podcasts have become more like listening to a radio show on NPR than like reading a person's essayistic blog posts.

Podcasts range from a purely amateur approach, using a computer's onboard microphone, to fully produced audio that includes opening and closing music, professional sound equipment, and possibly even some post-production work to improve the quality of the sound.

So, enough already. You have the podcast overview behind you; the rest of this chapter immerses you in the podcast world. You can find out about one feature of podcasts that more traditional text blogs also use — feeds. The following section fills you in on all the details.

Understanding Feeds

We all lead busy lives and can't always be online checking for new stuff. (Well, not every day, at least.) Bloggers quickly realized that fact, so they came up with a notification system that lets people know when new content is available. Blog publishers and podcasters provide *feeds* on their sites — essentially, a way of channeling their recent episodes to someone's PC. Users *subscribe* to those feeds by registering the feeds with a software program the users have on their PCs. This software runs through the list of subscribed feeds on a regular basis and checks each one for updates, notifying the user of any new content that it finds.

The feed for a blog or podcast is generally created in a special file format called RSS (Really Simple Syndication) or Atom (a competing format). The file format doesn't really matter to you as a consumer of podcasts and blogs, but you may run into these terms in your feed-reading software or on the Web site for a particular blog or podcast.

The feeds generally contain the full text of each entry, along with a link back to the Web page for that particular entry. With podcasts, this feed file also includes a link to the media file for each episode, so the user's software can download new entries as soon as it finds them. After you find and subscribe to a set of podcasts, the software automatically delivers new content to your machine every day.

Not all podcasts release new episodes daily, and many don't have any sort of regular schedule at all. Of course, most podcasts are completely free, so how can you really expect a regular schedule?

A feed can provide only a single media-file link per entry, but many podcasts produce their episodes in multiple file formats (.mp4 and .wmv for video files, for example, or .wma and .mp3 for audio files). Those podcasts generally handle this issue by having several different feeds, one for each file format they support.

The basic process for watching or listening to podcasts through your Zune follows these steps:

1. Find a podcast you want to check out.

2. Find the appropriate feed for that podcast.

3. Subscribe to the podcast by using some type of feed-reading software.

4. Configure the feed-reading software and the Zune software so that new episodes are downloaded and added to your Zune library.

5. Sync the podcast episodes onto your Zune.

We go through each of these steps in detail in the section "Finding the Right Podcasts," later in this chapter, but we get the software discussion out of the way in the following section before we explain how to find the podcasts you want.

Choosing Podcast Software

When the Zune was released, it had quite a few new and interesting features, but a lot of influential people on the Internet were quick to jump on one particularly glaring omission: The Zune has no software support for podcasts.

To be clear, the critics are unhappy because the Zune software on your PC can't help you find, subscribe to, or manage podcasts, specifically. You certainly can get podcasts onto your Zune in other ways (which we cover in the following sections), but the Zune's main competitors (the iPod and iTunes) include very complete podcast support, so some critics consider the lack of this type of software made specifically for the Zune a major issue.

Many of the most vocal critics of the Zune's lack of podcast support are podcasters themselves (people who publish podcasts), so they may have a somewhat distorted view of how important podcasts are for the first release of the Zune.

We suspect that although this feature wasn't included in the launch of the Zune, it's a high-enough priority for the Zune team that they'll probably ship out some form of podcast support as an update before too long. In the meantime, though, you need to use some other piece of software to subscribe to and download podcasts, and you may need some additional software to browse through a directory of available podcasts. You can choose from quite a few applications for this purpose, but we cover four possibilities in the following sections: iTunes, Juice Receiver, Doppler, and Internet Explorer 7. In each case, we show you how to subscribe to a new podcast, as well as how to configure the software so that new entries get all the way into your Zune library.

iTunes

Yes, we realize that the respective manufacturers didn't intend for you to use Apple's iTunes with Microsoft's Zune; iTunes is the software that ships and works with iPods. It turns out, though, that iTunes is also a great PC podcast client, even if you never use it with an iPod at all.

You can get iTunes installed very easily. In fact, you have to work to *not* get it installed because it automatically comes with Apple's media player (QuickTime) by default. If you've installed QuickTime (to watch a movie trailer online, for example), you likely already have iTunes. But if you don't have iTunes, you can easily get it. To install iTunes on your machine, follow these steps:

1. **Type** `www.quicktime.com` **into your Web browser's address line and press Enter.**

   Apple's QuickTime page appears.

2. **Click the large Free Download button in the middle of the page.**

   The actual download page appears. You have two choices on this page (see Figure 10-1): QuickTime with iTunes or just QuickTime.

3. **Pick the QuickTime with iTunes option.**

   The three check boxes below the download options offer you various subscriptions. If you want to avoid any unnecessary e-mails, deselect the check boxes.

4. **Enter your e-mail address in the box labeled Email Address.**

   You have to enter a valid e-mail address to download QuickTime and iTunes, but feel free to use a secondary e-mail address if you have one set up for spam and are worried about giving out your main address.

5. **Click Free Download Now.**

   In Internet Explorer, a prompt appears asking if you want to run or save the file `iTunesSetup.exe` (as shown in Figure 10-2). Other browsers save the file to disk by default.

6. **If you're using Internet Explorer, click Run in the prompt that appears to install iTunes. If you're using another browser, it asks you for a location to save the installation file. Select a location and click Download, then go find the downloaded file — if you don't remember where you saved it, search your machine for `iTunesSetup.exe` — and double-click it to install iTunes.**

   We're talking an approximately 35MB download, which can take some time if you use a dial-up connection.

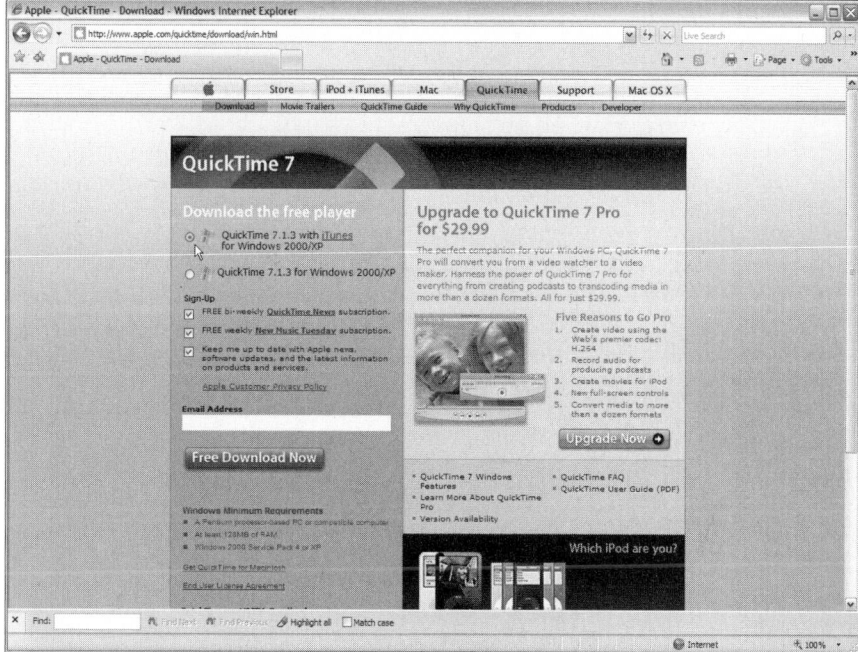

Figure 10-1:
Make
sure you
choose the
installation
option that
includes
iTunes.

Figure 10-2:
You need to
download
and run the
setup
application
to install
iTunes.

7. **When the Installation Wizard appears, click Next and accept the license agreement by selecting the I Accept option and clicking Next.**

   The Choose iTunes Installer Options dialog box appears (see Figure 10-3).

8. **Uncheck all three check boxes in this dialog box but leave the rest of the options set to their defaults.**

   If you don't uncheck the three options, the first option puts some extra icons on your desktop, the second option sets QuickTime as the default player for a variety of media files (a job that your Zune software is likely handling), and the third option installs additional software that lets you know when you need to update iTunes. The first and third check boxes aren't a big deal. although leaving the second check box checked won't crash your machine or anything drastic like that, the next time you double-click an MP3 file on your computer, that file opens and plays in iTunes rather than the Zune software, Windows Media Player, or whatever you had previously set to handle those files.

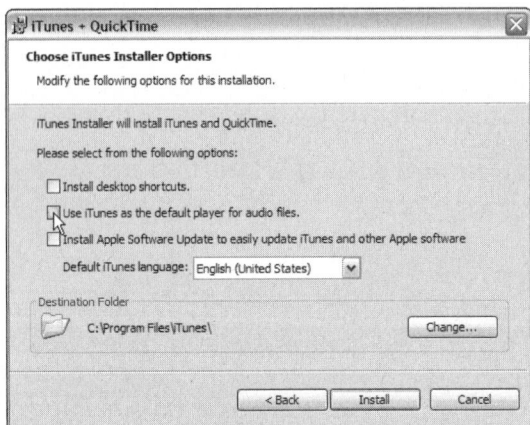

Figure 10-3: In the Choose iTunes Installer Options dialog box, you can control how iTunes changes your system settings.

9. **Click Install to finish the Installation Wizard.**

   Your computer starts copying files and configuring settings. You may want to go get a soda while you wait for the Congratulations message to appear saying the installation is complete.

10. **Click Finish to save your settings and close this dialog box.**

    You may be prompted to restart your computer to complete the installation. You probably need to restart only if the software installation had to update the version of QuickTime on your machine.

11. **Restart your PC, if necessary.**

12. **After your computer restarts, choose Start⇨All Programs⇨iTunes and click the iTunes icon.**

    After you agree to yet another license agreement (by clicking Accept in the iTunes Software License Agreement dialog box), you should be up and running with iTunes.

Finding podcasts in iTunes

With iTunes up and running on your computer (see Figure 10-4), click the iTunes Store link to jump into Apple's online store of music, videos, and podcasts.

iTunes Store link

Figure 10-4:
Click the
iTunes Store
link to open
the iTunes
equivalent
of Zune's
Market-
place.

The store's home page contains highlights from every category of content (as
you can see in Figure 10-5). Click the Podcasts link in the iTunes Store menu
(in the upper-left of the page) to open the podcast-specific home page.

Out of all the podcast-related software and Web sites currently available, the
iTunes Podcasts page (shown in Figure 10-6) is probably the single best place
to find podcasts. You can view podcasts by category or popularity, or you
can check out the featured podcasts right there on the main page.

If you click any individual podcast — the ABC World News podcast, for
example — a page appears showing that particular podcast with a list of
recent episodes below the description of the show itself, as shown in Figure
10-7. If a podcast has multiple feeds available for different audio or video formats, each individual feed may appear as a different podcast in iTunes.

Only formats that the iTunes/QuickTime player can play (such as MP4 and
MOV files) ever appear on an iTunes page; if a podcast provides a WMV
(Windows Media Video) formatted feed (which would work well for your
Zune), you won't see it and can't subscribe to it by using iTunes.

Figure 10-5:
The iTunes
home page
highlights
every type
of content
iTunes
offers.

You can click the Subscribe button on an individual podcast page to start your subscription, or you can download an individual episode by clicking one of the Get Episode buttons. When you click a Get Episode button, that particular episode starts to download, and a new icon appears along the left side of the iTunes application indicating how many items are currently downloading. You can click that Downloads icon to see a status list of current downloads, including the progress of each item, as shown in Figure 10-8. How long an episode takes to download depends on the size of the episode and the speed of your Internet connection.

If you subscribe to a podcast, instead of just downloading a single episode at a time, that podcast shows up in the Podcasts area of your Library. (You can get to your subscription podcasts by clicking the Podcasts link under Library on the left side of the iTunes interface.) If the iTunes software downloads new episodes, the number of downloads appears inside the gray oval next to the Podcasts link. If no new podcasts are available, the oval doesn't appear at all.

Figure 10-6:
Use the
Podcasts
page in
iTunes
to find
podcasts
that match
your
interests.

The iTunes software gives you some control over how your podcast subscriptions work. To set up your preferences, just click the Settings button at the bottom of the Podcast window of the Library (see Figure 10-9). Clicking that button calls up the Podcast tab in the iTunes Preferences dialog box. In the Podcast tab, you can configure three important values:

✔ **How often iTunes checks for new podcasts:** You probably don't need iTunes to check for new podcasts every hour (which is the default setting). We recommend going for once a day.

✔ **Whether iTunes automatically downloads all new episodes, downloads only the most recent new episode, or doesn't download anything at all:** We recommend that you start by setting it to automatically download the most recent new episode.

✔ **Whether iTunes keeps all episodes on your computer or selectively deletes older episodes:** Personally, we suggest you set it to keep all episodes, at least until you've used podcasts for awhile.

Subscribe button

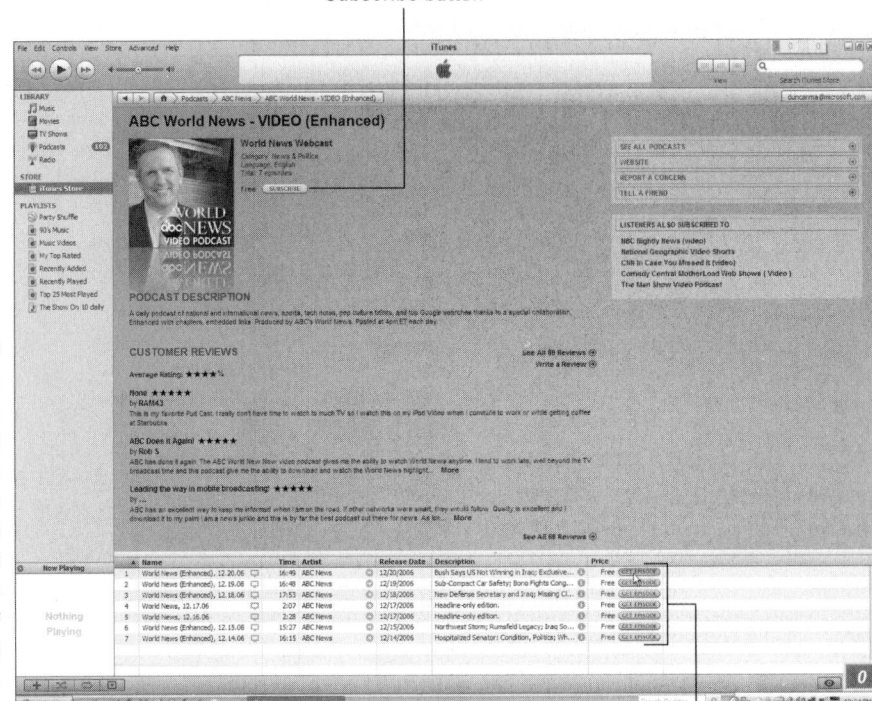

Figure 10-7:
Each
podcast has
its own
home page
that gives
you a
description
of the show
and a listing
of episodes.

Get Episode buttons

Getting your iTunes podcasts onto your Zune

After you download one or more podcast episodes from iTunes, start your
Zune software. The Zune software should automatically find any files added
to any of your monitored folders. (Check out Chapter 4 if the idea of monitored folders doesn't ring a bell.) The Zune software automatically monitors
your My Music folder, and iTunes downloads (by default) all of your podcasts
into a subfolder of your My Music folder. So the Zune software should find
your recently downloaded podcasts without any extra work on your part (see
Figure 10-10).

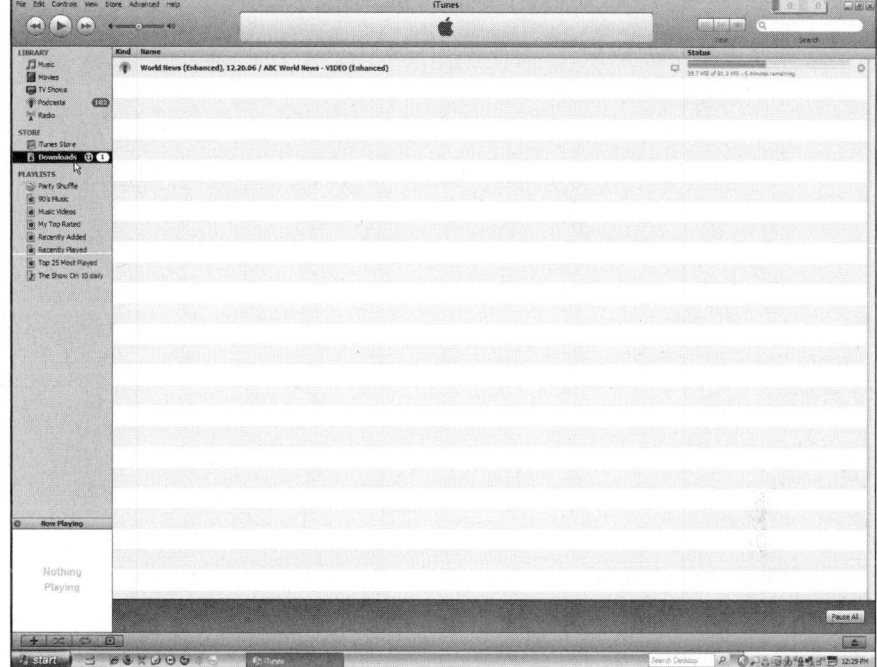

Figure 10-8:
Check the
status of
your
podcast
downloads
by clicking
the
Downloads
icon.

If the podcast hasn't shown up in your Zune library, the Zune software may not have found that podcast yet. You may have to give the Zune software a little time to find the files. If you're too impatient to wait (or if it doesn't seem to be showing up on its own), follow these steps:

1. **Right-click the Library heading on the Navigation pane of the Zune software display.**

2. **Choose Add Folder to Library from the menu that appears.**

   The Add Folder to Library dialog box appears.

3. **Click OK in the dialog box.**

   A file system scan starts, which should speed up the discovery process.

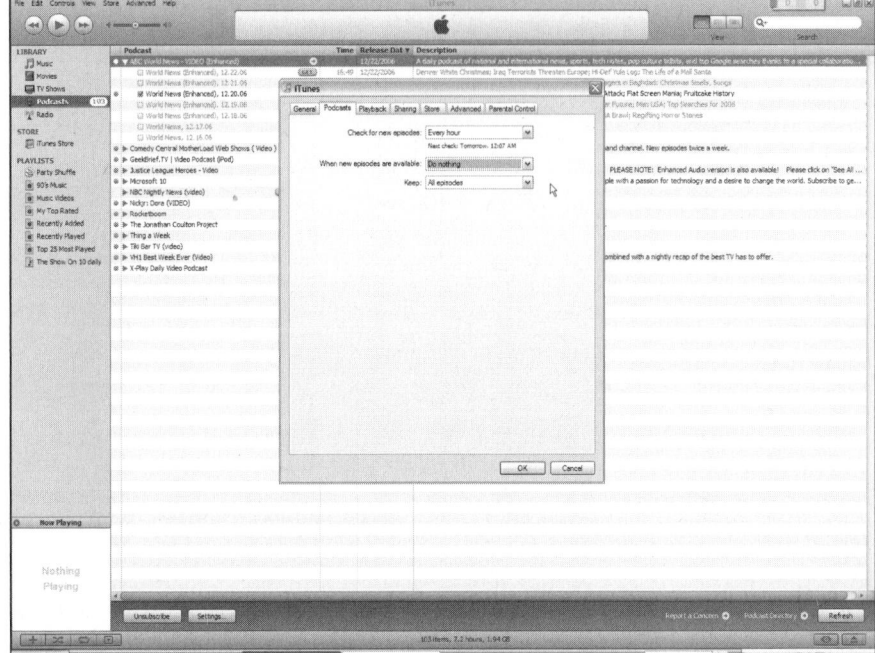

Figure 10-9:
You can
control how
iTunes
treats your
podcast
subscrip-
tions.

After you can see the podcast file in your library, drag the file onto the sync
list for your Zune. Your Zune software converts and copies the podcast to
your device, just like any other video.

Figure 10-10:
Your Zune
software
should auto-
matically
pick up
podcasts
downloaded
in iTunes.

Juice Receiver

Juice Receiver (Juice, for short) is a much more specific application than iTunes — its only job is to download podcast feeds. What may seem like a limitation is actually a plus. By being all podcast, all the time, Juice concentrates on doing one thing very well. Case in point: Juice addresses our main beef with iTunes (which we talk about in the section "Finding podcasts in iTunes," earlier in this chapter) because it can subscribe to feeds in any format, including Windows Media Video (.wmv) or Windows Media Audio (.wma). So, for podcasts that provide a WMV feed (especially podcasts already within the acceptable specifications for your Zune), you can download those files directly and skip the whole conversion step. You end up with quicker syncs and, most likely, better-looking video on your device.

To download and install Juice, go to www.juicereceiver.com. The Juice home page has download links for various operating systems, including Windows. Click the Windows logo to start downloading the installation files. You can run those files as soon as they download or save them to your computer to run later. When you run the installation, one screen includes a choice to have Juice run at Windows startup (see Figure 10-11). Select the Add to Startup Group check box if you want Juice to check for new podcasts and download them without you having to remember to fire Juice up.

You can subscribe to new feeds in Juice (so that Juice automatically checks and downloads them) through one of two methods:

- **The Subscriptions tab:** Use the Add button to manually add feeds to the Subscriptions list (see Figure 10-12).

- **The Podcast Directory tab:** As shown in Figure 10-13, use this tab to pick from several different online directories. Unlike iTunes, Juice doesn't have a single podcast directory complete with ratings and pictures, but directories such as PodNova contain massive lists of podcasts organized into different categories.

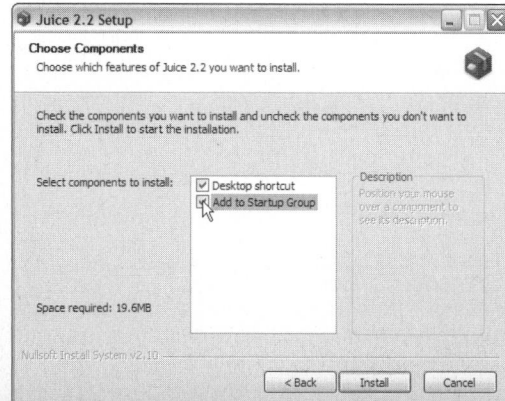

Figure 10-11: Run Juice at startup to keep your local podcast content up to date.

In the Juice software, you can change various settings through the Preferences dialog box. (Choose File⇨Preferences from the main menu to open the Preferences dialog box.) These settings include into what directory you want new podcasts downloaded, as shown in Figure 10-14. To make sure your podcasts show up in your Zune software, set the Download Podcasts into This Folder option in the Preferences dialog box to a folder location under your My Music or My Videos folder. By default, podcasts are downloaded into a My Received Podcasts folder under your My Documents folder, so you can also get your podcasts into your Zune software by adding that specific location to your Monitored Folders list.

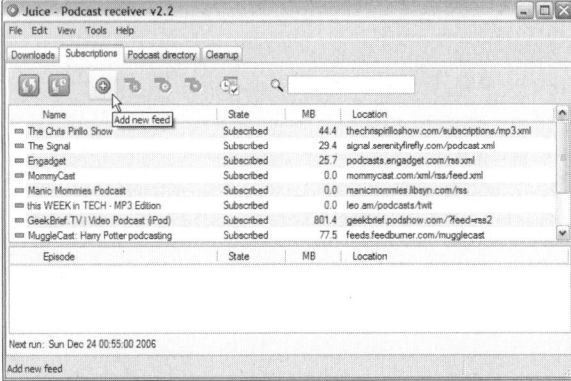

Figure 10-12:
Add a podcast's URL manually by using the Add button in Juice's Subscriptions tab.

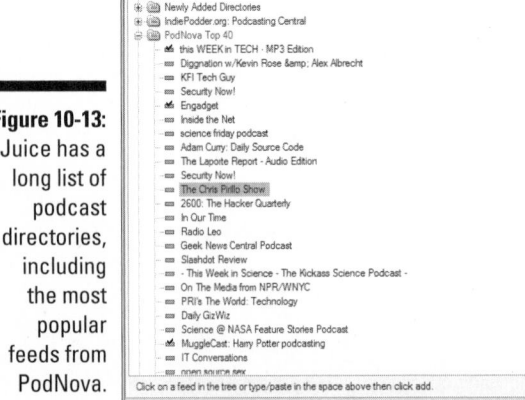

Figure 10-13:
Juice has a long list of podcast directories, including the most popular feeds from PodNova.

Juice is well integrated with Windows Media Player and can even create playlists for each podcast you subscribe to, and it also works well with your Zune!

Doppler

Doppler is a podcast client in the same style as Juice Receiver (which we talk about in the preceding section), but Doppler has some unique features. We personally find that the Doppler user interface looks more professional and has slicker graphics than Juice Receiver's, but Juice was our first podcast application and has remained the application of choice on most of our computers. Like Juice, Doppler has the ability to connect to external podcast directories, but it doesn't start out with the large directory list that Juice gives you; instead, it includes only three feed listings, and you have to add additional directories as you find them.

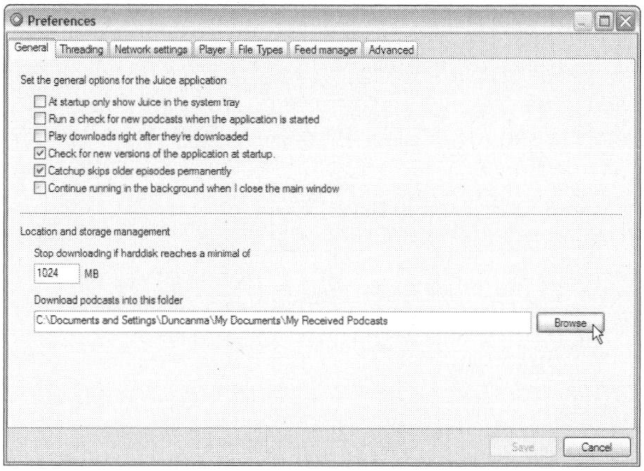

Figure 10-14: Use the Preferences dialog box to choose a folder location for your podcasts.

To install Doppler on your PC, follow these steps:

1. **Go to www.dopplerradio.net.**

   Find the Downloads heading along the right side of the page.

2. **Click the Doppler for Windows link that appears under the Downloads heading.**

   A page with a large Download Doppler link appears. Also on that page, you can find a link to download the .NET Framework, which you need on your computer to use Doppler.

3. **Click .NET 2.0 Framework Redistributable Package and follow the prompts to install the .NET Framework.**

   Although you may already have the .NET Framework installed on your PC, run the Framework installation, just to be sure. Reinstalling it won't cause any problems.

4. **After you have the .NET Framework installed, click the large Download Doppler link.**

   A File Download dialog box appears asking whether you want to open or save the Doppler installation file.

5. **Press the Open button in the dialog box.**

   A Zip file opens in WinZip (if you have that program installed) or Windows Explorer (if you don't have WinZip).

6. **Double-click the `DopplerSetup.msi` file to run the installation application.**

   During the installation, you have the option to make Doppler start up automatically when you log in to Windows (see Figure 10-15). The Juice Receiver also has this option, and it serves the same purpose in Doppler; if Doppler is running all the time, it can keep your podcast subscriptions up to date without you having to remember to run the application.

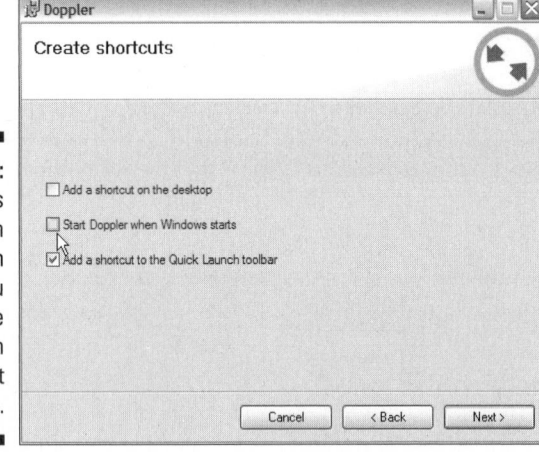

Figure 10-15: Doppler's installation program gives you the choice to run Doppler at startup.

After you install Doppler, you can launch it for the first time. As part of this first run of the application, you're prompted to pick a location for all your downloaded podcasts. Whatever location you pick, either make sure it's under an already monitored folder (such as the My Music\Podcasts folder shown in Figure 10-16) or go into your Zune software and add the download folder into the list of monitored locations. (For more on the monitored list, check out Chapter 4.) You need to pay particular attention to where you put your podcasts if you want any downloaded content automatically picked up and added to your Zune library.

To add a new feed in Doppler, follow these steps:

1. **Click the Add button near the lower-right corner of the Doppler application.**

   A dialog box (as shown in Figure 10-17) appears.

2. **Paste the URL of the podcast's RSS feed into the URL field in the dialog box.**

3. **Click Finish to add that podcast as a subscription to the Doppler application.**

Figure 10-16:
Put all your
downloaded
podcasts in
a folder your
Zune can
find, such
as your
My Music
folder.

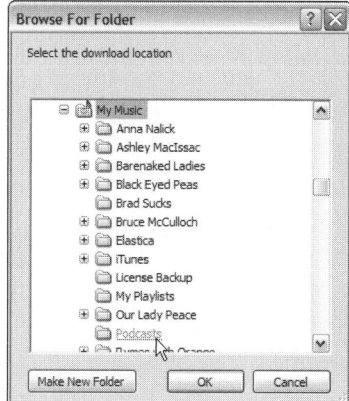

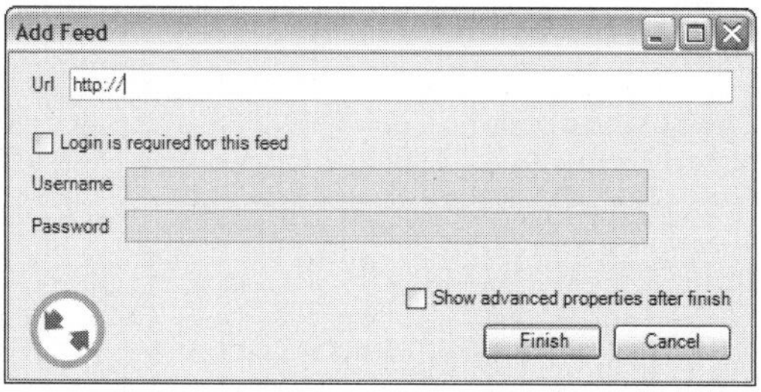

Figure 10-17:
You can
manually
add a
podcast to
Doppler
quickly and
easily if you
have the
URL of the
RSS feed.

Doppler provides basic support for podcast directories through an Import from Podcast Directory option on the File menu (see Figure 10-18). A *podcast directory* is an online catalog of available podcasts, and both Juice and Doppler allow you to find podcasts by using one or more of these catalogs. iTunes is quite different in that respect because it includes its own full-featured catalog. Choosing the Import from Podcast Directory option in Doppler lets you pick a podcast directory (by selecting one from the drop-down menu at the top of the dialog box), browse for something interesting, and then import a feed directly into Doppler without having to worry about RSS URLs or Website addresses.

A small, but very useful, feature of the Doppler application is its ability to change the Genre property of any content that it downloads. In an ideal world, all podcasts would already have "Podcast" in the Genre property, so you could very easily separate podcasts from your other music and video. But in reality, many media files leave this value blank, and those files that do add something aren't consistent in what term they use (some use Podcast, others use Podcasts, and still others use terms such as Talk or Web Radio). When you use this Genre-changing feature, all your downloaded media files end up with the same value in the Genre property, greatly simplifying your life when you try to find your podcast files in the Zune library. You can set the value that you want to use for the Genre in the Options dialog box, as you can see in Figure 10-19. Access this dialog box by clicking the Options link on the Tools menu.

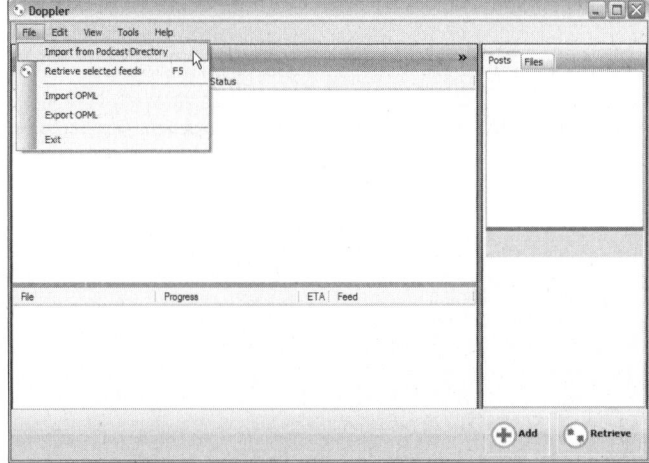

Figure 10-18: With Doppler, you can import feeds from a select group of podcast directories.

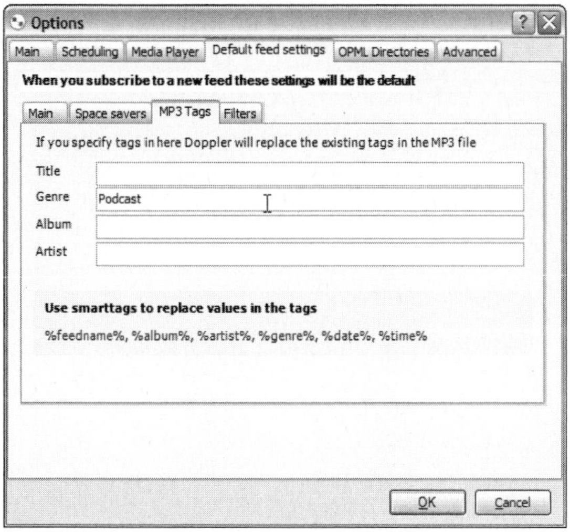

Figure 10-19:
The Options dialog box lets you assign custom tags to your feeds.

Internet Explorer 7

With Internet Explorer 7, the ability to download RSS feeds is built right into the browser. When you click a link to an RSS feed in IE7, a special view of the feed appears that includes a Subscribe to This Feed link near the top of the page (see Figure 10-20).

Clicking this link adds the feed to IE's built-in feed storage and automatically keeps that feed up to date. You can even configure IE to download any enclosures (such as audio or video files) included in a particular feed by following these steps:

1. **Right-click the feed in the feed list.**

2. **Select Properties from the menu that appears.**

    The Feed Properties dialog box appears.

3. **Check the Automatically Download Attached Files option, as shown in Figure 10-21, and click OK.**

Subscribe To This Feed link

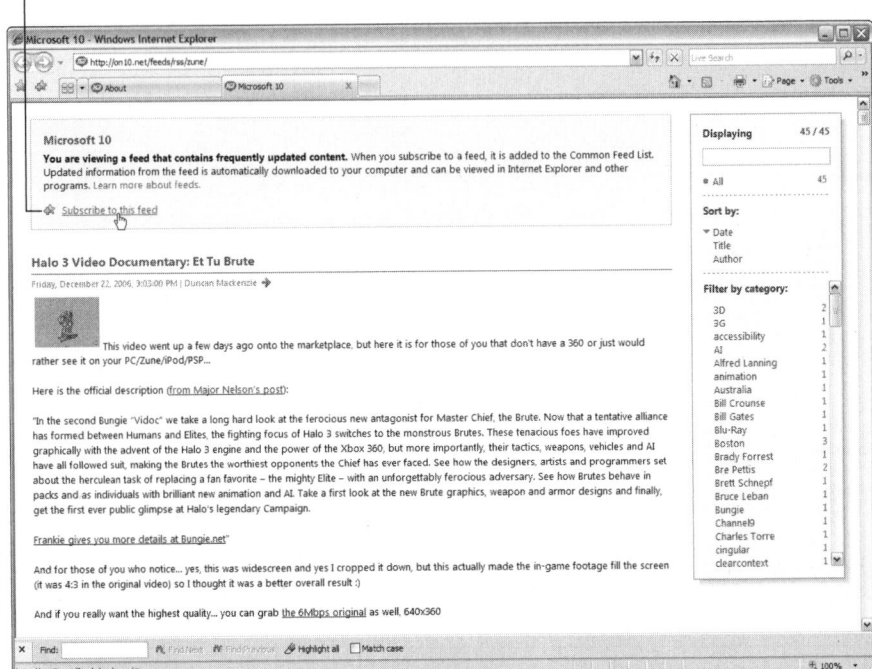

Figure 10-20: When you view a feed in IE7, a Subscribe to This Feed link appears at the top of the page.

With IE set to auto-download, any new video or audio files included in the RSS feed (also known as *enclosures*) are downloaded to your machine, ready to be added to your Zune library and synced to your device. Now, you need to find those files because they aren't downloaded to any expected location, such as your My Videos or My Music folder. Instead, they're stored in an automatically created folder under your Temporary Internet Files location. In Vista, this path is something like `C:\Users\<user name>\AppData\`
`Local\Microsoft\Windows\Temporary Internet Files\Enclosure`. In XP, you have a similar path, except that it starts with `Documents and` `Settings` rather than `Users`. In that Enclosure folder, each feed that you've set to download automatically has its own folder.

If you add the Enclosure folder as one of your monitored folders (as shown in Figure 10-22), any new podcast files are automatically picked up into the Zune's library. (For more on adding folders to your Monitored Folders list, flip back to Chapter 4.)

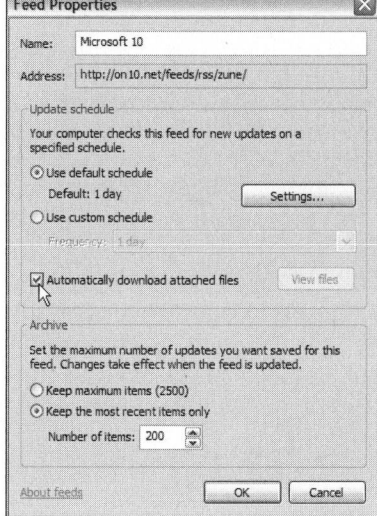

Figure 10-21:
Use the
Feed
Properties
dialog box
to configure
how often
IE7 updates
a feed and
whether it
downloads
enclosures.

Finding the Right Podcasts

You're an individual, with your own interests, opinions, and tastes . . . and
you can probably find a podcast that fits you perfectly. When the Zune
was released, the popular podcast directory Podcast Alley (www.podcast
alley.com) listed over 27,000 podcasts. To be brutally honest, the vast
majority of the podcasts out there are garbage; it's just the nature of this type
of content. So the real trick is tracking down the select few podcasts to which
you actually want to subscribe. The best tools for finding your perfect podcast are the online directories (which you can access from within Doppler or
Juice, or directly on the Web) and the podcast pages within the iTunes store.

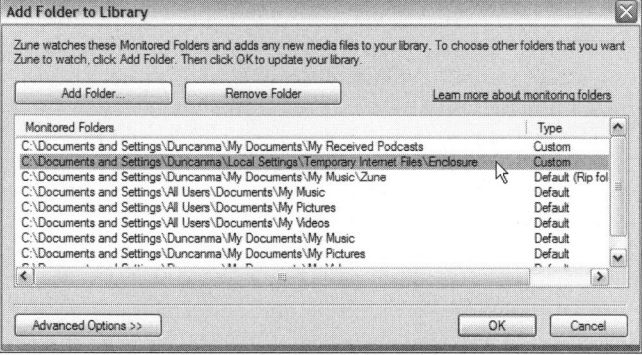

Figure 10-22:
Add the
Enclosure
folder to
your Zune
library to
pick up any
podcasts in
that folder.

Using the online directories

Many Web sites are devoted to helping you dig through the massive number of podcasts out there. Two are especially noteworthy because they're updated often and include a large number of feeds: Podcast.net and PodNova. These two sites serve the same general purpose — they're public directories of podcasts. But different people maintain them, and they may contain a slightly different catalog of feeds. In general, you can find popular feeds in both directories, but if you're looking for a complete list of feeds on any one topic, you might want to check several different directories. Here are some good starting sites:

- ✔ PodNova (www.podnova.com)
- ✔ Podcast.net (www.podcast.net)
- ✔ Podcast Alley (www.podcastalley.com)
- ✔ PodShow.com (www.podshow.com)

Using the iTunes Store

Our personal favorite way to discover new podcasts is through iTunes because it allows you to browse through different categories, includes descriptions of all of the podcasts in the directory, and it even has pictures! The key to finding great podcasts through iTunes is to find the editorialized lists (Editor's Picks, People's Choice) and the dynamic lists (such as the Top Podcasts list, shown in Figure 10-23). Unlike the podcast directories we mention in the section "Choosing Podcast Software," earlier in this chapter, iTunes is run by full-time employees of a large company (Apple), so it usually has high-quality editorial picks. iTunes also gets a lot more traffic than any other podcast directory, so the dynamic lists that show podcasts by traffic give you a really accurate source of information.

iTunes has another great feature for finding new podcasts — the Listeners Also Subscribed To section. When you click an individual podcast, the iTunes home page for that podcast opens. The podcast page includes a link to the podcast's Web site, a description of the podcast, a listing of episodes, and the useful Listeners Also Subscribed To section, which lists related podcasts that you might enjoy. Figure 10-24 shows the home page for a grammar podcast, and the Listeners Also Subscribed To area shows links to a variety of other podcasts, including one on manners!

Remember to check the Web site of a promising podcast to see if it has a WMA or WMV feed that you can subscribe to by using Juice Receiver, Doppler, or IE7. If the podcast comes in only QuickTime formats, such as .mov and .mp4, you might as well subscribe from within iTunes because iTunes can download your feeds as well as any other program.

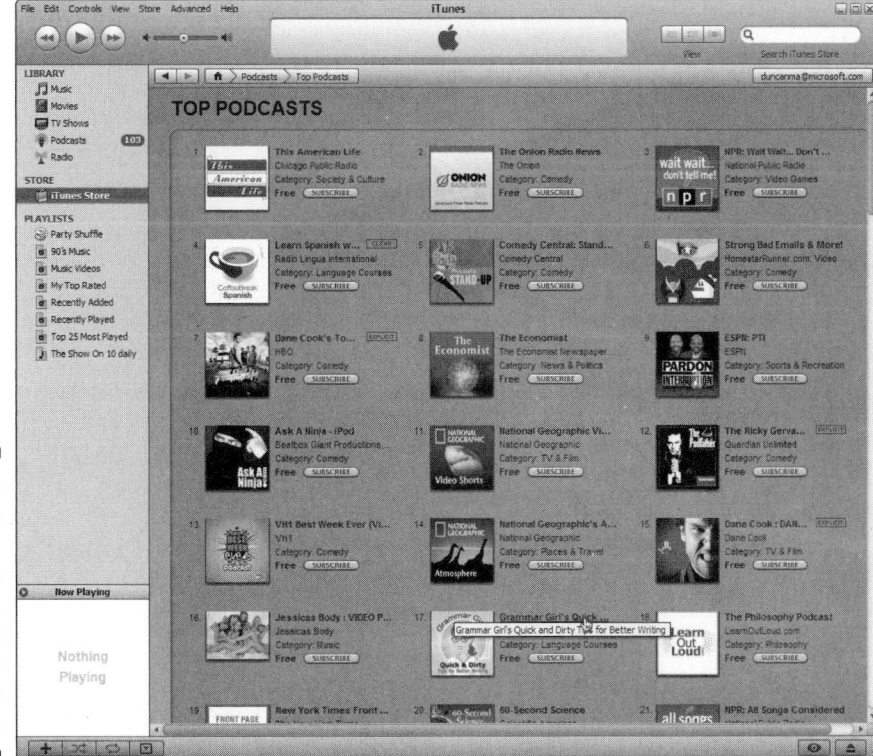

Figure 10-23: Dynamic pages, such as Top Podcasts, can help you find the latest and greatest.

The world of Web video

In 2006, Time Magazine's Person of the Year was You, their way of recognizing the massive amount of content and discussion being published to the Internet by individuals rather than traditional broadcasters. One trend that has sprung up over the past few years is the enormous increase in the amount of video being published online, with 65,000 new videos being posted every single day to just one video site alone (YouTube, which is probably the most popular of them all). In addition to YouTube, you can find several other large video sites online, including Google Video, Soapbox (from Microsoft), and iFilm.com, as well as many small video sites. Currently, the bulk of online video is displayed using a video format based on Adobe's Flash technology, which means that the videos can play in nearly any browser on nearly any type of computer.

None of these video sites offer the ability to download any of their content, though. You can't download from YouTube, Soapbox, and the other major sites for two reasons:

- ✔ **Commercial:** The podcast sites want everyone to watch their videos on their sites, not pass those videos around via e-mail or carry them around on their Zunes.

- ✔ **Legal:** These major sites have policies in place to remove content if it's infringing on a copyright or is in some way offensive. These policies are very important to these sites from a legal point of view, and they hinge on the site being able to control people's ability to watch a video. If a million people can easily download a video, the site can't really remove the video from everyone's computers, Zunes, and so on if they find out the video is inappropriate in some way.

So if you want to use your Zune to watch the latest hilarious video of some guy riding a bike into a lake (don't worry, you can also find other videos), you don't have any official way to do it. You can use one of many unofficial ways, all of which work by copying an `.flv` file onto your local machine. An `.flv` file is a standard Flash video that you can then convert into a format that will work with your Zune. Unfortunately, conversion isn't always easy, and most of the tools that can consistently handle the task end up costing you money. We can't really recommend any of these commercial tools, mostly because it's impossible to guarantee they'll be able to handle all of the `.flv` files that you're likely to see. Instead, we suggest you visit `www.ripzor.com`, a site that handles downloading `.flv`-format videos from YouTube, iFilm, and Google Video. (They don't handle Soapbox at the time this book was printed.) On the Ripzor site, you can find links to `.flv` conversion tools that you might want to give a try (they're free, after all!). This site appears to be well maintained, so as the `.flv` conversion world changes over time, their content will probably be updated, as well.

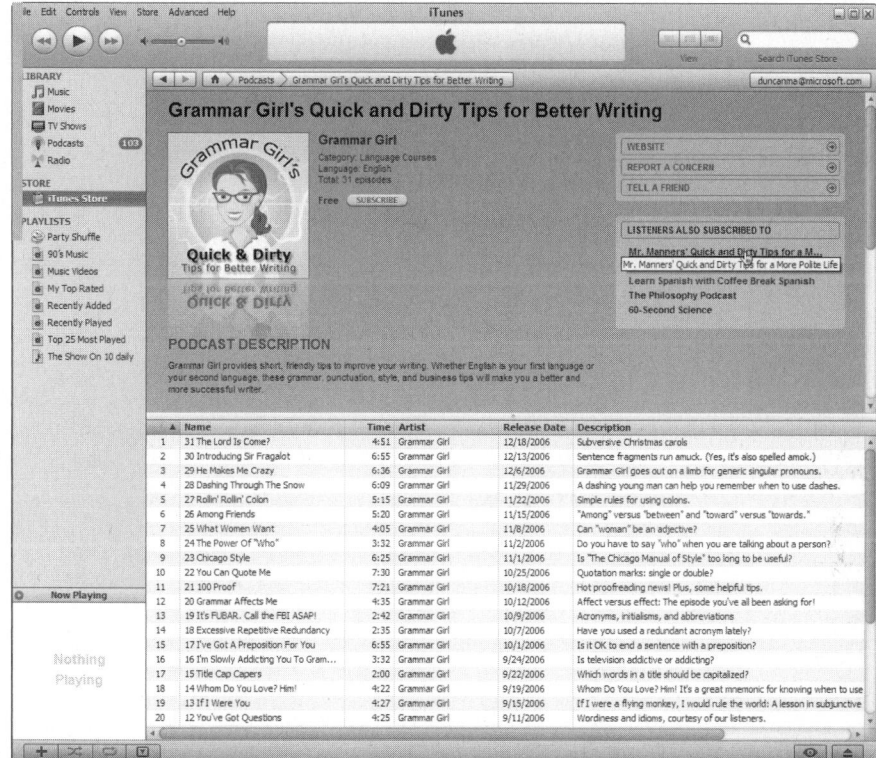

Figure 10-24:
From a
podcast's
home page,
you can find
links to
other
related
podcasts.

Recommended podcasts

We don't know enough about you to be able to pick out the perfect podcasts, but this section includes a list of popular ones that might be worth checking out. At the very least, they can give you some sample content for your Zune! See if any of these podcasts tickle your fancy:

- ✓ **Geek Brief TV (`www.geekbrief.tv`):** Funny, timely, and brief news about gadgets and other technology topics.

- ✓ **MuggleCast (`www.mugglenet.com/mugglecast`):** For Harry Potter fans, this podcast is a must-listen. MuggleCast has been consistently one of the most popular podcasts on iTunes for a long time now.

- ✔ **Major Nelson's Podcast (`www.majornelson.com`):** If you're a fan of Xbox 360 and Xbox Live, this is a perfect podcast for you. Major Nelson is the gamertag of Larry Hryb, the Director of Xbox Live at Microsoft and an all-around gaming celebrity.

- ✔ **The Signal (`http://signal.serenityfirefly.com`):** This podcast is all about the TV show *Firefly* and the movie that followed after, *Serenity*. It's a very popular podcast considering the series isn't even on the air anymore!

- ✔ **National Geographic's Podcasts (`www.nationalgeographic.com/podcasts`):** This great magazine has 13 free video podcasts. Topics range from great nature videos to the latest in world music, and they have a great news video podcast covering the latest in nature- and science-related information. Check out the Video Shorts podcast for five-minute clips with great titles such as "Octopus vs. Shark."

- ✔ **Microsoft's Channel 10 (`http://on10.net`):** Okay, so we're biased . . . building this Web site is Duncan's day job. This site covers technology, gadgets, and gaming, with a bunch of videos each week, and you can get every video in a Zune-optimized format.

And you can find many more podcasts on nearly any topic you can imagine!

Exploring the World of Podcasts on Your Own

This chapter gives you a good start into using your Zune for listening to podcasts, but the real task lies ahead of you — tracking down those podcasts that are worth listening to. Start with some of the suggested podcasts listed in the preceding section, and then start adding and removing podcasts as you figure out which ones you like and which ones you aren't that into. Eventually, you'll have a core set of podcasts that you listen to all the time, and you may have some others from which you download only the occasional episode. If you have the time, though, keep an eye out for other podcasts that you might like. You never know what content is going to make its way to the Web!

Part III
Enjoying Your Content

The 5th Wave
By Rich Tennant

"Why can't you just bring your Zune like everyone else?"

In this part . . .

This part is all about using your content after you get it into digital form. Listening to music, watching videos, and showing off photos — your options truly open up after you go digital.

Chapter 11 covers how you can use your Zune at home, hooked up to your stereo or your TV, including some of the accessories that make it easier to get the most out of your device. Chapter 12 dives into how you can organize video on your device (and on your PC) and how the video playback controls work.

For those of you with an Xbox 360 in the house, Chapter 13 is required reading. With the Zune software, Windows Media Player and maybe Media Center (all available on your PC), you can get your content from your PC to your Xbox 360 in a ton of ways. You can even hook your Zune up to the Xbox 360 directly, and Chapter 13 covers how.

Chapters 14 and 15 are for the Zune user who's always on the move. Chapter 14 covers using the Zune in your car, letting you ditch those CD carrying cases and start carrying around 30GB of your favorite music in a much slicker package. Chapter 15 talks about using your Zune when traveling and when you're at your second home, the office.

Finally, Chapter 16 digs into the online community that exists around the Zune — *the* place to go when you want to get the latest news or discuss the Zune with fellow Zune enthusiasts.

Chapter 11

Using Your Zune at Home

Digital music systems allow you unparalleled access to your music. The Zune is no exception. You can put your Zune in your pocket and stroll around the house with it easily enough, but if you have a $1,000 entertainment system sitting in the corner, you could do a bit better than just cranking the tunes through your Zune earbuds.

In this chapter, we explore options for enjoying your Zune content in new and exciting ways. We tell you about hooking your Zune to your sound system, you can find out about some devices that connect to the Zune directly, and we even suggest some inexpensive home-brew options for playing your Zune music at home.

Getting Your Zune Music Anywhere You Want to Be

You have a few different choices for playing your music at home. Take a look at the options before we get into the details:

✔ **The cable route:** With the help of a simple cable, plug some speakers into the headphone jack of your Zune device. You can also use a cable to connect your Zune directly to the stereo receiver of your home sound system.

✔ **The docking route:** Plug the port at the base of your Zune device into a dock of some kind (the Zune dock, for example) and then use some audio cables to connect the dock to the auxiliary inputs in the back of your stereo.

✔ **The Xbox 360 route:** You can share your Zune music collection through your PC and then access your content from your Xbox 360. Read Chapter 13 for the complete details on how to do this.

✔ **The dedicated Zune speaker system route:** A dedicated Zune speaker system is designed specifically to play your Zune tunes. You plug your Zune into one of these systems the same way you plug your Zune into a standard docking device.

All these solutions have their own pros and cons. The solution that you choose most likely depends on your budget and your willingness to spend time wiring all this stuff together. The good news is that you can get something simple set up pretty easily, and you can get even the more complex systems hooked up correctly without too much trouble!

Connecting directly to speakers and sound systems

The first (and probably easiest) way to connect your Zune to a sound system is to take advantage of the Zune headphone jack — the same jack you use when you're using your earbuds. You can either plug in a set of powered speakers or hitch up your Zune to a full-blown entertainment system with what's known as a *Y-cable* — a cable with an ⅛-inch stereo plug at one end and two RCA phono plugs at the other — going from the headphone jack on your Zune to a set of auxiliary inputs at the back of your stereo receiver.

Imagine that you have a nice set of powered PC speakers sitting in the basement, and you want to wire up a little sound system that you can use when you're working on the car in the garage. This speaker hookup is a pretty easy project. Here's what you need:

✔ **Speakers:** You need a working set of *powered* speakers — they either have to be battery driven or have a power cord you plug in somewhere. The speakers need to be powered because headphone jacks have limited output power. You can't turn a Zune up loud enough in most cases to get a satisfactory sound.

✔ **An ⅛-inch mini plug:** The speakers that you're setting up need to have a cord with a standard ⅛-inch mini plug, like the one you'd plug into the PC at the speaker output. This plug goes into the Zune headphone jack at the top of the device.

✔ **A Zune, of course!** Don't stay home without it!

To get all these electronics put together, follow these steps:

1. **Set up the speakers in the location you want them in your shop.**

   Make sure that you can easily get to the cable with the mini plug.

2. **Plug the speakers' power cord into the power source.**

   If your speakers use batteries, make sure they're fully charged and inserted correctly.

3. **Plug the mini-plug end of the speaker cable into the Zune.**

4. **Use your Zune normally.**

   The music comes through the speakers.

You may have to adjust the volume on the speakers to get the levels just right. After you do that, you can easily enjoy your favorite music right in the comfort of your garage. Of course, this trick works in any room in the house.

One downside of using the Zune headphone jack to play music is that the Zune doesn't charge while the music plays. (Okay, it doesn't charge if you use earbuds either, but at least you get to walk around and see the sights while you drain your battery.) Just keep in mind that you can power your Zune with the Zune AC adapter if you want.

Playing music through a dedicated speaker system

Two third-party dedicated speaker systems were on the market when we were writing this book — the VAF Octavio 1 and the Altec Lansing M604.

VAF Octavio 1

VAF Research is an Australian company that creates high-end speakers and audio components. The VAF Octavio 1 is one of the first licensed accessories for the Zune and features a Zune cradle for docking your Zune, charging it, and playing back Zune content.

The Octavio 1 features the following components:

✔ **Customizable colors:** The Octavio has three interchangeable skins that let you choose the look that fits your décor.

✔ **100-watt amplifier:** Enough power to fill a pretty big room with sound.

✔ **200mm bass diaphragm:** This feature provides for a deep, rich sound.

✔ **Two 130mm woofers:** All that power has to go somewhere and this is where most of it is directed.

✔ **Digital equalization:** One of those things that gives you really good sound balance.

✔ **Full-featured remote control:** This allows you to control the Zune from across the room.

✔ **Audio and video out:** This feature lets you connect the Octavio to your television and to your home stereo system.

Altec Lansing M604

The Altec Lansing M604 is another great home audio solution for the Zune. This speaker system features a Zune cradle and a slim profile that makes it great for small spaces in your house.

With the M604, you can charge your Zune and even use it as a dock by connecting it to a nearby PC. Other features of the M604 include

✔ **Video pass-through:** This allows you to play your Zune content through a television.

✔ **Alternate audio source:** Have a non-Zune MP3 player? The M604 lets you set any MP3 player you have in a built-in tray and connect it through an audio output cable to play content from that player.

✔ **Volume control:** This is on the device and via the remote control that comes with the M604.

✔ **Treble and base control:** This is right on top of the M604.

✔ **Wall mountable design:** This feature lets you hook the M604 to a wall to save space in your house and give you something cool to look at.

✔ **Headphone jack:** Lets you switch seamlessly between the speakers on the M604 and your own set of headphones. (Great when everyone else in the family is going to bed!)

Docking system basics

The Zune Home A/V Pack features all the pieces you need to play audio and video from your Zune through your television or your home entertainment system. The Zune Home A/V Pack includes the following components:

✔ **Zune dock:** The Zune dock has a Zune connector in its base, just waiting for a Zune to come around and plug itself in. Although you can use the dock to hold the Zune during synchronization and playback — it has connectors in the back of the dock so you can plug in the necessary sync cable from a PC, as well as connect the Zune AC power adapter — we're interested right now in the handy jack in the back, which allows for the delivery (via cables) of audio and video to a television or home entertainment system.

✔ **Zune AC power adapter:** The Zune AC power adapter provides power to the Zune through the Zune sync cable. You can connect the sync cable directly to the Zune or you can plug it into the Zune dock.

✔ **Zune sync cable:** You can use the Zune sync cable to synchronize the Zune with a PC. When the Zune is synchronized with a PC, the USB power from the PC charges the Zune battery. You can also use the Zune sync cable to power the Zune directly from the Zune AC power adapter.

✔ **Zune A/V cable:** You can use the Zune A/V cable to route audio and video signals from the Zune to a television or powered speaker system. It has a special mini jack at one end that takes the signals from the headphone jack on the Zune and splits the signals into three parts: audio left, audio right, and video. The audio and video are sent through standard RCA jacks that plug into most newer televisions and stereos.

✔ **Zune remote control:** You can use the Zune remote control to make your Zune do Zuney things when it's in the Zune dock. Although you can use the Zune controls while the Zune is in the dock, the remote makes controlling your docked Zune much easier. (Pushing the buttons of a docked Zune can be quite difficult.)

Each of the pieces in the Zune Home A/V Pack is designed for you to use either as part of a system where all the A/V Pack components plug together or as stand-alone accessories. (In fact, most of these items are sold separately, if you want to create a custom setup.)

Getting your docks in a row

In this section, we tell you how to use your Zune A/V cable to connect your Zune-and-dock combo to a home entertainment system or a television. (Okay, technically, you can plug the A/V cable right into the headphone jack of your Zune, but we like the stylish flair a dock can provide for your Zune.) A more practical reason to use the dock though, is that it lets you play music and video all day without having to worry about charging the batteries. Your Zune is ready to go on the road in an instant, fully charged and you can enjoy it all day long.

Now, the Zune A/V cable has a little ⅛-inch mini plug for the Zune end of the cable and RCA jacks (as they're called in the trade) for the TV or home audio system end. To connect your Zune using this cable, you need to have open RCA jacks on the back (or the front) of the system you want to connect to.

To connect the Zune dock to a television or home entertainment system, follow these steps:

1. **Place your Zune dock somewhere within a few feet of the entertainment system to which you want to connect.**

2. **Plug the ⅛-inch mini-plug end of the Zune A/V cable into the back the Zune dock.**

   Again, you can plug the mini plug directly into the headphone jack if you want.

3. **Plug the RCA plugs at the other end of the A/V cable into the RCA jacks that you want to use on your system.**

   Your system should have two or three jacks to plug into, depending on what kind of system you're using. If you're plugging into a TV, be sure to plug the white end of the Zune A/V cable into a white jack, the red end into a red jack, and the yellow end into a yellow jack. Here's a breakdown of what each colored connection does:

   • **White:** The white end carries the left audio signal.

   • **Red:** The right audio signal comes through the red end.

   • **Yellow:** The yellow end of the Zune A/V cable is the composite video out, so you use that end if you're connecting to a television or a system that has a television connected to it.

4. **Dock your Zune and test the audio connection and settings.**

   Test your system by changing the audio/video input selected on your system to the one to which you connected the Zune A/V cable. Use the controls on the Zune to navigate to a song and play it.

If you're having trouble hearing the audio, remember that you need to turn up the volume on both the Zune and the audio system (or television) to which you're connecting. If the volume on either one of the devices is set to zero, you won't hear anything coming out of your system.

Connecting the power

If you want to keep your Zune connected to your home A/V system for any length of time — whether you're using a generic Y-cable or a Zune A/V cable to do the job — it's a good idea to keep your Zune device plugged in and charging. The Zune charges through the Zune sync cable connected to the port at the bottom of the Zune (or on the back of the Zune dock). Now, you can connect the sync cable in a couple of ways:

- ✔ **To your PC:** You can connect the sync cable directly to a USB port on your PC and let it get its juice that way. But not everybody has their PC right next to their home entertainment center.

- ✔ **To the AC power adapter:** If you're one of those people who believes a computer's place is in the home office and the TV's place is in the family room — and never the twain shall meet — you should plug your Zune sync cable into the Zune AC power adapter and then plug that into a standard wall outlet. Your Zune will have no trouble getting its juice that way.

If you want to pump music to your TV or home entertainment system from your Zune (through the dock) while the Zune is connected to the PC, you need to close the Zune application on your PC.

Using the Zune remote control

Trust us, if you're using the Zune dock, you can control your Zune much more easily with the Zune wireless remote control than with the manual controls. (The Zune on its own is an ergonomic marvel — but start adding cables and a dock, and you end up with quite a handful.)

Keep in mind that the wireless remote control operates like most other remotes out there. It communicates with the Zune through the Zune dock via infrared signals — meaning that you have to have a direct line of sight to the dock when you're using the remote. Oh, and it also helps if you point the remote at the dock while you use it.

Using the wireless remote is pretty straightforward, although the buttons don't map exactly with the Zune device itself. The following list fills you in on what each button does:

- ✔ **Previous/Next buttons:** These buttons let you move from one song to another on the Zune.

- ✔ **Control pad:** The control pad works the same way as the control pad on your Zune device. You can navigate the menus using up, down, left, and right on the pad and you can click in the center to execute a menu item.

✔ **Volume Up/Down:** This control changes the volume of the Zune.

✔ **Back and Play/Pause:** These two buttons work like the buttons on the left and right of the control pad on the Zune device.

You use the Zune wireless remote with the Zune by docking the Zune device and then pressing the buttons on the remote. If the Zune is off, pressing OK on the remote automatically wakes the Zune.

Because the Zune wireless remote has a few more buttons than the device itself, take a few minutes to get familiar with the remote when you first try it out.

Playing content through your TV

If you connect the Zune to a TV, you can control the Zune menus and watch videos through the TV. To get your Zune's display on your TV, however, you first need to set the display option on the Zune so that the video image goes to your TV screen, rather than the screen on your Zune device.

To set the Zune to play video through the Zune A/V cable out to your TV (either via the dock or directly through the Zune), follow these steps:

1. **Plug your Zune into the dock.**

   If your not bothering with a dock, you can skip this step.

2. **Using your Zune A/V cable, connect your dock (or Zune) to the Video In jacks on your TV.**

   Most newer TV models put the Video In jacks right on the front of the TV, but your model may have stuck them in the back.

3. **Make sure your TV is set to the right input source.**

   Depending on your setup, this could be labeled LINE1, LINE2, AUX, or some similarly-named input source. Check your TV operating guide if you're not sure how to set your TV's input source.

4. **Using your Zune's control pad, navigate to Settings and then click Display.**

   The Display window appears onscreen.

5. **In the Display window, make sure the TV System setting shows your local signal type.**

In general, you shouldn't need to change this setting unless you travel to another country. In North America, this setting should be NTSC. Almost anywhere else in the world, the setting should be PAL.

6. **In the Zune Display window, toggle the TV Out setting to On.**

   At this point, the Zune screen should darken and the video menus from the Zune should show up on your television. You can control the menus on the TV by pointing the Zune wireless remote at the Zune dock. The screen displays horizontally for both the menus and for the video output.

To switch off the TV output, you have two options:

✔ Navigate to Settings, choose Display, and toggle the TV Out setting to Off.

✔ Turn off the Zune and turn it back on.

Other Zune home audio accessories

We think the Zune A/V Pack is a great deal, but it's not the only game in town when it comes to things audio/visual. Be sure to check out the following third-party accessories — one of them may be just the thing for your Zune home entertainment pleasure:

✔ **Incipio Home A/V Cable (www.incipio direct.com):** The Incipio Home A/V Cable features both audio and video output through RCA jacks that connect through the headphone jack at the top of the Zune. The unique feature of the Incipio is the retractor in the middle of the cable that lets you easily set the cable to whatever length you need to play your content through your TV or home audio system. (Search for "AV Connection Kit" from the main Incipio Web page to get to the product page.)

✔ **Monster StereoLink (www.monster cable.com):** Monster has a reputation for creating some of the best component cables you can buy for any home entertainment system. The Monster StereoLink for the Zune is no exception. This beautiful cable makes connecting your Zune to an audio component a snap. As with all the Monster cables, this one has a substantial, quality feel to it.

✔ **Monster TVLink (www.monstercable. com):** The Monster TVLink has the same great quality connectors as the Monster StereoLink, but this cable adds an RCA output jack for video, making it possible to watch your Zune content on a television.

Chapter 12

Watching Video on the Zune

*T*he Zune has a large, bright video screen, and you can hook up your Zune to your TV in a snap, so you're not going to use your Zune just to listen to music, are you? Back in Chapter 5, we talk about all the various ways you can get video onto your computer and then onto your Zune. In Chapter 9, we cover how you can make your own videos. And (as an added bonus) in Chapter 11, we show you how you can hook up your Zune to your TV. If you check out those chapters, you should have a lot of sources lined up for getting video onto your computer for syncing to your Zune.

This chapter talks about finding and watching that content. Along the way, you can find out about the metadata stored with your videos and how that metadata affects the video experience on the Zune. Hooking your Zune up to your TV works really well for watching video, of course; check out Chapter 11 for details on how to get that connection set up and working.

Finding Videos by Using the Zune Software

If you're at all like us, you have tons more video clips on your PC than you want to carry around on your Zune, so your first task (should you choose to accept it) is to organize the clips on your PC and set aside the ones you want to transfer to your Zune. Luckily for you, your Zune desktop software is just the program you need for the job.

Within the Zune software itself, you're generally in one of three modes; you're either looking at pictures, music, or videos. So you need to switch over to the Video mode (if you're not already in it) by clicking on the Video icon in the upper-left corner of the main window (see Figure 12-1).

Video icon

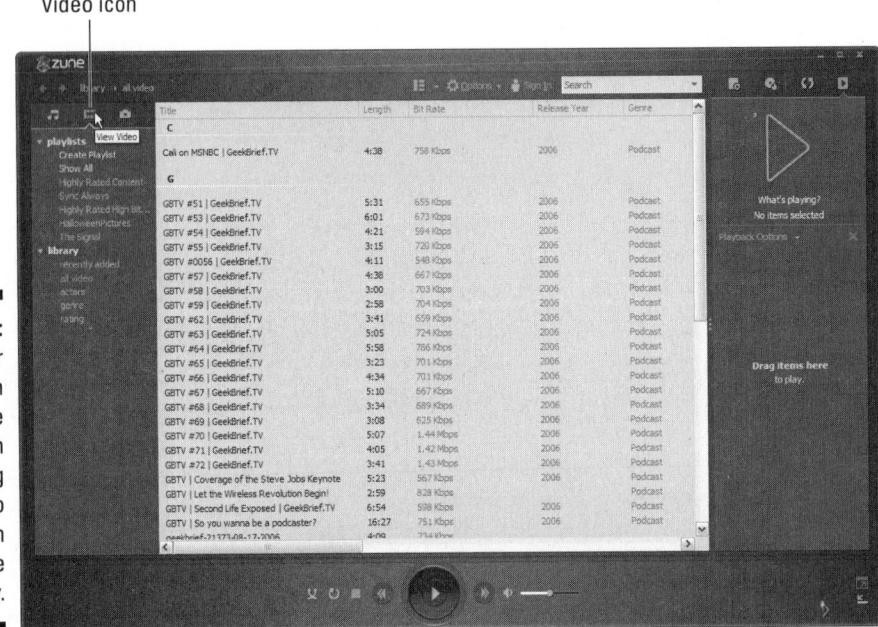

Figure 12-1:
Set your sights on Video mode when browsing video content in your Zune library.

The Zune software on your PC maintains its own library of videos, and that software adds videos to its library whenever it finds them in one of your monitored folders. If you want to add videos that aren't in a monitored folder, you can either drag them into the library manually or add more folders to the list of monitored locations. Check out Chapter 5 for more details on getting all of your videos into the Zune software on your PC.

Browsing for videos

After you switch to Video mode in the Zune desktop program (see the preceding section for more on that), a set of browsing options appears listed under the Library heading in the left navigation menu. Okay, the options aren't that extensive, but they *do* let you pick from a few predefined views. Three of these views allow you to group your videos by one of three fields — Genre (Comedy, Drama, Podcast, and so on), Actor, or Rating (the star value you give your content). Videos that aren't from a professional source often don't have information associated with them, so you have to enter in values for Genre and/or Actor yourself. Rating is a value that you have to pick for all of your videos because it reflects your personal opinion of that video. The other two options are the always-popular Recently Added view and All Videos view. We personally find the Recently Added option (see Figure 12-2) to be the most useful choice in the list because often either we want to know what's been automatically downloaded since we last synchronized (podcasts, for example), or we want to find a video that we manually added to the machine (possibly as recently as a few minutes before).

What falls into the Recently Added category depends on when Zune found the video, not the date of the file.

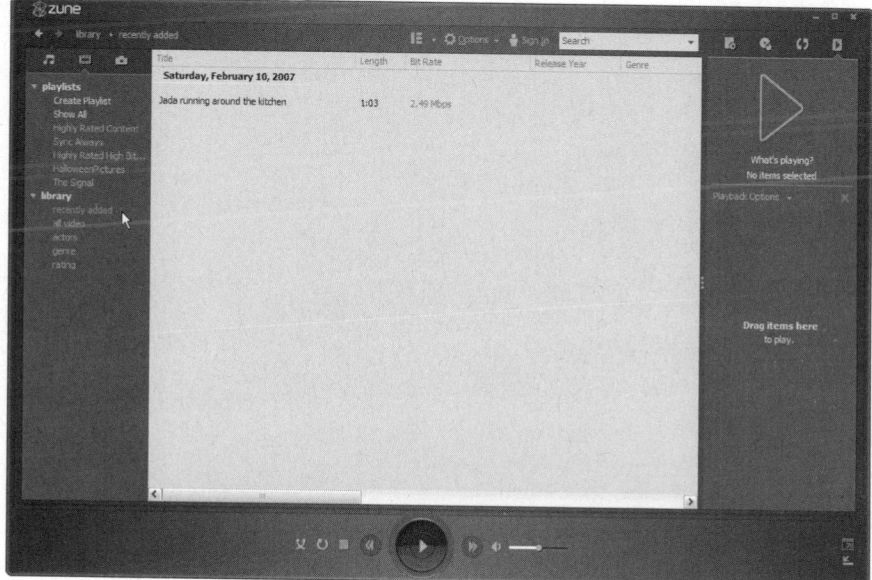

Figure 12-2:
Using the
Recently
Added
category.

In the case of the very recent additions, the Zune software usually picks them up pretty quickly, but not always. We can't even promise it'll pick up your new videos eventually because we've never had the patience to wait. When we add a video to a monitored folder, then check the Zune library and can't find it, we force Zune to find it. You can wait, if you have more patience than us, or you can do what we do by following these steps:

1. **Right-click the Library heading in the Navigation pane (on the left of the software display).**

2. **Select Add Folder to Library from the menu that appears.**

3. Click OK in the dialog box that appears.

These steps don't actually add a folder to your Monitored Folders list, but if you follow them, you force a scan of the monitored folders for new content (see Figure 12-3).

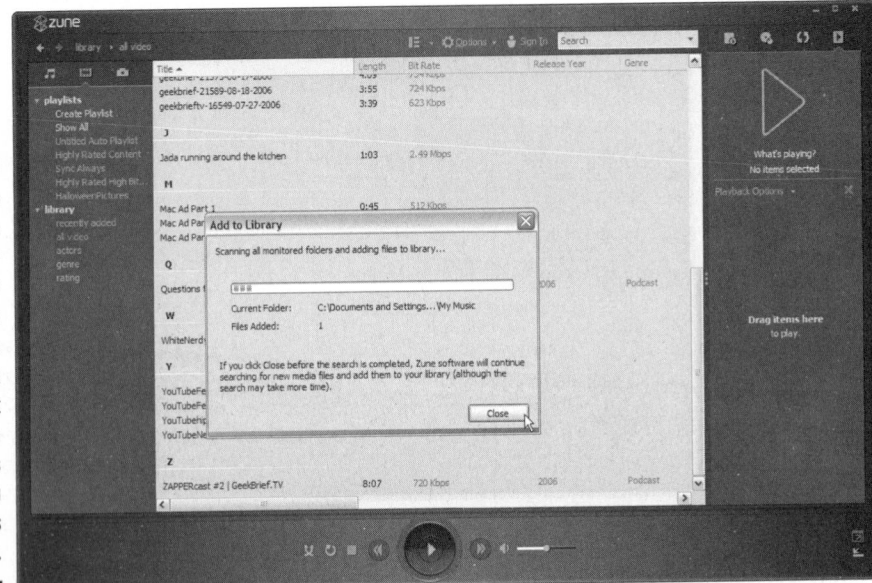

Figure 12-3:
Closing the
Add Folder
to Library
dialog box
makes this
dialog box
appear, but
the scan
continues
even if you
close this
dialog box.

If a video still doesn't show up, even after a full scan, an error in the video file (such as corruption in the file, insufficient security permission, or a video format that the Zune doesn't understand) might be preventing the Zune software from using that video. Try double-clicking the video file to play it in your Zune application or try dragging it into the Library window (into any library view, such as the view of songs by album) manually. If it still fails to play, the Zune software displays an error message that might help you figure out what's wrong with the file.

The other main view that you may find useful is the All Videos view, which is just a list of every video in your Library. By default, this list is sorted alphabetically (with headings for each letter, as shown in Figure 12-4), but you can change the sort order by clicking on the appropriate column name (see Figure 12-5). Click a column name to sort in ascending order (lowest to highest), click again to switch to descending order (highest to lowest), and click a third time to turn off sorting by that column, returning you to the default sort.

Title column in alphabetical order

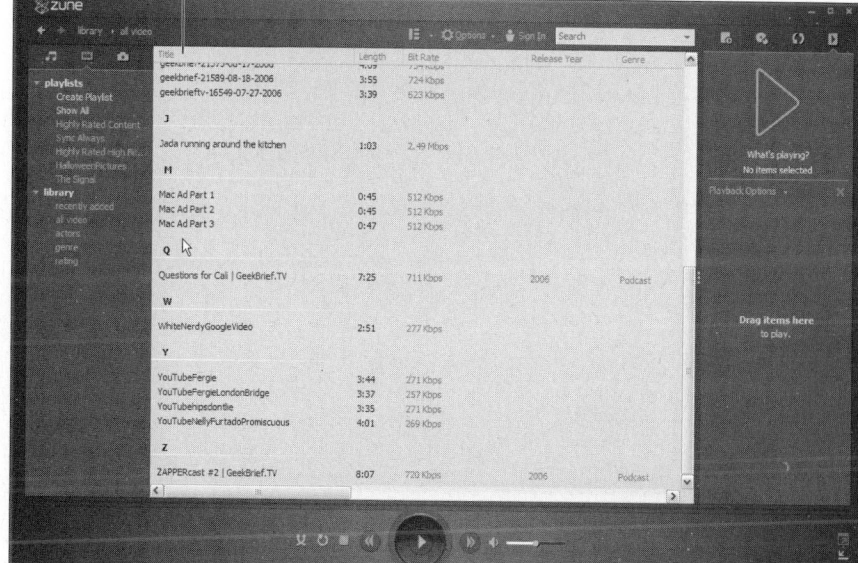

Figure 12-4:
The All Videos view sorts your videos alphabetically by default.

Switching to descending alphabetical order

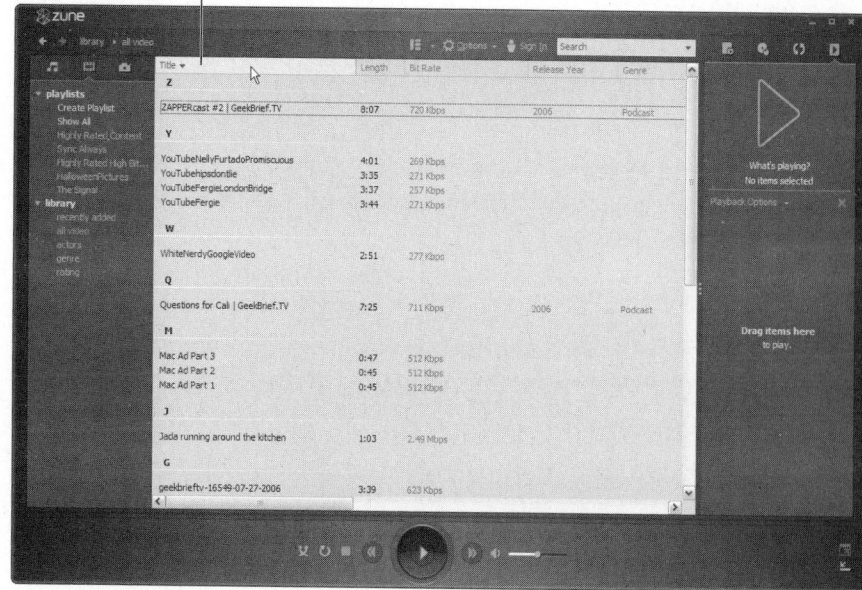

Figure 12-5:
Clicking on a column header lets you switch between sorting ascending, sorting descending, or not sorting by that column at all.

This ability to sort your All Videos list is quite powerful because you can add and remove columns as desired. Say you want to sort clips by Director, Date Added, or some other (nondefault) criteria. No problem. Just follow these steps:

1. **Right-click any column heading and pick Choose Columns from the menu that appears, as shown in Figure 12-6.**

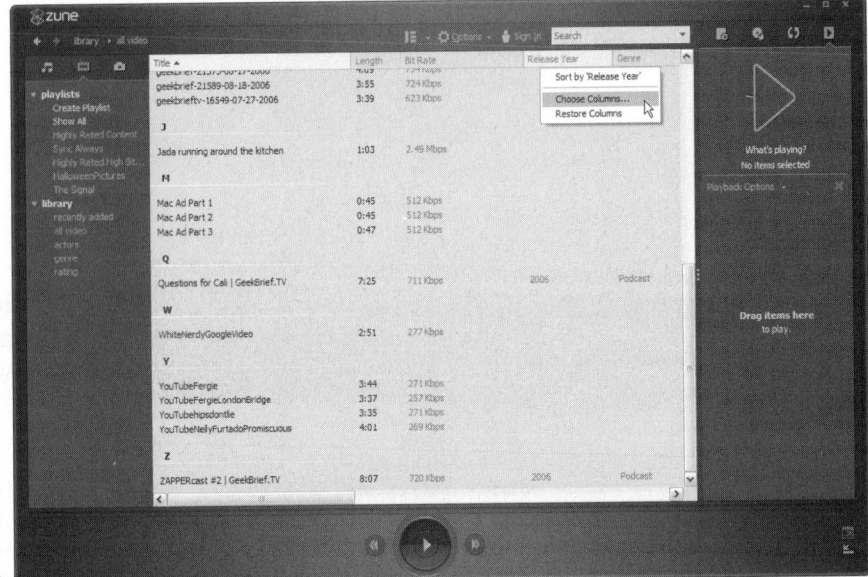

Figure 12-6: Right-click a column heading to access the Choose Columns option.

The Choose Columns dialog box appears, as shown in Figure 12-7.

2. **Select the check boxes associated with the columns that you want displayed.**

You have quite a lot to choose from here. Just keep in mind that the more columns you add, the skinnier each one will be in the final display.

3. **Use the Move Up and Move Down buttons to arrange the order of the columns you choose to display in Step 2, then click OK.**

The new settings are saved, and the dialog box closes.

The Zune software saves your current set of columns and their order when you close and reopen the software, but it always resets the sort order to alphabetical (by title) every time you go back into the software. In fact, the software resets the sort order if you just click to a different view (Recently Added, for example) and then return to the All Video view.

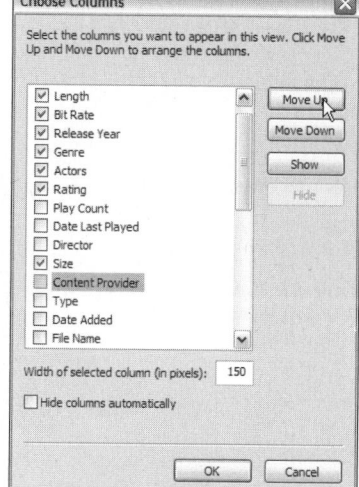

Figure 12-7:
In the
Choose
Columns
dialog box,
you can
show, hide,
and reorder
columns.

If you want to return your column settings to the initial configuration, right-click a column header and select Restore Columns from the menu that appears.

Creating auto playlists

Standard playlists are great because they let you create, in essence, a customized view of your video library. You get to handpick what you want to see based on your mood of the moment. But you do have to handpick them — meaning you have to find the videos you want and manually drag them to a playlist you've created. Auto playlists take the drudgery out of playlist creation because the Zune software dynamically generates playlists based on search criteria you provide. You decide what you're looking for, and the Zune software scours the library for just that content. (Please note, though, that auto playlists are limited to just one kind of content; you have to stick to just music, just pictures, or just video — you can't mix and match.)

You can open the New Auto Playlist dialog box, your go-to place for creating auto playlists, by following these steps:

1. **Right-click the Playlist option in the Navigation pane.**

2. **Select Create Auto Playlist from the menu that appears.**

   The New Auto Playlist dialog box appears, ready and willing to help you create new playlists.

You can add criteria (by clicking the plus sign) to three different areas in the New Auto Playlist dialog box, marked areas 1 through 3 in Figure 12-8:

- **Area 1:** Content that gets included if (and only if) it meets all the criteria you set for the area.

- **Area 2:** The "also" area, in which you can set up a second set of criteria for content. Content shows up in the final playlist if it meets the criteria in area 1 *or* area 2.

- **Area 3:** You can filter the complete list by what you select in area 3. Your options for area 3 include limiting the list to a certain number of items, a total size, or a total duration.

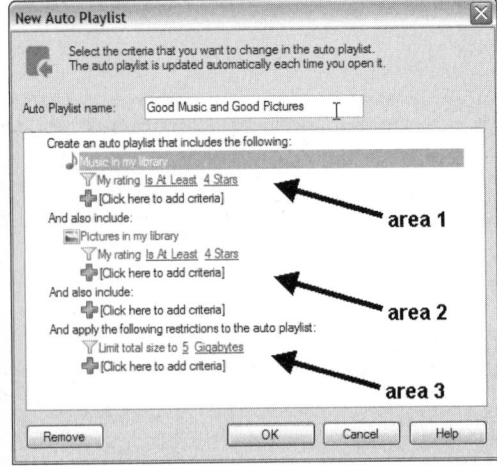

Figure 12-8: The three areas of the New Auto Playlist dialog box allow you to create your own playlist criteria.

Not too complicated, but an example never hurts. Say, for example, you want to make a playlist that contains highly rated videos (four or five stars) that are encoded at a high bit rate (1 Mbps or higher). Follow these steps to do it:

1. **Right-click the Playlists option in the Navigation pane on the left of the software display and choose Create Auto Playlist from the menu that appears.**

   The New Auto Playlist dialog box appears.

   By default, the list of criteria already has one filter set, constraining you to music. (Refer to Figure 12-8.) Time to change that!

2. **Select this initial criteria, click the Remove button at the bottom-left of the dialog box, and then pick Videos in My Library as the new filter by selecting that option from the Initial Criteria drop-down menu.**

3. **To add a criteria based on rating, click either the plus symbol (+) or the Click Here to Add Criteria link.**

   A drop-down list appears with options for the field on which you want to filter your content.

4. **Pick My Rating (the number of stars that you've given to a video or song).**

   The default values already filled in actually match our goal in this case, but you can edit either the operator (you can change "is at least" to "no more than" or "is") or the value (the number of stars, in this example). You can't change the field; to do that, you need to remove the criteria and add new criteria.

5. **Click the plus symbol (+) or the Click Here To Add Criteria link and add a filter based on bit rate that uses the "is at least" operator and "1 Mbps" as the value.**

6. **Enter a name for your new playlist in the Auto Playlist Name field at the top of the dialog box and click OK to save.**

   Your settings are saved, and the dialog box closes.

Now, if you check out the area under the Playlists heading in the Navigation pane to the left of the display, you should see your new playlist right under the Create Playlist option. Click the playlist name to see the dynamically generated content (which may end up being absolutely nothing at all, unless you have some videos with the appropriate bit-rate setting and with a four- or five-star rating). If you want to see the playlist in action but don't currently have any videos that qualify, head over to your All Videos view and rate a few high-bit-rate videos with four or five stars. Alternatively, you can right-click your new playlist in the Navigation pane or in the Playlists view (which you can see in Figure 12-9) and select Edit from the menu that appears to modify the criteria until you get some results. (To get to the Playlists view, just click — don't right-click, please — on the Playlists link.)

Playlists, especially dynamic ones, are very useful when it comes time to sync content to your Zune, as you can see in the following section!

Figure 12-9:
You can look over all your playlists in the Playlists view.

Synchronization and Background Conversion

When you sync your Zune with your PC, your Zune software converts music, videos, and pictures when it needs to so that the files can work on your Zune device. In the case of video, that conversion process can take a very long time — a full-length movie, for example, could possibly take several hours to convert. The actual transfer of content to the device takes relatively no time at all, compared to the conversion process.

Wouldn't it be nice if the Zune software could start converting video even before you hook up your Zune and start syncing? Imagine the conversion process could start right after a new video or podcast is downloaded, maybe even in the middle of the night. Then, when you came along and started syncing, you would only have to copy the file(s).

Well, if you've been browsing through the various dialog boxes and options in the Zune software, you may have seen the Allow Video Files to Convert in the Background option, which hints at exactly what we're talking about. This option can make your dream a reality, converting your video (and audio) files ahead of time and keeping the converted version around for you to quickly sync to your device.

There's one catch. Getting the option to work can be a bit tricky. The key here is automatic synchronization; background conversion of video and audio occurs only if you have automatic sync enabled. Even though it's the default, automatic sync can cause a lot of problems for you, so enabling it for background conversion of media might not be worth the hassle. One of the problems of automatic synchronization is that it wants to copy over all of your music, all of your video, and all of your photos when you might only want a selection of media. A good way to reduce this problem is to use playlists and then choose to automatically sync just those playlists, instead of using the default All Music or All Videos setting. You could use normal playlists for this purpose and then add or remove items to control what gets synchronized, or you could create an automatic playlist based on user-controlled criteria. (Chapter 4 has all you need to know about setting up playlists — regular or auto — for automatic syncing; you may want to flip back to bone up a bit on the process.)

After you set up an automatic sync (as outlined in Chapter 4), and as long as you've rated at least one of your video or music files four or five stars (because of the criteria you use in the automatic playlist example in the preceding section), those files begin to convert in the background. Keep in mind, though, that this background conversion occurs only if the Zune software is running and left idle for ten or more minutes, and if you've told the software to do it. (It's just a dumb machine and needs to be told everything.) Follow these steps to let your wishes be known:

1. **Click the Options icon (at the top of the Zune software), select any of the submenus (Playback, Library, and so on), and then click More Options.**

   The Options dialog box makes an appearance.

2. **In the Options dialog box, click the Devices tab and then click the Advanced button.**

   The File Conversion Options dialog box opens (see Figure 12-10).

3. **Select the check boxes for both the Allow Video Files to Convert in the Background option and the Allow Audio Files to Convert in the Background option.**

4. **Confirm where you want to temporarily store the converted files.**

   If you need to change the location, use the Change button.

5. **Set the amount of disk space (in MBs) that you want to use for preconverted files.**

   The Amount of Disk Space to Use setting limits how much media the software can convert ahead of time; if the software doesn't have any space left under that limit, background conversion stops and the video or audio encoding has to occur when you sync.

6. **Click OK to save your settings and close the dialog box.**

You're all set to take care of your converting in the background, where it belongs.

Figure 12-10:
The File Conversion Options dialog box lets you control background audio and video encoding.

Finding Videos on Your Zune

After you load your Zune up with a ton of TV shows, movies, and even a bunch of viral videos from YouTube, how do you find a video on your device? The video browsing options on the Zune are more limited than for music. You can't view videos by actor, playlist, or even (and this one really annoys us) genre. You can only view a list of all your videos in alphabetical order or select one of several filtered views. These views can include Movies, TV Shows, and Music Videos, but you see a particular option only if at least one video fits into the category.

The categorization of a video, the video title, and the description you see on your Zune all come from the metadata of the video file. (*Metadata* is a general name for all the additional information attached to a file, such as title, description, tags, and more.) The Zune software and the Zune device put that metadata to good use when you're browsing by displaying the metadata info about a video when you select that video.

If you have a video file named `zunedemo.wmv`, for example, it shows up on your Zune as `zunedemo` unless you've edited the Title metadata to something a bit more informative. To edit the metadata, follow these steps:

1. **Find the video file on your computer.**

Unfortunately, you can't edit this information through the Zune software.

2. **Right-click the file to bring up a menu of options.**

3. **Click Properties.**

   The file's Properties dialog box appears.

4. **Select the Summary tab.**

5. **Click the Advanced button to see the screen shown in Figure 12-11.**

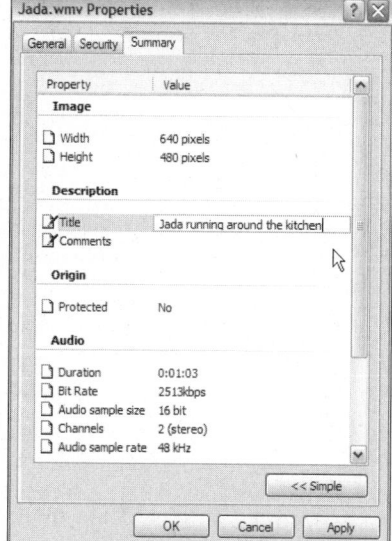

Figure 12-11:
You can edit
many of
the more
common
metadata
fields in
the file's
Properties
dialog box.

6. **Enter the title you want in the Title field.**

7. **Add this file to your Zune library either by waiting (if the file is in a monitored folder) or by dragging the file into a library view directly (any open view, such as the album listing, works).**

   As shown in Figure 12-12, the file shows up in your Zune library using the title that you enter in Step 6 rather than the filename it would have used by default.

Additional metadata fields will transfer to the Zune, but you can't easily edit them by using the Zune software. Check out Duncan's Web site, www. duncanmackenzie.net/zune, for a simple application that lets you browse through your video files and set the key pieces of media information that transfer to the Zune (including the media type, description, and title).

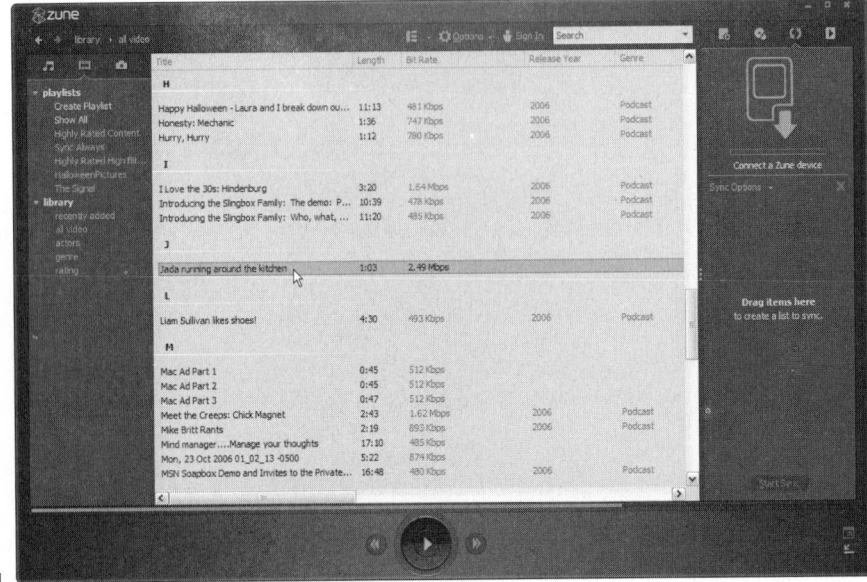

Figure 12-12:
The Zune
library, and
the Zune
device,
use any
available
metadata
for a
media file.

Using Playback Controls and Options

After you find a video that you want to watch, press the OK button in the
center of your Zune's control pad to bring up the Details view of that particular video (see Figure 12-13). On the Details view, you may see information
such as a description of the video, depending on what's available in the metadata for that particular file. You also get one or two options at the top of the
screen. You see either just Play or a Resume option paired with a Play from
Beginning option, depending on whether you stopped watching the video
before it was finished at some point in the past. A particularly nice feature of
the Zune is that it remembers the point at which you stopped watching any
number of video files. If you're 50 minutes into a great movie and then show a
few minutes of a different video to your buddies, you haven't lost your place
in the movie.

After you choose what you want to do (either play from the beginning or
resume where you left off), the video starts playing. At this point, the display
switches to Landscape (or Portrait) mode meaning that you need to turn
your Zune 90 degrees to the left. After a video starts playing, the control pad
changes its functions to reflect how you have to hold the Zune to watch the
video (see Figure 12-14).

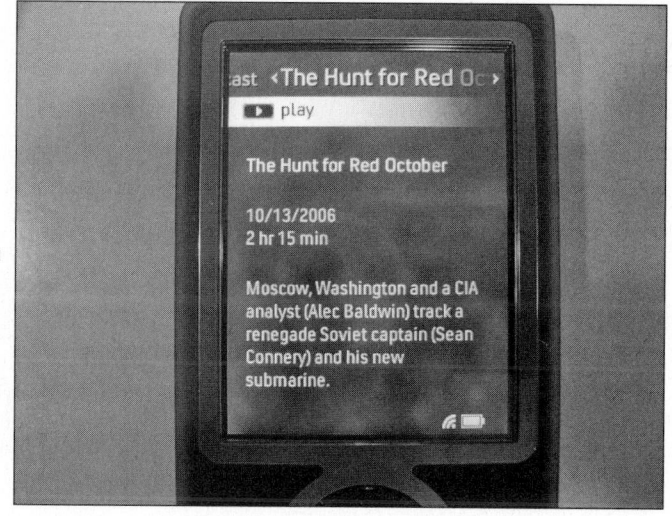

Figure 12-13:
If a video
has a
description,
you can see
it on your
Zune.

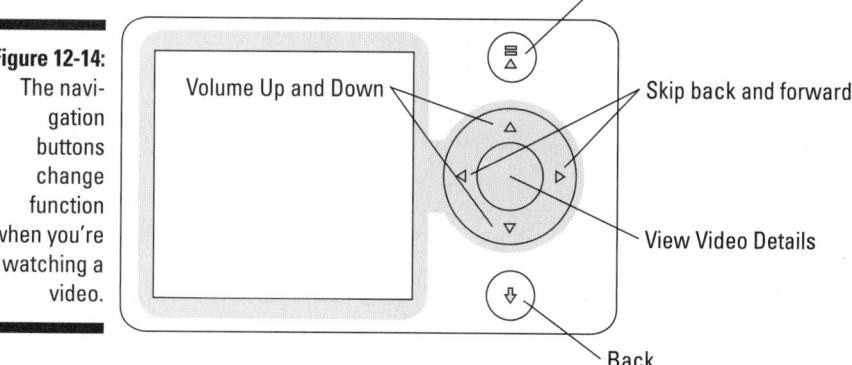

Figure 12-14:
The navi-
gation
buttons
change
function
when you're
watching a
video.

Play/Pause

Volume Up and Down

Skip back and forward

View Video Details

Back

Clicking to the right becomes Skip Forward, which advances you 30 seconds
into the video. Clicking to the left is Skip Back, jumping you only 10 seconds
or so back. The different amounts of time correspond to how you would normally use this feature when watching a TV program, skipping forward to
jump over commercials and then skipping back because you went a little too
far forward or to quickly review something you missed. If you hold down left
or right, the Zune scans through the video in forward or reverse. Up and
down on the control pad are Volume Up and Volume Down, and pressing the
center of the control pad (the OK button) displays the same information you
can find on the original video Details page (refer to Figure 12-13) overlaid on
top of the still-playing video. Press the OK button to make the video details
disappear, or simply wait a few moments.

Extending Battery Life

If you're traveling and plan to watch any videos, especially a few full-length movies, you're going to need to keep an eye on your battery life. Watching videos is probably the most battery-intensive activity you can perform with your Zune because the screen has to stay active the entire time (compared to playing music, when the screen can be off, or to viewing photos, which uses the screen but has to read a lot less data from the disk). All the Zune specifications suggest that you can get around 3½ to 4 hours of video playback time, but this isn't an exact figure. To get the most juice out of your battery, follow these tips:

- ✓ **Turn Wireless to Off:** No ifs, ands, or buts here; having your wireless connection on drains battery, pure and simple. Of course, turning your wireless connection off means that no one can contact you and send songs, but you'll often find yourself in situations in which you know no one will be trying to send you anything.

- ✓ **Set the screen brightness lower:** We personally find that the Medium setting works fine but Low is too dark for most videos. Don't sacrifice your viewing experience, though — just set the brightness as low as you find acceptable.

- ✓ **Encode your video (and music) at a lower bit rate:** The higher the bit rate, the more data has to be read from disk for every second of video. Reading data from disk uses more battery than just playing back out of the buffer, so a lower bit rate results in longer battery life.

For a brush-up on how to change all these settings, flip back to Chapter 3.

If you still find the battery life doesn't meet your needs, it's time to pull out the big guns. Several companies sell external battery packs that work just fine with the Zune. The Mobile Power Pack from the folks at BatteryGeek (www.batterygeek.net) provides interfaces for many different devices and a standard USB connector for devices such as the Zune. According to BatteryGeek, this power pack can add up to six additional hours of video playback.

Belkin (www.belkin.com) also makes a battery pack they call the TunePower. It wraps around the Zune like a case and is supposed to add six hours or more of battery life to your Zune, making it very similar to the power pack from BatteryGeek.

Either power pack should work to extend your battery for a long stretch of viewing, but if you're taking a multiday trip, make sure you have the ability to charge your Zune each day. If you, like us, carry a laptop everywhere you go, then you need only your USB sync cable. If you travel without a computer, you can get one of the many USB power adapters available (some labeled to work with the iPod). Duncan picked up Belkin's Power Pack for iPod Shuffle, which included both an AC-to-USB adapter and a DC/cigarette-lighter adapter for the car. Both adapters come in iPod white, but they work perfectly well with the Zune.

Finding More Information on Zune Video

Watching video on the Zune is all about getting the video from your PC to your Zune and then being able to find the video after it gets to your Zune. The Zune lacks a few video playback features, such as support for video playlists in the Zune itself (though you can create playlists in the Zune software on your PC) and the ability to rate a video while you're watching it (something you can do for music only at this point). Overall, though, it's a great device for making your videos portable. With a large, bright screen and the ability to hold more than 30 full-length movies, you'll never need to carry any other video player with you again.

To find out more about the metadata supported by the Zune, and other information about how to attribute and encode the video for your device, check out www.zune.net/support/howto/start/providecontent.htm. This page has all the nitty-gritty technical details on the bit rate, dimensions, encoding method, and metadata that you should use when creating your own files. All of this information also applies when you're converting an existing video for use on your Zune or when you're simply editing the metadata of a file before syncing it.

Chapter 13

Getting Music, Video, and Pictures to Your Xbox 360

*T*he Xbox 360 and the Zune are close friends; a lot of the same people built them both, and it shows. If you need proof, check out Zune Marketplace. Although it may look more like the Urge site you access through Windows Media Player (WMP), Zune Marketplace uses a Live ID account, a gamertag-style username, and Microsoft Points as its currency. Sound familiar? You guessed it — it works just like Xbox Live, the Xbox Live Marketplace, and the Xbox Live Video Marketplace, so it shouldn't come as any big surprise that the Zune and the Xbox 360 both have features that make them work really well together. Admittedly, how the two devices work together still has room for improvement (you can't synchronize shows that you download from the Video Marketplace on the Xbox 360 to your Zune, for example), but at the moment, they can work together to provide a great experience around your home.

The Zune device and the Zune software on your PC probably contain a lot of content that you want to enjoy elsewhere in your house. This content is likely mostly music, but you may also want to access photos and videos without having to be at your PC. The Xbox 360 is uniquely suited to help you free your content from your home computer because it's probably already sitting in your family room or living room, hooked up to your TV and maybe even a sound system of some sort. If you can just get your content routed to the 360 somehow, you have that content in the best possible location for viewing and listening.

No worries there. You don't have just one way to get all your ripped music, Zune Marketplace music, photos, and videos on their merry way to your Xbox 360 — you have four!

The Four-Fold Path to Getting Your Content Playing on the Xbox 360

If you have your Xbox 360 on a network with your home PC (or PCs), you can choose from several options for getting media over to your Xbox 360. Which of the following options you should use to get your music and media playing through your Xbox 360 depends on your specific setup and the content you're most interested in:

- ✔ **Use the Zune software itself.** The Zune software has the ability to share data with any or all of the Xbox 360 devices on your network, allowing you to stream music, video, and images in your Zune library.

- ✔ **Use recent versions of Windows Media Player.** Windows Media Player (starting with version 11) has the ability to stream out content that's listed as part of its library, but it's not limited to working with Xbox 360 devices. It can work with any device designed to work as a Universal Plug and Play media client, which includes the 360 but also covers a variety of devices from companies such as D-Link, Roku, and more.

You can also use Windows Media Connect 2.0 to make your content available to the Xbox 360, but because it's now built into Windows Media Player, you can't download it on its own anymore. If you do have Windows Media Connect 2.0 installed, and if you don't want to update to Windows Media Player 11, you can stream content to your 360 or any other compatible devices with Windows Media Connect. You may also have Windows Media Connect 1.0 installed on your machine, but that earlier version doesn't work with all the devices supported by version 2.0 and Windows Media Player, including the Xbox 360. Unfortunately, if you have only version 1.0, you may be out of luck trying to upgrade to 2.0 on its own because the only way to upgrade at this point is to install the latest version of Windows Media Player.

- ✔ **Use your Xbox 360 as a Media Center extender.** The Media Center Extender feature, built into the Xbox 360, allows you to connect to a PC on your network that's running Windows XP Media Center edition 2005 or the Windows Vista version of Media Center. You get the Media Center's full user interface right on your TV, which you can access by using your Xbox 360 controller or remote. Going far beyond the features that any of the other options offer, the Media Center interface lets you watch live TV (if you have a TV tuner in your Media Center PC and it's hooked up to your cable or antenna), as well as schedule and watch recorded TV shows. You can also view photos, videos, and any other features of the Media Center interface. And, if you have your 360 hooked up to an HDTV, your TV displays the Media Center interface in all its high-definition glory.

✔ **Use the direct method.** Yes, you can hook your Zune up directly to your Xbox 360 through the USB ports on either the front or back of the 360. The 360 has a special understanding of the Zune, and you can access all your Zune content through the 360 after you connect the two devices.

Getting Your Xbox 360 onto the Network

For three of the four methods for getting Zune content onto your Xbox 360 (which we discuss in the preceding section), your Xbox 360 has to be on your home network along with your computer, which may or may not already be the case.

Answer these handy questions to determine your current networking situation:

Can you access Xbox Live from your Xbox 360?

Can your home computer access the Internet?

Do you have a broadband (cable or DSL) connection to the Internet?

Do you have a router or wireless access point between your Xbox and the cable or DSL modem?

Are you running the Zune software on your home computer?

Do you have either a wired or wireless network connection to your 360?

If you answered "Yes" to all these questions, you're set for accessing your media at home, using the Internet, and using Xbox Live.

A note about wireless

When you're streaming media, you get much better results with a wired network connection than with wireless. If you do decide to go with a wireless connection, though, you may want to consider using something other than 802.11b. You can now find wireless access points that support 802.11b, along with 802.11a, 802.11g, or 802.11n (or all four), and because the wireless network accessory for the Xbox 360 supports a, b, and g (it doesn't support n at this time), you *do* have options. And we're here to tell you that, although 802.11b is by far the most common form of wireless networking available today, the other 360-compatible technology options (a and g) are faster and therefore can stream media at a higher bit rate and with fewer dropped connections.

In reality, you need affirmative answers to only the last two questions. If you don't have broadband access, but you've still set up a home network by using either a wired or wireless connection to your Xbox 360, you can still share media between your PC and your Xbox 360.

To check whether you have your network set up correctly, go ahead and try this simple test by following these steps:

1. **Fire up your Xbox 360 and press right on the D-pad of your controller several times to bring up the System blade on the Xbox 360 dashboard, as shown in Figure 13-1.**

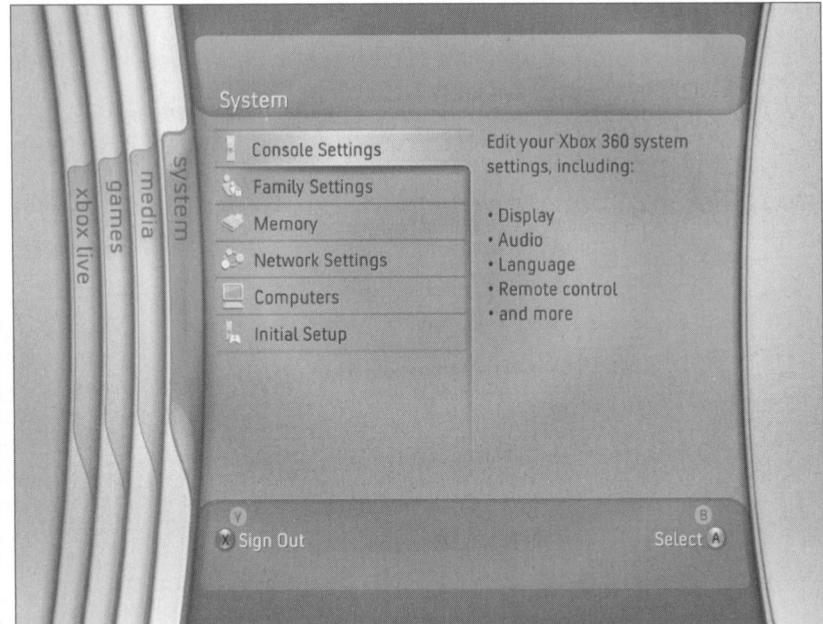

Figure 13-1:
The System blade of the Xbox 360 dashboard lets you configure your network.

System

Console Settings
Family Settings
Memory
Network Settings
Computers
Initial Setup

Edit your Xbox 360 system settings, including:

• Display
• Audio
• Language
• Remote control
• and more

xbox live | games | media | system

Sign Out   Select

2. **From the System blade, choose Network Settings⇨Test Xbox Live Connection.**

The system runs through a series of tests to confirm that it can connect to the Internet, resolve Web addresses, and send all the right types of data. It also tests the NAT (Network Address Translation) feature of your router. The NAT test may come back with Open (which is good), or it may return Moderate or Strict (which may cause you problems with gaming over Xbox Live, such as a failure to connect or perhaps a failure to join games).

If you have problems with the NAT, ICMP, or MTU tests (which all test the successful transmission of certain types of data), you may need to replace your router with one that Microsoft has approved for Xbox Live. You can find more information about routers and network setup at www.xbox.com — just type **"Introduction to Home Networking"** (including the quotes) into the search box at the top of the page and then click Search.

If all the built-in tests on the 360 report back success, you're ready to connect the Xbox 360 to your PC. We talk about how to get your PC and 360 working together in the following sections.

Turning On Sharing in the Zune Software

When you originally installed your Zune software on your PC, one of the setup screens asked if you wanted to share music with any Xbox 360s on your network. This option is set to On by default, so you probably already have sharing up and running, even if you don't realize it. Whether you have sharing activated or not, you can access the media sharing settings of the Zune software by following these steps:

1. **Right-click Library in the Navigation pane along the left side of the software.**

   The shortcut menu appears.

2. **Pick Media Sharing from the shortcut menu.**

   The Zune Media Sharing dialog box (see Figure 13-2) appears.

In the Zune Media Sharing dialog box, you can turn sharing completely off, change what type of content is shared, and restrict which Xbox 360s can access your music. To change the settings in this dialog box, follow these steps:

1. **Select the Share My Media check box if you want to share any Zune content with one or more 360s.**

   Of course, if you don't want to do any sharing at all, you can make your feelings known here. Just keep the check box unchecked. When you have sharing turned on, it runs on your machine all the time (using memory and CPU time), so you may want to turn it off if you don't need it.

   In some cases, people with their computers set to go into a sleep (or standby) mode after a certain amount of idle time have noticed that their computers never go to sleep if they have Zune Network Sharing on. (You can configure the Sleep/Standby option by choosing Start↪Control

Panel⇨Power Options). The Network Sharing software keeps your machine from being completely idle, and therefore your computer always thinks it's being used. If you need your computer to get its beauty sleep, you may need to disable sharing through the Zune software.

2. **Enter an easy-to-recognize name in the Media Library Name box field.**

   The default name is your login, but you may find it more useful to name it something such as Duncan's Zune, using 16 characters or less.

3. **Uncheck the check boxes to the left of the kind of content you don't want to share (if you don't want to share all your content).**

   You can choose to share (or not share) music, videos, pictures, or any combination of the three. By default, you share everything.

4. **Select the radio button corresponding to how you want to deal with sharing access to other Xbox 360s.**

   By default, any Xbox 360 on your network can access this material, but you can change these defaults if you want. With the default settings, anyone can fire up a 360 and connect to your Zune library, viewing all the music, pictures, and video content that you have, and you don't even get a notification when they do it.

Figure 13-2:
Sharing options on the Zune allow you to decide whom you give access to what.

For most people, having a random Xbox 360 appear on their network is very unlikely (although wireless networking increases the odds somewhat), but if you're on a shared network or use wireless in a crowded environment (such as in a dorm, apartment, or condo), you should definitely select the Only Share with These Xbox 360s option.

5. **If you select the Only Share with These Xbox 360s radio button, turn your Xbox 360 on (if it isn't already) so your Zune software can find it on the network.**

   Every 360 that the Zune software finds appears in the big field of this dialog box.

6. **Approve the 360s in this field with which you want to share by clicking them (each click toggles that Xbox 360 between being approved or blocked).**

7. **Click OK to accept your settings and close the dialog box.**

8. **With sharing enabled, go to your Xbox 360, navigate to the System blade, and select Computers.**

   Two options appear on your TV, Windows Based PC or Windows Media Center.

9. **Select either or both options to remove any previously created connections.**

   Your Xbox 360 can be associated with only one PC for media sharing and one PC (likely the same one) for running Media Center. The options on this page allow you to remove an existing association so that you can then reconnect and possibly select a different PC or (in the case of media sharing) a different media share running on the same PC.

   Normally, you wouldn't need to remove your PC connection; after you hook up your Xbox 360 to your PC, that connection is all you need. You may need to disconnect and then reselect a PC, though, if you decide to use shared music from another machine, re-install Windows onto your existing machine, or purchase a new machine that you want to connect to your Xbox 360. In any of those cases, whether you're using Zune sharing, Windows Media Player, or Windows Media Center, the two options on this screen remove your old connection(s) and allow you to create new ones.

   To set up a new connection, you have to move on to Step 10.

10. **On your Xbox 360 dashboard, go back to the Media blade and select either the Music, Pictures, or Videos option.**

    It doesn't matter which option you pick because this step just creates the PC-to-Xbox-360 connection for media sharing, and that connection's used for all three kinds of media, not just the one you select now.

    The set of options that appears includes Computer as a choice.

11. **Select the Computer option and press the A button on your remote control or game controller.**

    A list of all sharing services located on your home network appears.

If you renamed your Zune sharing service (by using the Zune Media Sharing dialog box; refer to Figure 13-2), you see that new name in the list, but the Zune icon to the right of the name tells you which service (if you have more than one) comes from the Zune software.

12. Select the item with the Zune image to the right of it.

The top level of browsing content from your Zune library appears on your TV.

You should have to go through this long list of steps only the first time you want to hook up to a new computer. Normally, you go directly to this view after picking Computer because you don't need to select a sharing service after you follow these steps the first time. From here, you can browse your music by album, artist, playlist, song, and genre; find the song(s) you want; and start playing them in the Xbox 360's music player.

The Zune software installs the Zune Network Sharing Service (Zune NSS), which runs all the time (if you have sharing enabled) under a special system account called Network Service. For good or bad, the sharing is always active, even if you're not logged into your machine. Because the Zune NSS doesn't run under your personal account, you may occasionally run into problems if some or all of your media is located on another server. The sharing service won't be able to access those files, so they won't be available to your Xbox 360.

You can solve this problem and enable the Zune sharing service to access your files off another computer by setting the Zune NSS to run with your username and password if you want, although this change affects the sharing service for all users of your machine. To make this change (which you should make only if you need to share media located on another machine on your network), follow these steps:

1. Choose Control Panel➪Administrative Tools➪Services.

The Services window appears, complete with a listing of all the services on your machine, as shown in Figure 13-3.

2. Find the Zune Network Sharing Service (it should be at the very bottom of the list), right-click it, and then pick Properties from the shortcut menu that appears.

The Zune Network Sharing Service Properties dialog box appears.

3. Click the Log On tab of the Zune Network Sharing Service Properties dialog box.

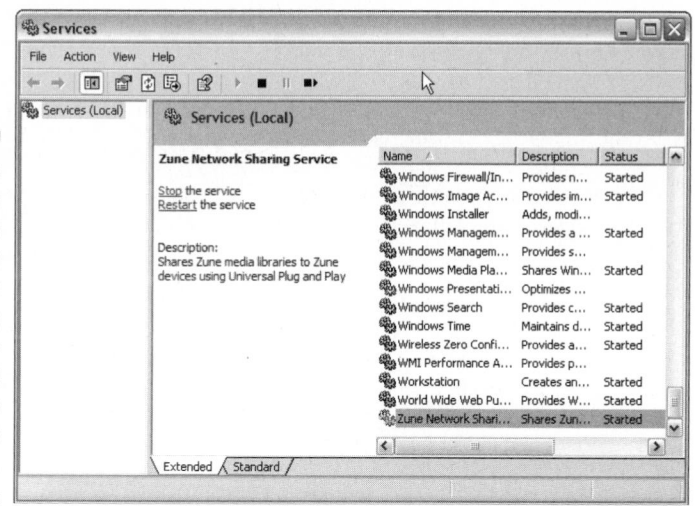

Figure 13-3:
You can
control the
Zune
Network
Sharing
Service
account
through the
Services
window.

4. **Type in your username and password (see Figure 13-4), then click OK.**

If you change your Windows password in the future, you need to come
back and change it here, as well (or else the Zune sharing service will fail
to run and your files won't be available to the Xbox 360).

Figure 13-4:
Set the
username
and pass-
word for the
account you
want the
Zune sharing
service
to use.

Windows Media Player Sharing

Windows Media Player 11 provides built-in sharing — much like the Zune software does — but it supports more options, more devices, and nearly all the same features as the Zune. In addition to the Xbox 360, Windows Media Player lets you stream your content out to devices such as the Roku Soundbridge, Sonos, and others. The one missing feature from WMP 11, though, is the ability to share MP4 videos. The Zune software can share these kinds of videos, going above and beyond the functionality of WMP 11.

You can configure sharing in Windows Media Player pretty easily. Just follow these steps:

1. **Right-click the Library option in the Navigation pane along the left side of the application window (see Figure 13-5) and select Media Sharing from the shortcut menu that appears.**

   The Media Sharing dialog box appears.

Figure 13-5:
Right-clicking the WMP Library option gives you access to the Media Sharing options.

2. **Turn sharing on by checking the Share My Media To check box and selecting your Xbox 360 device. (Or turn sharing off by unchecking that check box.)**

   If you have one or more devices listed on the Media Sharing dialog box, you can select each of these devices individually to configure their settings.

3. **After you select a device, click Allow or Deny to control overall access to your shared media (all of the media in your Windows Media Player library, which is probably located on that same PC), and then click Customize to configure settings specific to that device.**

   The Customize dialog box (see Figure 13-6) appears. This dialog box gives you a much wider range of choices than the Zune software does, including the ability to filter content based on star rating and parental rating. If you have all your media on your PC, for example, and two Xbox 360s in the house, then Windows Media Player allows you to control the content shown to each 360. You don't have this kind of control when using the Zune software; you can turn off the sharing of music, video, and/or pictures, but you can't filter any deeper than that.

4. **Click OK after you make the configuration changes you want.**

   The Customize dialog box closes, and you return to the Media Sharing dialog box.

Figure 13-6:
The Windows Media Player sharing options include restrictions based on media type, star rating, and parental rating.

Media Sharing - Customize
Choose what you share with this device.
Media types to share with Xbox 360'
☐ Use default settings

Media types:	Star ratings:	Parental ratings:
☑ Music	○ All ratings	○ All ratings
☑ Pictures	◉ Only:	◉ Only:
☑ Video		
	Rated 3 stars or higher ▾	☑ Music: Unrated
		☐ Music: Explicit
	☑ Include unrated files	☑ Music: Explicit content
		☑ Pictures: Unrated

How do I customize sharing?   [OK]   [Cancel]

5. **Click the Settings button in the Media Sharing dialog box to access the Default Settings dialog box.**

   The Default Settings dialog box appears, as shown in Figure 13-7.

6. **Enter a name for your WMP 11 sharing service in the Share Media As text field.**

   Although it doesn't really matter what you name the sharing service, you may want to include WMP in the name, along with your name, so you can easily find the service when you're connecting from the 360.

7. **Use the check boxes to indicate what content to share (music, pictures, or video), as well as whether to give new devices permission to connect by default.**

8. **Click OK to save your settings and close the Media Sharing dialog box.**

Figure 13-7:
The Media
Sharing
dialog box's
default set-
tings allow
you to spec-
ify sharing
settings
for new a
device and
control
whether
new devices
need
approval.

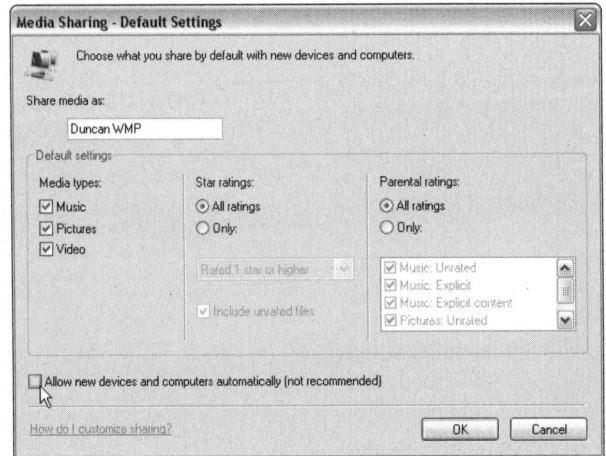

Library and Digital Rights Management Issues

Sharing from the Zune software and from the Windows Media Player software both work in the same basic fashion; they expose their library catalog to the remote device and then stream a selected piece of content to that device. If a file isn't in the software's library, that file won't show up on the remote device. You probably won't have to worry about this issue if you use only one of these two software programs — as long as you do your sharing from that same program, you should be set. But if you use the Zune software most of the time and then set up sharing through Windows Media Player 11, for example, problems with the library or with Digital Rights Management (DRM) may prevent you from playing your media. We talk about these issues in the following sections.

Library issues

When you hook up to the Windows Media Player 11 Network Sharing service, that service doesn't immediately scan your hard drive in response to your request for a list of albums, artists, and songs. It actually pulls that information from the Windows Media Player library. That library is updated while Windows Media Player itself is running, not just whenever new music is added. If you hardly ever run Windows Media Player — if you're always using the Zune software, for example — the WMP library could be quite out of date.

Unfortunately, you don't have an easy solution to this problem. If you absolutely, positively need to use Windows Media Player (to stream to a non-Xbox-360 hardware client, for example), you're stuck with using two different pieces of software and two different media libraries. If you leave your machine running most of the time (which you need to do if you're planning on accessing it from your Xbox 360, anyway), just leave Windows Media Player up and running all the time. Occasionally running WMP also works, but then you run the risk of forgetting to use it at all and having it fall farther out of date over time.

If you don't want to use the Windows Media Player's Sharing feature, and the Zune software's simpler version is all you need, you shouldn't have any problems. Use the Zune software to download music from the Marketplace, rip your CDs, and sync with your Zune. Then, when your Xbox 360 connects to the sharing service for streaming, the list of media is guaranteed to be up-to-date.

Digital Rights Management and network sharing

With network sharing, you may need to check what digital rights you have to your music. Protected music, such as music from the Zune Marketplace, can appear in the libraries of both Windows Media Player and the Zune software, and you can stream protected music to your Xbox 360 from either one. Your music license isn't refreshed (updated to work for the next 30 days) automatically when you're using sharing, though; that happens only when you're using the actual software on the PC. Even then, the license for Zune Marketplace music gets refreshed only when you use the actual Zune software to listen to your protected music. If you're connecting your Zune to your PC every day or so and copying over music, you don't need to worry too much about keeping your music licenses up-to-date, but if you don't use the actual software very often, you may find that your protected Zune Marketplace music stops playing through your Xbox 360 from time to time. When that happens, you can refresh the rights on your protected music by simply signing into the Zune Marketplace through the Zune software.

The Direct Method

You can hook up your Zune device to an Xbox 360 directly, avoiding all the steps that we talk about in the section "Turning On Sharing in the Zune Software," earlier in this chapter. This option can work to connect your Zune to your or anyone else's Xbox 360. To make this connection, you need your Zune, your Zune sync cable, and an open USB port on the 360.

 The Xbox 360 has three USB ports on it — two on the front and one on the back; hopefully, you have one of the two ports on the front open because you can generally access those ports more easily (it can be hard to reach around the 360 if it's sitting inside an entertainment center).

To hook up your Zune to an Xbox 360, follow these steps:

1. **Plug the Zune connector on your Zune's sync cable into the Zune and then plug the USB connector into the Xbox.**

2. **Navigate to the Media blade on your 360 and then select Music, Pictures, or Video, depending on what kind of media you want to view or listen to from your Zune.**

   Regardless of which media type you pick, the menu that appears includes one item that starts with a Zune icon. The Zune icon has either the name of your device or Portable Device listed to the right of it.

3. **Select the Zune item in the menu.**

   A page appears in which you can browse the contents of your Zune (filtered down to the current media type: music, pictures, or videos).

Pictures have no grouping at all. Even though you likely have several different folders of pictures on your Zune, all of those pictures appear as one long alphabetically sorted list on the Xbox 360's interface. Because of this lack of grouping, you can have a very hard time finding the picture you're looking for, especially if you've left the picture names in some numerical format (such as DSC0001.JPG for a Sony camera). In addition to the list of individual pictures on the right side of the screen, you also have a Play Slideshow button on the left side. Selecting this option randomly flips through all of your pictures, still ignoring their folder structure.

Videos work in the same basic fashion as pictures, without the Play Slideshow option; you get a list of all the videos without any grouping at all.

Music is the exception here. When you select the Zune item from under the Music menu, a list of folders appears. This list includes six or so items (the number could vary, depending on whether you've received any pictures or music via wireless sharing), including Albums, Music, Pictures, Playlists, Received Pictures, and Video. Oddly enough, only two of these options lead to any music you can play:

- ✔ **Music:** This option shows you a list of artists. Clicking an individual artist shows you a list of all the albums and loose songs on your Zune from that artist.

- ✔ **Playlists:** This option lists every playlist from your Zune. Selecting a playlist shows you the list of songs on that particular playlist, allowing you to select an individual song or just start playing through the list from the top.

The other four options appear only because they reflect the folder structure of the Zune itself, but selecting any of them displays an empty list (they don't contain any music files, so the 360 shows them as empty folders).

What to Do without a Home Network

You can hook your Zune up to your Xbox 360 directly (as we explain in the preceding section), which allows you to play all of your music, watch your videos, and view your photos through the 360, with no network required. You can also burn your own CDs or DVDs of music, videos, and photos, and then put those discs into your 360 to access their content right on your TV.

You can't burn your Zune Pass (subscription) music to CD or DVD, but you can burn music that you individually purchase or music that you rip off your own CDs. You can also burn unprotected music, such as MP3s or WMAs ripped from your own CDs, onto a CD as data files (instead of creating an audio CD), and the Xbox 360 can still access and play those files. A data CD can hold much more music than an audio CD.

For videos, just burn any WMV files you have onto a CD or DVD and bring it over to your 360, and that file should play without a problem. The resolution that's ideal for playing on the Zune (320 x 240 pixels) is much lower than what the Xbox 360 is capable of supporting, though, so experiment with higher quality and larger resolution video files if you have them available. Your Zune-formatted WMV files can certainly play through your 360, and depending on the size of your TV, you might not even mind the low resolution all that much. Unlike the Zune software, the Xbox 360 can't play MP4 movies, so stick with Windows Media Video (WMV) ones.

Finding More Information

For more on getting media content onto your Xbox 360, check out some of these other resources:

- ✔ You can get an intro to digital media at `www.xbox.com/en-US/support/systemuse/xbox360/digitalmedia/intro.htm`.

- ✔ Look into your connection options (for getting your Xbox 360 onto your network and connected to the Internet) at `www.xbox.com/en-US/support/connecttolive/xbox360/connectionmethods/intro.htm`.

- ✔ *Xbox 360 for Dummies,* by two of the geniuses writing this book (Wiley Publishing, Inc.), covers accessing media by using Windows Media Connect and Windows Media Center, along with information on getting your 360 onto the network.

Chapter 14

Hooking Your Zune Up in Your Car

*W*hether you're driving around the block or across the country, it's great to have your Zune — and your tunes — with you.

And, with your Zune player's sizeable hard drive, you don't need to lug a clattery old shoebox of CDs around anymore. With room for thousands of songs, you can use your Zune to serve up all the songs in your collection — and leave those CDs behind.

There's something special about getting behind the wheel and listening to your life's own soundtrack as the miles roll out behind you. And driving time is a great opportunity not just for listening to music, but also for catching up on audio books, podcasts, recorded lectures, or any audio files you may have.

In this chapter, we tell you how to keep your player powered up on those long drives, as well as different ways to connect your Zune player to your car stereo, including cassette adapters and direct audio connections. You can also find out about the Zune Car Pack accessory — which includes an FM transmitter to send your music via FM signals directly into your car stereo.

So what are you waiting for? Grab your Zune, hop in, and go!

Taking Your Zune on the Road

With its healthy storage capacity and compact size, you'll find yourself wanting to take your Zune with you all the time. Whether you're out running, walking, cycling, flying, or driving, it's a great joy and convenience to have your favorite pictures, movies, and videos with you while you're on the go.

Using Zune on the road, though, introduces a couple of special considerations:

✔ **Getting power to your player:** Sure, your Zune can run off its battery for some time, but for longer trips, you should take advantage of the power available through your car's electrical system.

✔ **Using your vehicle's stereo system:** You likely have a decent sound system in your vehicle already, so it makes sense to take advantage of that sound system.

✔ **Keeping your Zune for many years to come:** Although you may love having your Zune on the road with you, don't get in the habit of leaving it in your car, tempting any thieves who may be walking by. It's a good idea to just keep your Zune with you.

That way, you're sure to have the Zune around for your next drive!

The following sections take a look at ways you can deal with your power needs, as well as ways to unlock the power of your car stereo system.

Giving your battery a rest with car power adapters

Car power adapters (see Figure 14-1) are designed to power your Zune via your car's electrical outlet — you know, those round-shaped outlets that held cigarette lighters back in the old days.

Figure 14-1:
Car power adapters deliver juice to your Zune through your car's electrical system.

The rounded, lipstick-shaped end of a car power adapter slides right into your car's electrical outlet, providing much-needed juice to the adapter's connector port end — the same kind of connector you can find on the sync cable that you use to attach your Zune to your PC.

Various accessory makers — including DLO, Monster, and Belkin — offer car power adapters for Zune. These adapters are typically in the $20 to $40 price range, and they sometimes come bundled with AC adapters or other accessories. A Web search for "Zune car charger" returns several accessory makers' sites that offer chargers; you can often find good pricing on Amazon for these chargers, as well.

A car power adapter is also included in the Zune Car Pack, which we explore in some detail in the section "Going Places with the Zune Car Pack," later in this chapter.

Getting Zune tunes on your car stereo

With your power issues nicely resolved (which we explain in the preceding section), it's time to look at ways to connect your player to your car's stereo. The following sections fill you in on three options — direct audio connections, cassette adapters, and FM transmitters — so you can decide which one's right for you.

Direct audio connections

Some car stereos have auxiliary inputs that can accept music directly from an exterior source — in this case, your Zune player — and pump tunes to your stereo through a direct audio connection cable.

The type of connection available to you depends on the radio or stereo system installed in your vehicle. Many vehicle stereos — both factory and after-market systems — have one of the following types of input connectors:

- ✔ **RCA audio input jacks:** These connectors usually come with separate jacks for left and right channels, as shown in Figure 14-2.

- ✔ **3.5mm auxiliary inputs:** These inputs use a mini plug similar to what would fit in your player's headphone port.

- ✔ **CD changer ports:** Some car stereos include a port to accept a cable from a multidisc CD changer. You usually find such ports in the rear of the radio chassis.

You also have to use a specialized direct audio connection cable to connect these inputs to your player. Depending on the type of connection cable, the cable connects to your player through its headphone port or through the connector port at the bottom of the player.

This approach connects your Zune player directly into your car's sound system and allows you to control volume, balance, fade, and other functions through your car stereo's sound controls.

The benefits of the direct audio connection method are pretty straightforward:

✔ You get a strong, reliable signal directly into your car's sound system.

✔ Unlike the FM transmitters described in the section "FM transmitters," later in this chapter, outside radio signals don't affect the Zune's signal.

Potential drawbacks include

✔ Your car radio system may not have the necessary input ports to accept a direct connection to your player.

✔ Direct audio connection cables range from inexpensive and easy-to-find (for RCA cables) to more expensive connectors that are specialized for your particular stereo system (CD-changer port cables, for example).

A Web search for "Zune direct audio connector" gives you various hits on manufacturers of these cables. For audio connectors that use the headphone port to attach to your player, connectors made for the iPod can also work with your Zune's headphone port.

If your car stereo system doesn't support direct audio connection, or if you simply prefer another approach, keep on reading. The following sections fill you in on some other options — cassette adapters and FM transmitters.

Cassette adapters

Cassette players are becoming less common as standard equipment in vehicles . . . but if your vehicle has one, you can use it to play music from your Zune with a cassette adapter.

Cassette adapters (such as the one shown in Figure 14-3) receive a signal from your Zune player and make that signal readable through your car's in-dash tape player.

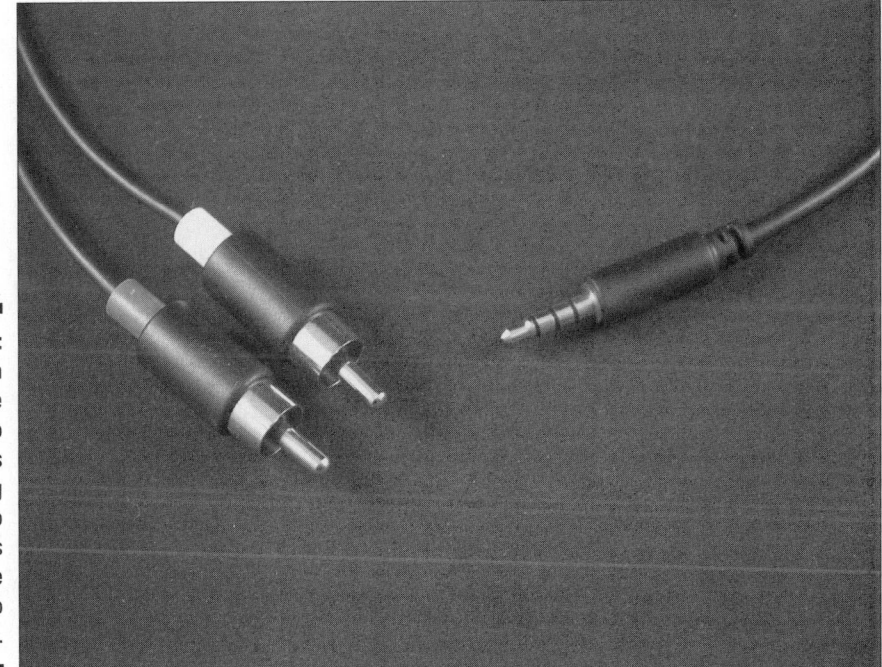

Figure 14-2:
You can make direct audio connections by using RCA audio connectors with some stereo systems.

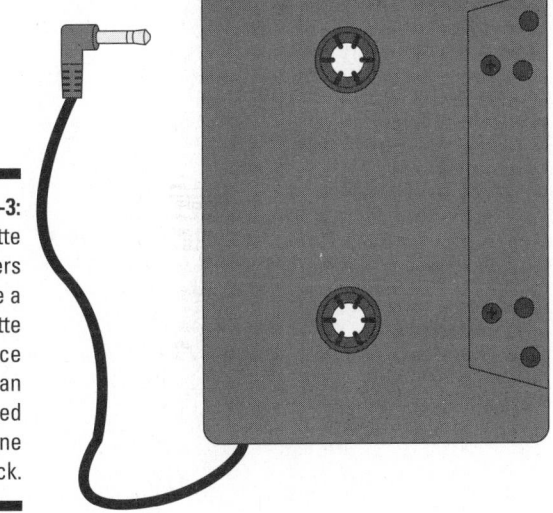

Figure 14-3:
Cassette adapters include a cassette interface with an attached headphone jack.

These adapters can vary from manufacturer to manufacturer. Some adapters work only in cassette tape players that accept cassettes with the tape opening facing the side, as shown in Figure 14-4; those models don't work with players where the cassettes are accepted with the tape opening facing the front or the back of the player. Be sure to pick up an adapter that works with your particular system.

After you insert an adapter into your tape deck, connect the wire attached to the adapter into your Zune's 3.5mm headphone port.

You can typically find cassette adapters for around $20. The following manufacturers, as well as many others, offer them at reasonable prices:

- ✔ Griffin (`www.griffintechnology.com`)
- ✔ Belkin (`www.belkin.com`)
- ✔ Sony (`www.sonystyle.com`)

Figure 14-4:
Double-check to make sure your cassette adapter fits with your car stereo system.

Some benefits of the cassette adapter method include

- ✔ It's an inexpensive solution compared to other options.
- ✔ Setup is very simple.

Here are some potential drawbacks:

- ✔ The sound quality may seem poor when compared with other options, particularly the direct audio connection method.
- ✔ You may need to clean your car tape player's playback head (using a cassette head cleaner) from time to time to maintain good sound quality.

FM transmitters

FM transmitters are Zune accessories that allow you to wirelessly transmit audio from your Zune player to your car's stereo system.

You may want to look into this approach if you use your Zune in multiple vehicles — for example, if you own more than one vehicle or frequently use rental cars. The transmitters are designed to work with any FM radio — you don't need any special equipment or connectors for your car stereo after you have the FM transmitter attached to the bottom of your Zune player, as shown in Figure 14-5.

FM transmitters have their own special benefits:

- ✔ FM transmitters are compatible with any FM radio.
- ✔ You don't need additional specialized connectors as you move among multiple vehicles.

You also have to consider the potential drawbacks:

- ✔ FM transmitters can be pricier than other options.
- ✔ Reception can vary based on where the vehicle's FM antenna is located and where you put the Zune player in the car.

For more nuts-and-bolts stuff about FM transmitters, see the "Understanding FM Transmitters" section, later in this chapter.

In fact, we look into the features of the Zune Car Pack in the following section.

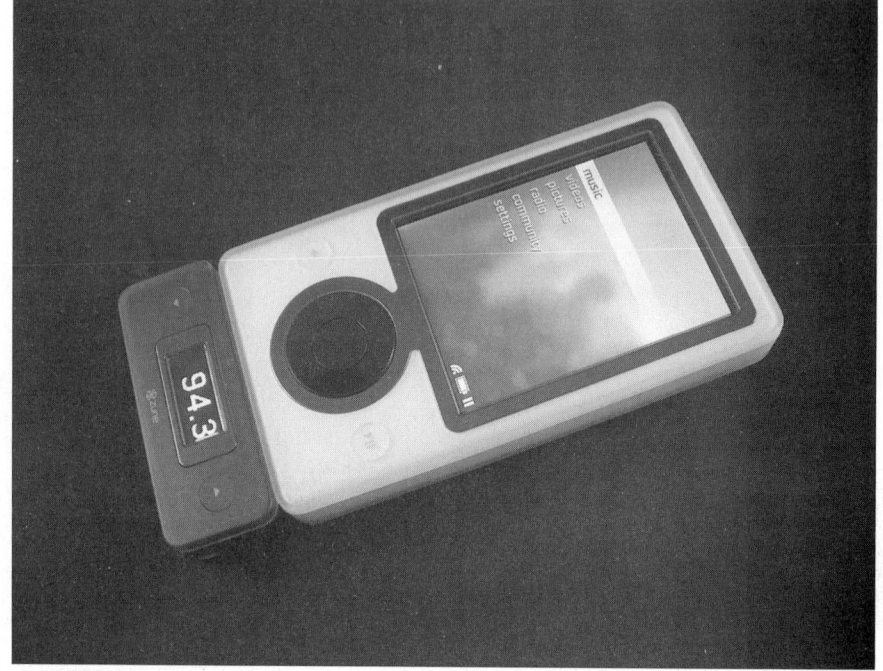

Figure 14-5:
FM trans-
mitters can
make taking
your Zune
player on
the road a
snap.

Zune FM transmitters are typically in the $50 to $100 price range, and you can find them at

- ✔ Monster (www.monstercable.com)
- ✔ Belkin (www.belkin.com)
- ✔ DLO (www.dlo.com)

Going Places with the Zune Car Pack

The Zune Car Pack can make using your Zune on the road an easy operation. With the Car Pack accessories, you have the essential elements for enjoying Zune music in your vehicle. The Zune Car Pack includes these items, shown in Figure 14-6:

- ✔ **A car charger:** Powers your Zune through your vehicle's electrical outlets
- ✔ **An FM transmitter:** Sends your Zune's tunes to your car stereo

✔ **The Product Guide:** Provides safety and health information related to Zune accessories

✔ **The Start guide:** Contains simple diagrams and instructions for operation of the FM transmitter and charger

You can shop for the Zune Car Pack, and other Zune car accessories, on Microsoft's Zune.net site at www.zune.net/en-US/accessories/car.

The Zune car charger

The car charger connects your Zune to your car's power system. You can, of course, use the charger to power your Zune while you're using it in your car, but you can also use it to recharge your Zune when the battery is low. The charger includes an indicator light to let you know the charging status of your Zune's battery.

The charger connects to your car's electrical outlet, with the other end attaching to your Zune through the player's connection port.

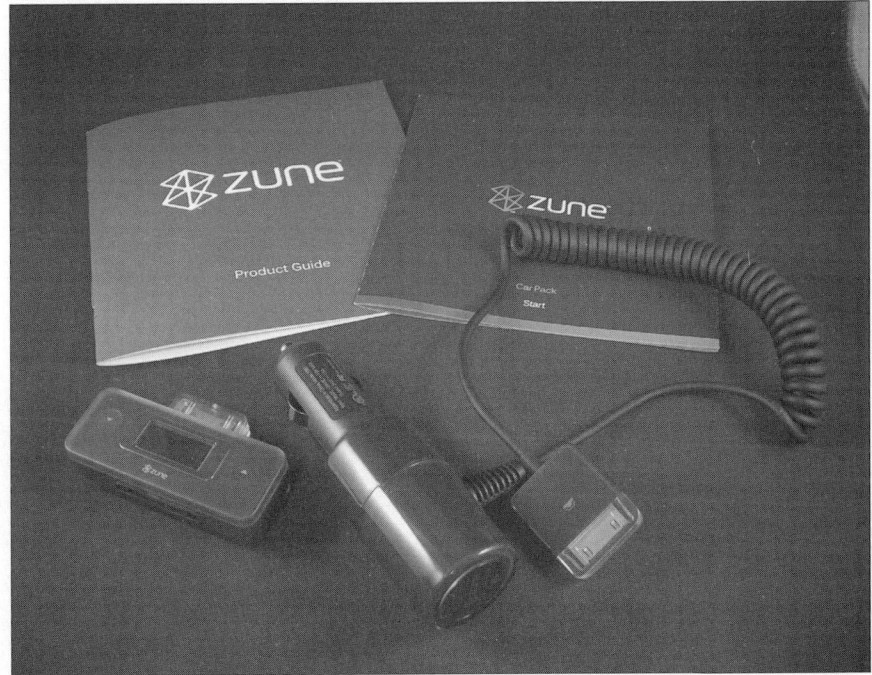

Figure 14-6:
The Zune Car Pack includes these accessories and instructions.

The Zune FM transmitter

The FM transmitter lets you play the songs you have on your Zune through your car stereo.

Similar to your Zune player itself, the FM transmitter has a doubleshot finish — a base color with a translucent blue highlighting that's molded into the edges of the Zune's body, as shown in Figure 14-7. Nice!

Figure 14-7: The Zune Car Pack includes an FM transmitter.

Understanding FM Transmitters

FM transmitters can deliver music to your car radio by acting like miniature radio stations. In effect, they send your songs from your player to your radio by broadcasting over open FM frequencies.

FM transmitters generate short-range FM signals, in a range of up to 30 feet. Your transmitter finds an available (unused) FM frequency so that you don't affect nearby radios by overriding an existing FM station.

To better understand how FM transmitters work, the following section takes a look at the attachments and controls on the FM transmitter that comes with the Zune Car Pack.

Looking into the parts of the FM transmitter

All FM transmitters contain these same basic components:

- **Connector:** Right on top of the FM transmitter's blocky little head is a Zune connector, which fits into your Zune player's connector port.

- **Display:** The transmitter includes a simple display, which shows the current FM frequency being used (refer to Figure 14-7).

- **Tuner buttons:** The buttons on the left and right sides of the display act as your tuner controls.

  Pressing the left button adjusts the frequency downward in 0.1 MHz intervals. Pressing and holding the left button causes the transmitter to *auto-seek*, to find the next available open FM frequency, downward. Similarly, the right button tunes and auto-seeks up the FM frequencies.

Arrive alive

When you're driving, your focus needs to be on safely operating your vehicle. Be aware of your surroundings and don't let yourself become distracted with the controls on your Zune player or on your car stereo system.

Keep these safe-driving-while-listening tips in mind:

- **Prepare for the road.** Connect your Zune and let it play before your wheels are rolling — then you don't have to fiddle with it while you're on the move.

- **Keep volume under control.** Never set the volume so high that important sounds around you are drowned out. Keep your volume levels such that you can still hear the sounds of other cars sharing the road with you, as well as sirens from police cars, fire engines, ambulances, and other emergency vehicles.

- **Avoid earphones.** Although you may be tempted to use the Zune's earphones while you're driving instead of routing the music through your car stereo, listening to earphones while driving is definitely a safety risk, and we don't recommend it in any way, shape, or form. Having music playing through your earphones can prevent you from hearing outside sounds that are important for the safety of you, your passengers, other drivers, and pedestrians! It could also be illegal, depending on your local traffic laws.

Using the FM transmitter

To set up the transmitter, simply follow these steps:

1. **Attach the transmitter to the base of your Zune player.**

2. **Plug the car charger's connector into the connector port at the base of the transmitter, as shown in Figure 14-8.**

Figure 14-8:
Connect the charger to the connector port on the FM transmitter.

3. **Plug the car charger into your vehicle's electrical outlet.**

   Okay, okay — technically, you can skip Steps 2 and 3, and run your Zune off its battery without the help of the car charger. But why pass on a great way to conserve your Zune's battery life?

4. **Press and hold either of the tune buttons on the transmitter.**

The transmitter automatically seeks and finds an available FM frequency.

5. **Turn on your car's FM radio and tune it to your transmitter's selected frequency, as shown in Figure 14-9.**

   Voila! Now you can hear your Zune playlists through your car's sound system.

If you hear static on the frequency selected by the auto-seek function, you can choose another frequency. Just press the left or right tuner button to adjust the frequency upward or downward. You can also try moving the Zune player (with its attached FM transmitter) to a different position or location within your car.

The transmitter draws its power from your Zune player. Plug your Zune player into your car's electrical outlet when you use the transmitter to ensure that you have sufficient power for your FM transmitter.

Figure 14-9:
Tune your car radio to your FM transmitter's frequency.

When not using your FM transmitter, you can tuck it away in your vehicle's glove box or console storage area. But first, cover the connectors of the transmitter and the charger with the clear plastic caps that come with them, as shown in Figure 14-10. These caps help prevent accidental damage to the connector pins.

Figure 14-10: Cover your accessory connectors with these protective caps, included with the Zune Car Pack.

Chapter 15

Using Your Zune on the Road

*T*he Zune is a great all-around device for carrying your portable entertainment, whether that entertainment be music, podcasts, photos, or videos. In other chapters, we take a look at each type of content, but in this chapter, we concentrate on the "portable" part of "portable entertainment" by discussing how you can use your Zune while you're away from home and on the road.

To get things started, we take a look at the Zune Travel Pack, an accessory that makes life on the road with the Zune much easier and more enjoyable. Then, we provide you with some tips for traveling with your Zune.

The Zune Travel Pack

The Zune Travel Pack contains a number of great accessories for the Zune, bundled into a single package. As the name implies, it's an honest-to-goodness travel pack, but you can use the items in the pack almost anywhere. In the following sections, we describe the various components of the Zune Travel Pack and tell you how to best use these accessories with your Zune.

The Zune AC adapter

We take a gander at the Zune AC adapter in Chapter 11, but elegant technology always deserves a second (or even third) look. The Zune AC adapter lets you use a standard electrical wall outlet to charge your Zune — which means you no longer have to stick around your PC to charge up. To use the Zune AC adapter, just plug the adapter into the wall, plug the sync cable into the adapter, and then connect the other end of the cable to your Zune.

This accessory is a real must when you travel — who has the time to sync your Zune to, say, your laptop when you're on the road? If you have the Zune AC adapter, you can just plug in at night and charge your Zune without worrying about the state of your Zune's battery. This leaves you free to use your laptop without worrying about what's tethered to it in your room.

You can see the Zune AC adapter in Figure 15-1.

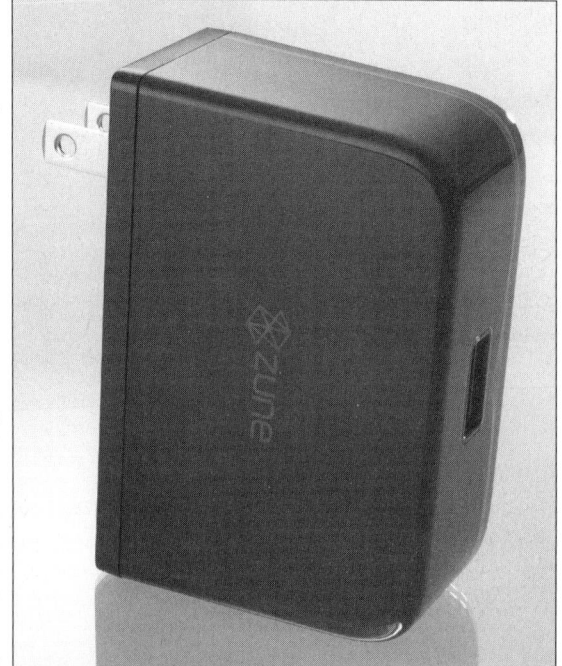

Figure 15-1:
The Zune AC adapter lets you charge your Zune without a PC connection.

The Zune dual connect remote

The Zune dual connect remote is quite a little contraption. It works as a wired remote control for your Zune. But wait, there's more! The Zune dual connect remote also allows you to plug two sets of headphones into the Zune at the same time (hence the "dual connect" part). So, you can easily listen to music or watch a movie on a plane with a friend! One of the best things about this remote is that it has two sets of volume controls. This way each listener can set the volume to a comfortable level for themselves.

The Zune dual connect remote connects to the Zune through the Zune's headphone jack. Figure 15-2 shows the Zune dual connect remote.

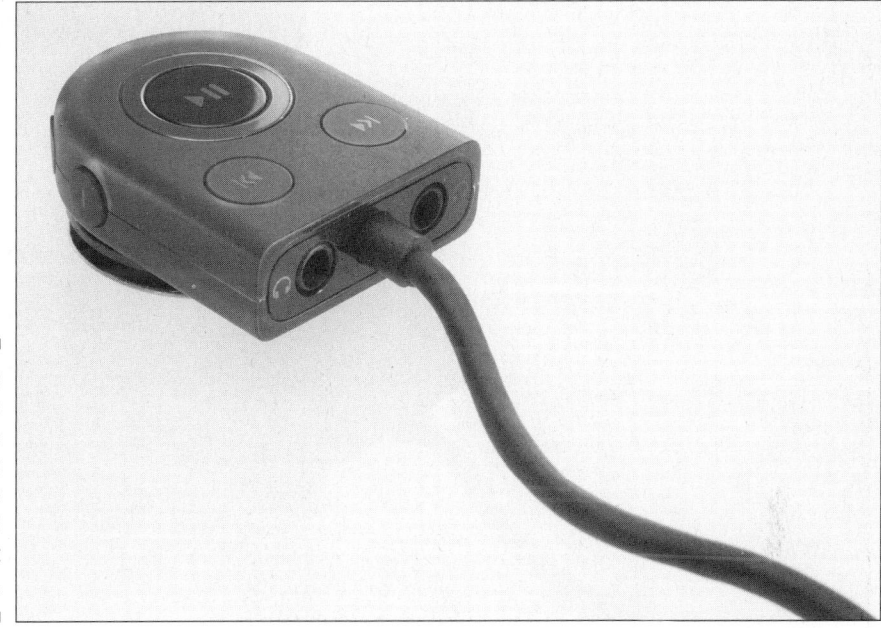

Figure 15-2:
Broaden
your Zune
possibilities
with the
Zune dual
connect
remote.

The Zune gear bag

The Zune Travel Pack contains a lot of stuff for traveling with your Zune on the road. So where are you going to store all that neat travel stuff? Why, in the Zune gear bag, of course! The gear bag features a secure place that can both hold and protect your Zune from inevitable bumps and drops while you travel. In addition, the gear bag features ample storage space for those Zune accessories you might want to take with you on the road.

Figure 15-3 shows a picture of the Zune gear bag.

Zune premium earphones

The Zune premium earphones are one of the best parts of the Zune Travel Pack. These earphones are the in-ear type, so they're a little different from the standard Zune headphones you get out of the box. If you like the standard Zune earphones, you might be wondering, "Why do I need the premium earphones?" Well, this is a travel pack, right? Travel generally means airplanes, and airplanes mean a lot of noise. The Zune premium earphones form a seal when you place them in your ears. This seal helps reduce the background noise that we all experience when we take public transportation. Trust us, after you start using in-ear earphones on an airplane, you don't want to go back to the standard variety.

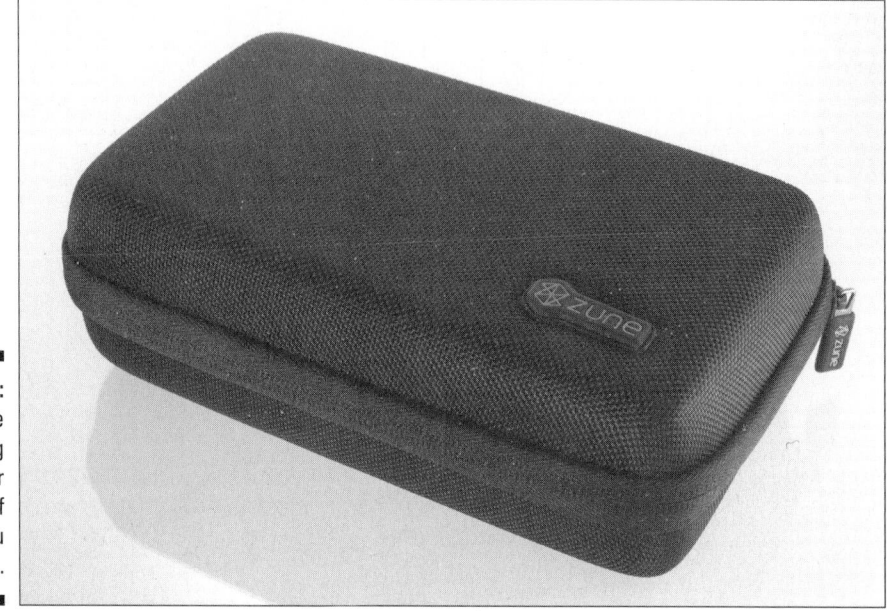

Figure 15-3:
The Zune gear bag holds your Zune stuff while you travel.

You can see a picture of the Zune premium earphones in Figure 15-4.

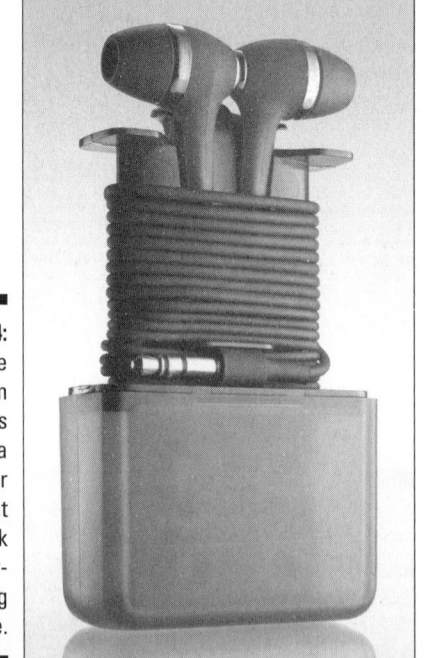

Figure 15-4:
The Zune premium earphones feature a soft rubber seal that helps block out surrounding noise.

Earphones that reduce noise by sealing to your ear are different from earphones that headphone manufacturers label "noise canceling." Noise-canceling headphones usually include a built-in computer that creates sound to counter or block any noise outside the headphones. These headphones usually cost a pretty penny, but prices have gone down significantly over the last couple of years. If you're sensitive to external noise when you use headphones, consider giving noise-canceling headphones a try.

Zune sync cable

Microsoft includes the Zune sync cable in your Zune Travel Pack for a couple of reasons:

- ✔ **So you always have a spare:** This extra sync cable lets you keep your original sync cable plugged into your docking station or desktop PC at home, and you can keep the extra in your travel bag.

- ✔ **To power up:** The Zune sync cable is just what you need to charge your Zune from a wall jack. Just plug the USB connector end of the sync cable into the Zune AC adapter and the other into your Zune.

You can see all the items included in the Zune Travel Pack in Figure 15-5 (the Zune sync cable appears on the right).

Figure 15-5:
Sync and charge your Zune by using the Zune sync cable, which comes in the Travel Pack.

Using Your Zune on the Road

Using your Zune on the road is easy, right? Well, yeah — but you do need to know how to carry the stuff you want with you on the road, how to protect your Zune, and how to keep your Zune charged. Although the Zune is amazingly resilient to problems such as the bumps and bruises of travel, due to its wireless functionality, it's different enough from the other music players out there that you need to take a few extra precautions.

Flying with your Zune

Your Zune can make flying a much more enjoyable experience. Here are some tips for using your Zune on airplanes:

- **Sync before you fly!** First things first: Sync and charge your Zune before you fly. You can easily forget to do this prep work, but you'll regret it if you don't sync and charge your Zune. Flights usually last a long time, and you won't be happy if you don't have all your stuff stored securely on your Zune. You'll feel even worse if your Zune runs out of juice halfway through your flight.

- **If you forget the preceding tip, charge through your laptop.** Don't forget that when you fly, you can charge your Zune through your laptop. If you have a long layover and get a chance to plug in your laptop, plug in your Zune at the same time to sync and top off your Zune's power before you take off again.

- **Turn off the wireless.** Your Zune has wireless capabilities that let you connect to other Zunes so you can share music and photos. Airline rules require that any devices that can send or receive a signal have that functionality disabled while in flight. (You will also get better battery life from your Zune by temporarily turning off its wireless feature.) So, you need to make sure that your Zune wireless connection is shut off when you travel by air.

- **Use high-quality earphones or headphones:** Plane noise can really get in the way of enjoying your favorite high-fidelity music. The Zune earbuds work great for everyday use, but you really want to think about upgrading your headset for those times you're on a noisy airplane.

  You have a few choices when it comes to headphones and earphones that reduce ambient noise on an airplane when you're listening to music. Each of these options has pros and cons. We recommend that you try a few different types of head- and earphones if you can, stopping when you find a solution that you find acceptable.

• **Earphones:** The Zune Travel Pack comes with a set of premium Zune earphones. These earphones have a rubber gasket in the plug that forms a seal when you place them in your ear canal. The gasket blocks out some of the outside noise that can disturb your listening while you travel.

Of course, a number of manufacturers make earphones of this type, and you can spend anywhere from $15 to $200 on these types of earphones. Are the more expensive buds worth the price? It really depends on who you ask. Some people swear by the more expensive earbuds, and some people can't get these expensive earphones to work well at all.

High-end earbuds often have strangely shaped plugs. If you're not hearing music the way you think you should be hearing it when using expensive earbuds, re-read the instructions carefully for insertion and keep trying. Getting the right fit seems to solve the vast majority of problems that users have with these types of earbuds.

Some earbuds come with plugs of varying shapes. Be sure to choose a size that seals in your ear comfortably for best results. You probably know your own ears; if the earphone keeps falling out, it's too small, and if it hurts, it's probably too large. If you have the time, check out all of the plugs that come with your earphones to fine the ones that are just right for you.

Because buying expensive earphones is a bit of an investment, check out your favorite review sites on the Internet and read some reviews. Sites such as `http://onheadphones.com` review the different types of headphones and earbuds you can find out there.

• **Earphones with noise cancellation:** Taking earphones to the next level, noise cancellation uses some nifty technical tricks to mask the noise outside of your headphones.

These earphones work by placing a small microphone outside of the earbud. Circuitry in the headphones generates a noise that cancels out the sounds outside of the earphones, making for a listening less distracted by exterior noise.

Noise-canceling earphones usually cost more than standard earphones. For some, the extra price is worth it, for others the experience is not so good. Noise-canceling earphones tend to have some bulk to them and the results can be disappointing if you buy into the marketing a little too much. Often users are disappointed that they don't hear absolute silence with the music turned off. You really need to try them to see if they're the right solution for you.

Remember, as you would with any other electronic device on an airplane, you're required by airline regulations to turn off the power to your noise-canceling earphones during your plane's take-off and landing.

Noise-canceling earbuds make great earplugs! Just turn them on and put them on when you're flying, and they immediately reduce the noise you're hearing from the people around you and the plane itself. Just leave the Zune off if you want to use your earphones this way.

- **Headphones:** People use two major types of headphones when they travel. One type sits flat on your ear when you listen to music, and the other forms a seal around your ear to help block out external noises. In this chapter, we talk just about the over-the-ear type of headphones because flat headphones really don't work well in situations in which you have a lot of noise around you. (Flat headphones work great in a quiet environment because they tend to be light and comfortable, but they let more outside noise in than any other type of headphone.)

As with the earphones, the quality of the different headphones available really varies, so read some reviews before you jump into spending a lot of money on these puppies.

You can find headphones that include the noise-canceling feature we talk about in the preceding bullet. If you're interested in noise cancellation, headphones can work even better than earphones simply because headphones are larger and therefore have more space for the circuitry needed to create the mask.

Of course, headphones have a downside when you travel — size. Headphones, especially over-the-ear headphones, are much larger than earphones and therefore add extra space and weight to what you have to carry around.

- **Don't forget your Zune!** Unless you're the type who gets to stretch out in first class on a regular basis, you know that planes can be cramped. You probably have a PC set up, a drink of some kind, maybe a PDA, and of course, your Zune. Keeping track of all of this stuff is tough, but you have to try, or you risk forgetting something when you get off the plane.

Here are some tips for keeping track of stuff on an airplane:

- **Use a good bag.** A good travel bag should hold your most important items, your laptop, your Zune, and anything else you travel with. Make sure it has enough space for all of your stuff. You can easily forget to put something in a bag that's overstuffed.

- **Use the same bag every time you travel.** If you have a designated travel bag, you can pick a compartment for each of your important items, making it easier for you to keep track of your stuff.

- **Don't put any personal items in the seat pocket in front of you.** Not even for just a minute. Out of sight, out of mind applies here!

- **Keep your Zune stuff together in a single case that fits into your larger bag.** You can more easily keep track of earphones, cables, and the other Zune accessories you carry around if they have their own case. (The Zune gear bag would be a good choice here — check out the section "The Zune gear bag," earlier in this chapter, to get the scoop on this official Zune case.)

If you do forget something on a plane, you don't have any time to lose. Contact your airline immediately and get them to start looking. The longer you wait, the smaller the chance that they'll be able to track down the item you've lost.

Using your Zune in your hotel room

Travel can be stressful. Your Zune can be your oasis of entertainment and information on what can be a lonely time away from your usual surroundings. In the following sections, we tell you a little bit about using your Zune in your hotel room in a city far away from home.

Checking out FM: No static at all

Are you a fan of National Public Radio or some specific genre of music? If so, don't forget that you have an FM radio in your Zune. You can usually find a station playing music or talk that you like, no matter where you go.

To find the right station for you, just follow these steps:

1. **On your Zune, navigate to Radio by selecting it from the main menu and clicking the OK button.**

2. **Click the right side of the control pad to browse through the available stations.**

3. **If you find a station you like, click the OK button to add it to your presets.**

When you want to navigate between your preset stations, hold down the right or left side of the click wheel to move between the stations.

Setting up a charging station

One of the biggest problems when traveling with any type of electronic gear is keeping stuff charged. You may get tired and forget to plug your Zune into your laptop at the end of the day, and the following day, you're sorely disappointed when you realize your Zune's charge isn't going to last.

Well, that's one of the reasons the Zune AC adapter comes in the Zune Travel Pack. You can easily plug your Zune into the wall outlet before you go to bed at night, and you have a freshly charged device in the morning.

One of the first things you should do when you check into a hotel is set up a charging station for your Zune. Just follow these steps:

1. **Find a power outlet in a good location (next to your bed, or on a desk) and plug your Zune AC adapter into the outlet.**

2. **Plug your Zune sync cable into the adapter.**

   Your charging station is all set up. Before you go to sleep at night, plug your Zune into your charging station, and your Zune will be charged and ready for a new day, come morning.

Find an outlet near the bed if you want to enjoy your Zune through the night. That way, if you fall asleep with your Zune on, it still charges while you sleep.

Syncing your Zune before you take off

Don't forget to sync your Zune in the morning before you take off for the day. If you're a Zune Pass subscriber, refresh your subscription content; and if you've set up your PC to download podcasts, you may want to update those before you take off, as well.

If you're taking pictures while you're on your trip and dropping them into your laptop's Pictures folder, syncing ensures that you can review those pictures on your Zune while you're on the plane home!

Labeling your Zune (outside and in)

We believe that people are honest. They'll try to find the owner of something if they can tell who the owner is. If they can't figure out the owner of a device, though, they won't know who to return it to.

To label your Zune, here's what we suggest:

✔ **Put a small contact-information label on the back of your Zune.**
Include at least your name and phone number on this label. With this
information, somebody can try to contact you if they find your Zune.

✔ **Consider having your Zune engraved with your phone number or
e-mail address.** Think of it as a stamp of personal ownership. (Keep in
mind that engraving your Zune might make it harder to sell later, if you
want to do that.)

✔ **Add a contact-card picture to your Zune that contains your personal
information.** This is the part where you label the inside. Create an electronic calling card for your Zune containing your contact info. The following steps tell you how it's done.

To create a picture containing your personal contact information, follow
these steps:

1. **On your computer, choose Start➪All Programs➪Accessories➪Paint.**

   The Paint program opens.

2. **Choose Image➪Attributes from the main menu.**

   The Attributes dialog box appears.

3. **In the Attributes dialog box, size the image to 240 pixels by 320
   pixels, as shown in Figure 15-6, then click OK.**

   The dialog box closes.

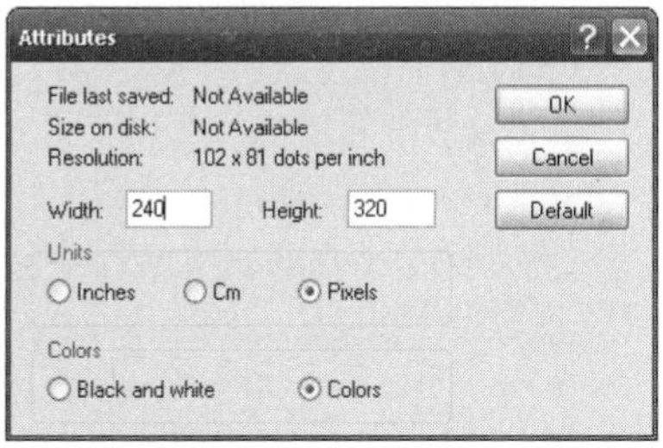

Figure 15-6:
Zune
images are
optimized for
a 240-pixel-
by-320-pixel
display.

4. **Use the Text tool in Paint to add any contact information you want to
   the card.**

   If you want, add a small picture of yourself to the card. This makes it
   easier for the person who finds your Zune to identify you if you want
   to meet.

5. **Save the picture file (as a JPG image) into a Picture folder that you sync to your Zune.**

   Give it a recognizable name, such as "IF-FOUND.jpg" or "MY CONTACT INFO.jpg."

   You can see a simple contact card in Figure 15-7.

6. **Sync your card image to your Zune.**

If you label your Zune (inside or out), somebody might actually be able to find you to return your device if you lose it.

Figure 15-7:
A contact card can make trackzing you down much easier if somebody finds your Zune.

Chapter 16

Tapping into the Zune Community

· ·

In This Chapter

▶ Reaching out to other Zunes

▶ Sharing wirelessly

▶ Checking out online communities

▶ Getting online help for your Zune

· ·

Zune works great as a stand-alone device, entertaining you with music, slideshows, videos, and radio. But one of the joys of owning and using a Zune is the opportunity it gives you to share. You can share not only your music and pictures, but also the interest, excitement, and downright passion that many feel about Zune.

A side benefit of being a Zune owner is the opportunity to interact with others in the Zune community. In this chapter, we explore some fun and useful ways to do just that.

Connecting with Other Zunes

Zune is a relatively new animal, and goodness knows competition is fierce in the digital media player market. Today, the market is dominated by Apple's iPod players, and many companies offer digital players, in addition to Apple and Microsoft. So, you probably won't bump into another Zune owner on the street or on the bus every day.

Finding Zunes in the wild

So, how do you find other Zunes out there in the wide world?

You have one powerful tool readily available to you. Unlike most other digital media players, your Zune player can detect the presence of other Zune players . . . through its wireless features.

Take advantage of your wireless Zune connections by looking for opportunities in which you might be in the company of other Zuners. You could find other Zuners in restaurants, on buses, at concerts, in airports, study halls, lunch rooms, campus libraries, student lounges . . . you name it! Use your player to scan your surroundings for nearby Zunes, and your Zune finds any other Zunes that are within a 60-foot wireless range.

Select the Community option from your Zune's main menu, and your player displays the device names of any nearby Zunes!

When in public settings, be sure to turn your wireless on (via the Settings menu) — otherwise, you won't know if other Zunes are trying to reach out to yours. (For more on the Settings menu, check out Chapter 3.)

When in a potential sharing area, check your Zune display occasionally. If your Zune is in your pocket or tucked away in a case, you may not notice the message displayed when another Zune owner attempts to wirelessly share music or pictures with you.

Some Zune owners have even taken to scheduling pre-arranged meeting places where Zunes can meet up to share music and pictures with each other. For example, some Zune owners arrange to meet once a month in a public setting, such as a coffee shop. The best way to find out about these gatherings is by checking the user forums listed in the "Joining Online Communities" section, later in this chapter.

If you're curious about other Zunes in your area, you can also check online maps of Zune locations. The maps, from sites such as Frappr (`www.frappr.com/zunerama/map`), allow Zune owners to introduce themselves and to mark their location on a map of the world.

Although these maps aren't too useful for wireless sharing purposes, it's fun to see the locations of Zunes around the globe!

Wireless sharing

When you find other people with Zunes, you can send them music or pictures wirelessly. This is one of the more novel aspects of the Zune experience! Zune is the first digital media player to provide this capability.

Mom was right — it's good to share

Zune's wireless sharing is a bold and groundbreaking new feature in the world of digital media players. Although it has limitations (as we describe later in this section), wireless sharing compares well with how cumbersome it is to share music by using other music players.

For example, say you've downloaded a cool new song to your player, and you meet up with a friend with whom you want to share the tune. If you both have traditional (non-Zune) players, you have only two options:

- **Let your friend borrow your earbuds to listen to the song.** That doesn't really give your friend a copy of the song — and, for a lot of people, the idea of using someone else's earbuds has a definite "Ewww!" factor.

- **Let your friend write down the name of the song and/or artist.** The idea here is that that he or she can run home with the little slip of paper, search for that song, and download it from a home computer. That's a big delay — and hardly convenient. "Hey, man, how do you spell 'In-A-Gadda-Da-Vida,' anyway?"

Life is easier if you and your friend both have Zunes. You simply send the song wirelessly to your friend's Zune, and about ten seconds later, he or she has a copy of the song on his or her Zune!

Your friend's use of the song has some real limits — as in, he or she can play it only up to three times in three days. After that, the song expires — but at least he or she has an opportunity to listen to it and an easy means to download a permanent copy of the song later, if desired. Some people are critical about the limits associated with sharing songs . . . but in reality, it's a big step forward compared to other non-Zune players.

Turn it on!

Turn on your Zune's wireless setting, that is. Just follow these steps:

1. **Go to the Settings menu on your player and highlight the Wireless feature by using Up or Down on your control pad.**

2. **Turn your Wireless feature on by pressing the OK button (the center button on your control pad).**

   The setting is a toggle — each time you press the OK button, the wireless setting switches between off and on.

   When you have wireless turned on, the Wireless icon (shown in Figure 16-1) appears at the bottom-right corner of your screen.

Figure 16-1:
The wireless icon appears to the left of the battery icon when a Zune's wireless capability is turned on.

Sharing a song

Next, find the song on your player that you want to share. You have a lot of ways you can do this — check out Chapter 4 if you need some reminders — but one way is to select Music from the main menu and press Up or Down on your control pad to browse songs. When you have the song you want to share highlighted, press the OK button to select that song.

At this point, you see a simple menu, shown in Figure 16-2, with a Play option, an Add to Quick List option, and a Send option.

Now the wireless magic starts! Just follow these steps to share a song with a another Zune:

1. Use Up or Down on the control pad to highlight the Send option in the song menu and press the OK button.

Your player displays a screen titled Nearby. If another Zune is nearby and also has its wireless turned on, you see the device name of that Zune. Figure 16-3 shows an example, in which a Zune has detected a nearby Zune with the device name Carrie's Zune.

If you have multiple Zune's nearby, each of those Zunes appears on your Nearby screen.

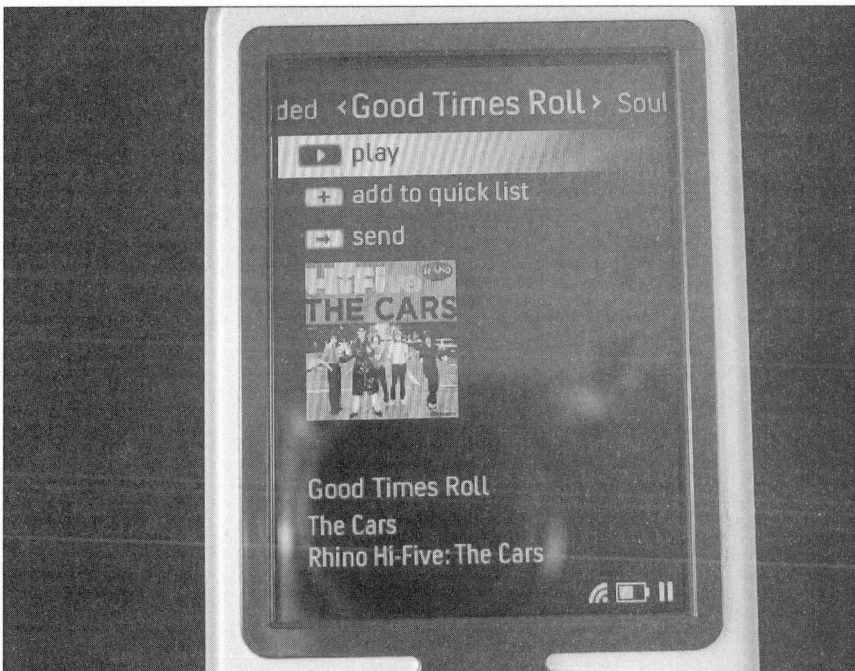

Figure 16-2:
Use the Send option to wirelessly share audio files.

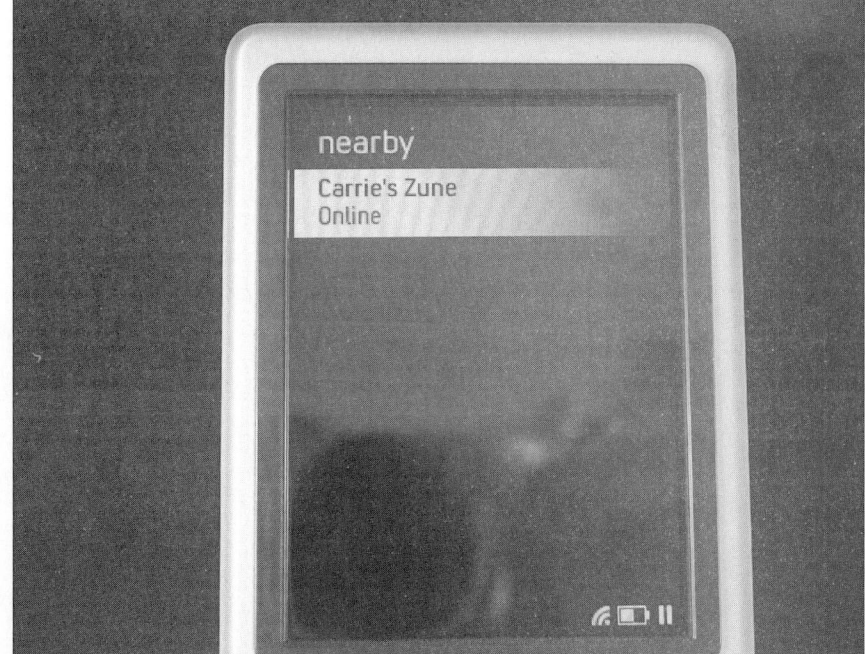

Figure 16-3:
The Nearby screen shows a list of nearby Zunes that have their wireless capability turned on.

2. **Select which Zune you want to send your song to by using Up or Down on your control pad.**

   If your Zune can find only one other Zune nearby, that Zune is already selected on your Nearby screen.

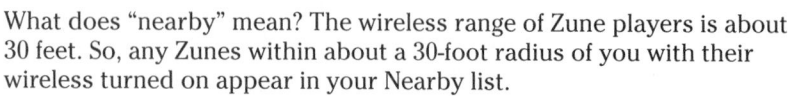

   What does "nearby" mean? The wireless range of Zune players is about 30 feet. So, any Zunes within about a 30-foot radius of you with their wireless turned on appear in your Nearby list.

3. **Press the OK button on your control pad.**

   You see a Connecting message and a Stop button

   On your friend's Zune, a message (shown in Figure 16-4) pops up indicating that your Zune wants to get social with his or her Zune. The ball's in the other Zune's court now!

If your friend is in an agreeable mood, he or she can press Yes to accept your offer to send files. (If he or she presses the No button, you may want to think about moving beyond your Air Supply collection.)

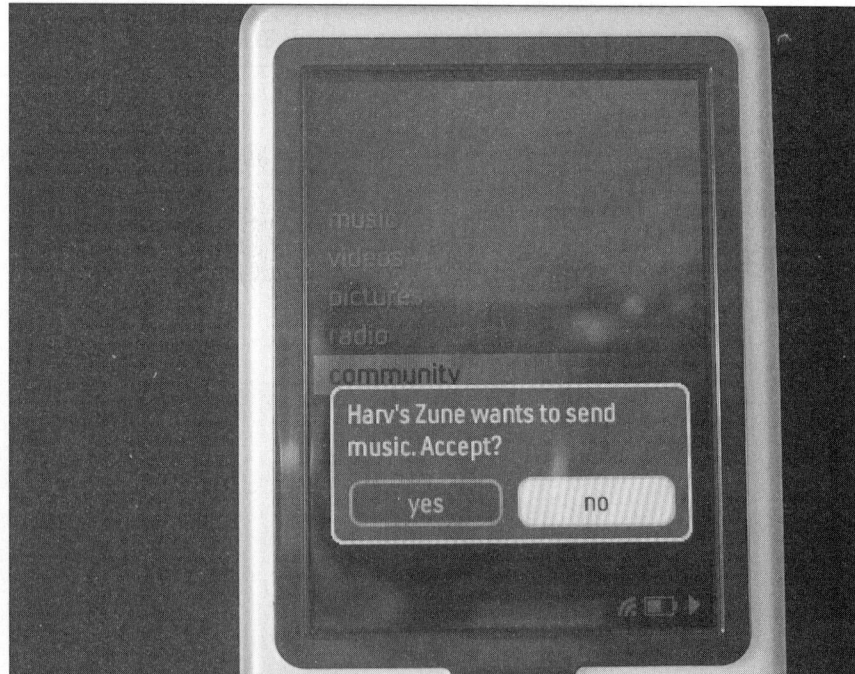

Figure 16-4:
You can always choose whether to accept files sent to you.

When your friend presses Yes, your Zune displays a Sending 1 of 1 message, and your friend's Zune displays a similar Connecting screen with a Receiving 1 of 1 message. When the transfer is complete — it takes all of a few seconds — a Done message pops up on your Zune's screen, and a Receive Complete message pops up on your friend's Zune. The message also advises your friend to check his or her inbox; that's where the Zune stores received files. As Figure 16-5 shows, your friend also gets a friendly reminder that the sent file is a sample song that he or she can play only three times in three days.

That's it! You've shared your song wirelessly, and your friend can immediately listen to it. How cool is that?

The lucky Zuner who just received the file can continue using his or her Zune in any way he or she pleases at this point. If he or she doesn't take any action after a few seconds, his or her Zune conveniently displays the received song in the player's inbox. Figure 16-6 shows an example of such a received song.

In the inbox, a reminder message appears about how many plays — and how many days — are remaining in the file's three-plays-in-three-days limit. This message counts down as the song is played or as the days go by.

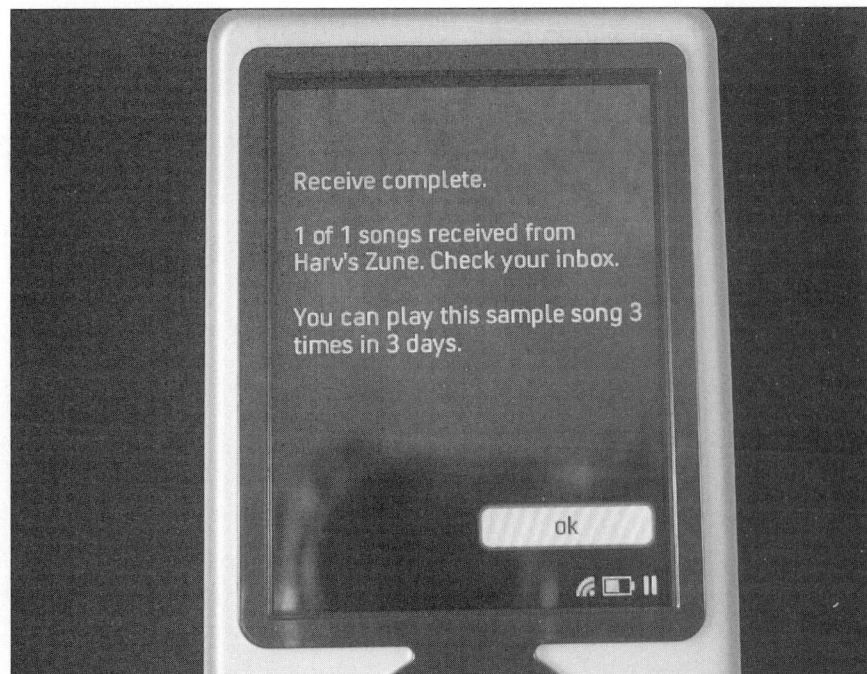

Figure 16-5:
A completion message confirms the receipt of files.

In this section, for simplicity, we refer to sharing songs, but you can share any kind of audio files — music, podcasts, audiobooks, or any sound file — with other Zunes.

I've received a song — now what?

What can you do with a song after you receive it?

Received songs are stored in your inbox. You can see your received files by selecting Community from the main menu on your Zune and then selecting Inbox from the top menu options.

Use Right or Left on the control pad to move through the top menu options, and then press the OK button after you highlight the option you want.

The inbox shows the files you've received since the last time you synced your Zune player. (Check out the example in Figure 16-7.)

When you select a song in your inbox (by highlighting the song and pressing the OK button), song information appears — including a reminder about how far you are in your three-plays-in-three-days limit.

In the example in Figure 16-8, the song has two plays remaining in the next three days.

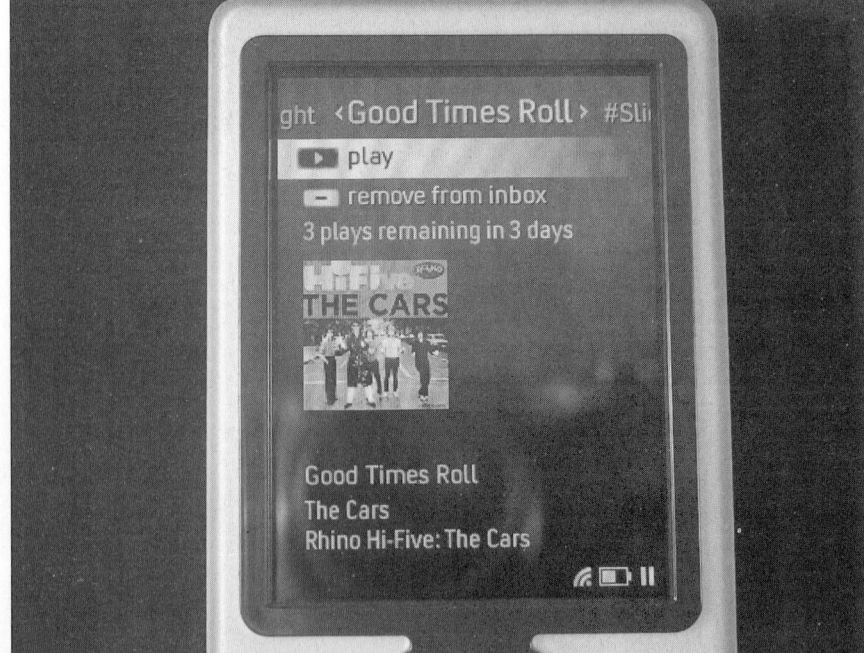

Figure 16-6:
Received songs are stored in the Zune's inbox.

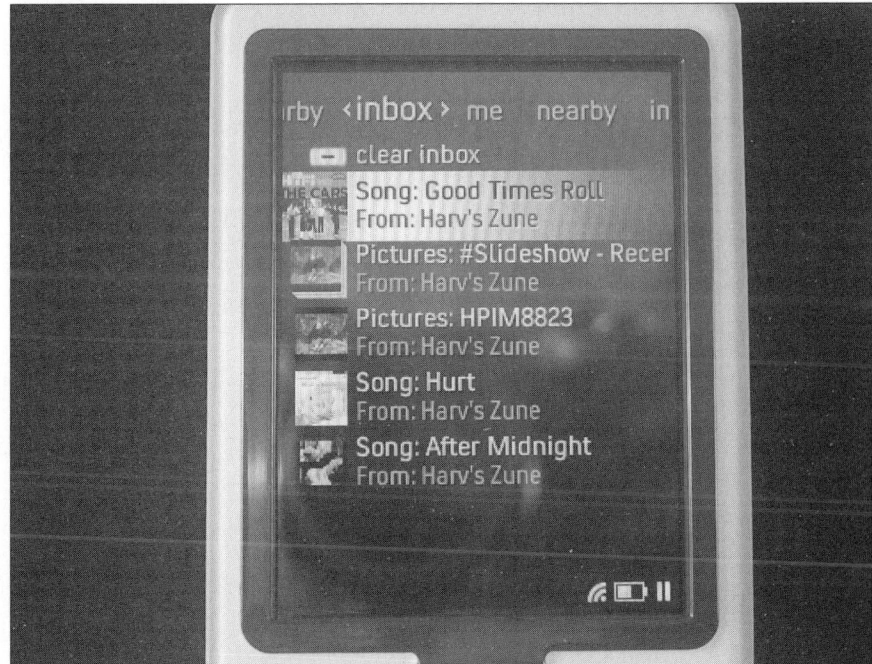

Figure 16-7:
The inbox displays your received files and shows where they came from.

Figure 16-8:
Your inbox reminds you how many plays, and days, are remaining for the sample audio file.

After you play the song three times, or have it three days or longer, the song is no longer playable. When you view the song in your inbox, it appears as Expired, as shown in Figure 16-9.

After you receive a song wirelessly, it's automatically transferred to the inbox in your PC's Zune software the next time you sync the player with your PC.

To view the contents of your Zune library's inbox on your PC, click the Inbox link in the Navigation pane on the left side of your Zune software window.

Figure 16-10 shows an inbox that has recently received pictures and songs. For each item in the inbox, you can see the title, artist, album, action, and Zune from which the file was sent.

If the item is a song that's not already in your library, you can select Download from the action column to pull down the song from Zune Marketplace. That way, you can get your own permanent copy of the song that was sent to you.

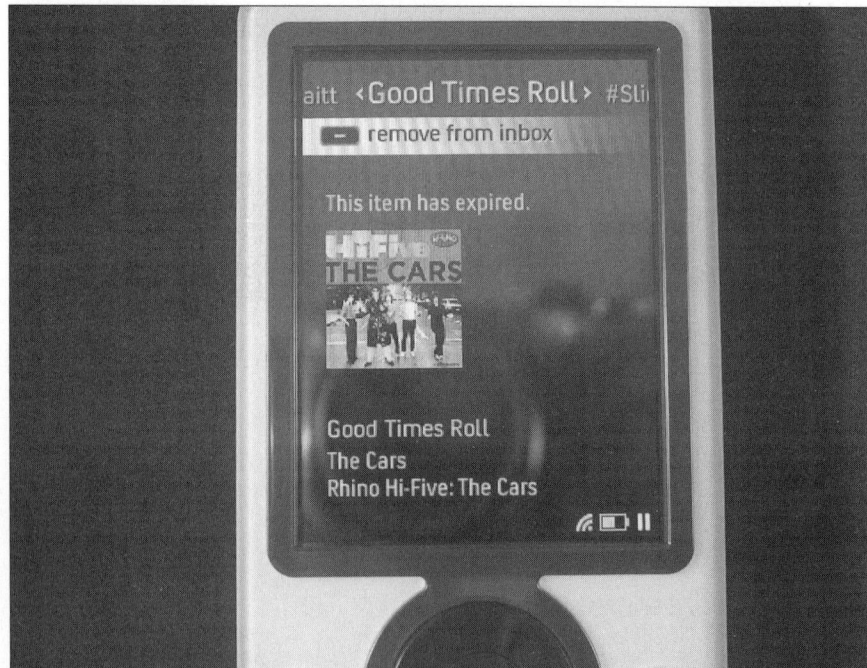

Figure 16-9:
The song displayed here has exceeded its three-plays-in-three-days limit.

Figure 16-10: Files you've received wirelessly sync to your PC's Zune software inbox.

Sending an entire album or playlist

You can wirelessly send an entire album, or an entire playlist, just as easily as sending an individual song!

To send an entire album, follow these steps:

1. **Find the album you want to send by selecting Music from the main menu, selecting the Albums view from the top menu options, and browsing through your album selections.**

2. **Use Up or Down on the control pad to highlight the particular album you want and then press the OK button.**

   You see the simple menu shown in Figure 16-11, which includes the Send option.

3. **From this point, the procedure is identical to the steps for sending an individual song.**

   A Nearby screen displays any nearby Zunes, and you can select a Zune to send the album to. Check out the section "Sharing a song," earlier in this chapter, for what to do from here.

Figure 16-11:
The Send
option
becomes
available
when you
select an
album.

Sending an entire playlist to another Zune works exactly the same way:

1. **Find the playlist you want to send by selecting Music from the main menu, selecting the Playlists view from the top menu options, and browsing through your playlists.**

2. **Use Up or Down on the control pad to highlight a particular playlist and then press the OK button.**

3. **In the menu that appears, choose Send.**

   Selecting the Send option displays the Nearby screen listing nearby Zunes. Select a Zune to send the playlist to and then follow the procedure outlined in the section "Sharing a song," earlier in this chapter.

Can all songs be shared?

You can use wireless to share *most* songs that you've downloaded from Marketplace, as well as all other songs on your Zune (songs that you've ripped from CDs, for example).

You can't share some songs wirelessly with other Zunes that you downloaded from Zune Marketplace. This is apparently because of different agreements associated with digital music rights.

When a song can't be shared wirelessly, you see a Can't Send Songs Because of Rights Restrictions message. (The receiving Zune displays a similar message.)

Sharing pictures

Sharing pictures wirelessly is even easier than sharing music. For one thing, no digital rights apply to picture sharing. After you send someone a picture, that picture is his or hers to keep forever, with no restrictions (such as the three-plays-in-three-days limit that's applied to audio files).

If you're familiar with how to send music files, you should find sending pictures pretty intuitive. Just follow these steps:

1. **Find the picture that you want to share.**

   You have a lot of ways to find a picture, and we outline them all in Chapter 6. One way is to select Pictures from the main menu, select a picture folder, and use Up or Down on your control pad to navigate to a particular picture.

2. **Select the picture that you want to share by using Up or Down on the control pad to highlight it. Then press the OK button.**

   The picture appears (in horizontal viewing mode) on your player, as shown in Figure 16-12.

Figure 16-12: The first step to wirelessly sending a picture is viewing the pic on the player.

3. **Press the OK button and use Up or Down on the control pad to choose Send from the menu that appears.**

   Your player displays a screen titled Nearby. If another Zune is nearby, and also has its wireless turned on, you see the device name of that Zune.

4. **Select the name of the device to which you want to send the picture, then press the OK button.**

   The Connecting message appears, complete with Stop button.

The receiving Zune displays a message asking whether it should accept pictures from your Zune.

After the other Zuner selects Yes, the transfer takes place. When all the bits are done flying between Zunes, the sending Zune displays a Done message.

On the receiving Zune, the message Receive Complete appears, along with an indication of how many pictures were transferred.

The receiving Zune can continue with any player function at this point. If the Zune user doesn't take any action after a few seconds, his or her Zune conveniently displays the received picture from the player's inbox. Figure 16-13 shows an example of such a received picture.

Figure 16-13:
Pictures
sent
wirelessly
show up in
your inbox.

Things to keep in mind about wireless sharing

Microsoft has imposed three Zune wireless-sharing rules, evidently put in place to prevent people from using wireless sharing for illegal distribution of copyrighted music. Here are the three rules associated with wireless sharing:

✔ You can't send the same song to the same Zune device more than once. In other words, you can't get around the three-plays-in-three-days rule by repeatedly sending the same song to your buddy.

✔ You can't wirelessly send a file that you yourself received wirelessly.

✔ The three-plays-in-three-days restriction is applied to *any* audio file shared wirelessly. This includes files downloaded from Marketplace, ripped from CDs, or even recorded or created by yourself.

You've sent your picture wirelessly from one Zune to another! The whole exchange takes just a few seconds. Very cool.

Sharing a folder of pictures

You can wirelessly send a whole folder of pictures to another Zune — all at once.

To send an entire folder, follow these steps:

1. **Find the folder you want to send by selecting Pictures from the main menu and then selecting the Folders view from the top menu options.**

2. **Use Up or Down on the control pad to highlight a particular folder, then press the OK button.**

   A menu appears.

3. **Choose Send from the menu.**

   The Nearby screen appears, displaying any nearby Zunes.

4. **Select a Zune to which you want to send the entire folder of pictures.**

5. **Press OK.**

   Voila!

Although you can share audio tracks and pictures wirelessly with other Zunes, you can't share videos wirelessly.

Some Zune owners have created special graphics, called *greeting cards,* that they can wirelessly send to others as a way of introducing themselves. These graphics are like business cards and can contain words of greeting, a short introduction, your Zune device name, and perhaps even your picture. You can see examples of these graphics in the Zune forums discussed in the following section.

Joining Online Communities

You can connect with other members of the Zune community through online Zune user forums. Every day, Zune owners from all over the world visit these forums to give opinions, ask questions, get technical support, and relate their Zune experiences.

Forums are a great way to get to know other Zune owners, find out about Zune accessories, get Zune help and advice, and get the most you can out of your Zune.

You can find several Zune forums on the Web by doing a Web search using the terms "Zune forum." According to ZuneList (www.zunelist.com, a site devoted to tracking Zune Web sites), these are the five most-visited Zune forums:

- ✔ ZuneScene (www.zunescene.com)
- ✔ Zunerama (www.zunerama.com) (See Figure 6-14)
- ✔ ZuneMax (www.zunemax.com)
- ✔ Zune-Online (www.zune-online.com)
- ✔ ZuneBoards (www.zuneboards.com)

Most forums have RSS (Really Simple Syndication) feeds available, which let you conveniently view recent forum posts from an RSS feed reader. The little RSS icon (see Figure 16-15) lets you know if a feed is available. RSS feed readers are integrated in some Web browsers, including Internet Explorer 7, and you can also get free feed-reader services from sites such as Google.

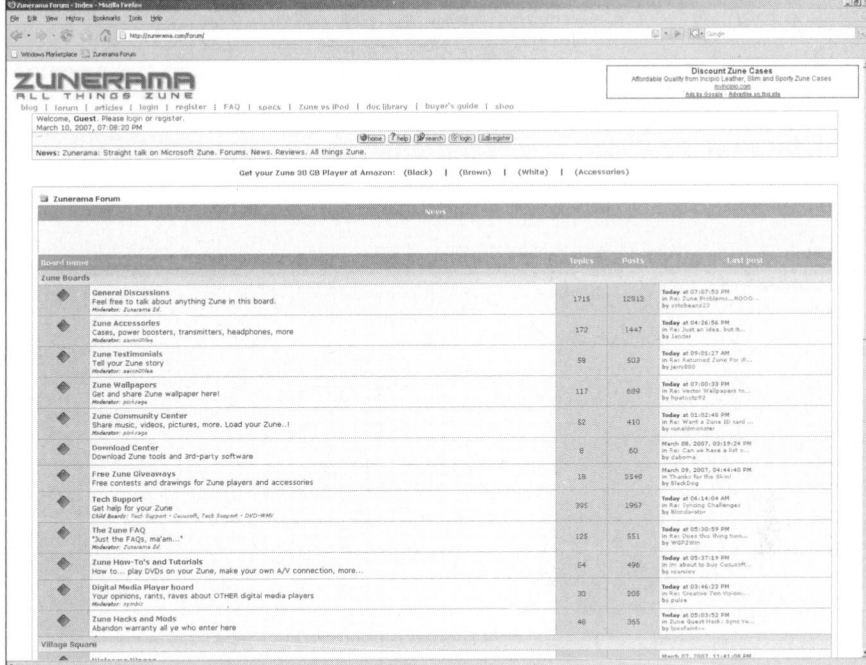

Figure 16-14:
Zune forums
provide an
online meet-
ing place
for Zune
enthusiasts.

Many forums hold contests and giveaways of Zune players and Zune accessories. In addition to the sites in the preceding list, you can find forums offering Zune freebies by doing a Web search for "Zune giveaways."

Figure 16-15:
RSS links
allow you to
conveniently
keep up to
date on
many Zune
forums and
Web sites.

Getting Zune Information Online

You can find a wealth of information through the Zune online community.

Want Zune tutorials? Answers to Zune frequently asked questions (FAQs)? Zune documentation? The latest Zune news and rumors? Information about Zune accessories? Zune wallpapers? How about Zune hacks and custom modifications?

All this information is at your fingertips! In the following sections, we discuss how to find this information, and we give you links to prominent Zune online resources.

The official Zune site

Microsoft's official Web site for Zune is Zune.net (`www.zune.net`). The site (shown in Figure 16-16) provides the obvious: an overview of the Zune player, Zune software, and Zune Marketplace. But it also includes these features:

- Links to music events and community sites
- Zune art that you can download and use as wallpaper for your Zune player
- Official made-for-Zune accessories and links to shopping pages for Zune players and accessories
- Technical support and troubleshooting information
- Zune Marketplace online account management

Semi-official Zune sites (from Microsoft employees)

Several Microsoft employees operate sites that provide glimpses into Microsoft's Zune team:

- **ZuneInsider (`http://zuneinsider.com`):** A blog from Cesar Menendez, a Microsoft employee working on the Zune team. (Check out Figure 16-17.)
- **Zunester (`www.zunester.com`):** A blog from David Caulton, another member of Microsoft's Zune team.
- **ZuneGuy (`www.zuneguy.com`):** Bill Wittress of the Zune business development team runs this blog.
- **Madison and Pine (`www.madisonandpine.com`):** A blog from Richard Winn, head of artist development for Zune.

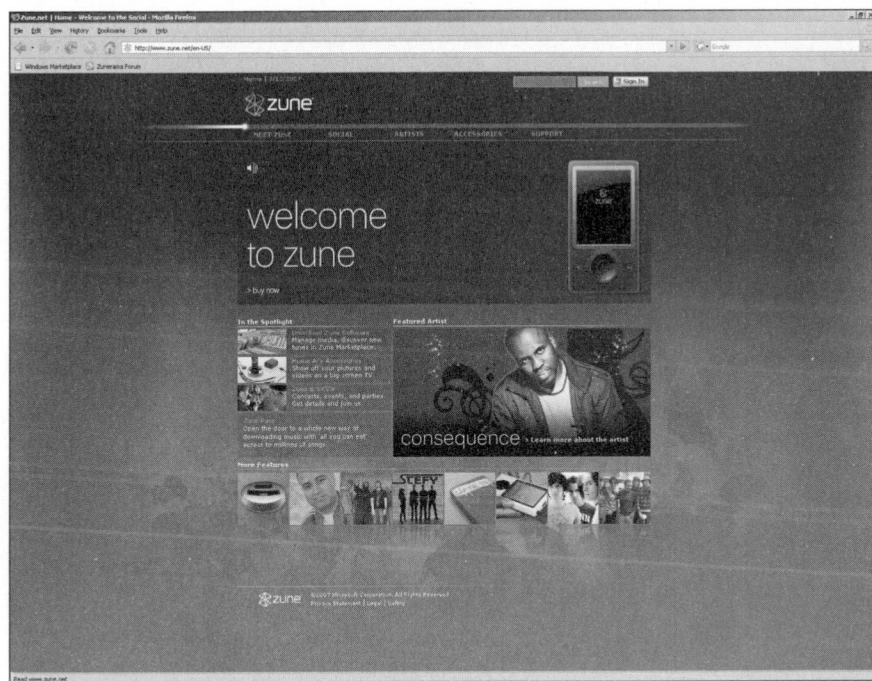

Figure 16-16:
Zune.net is
Microsoft's
official
Zune site.

Figure 16-17:
Several
Microsoft
employees
from the
Zune team
write blogs.

Sites about Zune sites

Several tracking sites monitor visitor traffic to Zune sites. You can use these sites to conveniently find the Zune sites that are most heavily used by other Zune owners. Tracking sites, also called *top sites,* include ZuneList (`www.zunelist.com`; shown in Figure 16-18) and TopZuneSites (`www.topzunesites.com`).

Your Average Joe Zune blogs

Not all Zune blogs are run by folks who have `@microsoft.com` as part of their e-mail address. Zune enthusiasts who just love the device also run blogs. The bloggers who run these sites write about Zune news, rumors, tips, and other information of general interest to Zune owners.

You can find a ton of Zune blogs out there! Browse through several blogs until you find a few that you like. Some Zune blogs aren't often updated, and others are updated several times per day. Most blogs have an article archive where you can view past entries.

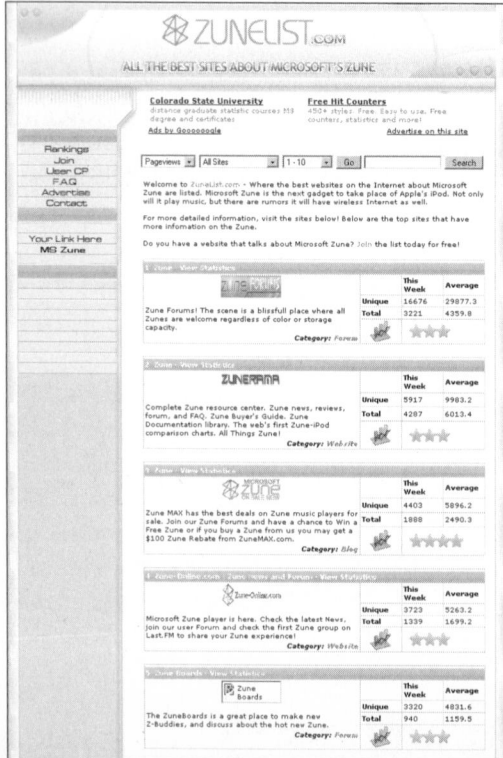

Figure 16-18:
Zune top sites keep daily track of the hottest Zune sites on the Web.

The *voice,* or writing style, varies from one blog site to another; and, of course, the insights offered through the blog vary from one blogger to another. Some blogs specialize in re-blogging information from other blogs and Web sites; others focus more on original content.

Do a Web search using the terms "Zune blog" or "Zune articles" to bring up a long list of Zune blogs. Blogs we like to check on a regular basis include

- **ZuneThoughts (www.zunethoughts.com):** Daily news, views, rants, and raves about Zune

- **ClicZune (www.cliczune.com):** Original commentary and analysis updated on a near-daily basis

- **Zunerama (www.zunerama.com):** As shown in Figure 16-19, original Zune stories and analysis, with photo and video reviews of Zune accessories

- **ZuneMax (www.zunemax.com):** Zune news and reviews, including new music from Zune artists, bands, and musicians

Figure 16-19: Zune blogs provide daily Zune news, articles, and analysis.

Zune FAQs

As you use your Zune, you may have questions from time to time. More often than not, your questions have probably been asked and answered by others before.

Fortunately, several sites maintain Zune FAQs — answers to frequently asked questions about Zune.

Whether your question is about your Zune player, the Zune software on your PC, or the Zune Marketplace, you can probably get your question answered at a good Zune FAQ site, such as the one in Figure 16-20 (`www.zunerama.com/zune-faq/faq.php`).

You can find these sites through a Web search for "Zune FAQ."

Zune tutorials

Everyday use of your Zune is quite straightforward. But, occasionally, you may find yourself puzzling over a less commonly used function or a more advanced task.

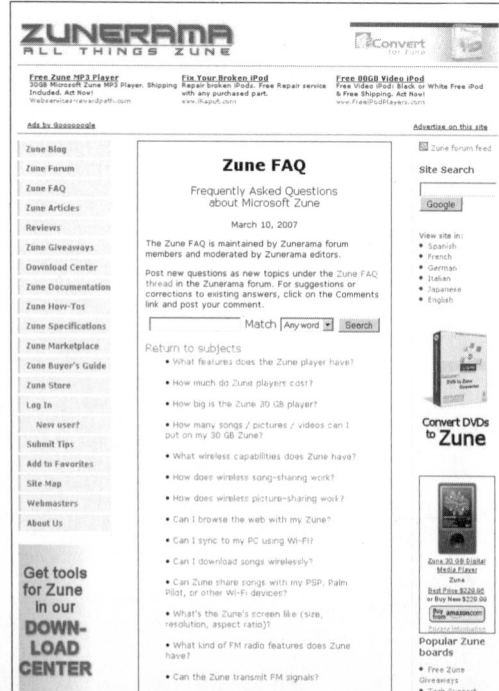

Figure 16-20:
Have a question? Get it answered in a Zune FAQ!

For example, perhaps you want to convert your family's home videos to a format that can play on your Zune. Or maybe your Uncle Stanley has given you a DVD of that last family reunion, and you want to rip that DVD and get the video on your Zune. Maybe you just want to connect your Zune to your TV and need a refresher on the cable connections.

Several sites provide Zune *tutorials* — step-by-step instructions on how to carry out these types of tasks. Figure 16-21 shows an example. You can find additional sites through a Web search for "Zune tutorials" or "Zune How To." You can also find good tutorials at

- ✔ www.zunerama.com/zune-how-to.php
- ✔ www.zuney.net/zune-tutorials
- ✔ www.zuneuser.com/forums/zune-tutorials-how-tos

Zune documentation

You can find a variety of Zune documentation online, including technical documentation, press releases, fact sheets, and specification sheets.

Look for sites offering libraries of Zune documentation through a Web search for "Zune documentation" or "Zune specifications."

Figure 16-21:
Get step-by-step instructions for advanced tasks from online Zune tutorials.

Getting Help for Your Zune

If you need to troubleshoot problems on your Zune, here are some ways to get help:

- ✔ **Use the Help info in the Zune software on your PC.** Press F1 or choose Options⇨Help⇨Zune Help from the Zune software main menu. An online user manual appears, featuring a Table of Contents and searchable index.

- ✔ **Use the online troubleshooting feature.** Choose Options⇨Help⇨ Troubleshooting Online from the Zune software main menu. This Web-based troubleshooting service troubleshoots for Zune, Zune Marketplace, and Zune accessories.

- ✔ **Check out a Zune FAQ.** See if your problem is addressed in a previously answered question.

- ✔ **Download a Zune manual.** You can find these manuals at `www.zune.net/en-us/support/resources/downloadmanuals.htm`.

- ✔ **Browse Zune user forums.** Look for posts from others who may have encountered similar problems and see how they resolved those problems.

- ✔ **Post a description of your problem in a forum.** Some forums have Technical Support boards specifically designed to allow members to help other members troubleshoot their Zune problems.

- ✔ **Call the Zune help desk.** 1-877-GET-ZUNE (1-877-438-9863). It's free and open seven days a week, from 6 a.m. to 10 p.m. Pacific Standard Time.

Part IV
The Part of Tens

The 5th Wave   By Rich Tennant

"It's like any other pacemaker, but it comes with an internal Zune docking accessory."

In this part . . .

The Part of Tens contains lists of stuff that we thought Zune owners might be interested in, such as a listing of cool accessories for the Zune, a rundown of what parents need to know to make the Zune safe for their children, and advice on how you can best protect your expensive new gadget.

Chapter 17

Ten Great Zune Accessories

*O*kay, so you have a Zune, and it rocks — but what if you need to hook it up to your car, your TV, or your home stereo? What if you're worried it's going to get scratched when you toss it into your carry-on bag for a trip? What if you want to use it while you're working out?

Sounds like you're in the market for an accessory; one of the many products that you can use to add to your Zune experience. Accessories for the Zune come in many different shapes, sizes, and price ranges, so there's something for everybody. Most products fall into one of the following five categories:

✓ **The essential cables:** To hook your Zune up to stuff.

✓ **Docks:** Like connectors, except they act more like a permanent cradle for the Zune. (They may — or may not — include speakers.)

✓ **Power adapters:** To make charging your Zune a bit easier.

✓ **Cases, sleeves, shells, and armbands:** All forms of protective gear that wrap around your Zune.

✓ **Headphones:** Even if they're not made for the Zune. (We show you some great upgrades from the earbuds that ship with the Zune in the section "Headphones," later in this chapter.)

Quite a few companies have jumped on board to make accessories for the Zune, leading to a lot of choices for you. You can also find products that, although not specifically designed for the Zune, nevertheless really add to the experience. Within each of the five categories mentioned in the preceding list, we pick out a few particular examples that we're impressed with and talk about them in detail in the rest of this chapter.

Connectors and Adapters

Depending on what you want to connect to your Zune, you may need an additional cable, which can be a problem because nothing comes in your Zune's box except for headphones and the Zune's USB sync cable.

The Zune USB sync cable

We know, we know — the sync cable comes with the Zune. So, why in the world do we call it an accessory?

Well, we thought a sync cable (a second sync cable, to be exact) fit on the accessories list for two reasons:

- ✔ **Multiplying cables:** You need the sync cable to do anything with the content on the Zune, so you might want to have one at home and an extra one at the office (or in your laptop bag, or wherever).

- ✔ **Disappearing cables:** You might end up buying a sync cable after you lose your first one. Personally, we've lost a lot of cables over the years. And because Microsoft didn't use a standard USB-to-USB cable for the Zune, if you lose your Zune's cable, you can't just grab one from your digital camera, camcorder, or cell phone.

If you decide you need a second Zune sync cable, it sells separately for around $20. (A Zune sync cable also comes in both the Home A/V Pack and the Travel Pack, which we talk about in the section "The Accessory Packs," later in this chapter.)

The A/V output cable

You can connect the audio/video output cable, which plugs into the headphone port on top of your Zune, to an audio system (by using the red/white RCA jacks) or to an audio/video display such as a TV (by using the yellow video cable, in addition to the audio ones). You'll find this cable invaluable if you end up in a hotel room that has inputs on its TV, and you can even use this cable at home if you want to show a video from your Zune on your TV screen. (Figure 17-1 gives you an idea what an A/V output cable looks like.)

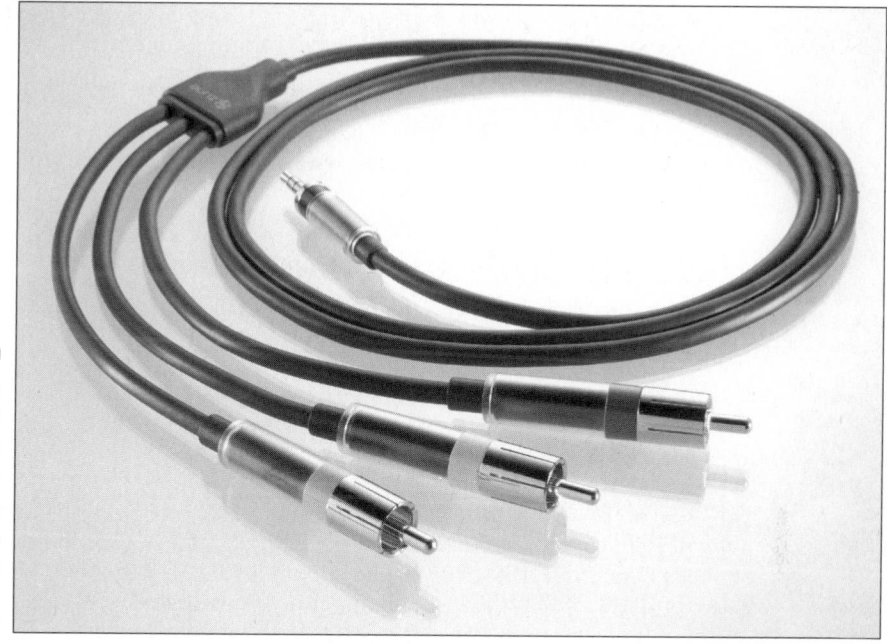

Figure 17-1:
The A/V
output cable
goes from a
mini-plug
jack to three
RCA output
jacks.

You can find this type of cable all over the place because it often ships with camcorders and other electronic gadgets — but keep in mind that not all mini-jack-to-A/V-output cables are wired the same. If you already have one of these cables from another gadget, try it out to see whether it works with your Zune. Sometimes, you can make the different wiring work if you rearrange the three output jacks (try putting the red jack into the yellow input, the white jack into the red input, and so on). Sometimes, though, the cable just won't work for the Zune at all.

To try out a cable, follow these steps:

1. **Hook up the mini plug to the headphone port of your Zune.**

2. **Put one of the RCA jacks into the yellow input on your TV or other device.**

3. **Make sure you're viewing the right input on your TV (switch to the appropriate input by using your TV's controls).**

   Depending on your TV, you may need to change your input source settings — through a source setting such as LINE1, LINE2, or AUX.

4. **Switch the Zune to TV Out mode by choosing Settings⇨Display⇨TV Out on the Zune device's main navigation menu.**

   If the connection works, great! You're done and can begin enjoying your Zune content through the connected device.

5. **If the connection isn't working, swap the RCA jacks around to try each of them in the video (yellow) input.**

6. **After you find a video jack-input combo that works, put the remaining two jacks into the red and white inputs for audio.**

   If nothing works and you need to get your Zune's screen back, just press the Zune's OK button or unplug the adapter.

The Zune's headphone jack is compatible with the iPod's jack, meaning that any A/V output cable for the iPod should work with the Zune — but you do need to swap the red and yellow cables.

The Zune output cable retails for approximately $20, and you can't avoid buying it if you want to hook your Zune up to a TV or similar device. If you're worried about only audio (for hooking your Zune up to a stereo system, for example), you'd probably be fine with a 3.5mm mini-jack-to-stereo-RCA-plugs cable. (You can find these guys at almost any store with electronics — Radio Shack, Best Buy, whatever — for anywhere from $2 to $15, depending on the brand.)

An A/V output cable comes in the Home A/V Pack (a bundle of accessories we cover in the section "The Accessory Packs," later in this chapter).

Monster (www.monstercable.com) sells the same basic cable, which they call the Monster TVLink Designed for Zune, for approximately $30. Monster's cable is longer than the Zune cable (ten feet long, compared to only a few feet for the Zune cable) and, like most Monster products, is considered higher-end than the typical cable.

FM transmitters

FM transmitters hook up your Zune to your car's lighter (or accessory power) and then broadcast the audio out of your Zune onto a specific FM frequency. After you have your transmitter hooked up, you can tune your car stereo into the FM frequency that you chose on the transmitter and listen to your Zune's music over your car speakers. You may have some problems finding a frequency that doesn't already have a station on it (which causes interference), especially in an urban area, but Microsoft's FM kit (created specifically for the Zune) includes a useful Auto Tune feature that seeks through the FM band, finds a clear channel for you to use, and then displays that frequency on a small display attached to the power adapter of the FM kit (see Figure 17-2).

Figure 17-2:
The Zune
FM trans-
mitter can
find the best
frequency
to use in
your car.

Belkin (www.belkin.com) makes an FM transmitter system that gets our unofficial award for Best in This Category: the TuneBase. It acts like a sleeve or cradle into which you slide your Zune, providing the functionality you expect (FM transmitting, storing multiple frequencies to choose between, charging while connected), along with a killer feature that you may not have seen in any other product. The TuneBase has a flexible steel rod connecting the cradle to the cigarette lighter or accessory power, and this rod holds your Zune up at a usable angle, allowing you to position your Zune as desired. Even if you can find another way to hook your Zune up to your car stereo (such as an aux-in jack, or something similar), you might still want to use the TuneBase just to charge and hold the Zune!

Monster (www.monstercable.com) makes an FM transmitter, as well — the CarPlay, which provides the same basic features as the one Microsoft came up with for the Zune (although the CarPlay does lack the auto-tuning feature that makes Microsoft's transmitter so unique).

All three of the FM transmitters charge your Zune while you use it in your car, which is a great feature for long trips.

Docking Your Zune

Docks give you a home base in a place (or places) where you plan on using your Zune on a regular basis. Instead of just hooking up the USB cable and setting your Zune down somewhere on that messy desk (or kitchen counter!), where you can't really even see the screen, a dock gives you a cradle into which you can slide your Zune. The dock holds your Zune upright, charges it, and provides output cables that you can leave permanently hooked up to your TV, stereo, or PC. You can find two main kinds of docks — those that include speakers and those that don't — although both types provide some of the same features.

Docks without speakers

When the Zune launched, you really had only one choice if you wanted a dock without speakers; the official Zune dock. You can place this small docking station next to your computer or home stereo so you can hook up your Zune by simply clicking it into the cradle (Figure 17-3 shows what the Zune dock looks like). In addition to the slot for connecting your Zune device, the dock has a connector port for hooking up the Zune USB sync cable to your computer or to a power adapter, as well as a headphone port that you can use with a standard audio cable to hook your Zune up to your stereo. (You can use the port with the Zune audio/video cable — or another A/V output cable — to hook your Zune up to your TV.)

This dock can work in two main ways, depending on how you want to use your Zune at home:

- ✔ **Connecting to A/V devices:** If you want to hook your Zune up to your home stereo system, your TV, or even just a set of external computer speakers, use the headphone jack to hook up the A/V output cable (for a TV), a standard mini-jack-to-RCA cable (for stereo systems), or the mini-jack cable for your computer speakers. (Figure 17-4 shows you how you could set up the TV connection.) At the same time, you can hook up the Zune sync cable to the dock and to an AC power adapter (we cover how this connection provides power to your Zune without using a PC in the section "Power Adapters," later in this chapter), and now you have a charging/listening station.

- ✔ **Hooking up to your PC:** If you mostly hook your Zune up to your PC just to charge and sync, you can hook the USB cable to the dock and then just slide the Zune into the cradle when you want to sync. You can still hook up a set of speakers in this scenario because the Zune plays music (or does anything, really) while it's connected to your PC, as long as the Zune software is closed. While the Zune software is running, though, your Zune displays a Connected message and won't play music or anything else.

Figure 17-3:
The Zune dock makes hooking your Zune up to charge, sync, or listen easy.

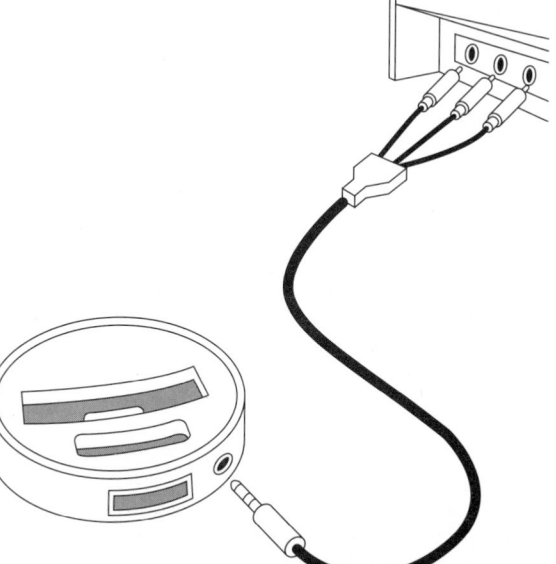

Figure 17-4:
A head-phone jack lets you leave your A/V output cable hooked up to the dock.

The dock makes hooking up and syncing your Zune a bit easier, and it certainly leads to a cleaner desk experience than having the USB cable running across your desk and the Zune just lying wherever you can find room. The question is, do you think a clean desk is worth $40?

If you want to get the Zune dock, consider the Home A/V Pack (which we discuss in the section "The Accessory Packs," later in this chapter); it includes the dock, a wireless remote, a power adapter, and the A/V output cable, and it costs around $100.

Docks with speakers

What if you want to hook up your Zune to some external speakers but don't have a stereo system conveniently available? For this scenario, you can get a dock that includes its own set of speakers so that you can bring the full Zune music experience out of your headphones and into your living room, bedroom, or wherever. (We're thinking about a dock for our desks at work!)

When the Zune was released, two companies had started selling speaker docks, with similar features but aiming at different audiences:

- ✔ **The Altec Lansing M604:** This cool little unit has a few unique features that make it worth noticing:

   - • **Universal cradle:** In addition to allowing you to dock your Zune, the M604 also accepts any other MP3 player through a mini-plug input and special universal cradle that comes with the dock.

   - • **Remote:** This dock comes with a wireless remote.

   - • **Video-out port:** With this video-out port, you can run a cable to your TV.

   - • **Wall mount:** Mounting the dock on your wall allows you to get your Zune and speakers up off the table or desk. It might even make a nice stylish addition to your wall.

   At around $200, this dock isn't cheap, but it's a stand-alone listening station for your Zune that might fit well in quite a few apartments, dens, or dorm rooms. Check out the Altec Lansing Web site at www. alteclansing.com for more info.

- ✔ **The VAF Octavio 1:** This dock is in a different class than most of the docks we've seen for any music player. The company behind the Octavio (VAF Research, at www.vaf.com.au) is known for high-end, high-fidelity speaker systems, and they've put that knowledge into building a dock unit for your Zune. This dock features charging, a wireless remote, and TV-out and auxiliary audio inputs (for your Xbox 360, your DVD player, or whatever else you want to run through a high-fidelity speaker system), but its single most important feature is the amazing sound you get from a speaker in such a small package. The Octavio can fill a good-sized room with quality sound in a package that's relatively compact, when you compare it to a full-sized stereo and speaker system. You do have to pay for this level of audio excellence; the Octavio costs around $500.

If you want a speaker system that works well with your Zune, check out either of these two dock systems. Go with the one that fits your budget, your space, and your style.

Power Adapters

We all have to deal with two Zune facts of life. One is that some computer USB ports don't have enough juice to charge your Zune, and the other is that the Zune doesn't ship with any other charging option.

We're the first to admit that it makes sense to use a computer to charge your Zune. You need to connect your Zune to your PC, anyway, if you want to take advantage of your Zune software, so it seems logical to go that route when charging. Personally, we always have a computer nearby, so we can hook up the Zune and charge it whenever it needs charging. On the other hand, if you're someone whose computer can't seem to charge the Zune, someone who wants to use his or her Zune in the car, or someone who likes to travel . . . then the power solution that ships with the Zune isn't going to cut it. Luckily for you, you can choose from a lot of options for Zune power supplies. You need only an adapter that outputs enough power and provides a USB port to which you can hook your Zune sync cable.

AC power adapters

The official Zune AC adapter provides a standard USB port (so you need to use your Zune sync cable to connect your Zune to the adapter). This adapter is made for the Zune, so you should definitely get enough power out of it. It's included as part of the Home A/V Pack and the Travel Pack (both of which you can read about in the section "The Accessory Packs," later in this chapter), or it sells for around $30 on its own.

Monster (www.monstercable.com) sells a slim power adapter (the SlimCharger) that includes a very small power brick, moves the USB port off the brick and onto a cable, and uses a fold-away plug. All in all, this small package is great for traveling. Like the official Zune adapter, this unit sells for around $30.

With a little searching, you can easily find a lot of other options out there, as well. Power adapters for USB devices are a common need, and many companies have created their own versions of these adapters. Be careful, though; just like some computer USB ports, the USB ports on some of these power adapters don't produce enough output to charge your Zune.

If a USB power adapter states that it should work for the Zune, that it's rated for 1000ma, or that it should work for all iPods, you should be able to use it to charge your device. Make sure you keep your receipt, though, in case it can't do what you bought it for.

DC power adapters (car-based)

The DC world mirrors the AC world — you can find a lot of choices out there, but not all of them are certified to work with the Zune.

Other than all the FM transmitters (which generally also supply power) that we discuss in the section "FM transmitters," earlier in this chapter, you can find just the one stand-alone car charger for the Zune — the Zune-branded car charger. It comes in the Car Pack, which also contains the FM transmitter, or you can buy it on its own for around $25.

Cases

We can think of a few (very) good reasons to get a case for your Zune, including to protect it from scratches and damage, for style, and to allow the Zune to sit up for video watching. We can't cover all the vast number of cases out there in this chapter, but we run through the general types of cases and present an example of each type in the following sections.

Protective cases

All cases protect your Zune, but a few take it even farther. One such case is the ToughSkin from Speck Products. This case is ridiculously rugged, but still allows you access to the controls on your Zune.

Speck also makes a few other cases for the Zune; you can check them all out online at www.speckproducts.com.

If you want a case for protective purposes, focus on protecting the screen of your Zune. The case should cover the screen in some way to prevent the screen from getting scratched. If you're worried only about the screen, Belkin (www.belkin.com) makes a screen overlay that you stick on over your screen. The overlay should keep your screen safe from everyday scratches that it might otherwise suffer from keys, coins, or whatever else might end up bouncing around next to your Zune. You can also visit a Web site such as www.screenguardz.com, where you can find protective films precut for your Zune. Just select Microsoft from the site's brand list, and you're set.

Leather cases

If you want to protect your Zune in style, check out one of the leather or canvas cases available for your Zune. Our personal favorite is a Vaja case (www.vajacases.com), the Classic (retails for approximately $60). With this case, you protect both the body of your Zune and your Zune's screen, and you can still easily access the navigation buttons, headphone port, and Zune connector. To top it all off, you can get the leather case of the Vaja Classic engraved with a logo or with up to three lines of text. Definitely a cool product.

One of the nicest features of an earlier Microsoft product, the Portable Media Center, was that every one of the manufacturers that made one provided some way to prop the device up for watching video without using your hands. You may long for this feature when you're trying to watch your Zune on a plane or the Zune is sitting on a desk in front of you. Sadly, the Zune itself doesn't provide any means for hands-free viewing, but you can buy a case that can make it happen for you. Belkin (www.belkin.com) makes a case they call the Folio Kickstand that protects your Zune when you aren't watching a video and holds it at a good viewing angle when it's time to enjoy a show.

Armbands

The Zune, on its own, works pretty well at the gym when you're sitting on an exercise bike or an elliptical machine, but what if you want to run? Or your workout clothes don't have any pockets? Sounds like it's time to strap that Zune onto your arm . . . which means you need an armband!

Belkin (www.belkin.com), DLO (www.dlo.com), and Speck (www.speck products.com) all make armband cases, ranging in price from $20 to $30. They all have the same basic feature — they let you strap a Zune onto your arm. Because none of them can make the Zune smaller — which is what you really want when you're trying to figure out how to put it onto your arm — you should probably base your choice on appearance and comfort. Speck's Active Sport case wins for the most exciting appearance (with a white exterior and fancy reflective stripes to keep you safe while running), but you need to try out the products in this category for yourself, so head on down to your local Best Buy or other retail electronics store instead of just browsing online.

Bags

All of the cases we talk about in the preceding sections allow you to access the Zune's controls while it's inside the case, but sometimes you just need a bag in which you can carry your Zune, your sync cable, and your other bits of gear. Your Zune comes with a tight little bag that works well for protecting your Zune's screen when you're about to toss it into your gym bag or your suitcase, but the bag has barely enough room for the Zune, so you certainly can't store your sync cable in there with it.

Microsoft offers a Zune-branded gear bag, either as part of the Travel Pack (which we cover in the section "The Accessory Packs," later in this chapter) or on its own (for around $30), which has room inside for the Zune and a few accessories (such as the AC adapter, your headphones, a sync cable, and so on). The gear bag includes soft netting inside to help keep everything together and to prevent your Zune and accessories from bouncing around.

If you want to save a few bucks by avoiding the Zune-specific items, any generic case that's designed to hold a point-and-shoot camera (or an iPod) can probably work almost as well.

Headphones

The Zune ships with a pair of (pretty good) headphones, but we've both moved on to different headphones. If you're in the market for a new pair of headphones for your Zune, you have a huge range of choices. You don't have to worry about searching for Zune-specific headphones — you can make your choice from the full range of available headphones with 3.5mm jacks (basically all of them come with that jack size these days).

You have a few different kinds of headphones to choose from, each of which has a fancy name:

- ✔ **Circumaural headphones:** Circumaural just means "around the ears" and indicates the large (and generally padded) style of headphones that people commonly use in recording studios (though you can also use them for home listening).

- ✔ **Supra-aural headphones:** This scary-looking term simple means "on top of the ears" and indicates that these headphones have large speakers that don't enclose the ears but do tend to cover them.

- **Earbuds:** These headphones should be familiar because they're the kind included with your Zune. These headphones rest inside the ear but outside of the ear canal.

- **Canalphones:** Also called inner-ear or in-ear headphones, these headphones fit into your ear canal.

In addition to the four types of headphones listed above, headphones also come as either open or closed. Open (or open-air) headphones allow you to hear external sounds from the world around you, and closed headphones isolate you from most external sounds. Use closed headphones while listening to music at home (they produce better sound with more bass), but stick to open-air headphones when you're out in public (so you can still hear what's going on around you).

Within both categories, you can find a range of quality. But in general, closed circumaural headphones that enclose the ears and isolate you from external sounds produce the best sound. Next up, and much lighter and smaller, are the canalphones, which also manage to isolate you from external noise by blocking your ear canal like a pair of ear-plugs.

Earbuds range in quality, too, but they often produce the worst sound of any type of headphone because they don't isolate you from external sounds. Earbud users usually play their music overly loud to compensate for the external sound interference.

Supra-aural headphones were more common ten years ago when they were the standard type of headphones shipped with any portable music device. Although you can find a large range of quality in these products, in general, they fall behind the circumaural in terms of sound quality.

Here are our personal favorites, assuming you don't want to spend more than $100 (you can find many headphones in all these categories that cost more than $100, if you want to shell out the big bucks):

- **Circumaural headphones:** Within the $100 price range, you'd do well with a pair of Sennheiser 500-series headphones, such as the HD515 or the HD555 model. Check them out at www.sennheiserusa.com, but don't buy them there — you can find them for about $60 less at sites such as www.newegg.com and www.jr.com.

- **Supra-aural headphones:** Although most of the $20 headphones we've purchased have fit into this category, they aren't really noteworthy. If you like this style of headphone and are willing to spend closer to $60, the Sennheiser HD-435 headphones are a great bet.

✔ **Earbuds:** You can get a good pair of earbuds for far less than the $100 price range; the Sennheiser MX75s (which cost about $50) are designed to stay in place and sound better than the earbuds that ship with the Zune.

✔ **Canalphones:** The best canalphones available for under $100 are either the Shure E2c Sound Isolating Earphones (www.shure.com), which run around $109 on the Shure site — but we've seen them as low as $60 through a search at www.pricegrabber.com — or the V-Moda Vibes (www.v-moda.com), which retail at $101 (a dollar over our limit, but who's counting?).

The Zune Premium Headphones (www.zune.net) are also canalphones, and they cost only $40, so you might want to try them out. You won't get sound as good as the Shure models can give you, or extras such as multiple sleeves, but they *are* cheaper.

Of course, you can find many more headphones out there — including many we've never used — so try a few pairs out and use your own personal judgment about the type and specific model of headphones that work best for you.

The Accessory Packs

Microsoft sells many of its most popular Zune accessories bundled up into various packs, including the Zune Car Pack, the Home A/V Pack, and the Travel Pack. You can get these packs at www.zune.net.

The Car Pack ($80) includes

✔ An FM transmitter

✔ The Zune car charger

The Home A/V Pack ($100) includes

✔ The Zune dock

✔ A USB sync cable

✔ A wireless remote

✔ An AC adapter

✔ The A/V output cable

The Travel Pack ($100) includes

- ✔ The Zune gear bag
- ✔ The dual-connect remote
- ✔ The AC adapter
- ✔ Headphones
- ✔ A USB sync cable

Finding Out More about the Available Accessories

If you're looking to find out more about the accessories we discuss in this chapter, or to see if any new ones have been released since this book was written, you need to hit the Web. Here are some useful sites for information on accessories:

- ✔ **Zune.net:** Microsoft's Zune site has an entire section on accessories at `www.zune.net/accessories`.
- ✔ **Zunerama:** This online Zune community site provides reviews of various accessories at `www.zunerama.com/review-main.php`.
- ✔ **Monster:** Monster Cable has a Zune page at `www.monstercable.com/mp3/zune.asp`.
- ✔ **Belkin:** Belkin's Zune page, including the Folio case, TuneBase, TunePower, and so on, is at `www.belkin.com/zune`.
- ✔ **Speck:** The makers of the ToughSkin case have Zune information linked from their main Web page at `www.speckproducts.com`.
- ✔ **Vaja:** The folks behind those leather cases that we rave about in the section "Leather cases," earlier in this chapter, have their Zune section at `www.vajacases.com/images/mp3/microsoft/zune/zune_en.html`.

Chapter 18

Ten Tips for Parents

Depending on the age of your children (if you have children at all), the Zune may be an adult-only device, or it may end up spending more time with your kids than with you. In fact, if your kids are into music and movies, maybe you bought the Zune for them. Whenever kids are involved with a device such as the Zune, a whole set of concerns and questions comes up. In this chapter, we lead you through ten tips for using your Zune, your computer, and your digital media files with kids.

Working with Child and Parent Accounts in Live ID

Both the Zune and the Xbox 360 take advantage of Microsoft's Live ID system (formerly known as Passport) for user identification; you need to have a Live ID to use their services. As a result, the Zune has inherited the Live ID model for maintaining parental control over a child's actions online. For this model to work, though, a couple of things have to be true:

✔ Your child should be using his or her own computer account (login), either on the same machine as you or on a different machine. If you're sharing the same login, your kid may be able to use your Live ID, thus bypassing the parental controls.

✔ You have to set up the Live ID for your child correctly.

Getting your child's Live ID right is the critical issue, so to help you understand the parental control system, Duncan researched the whole topic thoroughly by setting up a Live ID for his son, Connor. All that work on his part means that you just have to follow these handy steps to set up your own child's Live ID:

1. **Point your browser to `www.passport.com`.**

   The Windows Live ID home page, just the place to create new Windows Live ID accounts, appears.

2. **Under the Sign Up for a Free MSN Hotmail Account heading, click the Get Started Now link, as shown in Figure 18-1.**

   The Mail window appears. You also create a new Hotmail (free Web-based e-mail) account along with the Live ID.

   Do all these steps yourself, filling in the information for both the child and parent.

   If you happen to be already signed in with your own Live ID, you're prompted to sign out of that account (see Figure 18-2) before you can continue creating your new one.

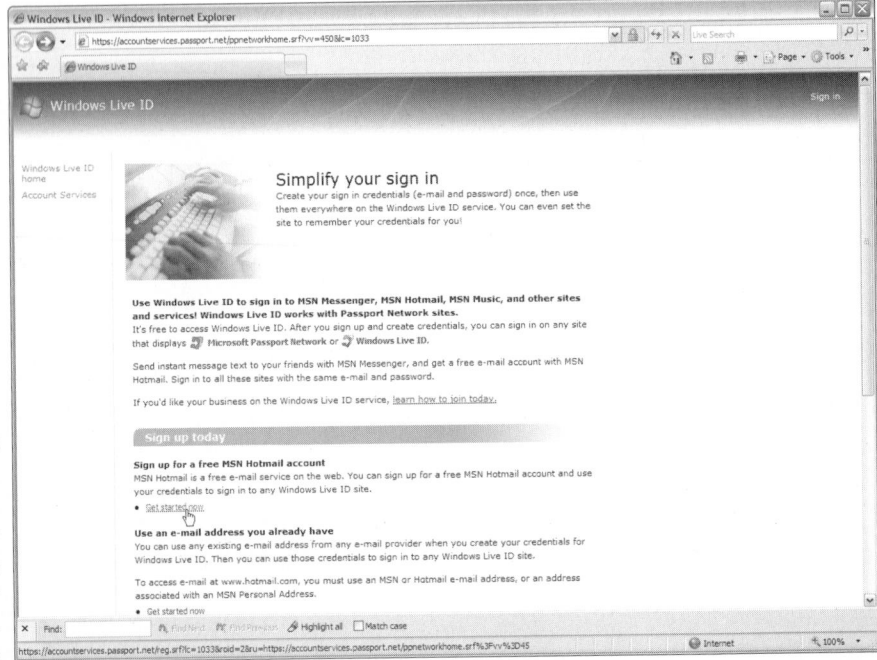

Figure 18-1:
Create a
new
Windows
Live ID for
your child.

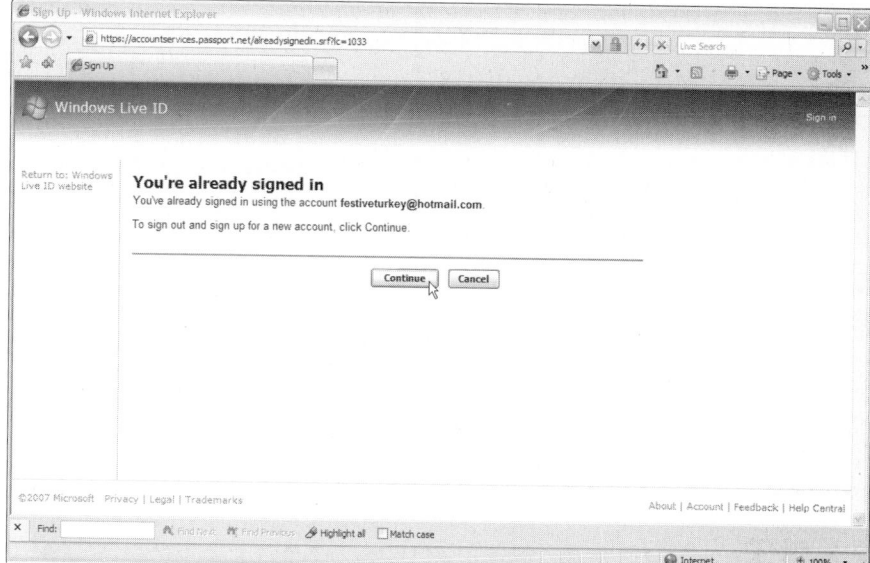

Figure 18-2:
Figure 18-2:
To create
a new
Windows
Live ID, you
have to sign
out of the
Live ID
system.

3. **Use the drop-down menu to enter your country. Then enter an e-mail address for your child in the E-Mail Address field and click the Check Availability button (as shown in Figure 18-3).**

   If no one else has signed up using that e-mail address, the Create Your Password page appears. If someone's already staked a claim to johnsmith@hotmail.com, you're told that address is no longer available, and you should try another.

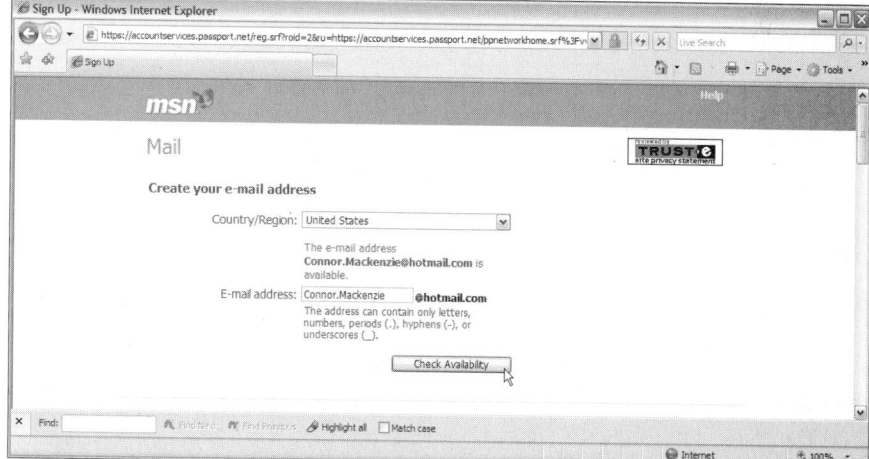

Figure 18-3:
Picking a
valid and
available
Live ID
username
can take
quite a few
tries.

TIP

It often takes a couple tries to come up with an address no one's used before. If you get frustrated, try something a bit off the beaten track.

4. When your e-mail address is accepted as unique, scroll down the browser to the Create Your Password section; type a password into the Password text box, retype that password in the Retype Password text box to confirm, and then specify a special question and answer that will enable you to reset your password if you ever forget it. (See Figure 18-4.)

Figure 18-4:
Creating a
question/an
swer pair
lets you
retrieve or
reset your
password in
the future.

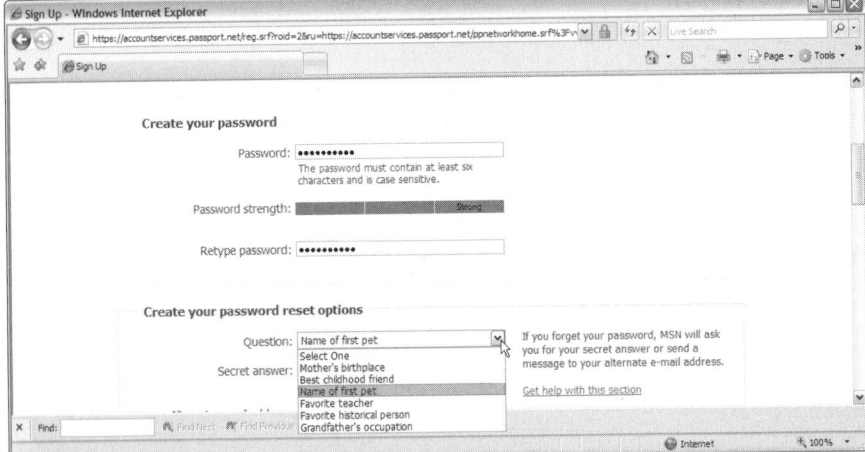

5. Scroll down the browser window until you reach the Enter Your Account Information section, then fill in the fields with the information pertinent to your child.

Again, you as the parent are filling in your child's information, not your own.

Most of this information (which you can see in Figure 18-5) is just what you'd expect. Microsoft uses the value you enter in the Birth Date field to determine whether the account holder is considered a child. The age under which a person is considered a child may be different in each country and region, but in the United States, the age is 13. (If the account holder is under 13, he or she needs an adult's permission to access Live ID services.)

If you enter a birth date of someone younger than 13, the site tells you that you need permission to continue, as shown in Figure 18-6.

6. Click the Get Permission Now button.

The Give or Deny Your Child Permission to Use Microsoft Online Services page appears.

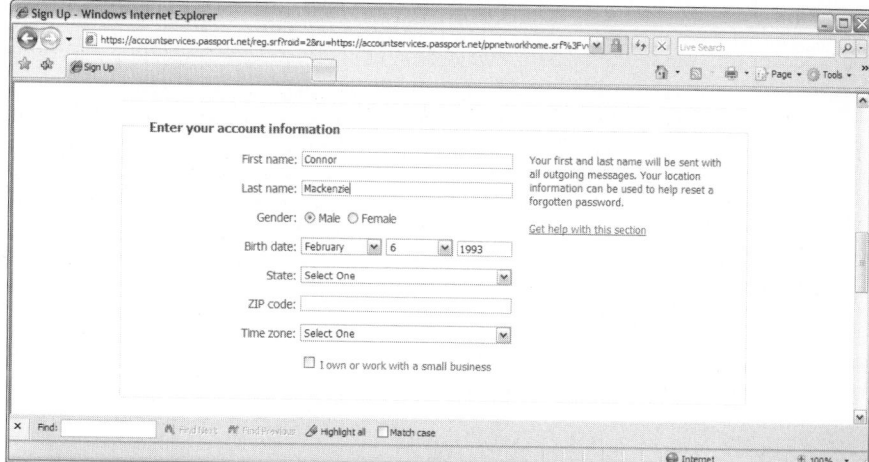

Figure 18-5:
Live ID
accounts
created by
(or for)
someone
under 13
become
special child
accounts.

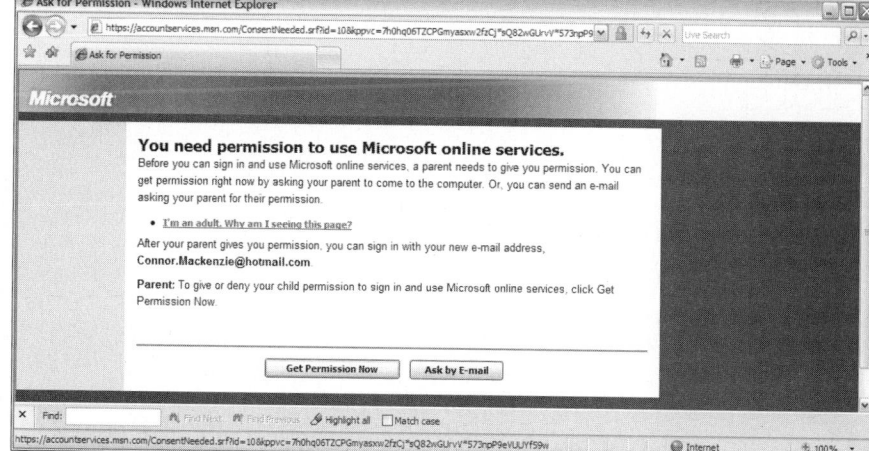

Figure 18-6:
You need to
sign in to
complete
the registra-
tion of a
child Live ID
account.

7. **Click Continue.**

   A page appears, asking, "Do you give your child permission to use Microsoft online services?" You can choose Yes or No.

8. **Select the Yes option and then click Continue.**

   A Sign-In Now page appears, but you aren't actually at the sign-in page yet.

9. **Select Sign In Now and then click Continue.**

   The Sign-In window appears.

10. **In the Sign-In window, sign in with your own (not your child's) Live ID.**

If you've been through this process before (maybe for a different child or service), the You've Given Permission page appears. You can skip the rest of the steps in this list — your changes have been made.

If you've never done this process before, you're asked to enter credit card information to verify that you're an adult.

11. **Enter your credit card information.**

Your credit card isn't charged, but you need to use an active card to validate your age. (See Figure 18-7.)

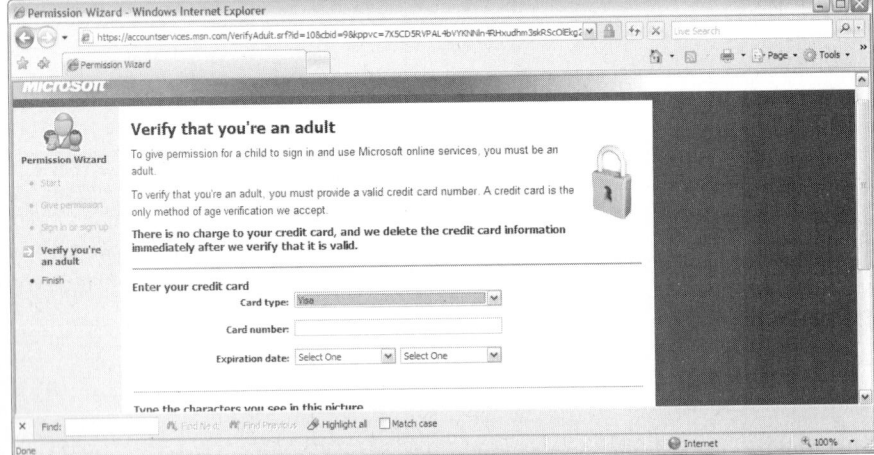

Figure 18-7:
You need to verify your age with a credit card to complete the registration of a child Live ID account.

12. **Click Submit to send your credit card information.**

Assuming the credit card information is successfully validated, the Status Verified page appears.

13. **Click Continue to complete the process.**

The You've Given Permission completion page makes an appearance, showing that your changes have been made.

After you create this child/parent relationship, you see it in action anywhere within the Microsoft network of sites. For example, when the child tries to go to Hotmail for the first time, he or she needs to ask the parent for permission. The parent can sign in right then to approve the request, or the system can send the parent an e-mail so he or she can approve the request from another location (such as a computer at work). The e-mail (shown in Figure 18-8) includes a link that the parent can use to sign in and then approve or deny the request.

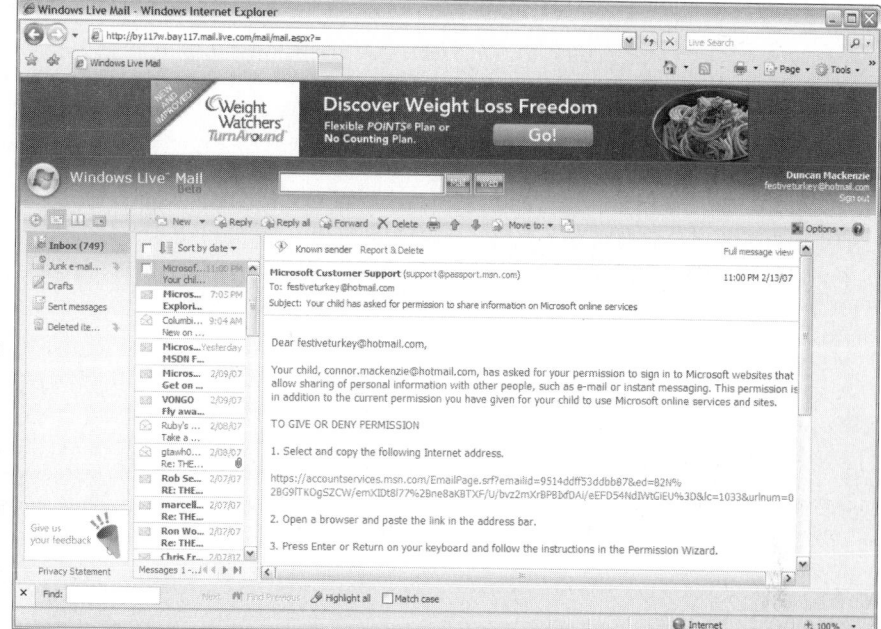

Figure 18-8:
Accessing
Live ID
online
services
requires
parental
approval.

Applying this child/parent relationship to the Zune software follows nearly the same process. If you've installed the Zune software onto your child's machine, you can go ahead and sign him or her into Marketplace. Just follow these steps:

1. **Enter your child's Live ID account information in the Zune software (you can see an example in Figure 18-9), then click the Sign In button.**

   The Profile page appears.

2. **Fill in all your child's information and then click Next.**

   The Parental Approval Required screen appears. Before your child can complete the account creation process, he or she needs parental approval (as shown in Figure 18-10).

3. **Click Next.**

   The Parental Age Verification screen appears.

4. **Enter your credit card information, complete with address, and then Click Next.**

   The Family Settings Options page appears (see Figure 18-11). You can modify those settings now, if you want, or you can take care of it later.

Figure 18-9:
The Zune
sign-up
process
requires
your child's
Windows
Live ID.

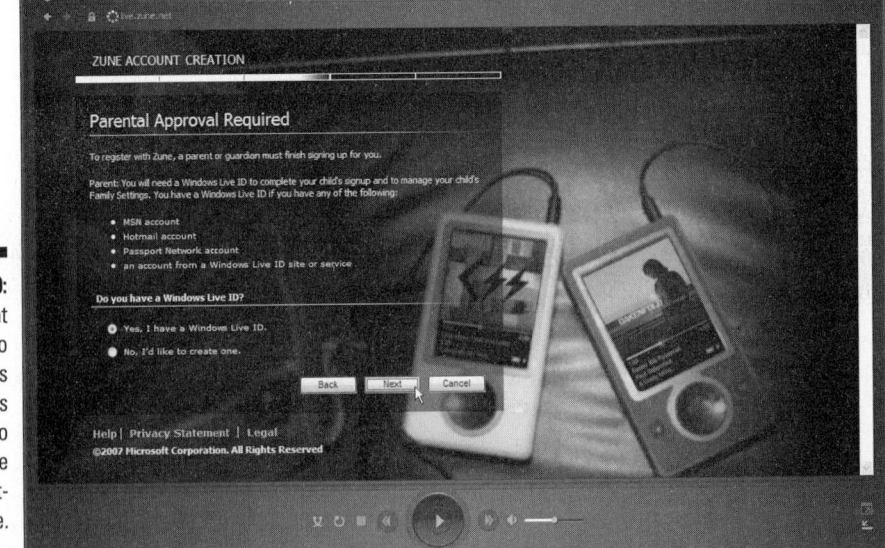

Figure 18-10:
A parent
needs to
approve his
or her child's
entrance to
the Zune
Market-
place.

Either now or later, you can set the family settings for this child account by following these steps:

1. **Go to the Account Management page.**

   Choose Sign-In➪Account Management from your Zune software's main menu to get there.

2. **Click the Family Settings button (second from the top).**

   The Family Settings dialog box appears. Your choices (as shown in Figure 18-11) include the ability to restrict the purchase of music from Marketplace and block explicit content.

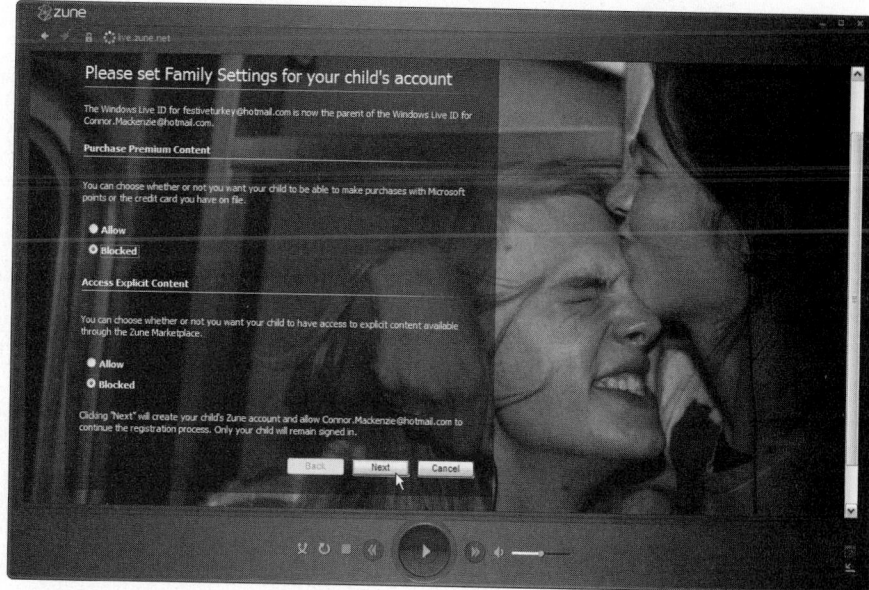

Figure 18-11: The Family Settings dialog box allows you to restrict your child's Marketplace access.

If you decide to block explicit content, which you probably will (remember that these rules apply only to children under 13), the child can't play that type of content through his or her account (as shown in Figure 18-12).

Of course, this style of parental control really affects only the Zune Marketplace (and other non-Zune Microsoft services, such as Hotmail and Messenger), and your child can find many other ways to get that explicit content onto his or her Zune device. The rest of the tips in this chapter deal with how to handle all the content in non-Microsoft locations out there.

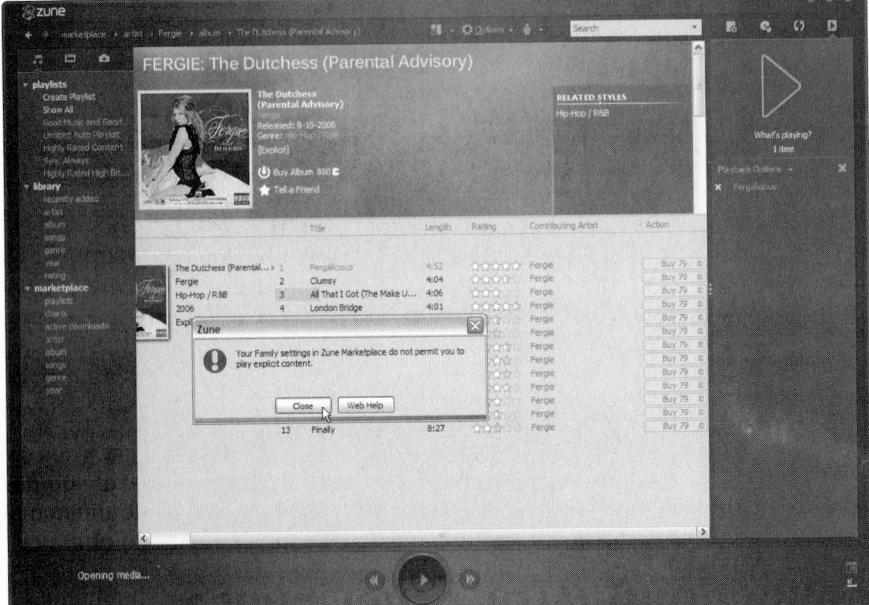

Figure 18-12:
Your child
can't access
explicit
content if
you've
blocked it.

Reviewing Your Kid's Media Library

If you aren't using the parental controls feature, either by choice or because your child is too old (13 or older), you may want to scan his or her Zune library from time to time to see what type of material he or she is downloading. You might think this check-up is intrusive, but you can make it a part of the deal up front — he or she gets to download whatever, use the computer, and use the Zune, but you reserve the right to check out the machine from time to time. Of course, assuming your child has a lot of content, this scan might take some work. Here are a few tips for checking out your child's Zune library:

- ✔ **Use the Recently Added view:** To browse Marketplace or ripped music your child has added to his or her library, use the Recently Added view. This view lets you see what he or she has added or downloaded lately. Use this view if you plan to glance through the library every week or so.

- ✔ **Create a dynamic playlist:** Set your dynamic playlist to look for newly added music over a specific timeframe (Figure 18-13 shows playlist criteria going back a month) and/or explicit content.

Filtering on the Explicit value requires clicking the More button at the bottom of the field list and finding the Parental Rating item in the full list of possible fields that appears. You have to type **Explicit** into the value box (you don't have a drop-down menu of possible values to choose from, but it will work fine, as long as you spell Explicit correctly. (For more on creating dynamic playlists, see Chapter 4.)

Browse: Of course, looking only at content that's marked Explicit doesn't take into account all the music or videos that aren't properly attributed (which might include material downloaded from a Web site or sent from a friend). To really see what your child has on his or her computer, you have to browse around in the Zune library (and also on the computer itself).

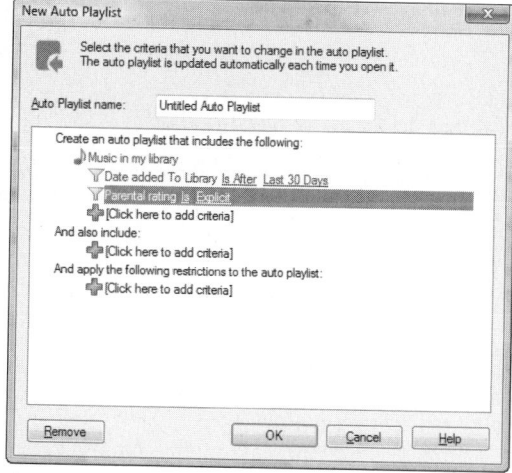

Figure 18-13: You can use auto playlists to find all recently added explicit content.

If you want to keep tabs on your kid's Zune and Internet activities, simply keep your PC out in a family area, not in your kid's bedroom or down in some den where you never go. Even if you aren't looking over your children's shoulders, you do get some idea of what they're doing and how much time they're spending on the computer. If you do decide that you need, or even just prefer, to put the PC in a bedroom, keep an open-door policy — they should leave the door open while they're awake and using their machine. With this policy, you can at least walk past whenever you want or drop in to chat as appropriate.

Duncan's thoughts on snooping

Ronald Reagan was fond of the saying "Trust, but verify," and although he may have been talking about the Russians during the Cold War, I believe the same guideline applies to your kids. Everyone is different, of course, so take my advice as just one parent's opinion, but if you aren't sure what's okay and what's not when it comes to monitoring your kid's computer, Internet, and music usage, then perhaps my thoughts can help you figure it out.

I believe you should give your kids freedom; freedom to use the Internet, download music with their Zune Pass, and have e-mail and Instant Messenger chats with their friends. This freedom comes as part of a package, though; they get to download new songs without having to ask you every time, but they understand that you can look at what they're doing at anytime without invading their privacy. Make it clear that you're looking only to make sure they're staying safe and aren't dealing with content that you feel is too inappropriate.

Yes, I said "too inappropriate." Just because you see something that seems slightly inappropriate

doesn't mean you should mention it to your kids. If you want to keep this deal intact, allowing you to snoop without having to hide it, you need to keep up your end of the bargain. You need to show your children that you respect them and trust them to make good decisions. If they've downloaded a few hundred songs, and you find that one or two of them contain some mild profanity, you may want to just let that slide. Save your parental veto on music, pictures, and video for materials you truly think are a problem; otherwise, you leave your kids feeling like their every move is being watched. Along the same lines, if you see something juicy, but not inappropriate, try to forget you ever saw it. For example, say you notice an e-mail from your child in which he or she is talking about a "totally adorable" girl or boy. If you mention this e-mail to him or her, you're simply hammering home the fact that you're monitoring his or her communications. Any feeling your child has of being respected and trusted has gone out the window.

Dealing with the Wide Open Zune

The Zune has no parental controls, no concept of a passcode, or any other sort of restriction. After content ends up on the Zune, anyone who uses the device can play that content. So, although the ratings of movies and TV transfer over to the device, those ratings are for informational use only; playing an R-rated movie takes the same number of clicks as playing a G-rated one.

What does this lack of restriction mean for you? Well, it depends on your situation. As one example, say you have an older child who has a Zune and whom you allow to watch or listen to content that you don't want your younger child (or children) to see or hear. In this case, you can make your older child's computer account off limits to the younger child, but you also have to make sure that no one leaves the Zune itself out in the open.

This example is for all you parents with Zune devices. Imagine you use the Zune for music and movies, and you've copied over a bunch of movies and TV shows that you like to watch. Now, you're preparing to take a vacation, so you copy over the latest hit kid's movie to your Zune. When you start your road trip, you pass the Zune into the back seat. A few clicks later, your kids are happily watching that R-rated horror flick you copied to your Zune ages ago, rather than some kiddie feature you just copied over specifically for them. Sadly, you don't really have a good solution to this problem. The Zune device has no mechanism to restrict content by rating or even to support multiple user profiles. To completely avoid this problem, you either need to make your Zune just for you or just for them, or remove any inappropriate content before you share the device with the kids.

Sharing One Zune between Several People

Other than the wide-open Zune issue mentioned in the preceding section, in which the content that one person watches may not be appropriate for a younger child, you can quite reasonably think of the Zune as a family device for a couple of reasons:

- **Price:** We're talking about a fairly expensive gadget, much more expensive than the portable cassette players of old, making it more suitable as a purchase for the whole family.

- **Control:** If the Zune belongs to the whole family, you can more easily lay down rules about how everyone uses it and what type of content (music or otherwise) everyone can place on it.

If you do want to share a single Zune with all your family members, you have to decide how to set it up for synchronization, handle the use of your Zune Pass, and handle purchases from the Zune Marketplace. You can establish these ground rules in more than one way because you can use the same Zune Marketplace login (Live ID) on up to three different machines, and you connect the same Zune to each individual computer (or individual login on the same computer). You need to assign one computer or login to be the home PC for the Zune, making that connection the main login. Any other computers or profiles get to connect to the Zune as a guest whenever they hook up (see Figure 18-14).

You can set up the Zune partnership on your home PC and then connect to the Zune as a guest on any number of machines that have music, photo, or video content on them (although your Zune Pass music is limited to three PCs, you can connect as a guest to any PC to grab nonprotected content). For simplicity's sake, you could limit all of your Marketplace downloads to that main PC and connect to the other machines only to grab non-Marketplace music, photo, and video files. Of course, if you have only the one machine and everyone uses the same login, just set up the partnership and off you go!

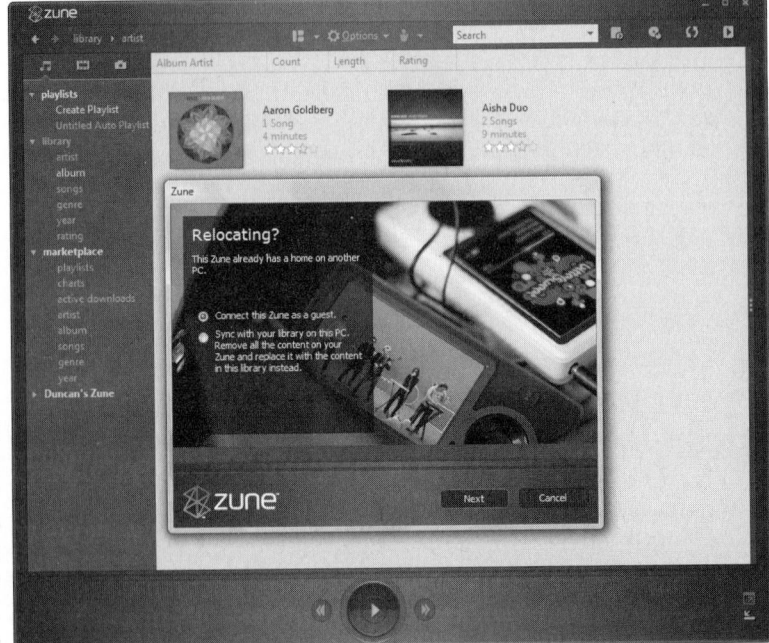

Figure 18-14:
Treat your
Zune like a
guest on
secondary
computers.

To keep track of the music content various users download, you may want to create one or more manual playlists (Joe's music, Cindy's music, and so on) and then drag those entire playlists into the Zune when syncing so that the playlists show up on the device. Playlists don't work for videos or photos, though, so you can use them to keep only multiple musical tastes safely contained.

More than One Zune in the Family

What if you have more than one Zune in the house? Well, if you have just two Zunes and no more than three computers, you're set. You can set up the same PC as the home PC for multiple Zunes, and you can set up different sync rules for each of them. If you go with the subscription model (Zune Pass) for downloading music, you can sync your Zune Pass music onto both Zunes, paying a single monthly fee to use that music on both Zunes.

If you have three or more Zunes, your setup can get somewhat more complicated. Zune Pass music can work on only two Zunes at a time, so if you download a particular song via your Zune Pass, you can use it on just two of your Zunes at the same time. Of course, you may not have an issue if the users of the three or more Zunes have different musical tastes. You get music rights on a per-song basis, so each person could conceivably listen to all the music he or she wants, and you're still only paying a single monthly fee. You can even use multiple PCs to sync content to your Zunes, but you can work with Zune Pass content on only three authorized computers.

Using the Account Management feature, you can remove authorized computers that you're no longer using, which is critical if you sell your machine or even just wipe it and reinstall the operating system. To access the list of computers, follow these steps:

1. **Sign into the Zune software by using your Live ID.**

2. **Choose Account Management from the Sign-In menu to the left of the Search box.**

   The Account Management page appears.

3. **Click the Rights Management button.**

   A list of the computers that are currently authorized to play music downloaded using your Zune Pass appears (see Figure 18-15).

4. **Click the Remove button to the right of a computer's information to get rid of that authorized computer.**

   This step makes room for you to add another computer, if necessary (if you've replaced a PC, for example), but Microsoft limits how often you can reassign computers. You can remove a computer from this list only once every 30 days to prevent you from removing and adding computers over and over again to enable more people on more machines to use your single Zune Pass.

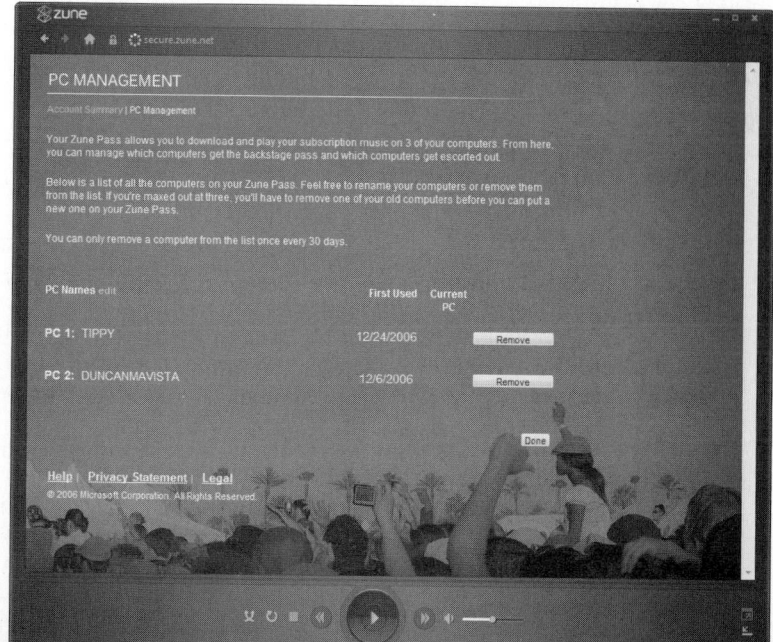

Figure 18-15: Your Zune software can show you the computers associated with your Zune Pass.

You can't add a computer by using this PC Management screen; computers are added automatically when you try to play your Zune Pass music on a machine that's not already on this list. If you need to remove a machine but can't because of a problem in the software, or because of the 30-day restriction, contact Microsoft Support and have them make the required change for you. You can find the Zune support options at www.zune.net/support.htm.

Keeping Safe Wirelessly

Built-in wireless networking is one of the distinctive features of the Zune, enabling you to share music and images between two Zunes. As a parent, you have to look at this feature carefully. From a positive point of view, your children can share the music they like between their Zunes and their friends' Zunes, making for a great social experience. They can also pass along photos, sharing their shots of a recent school field trip or pictures of a recent vacation that they want their friends to see. Very cool, very fun, and just the kind of thing a kid would be into.

Looking at the wireless feature with a cynical parent's eye, you need to be aware of the information that the Zune broadcasts over the wireless connection. Without having to talk or even stand all that close, another Zune user can find out the name of your child's Zune and what he or she is currently listening to. Your child's Zune might give another Zune user your child's first name, and the currently playing music info gives that other user a conversation starter with your child. If the person viewing this information is a new kid at the school, then that's great; they know your child's first name and can start a nice conversation about the music they both like. But what about when it's some creep who just likes hanging around the school?

Thankfully, you can reduce this problem without giving up the cool wireless features that make the Zune unique:

- ✔ Don't use your own name when naming the Zune; go with something like My Zuney rather than Joe's Zune.
- ✔ Change the wireless network settings to *not* show people what you're listening to by choosing Settings➪Wireless➪Online Status, then toggling from Detailed to Basic (see Figure 18-16). Basic lets other Zunes see your Zune's name and that your Zune is available, but it doesn't show any information about what you're currently listening to or watching.

You can see what your Zune looks like to another Zune owner by going to Community (an option in the top menu of the Zune, which you can get to by pressing and holding the Back button for three or four seconds) and selecting Me from the options along the top of the display. Figure 18-17 shows what another Zune would see if you have the Online Status option set to Basic, and Figure 18-18 shows what type of information is passed along if you have your Online Status set to Detailed.

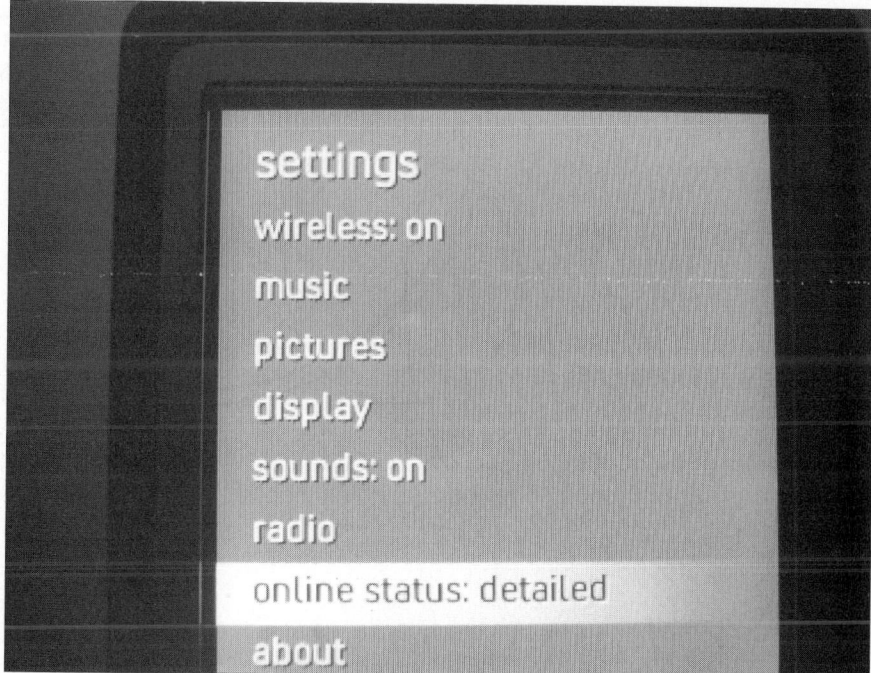

Figure 18-16:
Setting your online status determines what information other Zunes can see.

Figure 18-17:
With Online Status set to Basic, other Zunes see only that your Zune is around, not what you're currently listening to or watching.

Figure 18-18:
Detailed
status
includes the
name of the
video you're
currently
watching or
the song
you're
currently
listening to.

Figure 18-17 and Figure 18-18 show that Duncan hasn't followed any of our own advice; he named his Zune using his own first name, and he normally does leave his Online Status set to the Detailed view. Of course, he's an adult and honestly doesn't really mind if nearby Zune users know his name or what he's watching or listening to, so those settings work just fine for him.

Zune Sharing, WiFi, and Your Media

The Zune software, along with Windows Media Player 11 and a piece of software called Windows Media Connect, enable you to browse and view your content (music, photos, and videos) from a remote device (such as an Xbox 360). The Zune software itself shares only to Xbox 360s, but Windows Media Player (which is almost guaranteed to be installed on your PC) and Windows Media Connect can share to any device that has certain public standards. You can find out more about all three ways to share content in Chapter 13. This list focuses on what you need to know from a privacy point of view:

✔ **Approving connections:** All three sharing methods allow you to configure them so you can either allow *any* device (or any Xbox 360, in the
case of the Zune software) to connect or set it up so that you have to
approve each device that wants to connect.

You should go with the second choice (the Only Share with These Xbox
360s option in the Zune software) to ensure that someone can't get
onto your wireless network and slurp your private music, photo, or
video collection onto his or her own machine.

✔ **Placing your Zune under lock and (WEP) key:** Make sure your wireless
network is secured (for example, with a *WEP key,* which is essentially a
password for your wireless network), which prevents random computers
from connecting to your network without a password that only you have.

✔ **Putting up a firewall:** Make sure the Windows XP or Windows Vista
firewall feature is enabled, which can help keep other people off your
personal network.

Going Digital

If you and your family plan to use digital media and digital media players such
as the Zune, then to get the most out of all your content, you need to fully
embrace the digital lifestyle. The more media you have in digital form, the
more options you have for using your Zune — and the more you can do with
both your Zune and your PC. Here are some tips for making your world digital:

✔ **Make your photos computer friendly.** Get a digital camera, not a film-
based one, or pick the Photo CD option at the photo-processing place to
get a CD of all your images.

✔ **Get a digital camcorder.** Go for either a MiniDV, hard-drive-based, or
Flash-memory-based camcorder (Chapter 9 gives you more information
on cameras).

✔ **Transfer your creations to your PC.** After you record an event or take
some pictures, get the video or photos off of the video tape, memory
card, or hard drive as quickly as you can. Until you have the digital content on your PC, you can't do much with it.

✔ **Rip your CDs.** You can rip CDs by using the Zune software. (See Chapter 8
for more ripping information.)

✔ **Back up your content.** After you have your family photos, your home
movies, and even all your music on your PC, you don't want to lose even
a single photo. You can burn your own DVDs to store files or use some
form of backup service or software.

Headphone Safety

Many parents are concerned about how their kids use headphones. Recently, studies suggest that prolonged headphone usage at high volume can cause permanent hearing damage. Headphones are also considered responsible for several accidents in which pedestrians crossing the street while wearing headphones were hit by cars (some people think that the victims couldn't hear the cars coming because of the headphones).

Luckily, the Zune appears to have a lower output volume than some other portable music players, so your child can't as easily play it at an unsafe level. But, depending on the volume of the source material and the headphones used, your child could still have the music cranked up far louder than is safe.

You may have real problems policing your child's headphone usage, especially with older kids who listen to their Zune outside of the house and away from you. Try to keep them using open-air headphones — headphones that aren't sealed around the ears and don't fit into the ear canal. This type of headphone has two benefits:

- ✔ It moves the speaker slightly farther away from the ear.
- ✔ It allows the user to hear the noise of the world around him or her.

When your children are wearing their headphones, see if you can hear the music clearly from a few feet away; it's an unscientific test, but it probably means that they're playing their music much too loud.

Using iTunes and Other Software to Access Digital Media

Look into what parental control options are available in other software and even in other devices. Many DVD players, for example, include a parental control feature that allows you to block DVD movies based on their rating. Cable boxes also often include this feature; some TVs do, as well. The Xbox 360 includes a complete set of parental controls. All in all, you have a lot of places where you can enforce your guidelines for content by using some sort of technical means.

If your child likes to download podcasts by using iTunes, you can restrict access to explicit material in that program. In the iTunes Options dialog box (in iTunes, choose Edit⊏>Preferences to access this dialog box, and then select the Parental Control tab), as shown in Figure 18-19, you can choose what rating level of TV and Movies the current Windows account can view. Each Windows login has its own iTunes settings, so if multiple family members use iTunes under one Windows login, they all have the same settings. You can also restrict certain sources of content (such as podcasts), and you can enable the Restrict Explicit Content option.

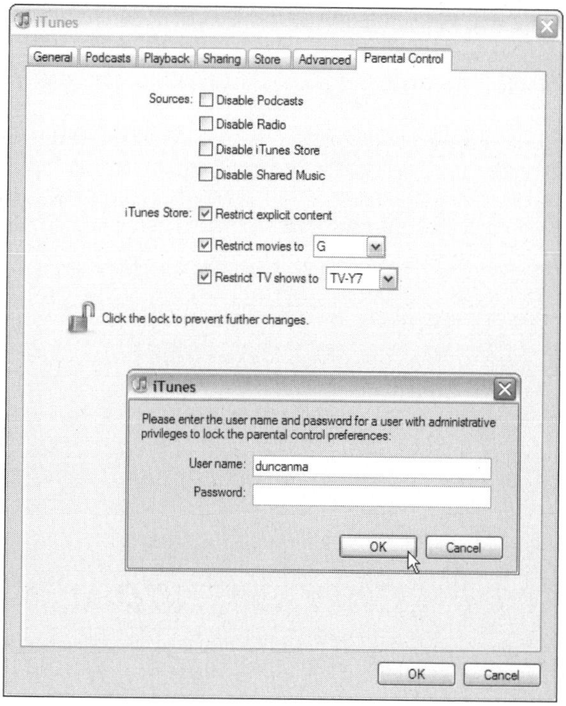

Figure 18-19: You can access the iTunes Parental Controls options only if you have administrator rights.

If you select to restrict explicit content in the iTunes Options dialog box, content of all sorts (including podcasts) that's marked as Explicit won't download or play back via the iTunes software. To change the parental controls in iTunes, you need to have Administrator access to the computer on which you're running iTunes. If your child is an administrator (or if you're not), this type of restriction can't help you regulate what your child can access.

Finding More Information

If you want to find out more about any of the ten tips covered in this chapter, check out these official resources:

- ✔ **Headphones:** The page www.zune.net/support/resources/hearing safety.htm has more information about headphones and hearing damage.

- ✔ **Online status:** You can find a detailed description of the Online Status setting (Basic or Detailed), and how to change it, at www.zune.net/support/howto/zunetozune/onlinestatus.htm.

- ✔ **A family-friend setup:** You can find out more about the parental controls, child accounts, and family settings features of the Zune software at www.zune.net.support/howto/marketplace/familysettings.htm.

Chapter 19

Ten Ways to Keep Your Zune Safe

*W*ith portable electronics becoming an extremely common accessory for many people, you might not have ever considered the cost of the gadgets that you carry around. Your Zune is likely one of your most expensive individual items, along with your cell phone or a portable gaming system if you have one, so you need to make sure you keep it safe.

Some of the biggest threats to the safety of your Zune include theft, damage, and loss. Because Zunes are expensive, relatively fragile, and small, these portable devices are vulnerable. In this chapter, we give you ten tips to reduce both the risk and the impact of these dangers.

The Risk of Theft

In recent years, with the popularity of MP3 players (especially iPods), the theft of portable electronics has become increasingly common. In the United Kingdom, iPod theft is such a concern that the government has put up posters with captions such as "Bye Pod." These posters are displayed just to remind people of the risk of iPod theft and to encourage preventative measures. Theft is a concern in any country, though, and portable electronics such as cell phones and MP3 players make very tempting targets. Few other things are so common, so small and light, and so expensive — a great combination of features for a thief. Reducing the chance of theft is the goal of the tips in the following sections, but in the section "Reducing the Impact of Losing Your Zune," later in this chapter, we also talk about how to make the loss or theft of your Zune less painful.

Keep your device out of sight when you're using it

When you're sitting on the bus, in the library, or just walking down the street, you don't need everyone to know that you have several hundred dollars worth of electronics on you. The first step in getting your Zune stolen is letting a thief know that you have something worth stealing.

So don't carry your electronics out in your hand; put them in a jacket pocket, in a pants pocket, or even in your backpack or purse. If you need to use the Zune's controls, you should be able to do that without taking it out, but if you need to look at the screen, you do have to pull it out and hold it in your hand. Some visibility of your device is unavoidable, and that's okay; you just want to arrange things so that not everyone walking down the street knows exactly what you're carrying. Of course, functionality is important, so find a place where you can run the headphone wire all the way up to your ears.

Ah, headphones . . . what about those? You can't really just keep those hidden away, not if you want the Zune to be of any use at all. People will notice that you have headphones on your ears. A pair of headphones on their own don't really tell a criminal very much, though: You could be listening to an old portable cassette tape player or a cheap flash-based MP3 player; the headphones that come with the Zune aren't so distinctive that anyone who sees them would recognize them, as compared to the iPod's distinctive white earbuds. A thief who sees white earbuds is pretty sure that the person wearing them has some form of iPod in his or her pocket, but black headphones like the Zune's could be from any player.

Lock your Zune away

What about when you aren't carrying your Zune? Maybe you're at work, at school, traveling, or just at the gym. In all these cases, and many more, you have to put your Zune down and likely walk away from it. What should you do? First, if it's at all possible to keep the Zune with you, do it. If you're in a public place, such as a coffee shop, library, or even on a plane or bus, and you have to get up for a bit, stick your Zune in your pocket and take it with you. You may have to leave some things behind if you aren't willing to pack up all your stuff whenever you get up, but something as small as the Zune can probably tag along with you.

Depending on your situation, though, you may not be able to bring the Zune everywhere you go, so the next best thing is to make sure it's in a safe place. If you have a locker at school, make sure it's locked and don't share your combination with your friends. You may trust them, but if someone gets your locker open, it's better if you don't have to suspect one of your pals.

Inside your locker, don't leave your Zune in plain sight; put it away in your books, your backpack, your jacket, or whatever. Even an obvious choice could slow the thief down, increasing the risk he or she is taking and hopefully making him or her decide to move onto an easier target. The same goes for when you're traveling on a plane or bus and need to leave your seat. If you can't just take your Zune with you, put it in your carry-on luggage or under a jacket — anywhere to make it harder for someone wandering past your seat to just pick it up.

Don't leave your Zune or Zune accessories in your car

Vehicles are easy targets for theft because they're left alone for hours at a time. If a thief looks in your car window, you want to make sure that he or she doesn't see anything worth stealing. If you decide to hook your Zune up to your car stereo, make sure that not only is the Zune out of sight (or better yet, not in the car at all), but any power cables, mounting brackets, or FM transmitters are all out of sight, as well. If someone sees a Zune power adapter in your car, he or she can probably figure out that you have a Zune in there, as well, and it suggests that you're into portable electronics. He or she might think it's worth breaking your window to check it out.

You should take your Zune with you when you the leave the car, but it seems a little silly to carry around all the cables and other accessories you use. Stash them away in the center console or glove box, whatever works in your particular vehicle.

What about iPods?

If you have an iPod and you're worried about keeping it safe, this tip applies to you, as well: Keep your iPod tucked away and hidden from view, and get yourself some nonwhite headphones or earbuds.

Get creative to stop thieves

The preceding three tips are pretty straightforward: If thieves don't know you have a Zune or where you keep it, they won't try to steal it. According to statistics from the U.S. Department of Justice for 2004 and 2005, portable electronics are the second largest category of stolen goods — after vehicles — ranking even higher than cash or credit cards. The vast majority of these thefts take place when the device isn't being used, so it seems that the most important time to protect your Zune is when you have to leave it alone (in your house, your bag, your locker, or your desk). To that end, you can devise your own creative ways to keep your Zune safe.

For example, check out the idea behind iDisguise's product (`http://idisguise.com`), a fake mint tin to hide an Apple iPod Nano or Shuffle (see Figure 19-1).

A quick online search for the terms "mint tin" and "iPod" turns up a ton of do-it-yourself projects for turning a mint tin into a stealth case for a music player, so you don't really need to go out and pay for one specially designed for this purpose.

Figure 19-1:
Hiding your music player inside a mint tin is just one idea to keep your Zune from being stolen.

Although iDisguise doesn't make a hiding case for the Zune, don't let that stop you from making your own. Find something the right size that doesn't look valuable (don't hide your Zune inside the box for something equally expensive!), and you have a nice little bit of camouflage when you aren't using the player. A quick look around our offices turned up several boxes that fit the Zune perfectly, including the box for four EXPO brand markers and several different boxes that were holding a dozen pens or pencils.

If you decide to stealth your Zune inside a box, we wouldn't recommend putting a hole for your headphone cord in it; that just draws attention. A hole for your headphones may also lead to leaving your headphones plugged in when you have the Zune in the box, blowing the whole point of the disguise. Instead, use the box just for when you're storing your Zune away.

Of course, a metal tin like the Altoids box would look a bit nicer, but we're sure you can find something suitable if you keep your eyes open. The Web site www.thetinbot.com/home sells metal cases that can most likely fit a Zune, but they're a bit too pretty for our taste. As a case, there's nothing wrong with these beautiful tins, but as a disguise, they stand out too much.

Another idea, and one that has also been done for iPods already, is to cut a Zune-sized area out of the middle of a book, like you can see in Figure 19-2.

Figure 19-2: If you're willing to do some craft work, you can find all sorts of unique ways to hide your Zune away.

Once again, we wouldn't add the cut out at the top for your headphones, and we'd make sure to use a book that has no real redeeming value anymore. In our case, we have plenty of books about obsolete versions of software that serve this purpose well.

Our final creative suggestion is to try an actual safe: a locked box normally intended for travelers, but well designed to hold your personal electronics. You can get one with the right dimensions to fit the Zune and several other pieces of electronics from www.thepodsafe.com. Make sure to look at the Travel Safe, not the Pod Safe that's on that same site; the Pod Safe works only with iPods.

The Risk of Damage

For many people, the risk that their Zune will get scratched or otherwise damaged is a much more realistic concern than theft. Portable electronic devices like the Zune have a reputation for being fragile; drop one on your kitchen table, and it may never work again. Between the two of us, we've broken a number of devices (one of our wives broke two MP3 players in a row, just by dropping them from a treadmill onto a carpeted floor), and it's a terribly easy way to waste your money. Some accidents can't be avoided, and some damage can't be protected against, but you can definitely do something about a lot of the small bumps and scratches that happen to a device like a Zune.

Protect your Zune's screen from scratches

The screen of any portable device is one of the most vulnerable components, mostly because even a few scratches can make it nearly unusable. Avoiding scratches to your Zune is hard because it's so easy to toss your Zune in a pocket with your keys, put it into a backpack next to a zipper, or have it bouncing around next to some coins in your jacket pocket. The best bet is to protect that screen so that you can stop worrying about where the Zune is and what might bump into it. You can start protecting it right away by using the simple Zune bag that ships right in the box. It may not be fancy, but it puts a soft layer of cloth between your Zune and anything that might scratch it.

Another option is to put a clear screen protector on top of your Zune. These are generally inexpensive and provide a layer of scratch protection without really changing the appearance or functionality of your device. Some of the available screen protector products include

- ✓ **The JAVOScreen Ultra Clear screen (www.javoedge.com):** Select Microsoft and Zune in the Quick Search options along the left side of this Web page.

- **Belkin's ClearScreen overlay (www.belkin.com):** You can see how this overlay works in Figure 19-3.
- **ScreenGuardz (www.screenguardz.com):** This site has several screen protectors available.

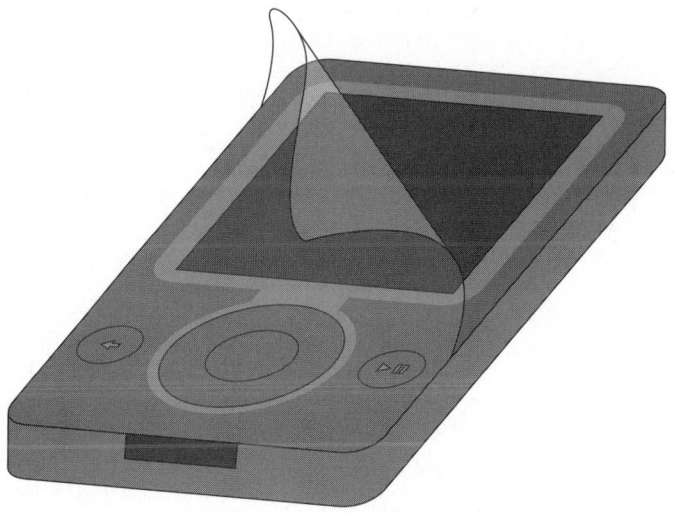

Figure 19-3: Screen protectors are a plastic film that sticks to the entire top surface of your Zune and helps you avoid scratches.

You can also protect your screen by putting your whole Zune into one of the many cases available, but make sure the case you choose includes a cover over the screen. Our personal favorite is the Classic from VajaCases.com, but Belkin, Speck, and many others make cases that include a clear cover over the screen.

Get a protective case

No, this isn't a repeat. Your Zune's screen is very important, and scratches are a big issue, but you can protect against scratches with a millimeter-thick layer of plastic. But what about impact damage from dropping your Zune, dropping something on top of it, or banging it on the edge of a counter on your way by? Any impact on your Zune could damage some of its internal parts or crack the LCD screen (leaving it essentially useless for video and making the menu system awfully hard to use). Not all damage can be avoided (we don't think any case would protect your Zune if it fell out of a moving car, for example), but a good protective case can really help reduce the likelihood that a little bump or drop will ruin your Zune.

The most protective case currently available appears to be the ToughSkin from Speck (www.speckproducts.com). This rubberized container is the only case we've seen that looks thick enough to help cushion any real impact.

If you're worried about water, dirt, and dust damage, another great option is the iBagz from www.ifrogz.com. This product is a thick plastic bag complete with Ziploc/Velcro closure and a special cable that lets you plug in your headphones while still keeping the bag waterproof. The thick plastic of an iBagz might protect against some impact damage, as well, but it's really intended to keep out water, dust, and sand. With your Zune in one of these cases in an inside pocket of a ski jacket, it would probably stay pretty safe while you're skiing or snowboarding.

Reducing the Impact of Losing Your Zune

Even with the preceding tips, you might still lose your Zune to theft, damage, or just plain loss. In any case, you've lost a fairly expensive piece of electronic equipment and all the content you had on it. The following three tips can help make the loss of your device as painless as possible.

Record your Zune's serial number in a safe place

If your Zune gets stolen or lost, you need to know as much information as possible to have any chance at all of getting it back. After you get your Zune — or right after reading this — flip it over and find the serial number near the bottom of the back (right above "Hello from Seattle"). Keep this number, which should start with *SN,* in a safe place where it isn't likely to be stolen along with your Zune. (So don't put it into your backpack where you always keep your gadgets.) We put our serial numbers into some form of online storage; nearly any other type of filing system generally means we'll never see it again. If you're better with your files than we are, though, or if you already have a place where you keep important papers, you should probably use that.

You also need to keep a copy of your bill of sale (invoice, receipt, whatever you received from the store when you bought it) for warranty purposes. You can find more information about the Zune's (1 year) warranty at www.zune.net/support/resources/warranty.htm, including the portion of the agreement that specifies that you need a copy of the original proof of purchase to receive repairs under warranty.

Make sure you provide the serial number if you have to file a police report about a theft or as part of an insurance claim (more on insurance in the following tip).

Make sure your homeowner's insurance covers the Zune

Homeowner's insurance policies often contain a certain amount of coverage for your personal property, even when you're outside the home. This may include a portable device like the Zune and may cover loss, damage, and theft or only one or two of those. You also probably have a deductible that may or may not apply to the loss of an item like the Zune, and (depending on the amount) it may not even be worth filing a claim for just the Zune (although if you lose the Zune along with many other items, the deductible applies only once and should seem more reasonable). If you don't know the details of your coverage, e-mail or call your insurance agent and ask these questions:

- ✔ Does my policy cover my personal property outside the home, such as jewelry and portable electronics?

- ✔ Am I covered against loss, theft, or damage, or only some of these events?

- ✔ In cases of loss, theft, or damage to my personal property, what deductible would be involved?

- ✔ Are there any guidelines for handling a theft or loss to ensure I'm eligible for insurance coverage? (Some insurance policies require a police report to be filed for any theft before they'll process a claim.)

- ✔ Am I covered for replacement cost (the cost of a new Zune to replace my lost one) or for value of the item (a reduced amount based on the age of the item)?

Some insurance companies recommend that you create a complete inventory of all items you own to make it easier to file a claim in the case of a fire or even the loss of an individual item. If you want to create a home inventory of your own, check out www.knowyourstuff.org for some tips and software to inventory all of your belongings. The most difficult part of a home inventory for many people is keeping it up to date, but adding at least high-ticket items such as your Zune would be useful.

Make sure all your Zune content is backed up

When you have a portable media device like a Zune, you can put a lot of important things onto it, including pictures, movies, and music. Normally, everything on your Zune comes from your personal PC, but you should make sure not to consider the Zune a backup of any of that media. If you were to lose your originals (from your PC), you'd most likely be disappointed to find out that the copies on your Zune are often of lower quality. Photos, for example, are reduced from their original resolution to 640 x 480. The quality of video and audio files depends on your settings but is often lower than the original.

The other issue is that if you end up with some content on your Zune that you no longer have on your PC (such as photos), you need to get that content back on your PC. To do this, you have two choices. One is to use the Zune software by following these steps:

1. **Connect your device to your PC and bring up the Zune software.**

2. **Select your Zune from the Navigation pane (on the left side of the software interface).**

3. **Find the content on your Zune that you want to save to your PC.**

4. **Click the Sync tab in the Task selectors area (in the upper-right of the software) to make the Sync List area visible.**

5. **Drag the desired content onto the sync list and click Start Sync.**

   The photos, music, and/or video are copied back to your PC.

This approach works only with a PC that you've set up as the Home computer for your Zune and only if you don't have automatic sync already set up.

The other option for backing up your Zune content is something known as the hard-drive hack, which sounds a lot scarier than it really is. This bit of registry manipulation tells Windows that your Zune should be displayed as a device under your My Computer icon, and therefore you can click it to browse through your videos, photos, and music, and copy anything you want back to your PC. This approach works great for us, and we use it as a quick way to get a copy of videos that we've already converted to the perfect format for the Zune. But hard-drive hacking is most definitely unsupported by Microsoft. Instead of trying to detail all of the steps involved, we'll just point you to www.duncanmackenzie.net/zune, where you can find all the details under the heading Hard Drive Hack.

Keeping Yourself Safe

Our final tip is about your own safety while you use your Zune. One of the great benefits of having a Zune is that you can have your own music and video no matter where you are; you can surround yourself with the media you want to listen to or watch whenever you want. This same feature can lead to two problems:

- ✔ You might end up using your headphones for hours and hours every day and cause yourself ear damage.
- ✔ You might not be very aware of your surroundings while you're using those headphones.

Using headphones all the time might not seem dangerous, but rising levels of hearing damage in young people around the United States suggest that hours of headphone use combined with too-high volume levels are very dangerous. For your own safety, use external speakers when possible (in your office or at home, hook your Zune up to a stereo), and when you're using headphones, keep the volume at a comfortable level.

We've seen conflicting recommendations about what type of headphones are the most dangerous. On the one hand, the use of *canalphones* (ear plug–style headphones that insert right into the ear canal) is considered hazardous because they project music so close to the inner ear. On the other hand, more external noise is blocked by this type of headphone, so you can often listen at a much lower volume level. The isolation from external sounds brings us to the second risk of headphones, though, a lack of awareness to your surroundings.

Many self-defense instructors stress the need to *be alert,* something that's hard to do if you can't hear anything going on around you, possibly making you a target for theft or worse. You also need to be alert and aware of your sur- roundings when you're driving a vehicle; consequently, headphone use while driving is illegal in several states and in many countries. (Instead of using headphones, use an FM transmitter or an aux-input jack to hook your Zune up to your car stereo.) The same safety concerns apply when riding a bike or running along a road, but no laws stop you from blocking out the world in those situations. In any situation in which you need to be able to hear at least some of what's going on around you, you may want to consider using open-air headphones instead of earbuds, canalphones, or noise-canceling headphones. Open-air headphones rest on your ears without forming any kind of seal, so most external noise manages to make its way to you — assuming you don't have the volume too high!

Where to Go from Here

The ten tips given in this chapter are intended to help you avoid the loss of your Zune, or at least to deal with that loss with the least amount of hardship. Keep in mind that you're not guaranteed, or even likely, to have to deal with these types of problems. If you handle your Zune with a bit of care to avoid damage and take some basic preventative measures to avoid theft, you should be able to hang onto your Zune without any problems . . . right until you decide you want to pick up the latest model a few months or years from now!

Index

• O •

• *W* •

• *X* •

SPORTS, FITNESS, PARENTING, RELIGION & SPIRITUALITY

0-471-76871-5

0-7645-7841-3

Also available:
- Catholicism For Dummies
  0-7645-5391-7
- Exercise Balls For Dummies
  0-7645-5623-1
- Fitness For Dummies
  0-7645-7851-0
- Football For Dummies
  0-7645-3936-1
- Judaism For Dummies
  0-7645-5299-6
- Potty Training For Dummies
  0-7645-5417-4
- Buddhism For Dummies
  0-7645-5359-3

- Pregnancy For Dummies
  0-7645-4483-7 †
- Ten Minute Tone-Ups For Dumm
  0-7645-7207-5
- NASCAR For Dummies
  0-7645-7681-X
- Religion For Dummies
  0-7645-5264-3
- Soccer For Dummies
  0-7645-5229-5
- Women in the Bible For Dummi
  0-7645-8475-8

TRAVEL

0-7645-7749-2

0-7645-6945-7

Also available:
- Alaska For Dummies
  0-7645-7746-8
- Cruise Vacations For Dummies
  0-7645-6941-4
- England For Dummies
  0-7645-4276-1
- Europe For Dummies
  0-7645-7529-5
- Germany For Dummies
  0-7645-7823-5
- Hawaii For Dummies
  0-7645-7402-7

- Italy For Dummies
  0-7645-7386-1
- Las Vegas For Dummies
  0-7645-7382-9
- London For Dummies
  0-7645-4277-X
- Paris For Dummies
  0-7645-7630-5
- RV Vacations For Dummies
  0-7645-4442-X
- Walt Disney World & Orlando
  For Dummies
  0-7645-9660-8

GRAPHICS, DESIGN & WEB DEVELOPMENT

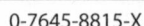

0-7645-8815-X

0-7645-9571-7

Also available:
- 3D Game Animation For Dummies
  0-7645-8789-7
- AutoCAD 2006 For Dummies
  0-7645-8925-3
- Building a Web Site For Dummies
  0-7645-7144-3
- Creating Web Pages For Dummies
  0-470-08030-2
- Creating Web Pages All-in-One Desk
  Reference For Dummies
  0-7645-4345-8
- Dreamweaver 8 For Dummies
  0-7645-9649-7

- InDesign CS2 For Dummies
  0-7645-9572-5
- Macromedia Flash 8 For Dummi
  0-7645-9691-8
- Photoshop CS2 and Digital
  Photography For Dummies
  0-7645-9580-6
- Photoshop Elements 4 For Dum
  0-471-77483-9
- Syndicating Web Sites with RSS
  For Dummies
  0-7645-8848-6
- Yahoo! SiteBuilder For Dummie
  0-7645-9800-7

NETWORKING, SECURITY, PROGRAMMING & DATABASES

0-7645-7728-X

0-471-74940-0

Also available:
- Access 2007 For Dummies
  0-470-04612-0
- ASP.NET 2 For Dummies
  0-7645-7907-X
- C# 2005 For Dummies
  0-7645-9704-3
- Hacking For Dummies
  0-470-05235-X
- Hacking Wireless Networks
  For Dummies
  0-7645-9730-2
- Java For Dummies
  0-470-08716-1

- Microsoft SQL Server 2005 For Du
  0-7645-7755-7
- Networking All-in-One Desk Ref
  For Dummies
  0-7645-9939-9
- Preventing Identity Theft For Dur
  0-7645-7336-5
- Telecom For Dummies
  0-471-77085-X
- Visual Studio 2005 All-in-One D
  Reference For Dummies
  0-7645-9775-2
- XML For Dummies
  0-7645-8845-1

Diabetes Cookbook For Dummies, 2nd Edition

0-7645-8450-2

Dieting For Dummies, 2nd Edition

0-7645-4149-8

Also available:
- Bipolar Disorder For Dummies
  0-7645-8451-0
- Chemotherapy and Radiation For Dummies
  0-7645-7832-4
- Controlling Cholesterol For Dummies
  0-7645-5440-9
- Diabetes For Dummies
  0-7645-6820-5* †
- Divorce For Dummies
  0-7645-8417-0 †

- Fibromyalgia For Dummies
  0-7645-5441-7
- Low-Calorie Dieting For Dummies
  0-7645-9905-4
- Meditation For Dummies
  0-471-77774-9
- Osteoporosis For Dummies
  0-7645-7621-6
- Overcoming Anxiety For Dummies
  0-7645-5447-6
- Reiki For Dummies
  0-7645-9907-0
- Stress Management For Dummies
  0-7645-5144-2

CATION, HISTORY, REFERENCE & TEST PREPARATION

C. S. Lewis & Narnia For Dummies

0-7645-8381-6

Genetics For Dummies

0-7645-9554-7

Also available:
- The ACT For Dummies
  0-7645-9652-7
- Algebra For Dummies
  0-7645-5325-9
- Algebra Workbook For Dummies
  0-7645-8467-7
- Astronomy For Dummies
  0-7645-8465-0
- Calculus For Dummies
  0-7645-2498-4
- Chemistry For Dummies
  0-7645-5430-1
- Forensics For Dummies
  0-7645-5580-4

- Freemasons For Dummies
  0-7645-9796-5
- French For Dummies
  0-7645-5193-0
- Geometry For Dummies
  0-7645-5324-0
- Organic Chemistry I For Dummies
  0-7645-6902-3
- The SAT I For Dummies
  0-7645-7193-1
- Spanish For Dummies
  0-7645-5194-9 ·
- Statistics For Dummies
  0-7645-5423-9

Get smart @ dummies.com®

- **Find a full list of Dummies titles**
- **Look into loads of FREE on-site articles**
- **Sign up for FREE eTips e-mailed to you weekly**
- **See what other products carry the Dummies name**
- **Shop directly from the Dummies bookstore**
- **Enter to win new prizes every month!**

ate Canadian edition also available
ate U.K. edition also available

wherever books are sold. For more information or to order direct: U.S. customers visit www.dummies.com or call 1-877-762-2974.
omers visit www.wileyeurope.com or call 0800 243407. Canadian customers visit www.wiley.ca or call 1-800-567-4797.